# Patterns and Meanings in Discourse

# *Studies in Corpus Linguistics (SCL)*

SCL focuses on the use of corpora throughout language study, the development of a quantitative approach to linguistics, the design and use of new tools for processing language texts, and the theoretical implications of a data-rich discipline.

For an overview of all books published in this series, please see
*http/benjamins.com/catalog/scl*




**Volume 55**

Patterns and Meanings in Discourse. Theory and practice in corpus-assisted discourse studies (CADS)
by Alan Partington, Alison Duguid and Charlotte Taylor

# Patterns and Meanings in Discourse

## Theory and practice in corpus-assisted discourse studies (CADS)


Alan Partington
University of Bologna

Alison Duguid
University of Siena

Charlotte Taylor
University of Portsmouth



John Benjamins Publishing Company
Amsterdam / Philadelphia

The paper used in this publication meets the minimum requirements of the American National Standard for Information Sciences – Permanence of Paper for Printed Library Materials, ANSI z39.48-1984.

Cover design: Françoise Berserik
Cover illustration from original painting *Random Order*
by Lorenzo Pezzatini, Florence, 1996.

**Library of Congress Cataloging-in-Publication Data**

Patterns and meanings in discourse : theory and practice in corpus-assisted discourse studies (CADS) / Alan Partington, Alison Duguid, Charlotte Taylor.

p. cm. (Studies in Corpus Linguistics, ISSN 1388-0373 ; v. 55)

Includes bibliographical references and index.

1. English language--Research--Data processing. 2. English language--Discourse analysis--Data processing. 3. English language--Study and teaching--Data processing. 4. Computational linguistics. I. Partington, Alan, editor of compilation.

PE1074.5.P385 2013

420.1'88--dc23 2012050684

ISBN 978 90 272 0360 1 (Hb ; alk. paper)

ISBN 978 90 272 0361 8 (Pb ; alk. paper)

ISBN 978 90 272 7212 6 (Eb)



John Benjamins Publishing Co. · P.O. Box 36224 · 1020 ME Amsterdam · The Netherlands
John Benjamins North America · P.O. Box 27519 · Philadelphia PA 19118-0519 · USA

# Table of contents

# Acknowledgements

The authors would like to thank Anna Marchi and John Morley for their help and encouragement.

Chapter 4 is a blended and reworked version of two articles published in the *Journal of Pragmatics* (2007 and 2011); Chapter 5 uses some material from an article published in *ESP across Cultures* (2008) and some material from a chapter in *Exploring the Lexis-Grammar Interface* (Benjamins 2009); Chapter 6 uses some material from an article published in the *Lodz Papers in Pragmatics* (2008); Chapter 9 uses some material from a chapter in *Situated Politeness* (Continuum 2009); Chapter 10 uses some material from an article published in *Corpora* (2010); the case studies in Chapter 11 use some material from an article published in the *Journal of Language and Politics* (2012) and from an article published in *Corpora* (2013). In each case the material here is updated, recontextualised and often considerably developed and extended.

# Introduction

The present volume has a similar format to that of its predecessor, namely *Patterns and Meanings: Using Corpora for English Language Research and Teaching* (1998), mixing theoretical discussions with practical demonstrations. It begins with introductory chapters defining terms and outlining the rationale and aims of the volume, the theoretical linguistic stance underpinning it and the overall methodologies to be used. After this introduction, each chapter begins by outlining a topic or an area in discourse studies, followed by descriptions of case studies which attempt both to shed light on particular themes or issues in this area and especially to demonstrate the methodologies which might be fruitfully employed to investigate such issues. Each chapter concludes with suggestions on activities which the readers may wish to undertake themselves. Finally, Appendix 1 contains a list of currently available resources for corpus linguistics research. Like the first *Patterns and Meanings*, it is thus designed to both provoke theoretical discussion and also serve as a practical vademecum for students and for use with students.

The topics for case study are just as wide-ranging in their scope as those in the earlier book, which included studies in lexis, phraseology, syntax, text grammar, evaluative meaning, metaphor and "unusuality" (defined as the creative upsetting and exploitation of readers and hearers expectations of regularity in language). All of these concerns are present in the current work and are augmented by studies into author style, irony, spoken interaction, including face and politeness and diachronic studies of both linguistic and social, cultural and political changes over recent time.

The ways it differs from its predecessor are accounted for mainly by the development of the field of corpus linguistics itself which has matured considerably in the intervening years. The variety of corpora we employ here is much wider than that in the earlier work, which reflects the far greater ease of data collection nowadays. Concomitantly, these corpora contain a wider variety of discourse types, and this very ease of data collection has allowed and encouraged many corpus linguists, including us, to take an interest in analysing and comparing the particular features of different discourse types and to thus establish the multidisciplinary field we have named *corpus-assisted discourse studies* (Section 0.3).

## 0.1 Discourse and discourse analysis

Since they are the object of our attention throughout this volume, we might look at how discourse and discourse analysis have been defined and discussed by previous authors. The literature provides a seemingly bewildering array of different definitions of "discourse" (see Jaworski & Coupland 2006: 1–37 for an overview). In reality they have more overlap than would appear at first sight.

The first set of definitions are structural. Discourse "is used to refer to any piece of connected language, written or spoken, which contains more than one sentence" (Thornborrow & Wareing 1998: 240) or "meaning beyond the clause" (Martin & Rose 2003: 1). Discourse analysis in this context consists of "attempts to study the organisation of language above the sentence or above the clause, and therefore to study larger linguistic units, such as conversational exchanges or written texts" (Stubbs 1983: 1). These approaches wish to stress that the organisational mechanisms at play in language above the clause level – "the rules and conventions underlying the use of language in extended stretches of text" ( Carter et al. 1997: 318) – namely, the norms of *cohesion* – are very different from those at work within the clause, that is, syntax, morphology and phonology. Few authors, however, would deny that utterances such as "Fire!", "Get lost" or "Your flies are undone" constituted discourses in themselves.

In another, perhaps now old-fashioned, approach, "[s]ome linguists use discourse in a loose way to distinguish speech from writing. 'Discourse' is used when talking about speech, whereas 'text' is used when discussing writing" (Carter 1995: 39). This view was developed to stress that the study of discourse is the study of language in interaction and speech is generally more interactive than writing, although we might note the existence of "speech-like" forms, such as epistolary and/or e-mediated communication, and so on.

In the third classic definition, the functional definition, discourse analysis is "the analysis of language in use" (Brown & Yule 1983: 1), "language that is doing some job in some context" (Halliday 1985: 10) and "[a]s such it cannot be restricted to the description of linguistic forms independent of the purposes or functions which these forms are designed to serve in human affairs" (Brown & Yule 1983: xiii). Under this definition, of course, practically all language communication is discourse; as David Lodge's Professor Bates puts it: "every utterance or written sentence always has a context, is always in some sense referring to something already said and inviting a response, is always designed to do something to somebody, a reader or a listener" (2008: 31).

This view of discourse as language-when-doing-something leads to the inescapable conclusion, paradox perhaps, that the discourse linguist never has real discourse in her hands since, by the time it gets to her dissecting table, it is no longer doing what it was intended for. It is, as it were, "once-was-discourse".

In other words, it has become text, that is, the product, the linguistic record or trace of discourse action and as Stubbs put it "[s]ince only text is directly observable, this is the basic data for corpus linguistics", or indeed any form of text linguistics (2007: 144). The discourse analyst tries to infer the processes of interaction from its textual product, s/he is thus actually a "text-to-discourse" analyst. But this is not a message of despair. Historians too must infer processes of interaction from textual sources, if they are lucky enough to have any. Many literary critics (another kind of historian) spend a great deal of time and ink making very educated guesses about authorial intentions and what the interactions among participants in a work might mean. All such scholars share "this central problem of hermeneutics" (Stubbs 2007: 145).

Some authors have taken the socially interactive theme and describe discourse as constructive (and constraining) of social relations and so discourse analysis is seen as studying the set of norms governing how activities are normally conducted using language, what kinds of language behaviour are normally permitted and not permitted and are normally frequent or infrequent, in a certain social setting: "the analysis of language as it is used to enact activities, perspectives, and identities" (Gee 1999: 4–5). This implies of course that there are as many different types of discourse (often termed "discourses") as there are social settings and purposes, each with its own set of norms, which is why analysts commonly refer to "the 'discourse' of advertising", and so on (Carter et al. 1997: 318). Indeed, a very large number of human activities are conducted almost entirely through language and in some sense actually consist of the language used to carry them out. As asserted by Professor Bates, obviously meant to be a rather keen proponent of this view of discourse:

> We live in discourse as fish live in water. Systems of law consist of discourse. Diplomacy consists of discourse. The beliefs of the great world religions consist of discourse. And in a world of increasing literacy and multiplying media of verbal communication – radio, television, the Internet, advertising, packaging, as well as books, magazines and newspapers – discourse has become more and more to dominate even the non-verbal aspects of our lives. We eat discourse (mouthwatering menu-language, for instance like "flame-roasted peppers drizzled with truffle oil") we drink discourse ("hints of tobacco, vanilla, chocolate and ripe berries in this feisty Australian Shiraz"); we look at discourse (those minimalist paintings and cryptic installations in galleries that depend entirely on curators and critics' descriptions of them for their existence as art); we even have sex by enacting the erotic discourse of erotic fiction and sex manuals. To be able to understand the culture and society you have to be able to analyse their discourses. (Lodge 2008: 32)

It would be a mistake however, sometimes committed by materialist social philosophers, to imagine that human interactions which exist *in* discourse consist solely *of* discourse. Politics, religion, law, diplomacy etc. must also be understood in terms of the needs, ideologies, beliefs, intentions, and so on, that underlie the use of language both in the minds of interactants but also within the society where the interaction occurs. It is, of course, the earnest hope of the typical discourse linguist that the study of language in use can of course open a window onto at least some of these, even if our problem of hermeneutics, that is, that inference from text to mental or social processes is fallible, applies more heavily still to this form of study.

It is often pointed out that superior knowledge and skill in the use of a particular discourse, especially competitive discourses, conveys very important advantages as, for instance, to a skilful barrister in witness interrogation (Taylor 2009a). However, what is probably mentioned less, perhaps because not so sinisterly dramatic, is that knowledge of the discourse conventions of a particular setting, especially when shared and agreed upon by participants, is generally of assistance in smooth cooperation and in getting the business in hand completed successfully as, say, in doctor-patient interviews.

Another social use of discourse, where is it also used as a countable noun, is in the sense of ways of talking about and constructing a particular topic, as for instance the discourse(s) of climate change (examined in Grundmann & Krishnamurthy 2010). We can view this meaning of discourse as cutting across the meaning above, so, for instance, one might compare the ways in which climate change is represented in different discourse types, such as mainstream newspapers, parliamentary debates, blogs, and so on.

Another distinction is made by some scholars between *discourse* and *text*, the former being the study of the relationship between language and its social context, the latter concentrating instead on the internal organisation of language: "[s]ome linguists use discourse to refer to language as a piece of communication within the context of situation and text to denote the formal devices used for establishing connections between sentences and their co-text" (Ulrych 1992: 149). This definition of text is practically identical to what we termed above the "structural" view of discourse.

Finally it is frequently stated that the object of study should be naturally-occurring "authentic" discourses (McEnery & Wilson 1996), which at some point in time served a communicative purpose. However the concept of naturally-occurring and "authentic" is not as unproblematic as it is usually taken to be. The illustration of "non-authentic" language which is usually given is that of ad hoc "invented" examples concocted by the linguist to make his or her points, and there can be no doubt that the kind of linguistics – "armchair" linguistics (Fillmore 1992) – which depends on this practice works very differently from text linguistics, including corpus linguistics. However, *all* language is in a sense "invented" by a speaker. Moreover, an invented example used to illustrate a point is also undeniably serving a communicative purpose, that, indeed, of illustration. Perhaps the only way around this theoretical impasse is to stress that the texts employed in corpus linguistics very generally predate the analysis and have been produced by some other party than the analyst (and yet a quotation from, say, Shakespeare brought forth as an illustration would also fulfil these requisites), and by defining *illustrating a linguistic point* as a *metafunction* rather than a fully-fledged function of language, that is, "talk about talk" rather than about the world. If we prefer, illustrating a point is language as *mention* rather than *use*, in Quine's (1940) celebrated and helpful distinction.

In the spirit, then, of adding to the plethora of definitions, ours is the simple and therefore inclusive one: discourse analysis studies how language is used to (attempt to) influence the beliefs and behaviour of other people.

During the development of this volume we will be examining discourse in the guises listed here, that is, as both structure and function. In Chapter 1 we examine discourse structure, in particular, the principles of discourse organisation that writers/speakers employ to communicate effectively. In the subsequent chapters we will, in the course of numerous case studies, observe the ways in which the meaning potential of lexis is actually activated in discourse in attempts to do things to hearers/readers, in accordance with the abovementioned functional view.

## 0.2 Corpus linguistics

### 0.2.1 What it is and what it does

Corpus linguistics can be defined most simply as: that set of studies into the form and/or function of language which incorporate the use of computerised corpora in their analyses. It is a form of text linguistics and as such is evidence-driven. It shares with other forms of text linguistics the purpose and rationale of describing the interactions between writers/speakers and readers/hearers as evidenced in the linguistic trace, that is, the texts, that these interactions leave behind. But also the overarching endeavour of describing (how it is organised) and explaining (why it functions as it does) the language system or some part of it, as evidenced in these interactions between writers/speakers and readers/hearers, in other words, a central interest of corpus linguistics is grammar. These enterprises, of course, entail considerable challenges. In fact, the possibilities of language behaviour permitted in abstract by the language system would appear to be far wider than the actual behaviour we observe (in texts) to be habitually performed by speakers/writers. The problem of inferring the norms of form and function of the system (which is, in any case, in a state of continuous transformation) from the actual subset of performed behaviour is immense and is the main reason linguistics is still far from a complete functional description of any natural language system.

Corpus linguistics proper is accompanied by a body of work recounting how various corpora have been compiled and/or annotated (Section 0.4.2) which we might refer to as "meta-corpus linguistics", which can be seen as either a sub-category of or an ancillary discipline to corpus linguistics.

Although this might seem extremely broad as a definition, it does capture the enormous range of studies which have been performed using corpus techniques, reflected in the huge variety of corpora which exist, from collections of Anglo-Saxon poetry, to the speeches of individual politicians, to Papal encyclicals. Corpora have been studied to shed light on the use of single lexical items (lexicology and dictionary making), typical phraseologies of a discourse type, textual cohesion, authorial style, figurative meaning, evaluative meaning, social, political, cultural and religious ideologies as expressed in text, and much else. This means that the topics of study are much wider than in any of the other areas of text study such as historical linguistics, literary criticism, text grammar, and so on. In fact corpus linguistics can contribute, can play a role, in all these areas.

Many corpora are *synchronic* in the sense that they contain a "snapshot" sample of language from a given limited period of time, for instance, the early Brown and LOB corpora contained a variety of texts from the early 1960s and were meant to be representative samples of, respectively, the US and UK English of their day. But corpora have made a considerable contribution to historical or *diachronic* linguistics and have now been around long enough for linguists to use them to track language changes over time, indeed LOB itself is now part of a set of corpora from different years which can be used for diachronic studies (see Chapters 10 & 11). Stubbs calls corpus linguistics inherently diachronic (like all text linguistics) since "it studies what has frequently occurred in the past" (2007: 131). But this study is often a precursor to generalising and therefore predicting how things are and will be done in the language now and in the future (see 0.2.2 below on induction). He also calls corpus linguistics inherently quantitative (see next section) and inherently sociolinguistic since it studies texts which are the record of "real communicative acts in a discourse community" (2007: 130–1, and see Section 0.1 above). As the work of Hoey (2005) shows, it is also inherently psycholinguistic, since corpora are also the repository of and evidence for writers' and speakers' acquired language primings, that is, their combined knowledge of how linguistic items can be used to communicate meanings (equivalent to their communicative competence, Hymes 1971).

Given this variety of topics treated and uses to which corpora have been put, it has been argued that it is better to see corpus linguistics not as a discipline or field of study but more a methodology, that is, a set of tools and general practices and ways of using those tools for the purpose of language analysis. Others reject this view as too simplistic and limiting, for instance, Leech argues that "computer corpus linguistics defines not just a newly emerging methodology for studying language, but a new research enterprise, and in fact a new philosophical approach to the subject" (1992: 106). Similarly, Stubbs claims that "a corpus is not merely a tool of linguistic analysis but an important concept in linguistic theory" (1993: 23–24), whilst Teubert describes corpus linguistics as "a theoretical approach to the study of language" (2005: 2). Taylor (2008) gives an overview of the way practitioners have described corpus linguistics. These include as a *tool*, a *method*, a *methodology*, a *methodological approach*, a *discipline*, a *theory*, a *theoretical approach*, a *paradigm*, or a combination of these.

In the view of the current authors, we need first to distinguish between the questions of what corpus linguistics *is* and what it *does*. The answer to the first might well be simply "a collection of tools and techniques for linguistic analysis". But what corpus linguistics does is a far more complex matter. It is clear that advances in the natural sciences, including leaps of theoretical paradigms, have very often depended on technological innovations which both allow new phenomena to be observed and new data to be collected (the microscope, the radio telescope) and also permit us to see familiar phenomena and data in new and more detailed ways (the optical telescope) (Partington 1998: 144, 2009a: 295–296; Stubbs 2007: 128–129). Equipment, methodology and theory – as well as the researcher – are interdependent:

> There is a sort of indivisible hermeneutic package – the observer (including mind), observational instruments, observations, object of observation. Alterations in any of the parts will affect the entire system, a process usually known as scientific advance. For instance: (i) the researcher can have a bright new idea of what to search for or how to use a tool in a fresh experimental way; (ii) tools can be constantly refined; (iii) observations can be made wider, deeper, more cohesive; (iv) any change in the observed system gives researchers the chance to fruitfully compare the new with the previous behaviour. Thus it is with corpus linguistics, just as it is for astrophysics or particle science. (Partington 2009a: 296)

And so, although the introduction of corpora use into the language sciences is not a theoretical advance in itself, the new tool and the new techniques developed to exploit it can and have led to improvements in our theoretical grasp of language. In this sense corpus linguistics can be described as a new, not theoretical, but *methodological* paradigm, where paradigm means an analytical model of the part of the universe under analysis, here, language structure and use.

This distinction between what corpus linguistics is and what it does was summarised by Thompson and Hunston "[a]t its most basic corpus linguistics is a methodology that can be aligned to any theoretical approach to language" (2006: 8) as long, we might add, that the approach in question holds that the study of texts is worthwhile (unlike, say, some Chomskian approaches) and that there is a value in "counting". However, Thompson and Hunston go on to describe two major theories which have come out of corpus linguistics. First of all, that meanings are not located in single words, but in "units of meaning" in Sinclair's terminology, and consequently that communicative discourse unfolds largely as a series of semi-fixed phrases (2006: 11–12). Chapter 1 of this volume deals with these theoretical developments at length. To these, we might add the corollary highlighted by work in semantic – or *evaluative* – prosody, a notion devised for the first time within corpus-based lexical grammar, that lexical items are very largely coselected by speakers in batches rather than singly and that therefore meanings in utterances, including and especially evaluative meanings, are prosodic – spreading over stretches of language – rather than atomistic in nature. This will be a major topic of Chapter 2.

### 0.2.2 Quantity, frequency, comparison and recurrence (or patterning)

As we noted above, the methodology of corpus linguistics is often referred to as inherently "quantitative", but the term needs further elucidation. Having a whole lot of language amassed in one place (that is, in a corpus) is not necessarily going to provide particular insights in and by itself. But texts in quantity make it possible to conduct word-frequency counts (single or multiple word groups) and to spot recurring patterns of usage if you also possess the tools to so analyse the data you have collected.

Word-frequency counts, although often informative in themselves, become more revealing still in comparison with similar lists derived from other discourse types in that they can thus highlight both the typical grammar and also the recurrent topics of a discourse type under study. In Chapter 10 we report how a comparison of word frequencies in UK newspapers in the years 1993 and 2005 sheds light not only on developments over the period in society and politics, but also on changes in newspaper prose style, stance towards the reader and newspaper organisation and production techniques.

Rather than the term quantitative, it might be better to say that most of the linguistic analysis performed using computerised corpora is born out of a *statistical* methodological philosophy, the search for – and belief in the importance of – recurring *patterns*. It is based on the twin concepts of frequency (a factor of [past] *observation*) and probability (a factor of [future] *predictability*). In other words, if something is seen to happen frequently in a language, then it is significant. It is significant precisely because this frequent occurrence, or *regularity*, can be used as the basis for predicting how other, as yet unanalysed, chunks of language will behave, and, in the end, for hypothesising a description of how larger parts of the discourse under study is constructed. It is in this sense that corpus research is often described as generally *inductive*, that is, it follows "the process of inferring a general law or principle from the observation of particular instances" (*OED*; see also Chapter 1 on induction). Very often these language patterns are not immediately obvious in the course of simple introspection, but they can become more apparent through the medium of the concordancer, a tool which searches through large quantities of texts and can collect together and display recurring patternings of words surrounding the search (or "node") item stipulated by the analyst. We will observe several concordances or extracts from concordances throughout this work (and see the example in 0.4.2).

### 0.2.3 Serendipity

Forms of research which are inductive and rely on the observation of authentic data are more likely than those which depend more exclusively on introspection and ad hoc data invention to lead to serendipitous discoveries, that is, the chancing upon hitherto unforeseen phenomena or connections among phenomena. Evidence-driven research is highly likely to take the researcher into uncharted waters because the observations arising from the data will inevitably dictate to a considerable degree which next steps are taken. The present work is well punctuated with serendipities.

Nevertheless, most corpus research, by steady and repeated observation of data, results in telling us more about what we know already. Although it may sound pedestrian, this process and outcome are not to be dismissed lightly. The vast majority of scientific research consists in the steady accumulation of facts about phenomena of which we already know something and, in a very real sense, deeper knowledge is also a different kind of knowledge; quantitative data accumulation can become qualitative advance as gaps in knowledge are filled enabling new and perhaps unexpected observations to be made. Moreover, corroboration of what is already strongly suspected is frequently a vital component of scientific advance.

But serendipitous discovery, when it occurs, can have a quality, a value, of its own. Some serendipities are not just lucky finds but findings which mean that fresh questions need to be asked in the field. Kuhn argues most convincingly that science advances via moments of revolution, we might also say "revelation", but that each revelation is also highly likely to suggest entirely fresh and more intricate "puzzles" (his term), to show us things we perhaps didn't even know we didn't know (1962/1970, 38–39). Serendipity shares this quality – of raising new puzzles – and the briefest contemplation of the history of linguistic research reveals that language is today considered to be infinitely more complex than it was felt to be by previous generations (Chomsky 2000: 122; Stubbs 2006: 26). There is no reason to doubt that we shall continue to discover ever further fascinating complexity.

## 0.3 Corpus-assisted discourse studies or CADS

### 0.3.1 Definition and aims

Corpus linguistics was defined in Section 0.2.1 as "that set of studies into the form and/or function of language which incorporate the use of computerised corpora in their analyses". CADS can thus be defined, in an equally essentialist fashion, as a subset of corpus linguistics: "that set of studies into the form and/or function of language as *communicative discourse* which incorporate the use of computerised corpora in their analyses".

The term was first coined in Partington (2004a) but much CADS research was being conducted *ante litteram*, probably even from close after the dawn of corpus linguistics. It was felt that a term was needed not only to describe the kind of study which incorporates quantitative/statistical methods in the study of discourse types but which also emphasised the eclectic nature of the approach. That corpus techniques were only one sort amongst others and that CADS analysts employ as many as required to obtain the most satisfying and complete results, hence "corpus-*assisted*". Moreover, compared to some other forms of corpus linguistics, more frequent use is made of other sources of information outside our corpus. In discourse analysis, one is analysing language in context and therefore to treat the corpus as an isolated black box is often methodologically unsound and unfruitful. It is often helpful to examine corpus-external data both to try and interpret and explain our data and also as a means of identifying areas for analysis. An early example is Krishnamurthy (1996) who compares corpus data with newspaper usage and dictionary definitions in his analysis of the use of the terms *ethnic*, *racial* and *tribal*. In the case study into the way antisemitism is reported in the UK press in Chapter 10, where to look for sources for further information on the topic (for example, a parliamentary enquiry, Home Office report and *Pew* International surveys into attitudes to minorities) actually came from indications found in the corpus data. It must also be emphasised that CADS is not tied to any particular school of discourse analysis, certainly not, for instance to *critical* discourse analysis (CDA). Unlike CDA, it has no overarching political agenda and has very different attitudes to and traditions of how language data should be managed.

In the formulation intended here, CADS arises from the pioneering work in particular of Stubbs (1996, 2001). Best known to the present authors is the body of research which has been conducted in Italy either by individual researchers or under the aegis of combined inter-university projects such as *Newspool* (Partington et al. (eds) 2004), *CorDis* (Morley & Bayley (eds) 2009) and the EU-funded *IntUne* (Bayley & Williams (eds) 2012). It has concentrated on political and media language, mainly because a nucleus of linguists in Italian academia work in Political Science faculties and are increasingly interested in the use of corpus techniques to conduct analyses of sociopolitical discourse. A parallel body of work inspired by a very similar methodological philosophy has been conducted by researchers at Lancaster University in the UK, where a group of corpus linguists has collaborated with a group of discourse analysts in the analysis of sociopolitical issues as reflected in the UK press (see for instance Gabrielatos & Baker 2008).

The aim of the CADS approach is the uncovering, in the discourse type under study, of what we might call *non-obvious meaning*, that is, meaning which might not be readily available to naked-eye perusal (including the kind of deeper knowledge mentioned in 0.2.3). There would be little point in involving corpus techniques to uncover meanings which were readily available to traditional types of discourse analysis. For instance, we hardly need a corpus of websites about travel to tell us that place names will be high on the list of lexis of such texts. We have no need for a corpus to discover that the names of characters will occur frequently in a novel or that the past will normally be the preferred tense for narrative.

It has long been recognised that much of what carries meaning in texts is not open to direct observation: "you cannot understand the world just by looking at it" (Stubbs [after Gellner 1959] 1996: 92). We use language "semi-automatically", in the sense that speakers and writers make semi-conscious choices within the various complex overlapping systems of which language is composed, including those of transitivity, modality (Halliday 1994), lexical sets (*freedom, liberty, deliverance*), modification, and so on. Authors themselves are, famously, generally unaware of all the meanings their texts convey (an extreme expression of this notion being the "intentional fallacy", Wimsatt & Beardsley 1946). By combining the quantitative approach, that is, statistical overviews of large amounts of the discourse in question – more precisely, large numbers of tokens of the discourse type under study contained in a corpus – with the more qualitative approach typical of discourse analysis, that is, the close, detailed analysis of particular stretches of discourse – stretches whose particularly interesting nature may well have been identified by the initial overview – it may be possible to better understand the processes at play in the discourse type. It may be possible, in other words, to access such non-obvious meanings.

### 0.3.2 A comparison between traditional corpus linguistics and CADS

Traditional corpus linguistics has, quite naturally, tended to privilege the quantitative approach. In the drive to produce more authentic dictionaries and grammars of a language, much early corpus work was characterised by the compilation of often very large corpora of heterogeneric discourse types in the desire to obtain an overview of the greatest quantity and variety of discourse types possible, in other words of the chimerical but useful fiction we call the "general language" ("general English", "general Italian", and so on). This has led to the construction of immensely valuable research tools such as the *Bank of English* and the *British National Corpus*. Corpus linguistics proper has also frequently been characterised by the treatment of the corpus as a "black box", that is, the analyst is not always encouraged to familiarise him/herself with particular texts within the corpus in case the special features these texts may possess should distort his or her conceptions of the corpus as a whole. There is a certain argument which runs that, if we are to construct from scratch a fresh descriptive model of the language which is as closely based on the observation of authentic discourse in action as possible, we need, grammatically speaking, a mental *tabula rasa* to free ourselves of the baleful prejudice sometimes exerted by traditional models and allow the data to speak entirely for itself (Sinclair 2004: 185–186).

The aim of CADS on the other hand is radically different. Here the whole aim of the exercise is to acquaint ourselves as much as possible with the discourse type(s) in hand. Unusually for corpus linguistics, CADS researchers typically engage with their corpus in a variety of ways. As well as via wordlists and concordancing, intuitions for further research can also arise from reading or watching or listening to parts of the data-set, a process which can help provide a feel for how things are done linguistically in the discourse-type being studied.

CADS is also typically characterised by the "ad hoc" compilation of specialised corpora, since very frequently there exists no previously available collection of the discourse type in question. Just as typically, other corpora of various descriptions are utilised in the course of a study for purposes of comparison. These may include pre-existing corpora – occasionally it is convenient to compare the behaviour of the linguistic items under study in a single discourse type (or *monogeneric*) corpus with their behaviour in one of the large *heterogeneric* corpora, such as the *British National Corpus* or the *Bank of English* – or they too may need to be compiled by the researcher.

In an important sense, all discourse analysis, and therefore, by extension, CADS, is properly comparative; it is only possible to both uncover and evaluate the particular features of a discourse type by comparing it with others. We are not deontologically justified in making statements about the relevance of a phenomenon observed to occur in one discourse type unless, where it is possible, we compare how the phenomenon behaves elsewhere. If, for example, it was discovered that a systematic metaphor existed of the type BUSINESS IS X (perhaps WAR), this would be significant only if this metaphor was particularly prevalent in this sectorial language. If metaphors were also found of the type that SPORT IS X and POLITICS IS X, this would mean that the metaphor was common to journalism as a whole, perhaps even to large numbers of discourse types of English (Partington 1998: 111).

Comparing data from one discourse type with that deriving from others can take a number of forms and we might attempt a typology of ways of comparing, as shown in Table 0.1:

**Table 0.1.** Types of comparison. DT = discourse type, tx = period of time

| | |
|---|---|
| Simple: | DT(a) compared to DT(b) |
| Serial: | DT(a) compared to DT(b), DT(c) … DT(n) |
| Multiple: | DT(a) compared to DT(b + c … n) |
| Diachronic: | DT(ta) compared to DT(tb) compared to DT(tc) … DT(tn) |

A simple comparison entails the contrast between language from one source with that from another, for instance, a body of studies has compared the linguistic features of the Brown corpus of American English with LOB, its sister corpus of British English. Discourses in institutional settings normally consist of questions posed by one set of institutional actors and responses by another category of participant. In a corpus suitably annotated for speaker category, the linguistic behaviour of each side can be compared, for example, to study whether they use key words and notions in the same or different ways (see Chapter 8). A further form of simple comparison in institutional talk is exemplified by Taylor (2006) who compares witness discourse produced under hostile examination, with that produced under friendly examination.

Another simple comparison could contrast, for example, a set of articles on the European Union from Newspaper (a) with one from Newspaper (b) (perhaps a political rival), whereas a serial comparison would entail measuring the article set from Newspaper (a) first against those from Newspaper (b), then against those from Newspaper (c), and so on.

A multiple comparison would involve comparing the article set from Newspaper (a) against a corpus containing the article sets from a number of newspapers – Newspaper (b), (c) … (n) – all grouped together. Those studies which employ the BNC or the Bank of English as the background or reference corpus are of this multiple-comparison type. Culpeper's (2009) analysis of character-talk in Romeo and Juliet was also of this type: "the comparative reference corpus was the speech of the six characters minus the one being investigated (e.g. Romeo's speech was compared with the speech of the other five characters)" (2009: 35).

Finally, a diachronic comparison entails comparing discourse from one source with discourse from the same or similar source at a different period of time. Chapters 10 and 11 describe several diachronic comparisons among data from corpora of UK broadsheet newspapers from 1993, 2005 and 2010 (see next section).

These forms of comparison may well need to be combined, the most appropriate combination depending on the precise nature of the research question. The majority of case studies in this volume will involve comparative analysis and we outline when appropriate the reasons for choosing both the type of comparison performed (whether simple, serial etc.) and the data-set(s) selected for the comparison(s).

Finally, as we will discuss in detail in Chapter 11, the comparison between corpora is not necessarily keyword-driven and focussed solely on difference. As Baker notes, the way that differences and similarities interact with each other is "an essential part of any comparative corpus-based study of discourse" (2006: 182) and we will address some of the methods available for this kind of comparison.

## 0.4 The corpora and tools for analysing corpora

### 0.4.1 The corpora

A considerable variety of corpora were employed in the course of the present studies. The most frequently used body of texts is the *Siena-Bologna Modern Diachronic Corpus* (the SiBol Corpus), which consists of two (sub-)corpora from different but contemporary periods in time, designed and compiled so as to be as alike as possible to eliminate potential maverick variables. The first, SiBol 93 contains all the articles published by the three main UK broadsheet or so-called "quality" newspapers, namely *The Times* and *Sunday Times*, the *Telegraph* and *Sunday Telegraph* and the *Guardian* in the year 1993. The second, SiBol 05, contains articles which appeared in the same three newspapers in the year 2005. The first contains around 100 million words, the second contains circa 150 million words. SiBol 93 and SiBol 05 are sometimes interrogated independently, but Chapters 10 and 11 outline a series of comparative studies where the contents of the two corpora were contrasted in order to track changes in newspaper language and in socio-political and cultural topics over the period of time between the two.[1] A third sister corpus, Port 2010 (so-called because it was compiled in Portsmouth) containing all texts from the same newspapers (excluding Sunday versions) from 2010 is also used in Chapters 10 and 11. These three corpora are now available via Sketch Engine (see Appendix for details). Chapter 11 makes use, along with the first two SiBol corpora, of a purpose-built collection of articles relating to antisemitism from the same three newspapers from the year 2009.

1. The *Guardian*'s Sunday sister paper, the *Observer* was available in 2005 but not in 1993, and so we exclude the *Observer* in many of our comparative studies.

We have given only approximate figures for corpus sizes because we discovered that different software gave us different results, since they take different views on the conundrum of what precisely counts as an individual word. Are numbers words? The string *eleven* would certainly be counted, but should we count *11*? *Ten thousand* would be two words but *10000*? What to do with hyphenated items? *Dataset* counts as a single word, *data set* as two, so how do we treat *data-set*? And punctuation: *UK* gets counted as a single word, whereas *United Kingdom* is two, and so how do we deal with *U.K.*? If one decides that a punctuation mark always marks a word division, this would make *J.K. Rowling* equivalent to *Joanne Kathleen Rowling*, but different from *JK Rowling* and *10000* would be counted different from both *10,000* and *10.4*. If one decides it does not then *M.P.* is always one word, but what it signifies – *Member of Parliament* – is three.

Chapter 4 (on irony) involves the use, alongside SiBol, of three corpora of semi-spontaneous interactive spoken discourse. The first two contain White House press briefings in transcription, one from the Clinton era, the other from the first term of the George W. Bush administration, where the official spokesperson of the American administration deals with questions from a group of journalists representing a variety of media outlets, and Ints which contains 250,000 words of transcribed televised UK political interviews.

In the first case study in Chapter 5 (on metaphor) we employ a circa 10 million-word corpus of newspaper texts from three countries, USA, UK and Italy from the period 1999–2007 and, in the second study, a 250,000-word corpus of review articles, more precisely, humorous opinion pieces.

For Chapter 6 (on stylistics) we compiled three corpora of literary works by downloading from the Project Gutenberg site, the first containing writings by the British humorous novelist P.G.Wodehouse, the second, other humorous works from the same period and the third, non-humorous contemporary novels.

Chapter 7 (on cross-linguistic analyses) employs twinned sets of corpora on newspaper data. The first set consists of articles referring to racism or xenophobia in English and Italian newspapers. While the second set contains articles which refer to migrants in the same newspapers and from the same time period. This means that corpora are comparable across the two languages, English and Italian, and comparisons may also be drawn between the newspapers construction of racism and their own representation of migrants.

Chapter 8 uses different corpora of spoken interaction, namely, two compilations of White House press briefings, one from the Bush era and another from the Obama administration and a corpus consisting of transcripts of the Hutton inquiry, a public inquiry into the circumstances surrounding the death of Dr. David Kelly in 2003.

Chapter 9 (on impoliteness) makes use of two distinct sets of corpora. The first set is composed of transcripts of institutional discourse from the UK House of Commons, the Hutton Inquiry and the *BBC* television programme *Breakfast with Frost*, which consists largely of interviews with public figures, while the second set is made up of media comment on these three spoken events. In addition, reference is also made to the BNC when it was necessary to check findings in a more general corpus.

As mentioned earlier, Chapters 10 and 11 contain several case studies in which data from the above-mentioned SiBol and Port 2010 corpora are compared.

### 0.4.2 Corpus annotation

Corpus annotation entails the adding of information to a corpus, either by the compilers or by third-party users. The two principal forms of annotation employed are known, respectively, as *part-of-speech* (or *POS*) *tagging* and *mark-up*. In the first of these each lexical element in the corpus or segment thereof is assigned a *tag* or label indicating its grammatical status (noun, adverb, preposition, and so on) in the context in which it appears. This is usually performed automatically or semi-automatically; the software makes a preliminary assignment but human post-editing is also sometimes carried out. Tagging is generally carried out for linguistic purposes, either as a precursor to parsing the text or to the check the accuracy (and therefore grammatical understanding) of the tagging system.

Editors may choose to mark-up an almost infinite variety of items in the texts contained in a corpus. They may wish to indicate structural units, such as introductions and closing sequences or headlines and body of newspaper articles (as in the case of the SiBol corpora). In spoken texts they may wish to add information about speech turns, pauses and paralinguistic features such as laughter, and perhaps the sex, age, occupation, and so on, of speakers. Or they may wish to indicate the occurrence of foreign words, slang, personal names, place names, dates, or almost anything an analyst might conceivably be interested in. Standardised editing protocols have been devised which enable marked-up texts to be machine-read in any platform environment. The most commonly used is the Text Encoding Initiative (T.E.I.).[2] Such editing/annotation is clearly highly painstaking and can require considerable investments of time and financial resources.

2. Text Encoding Initiative: ⟨http://www.tei-c.org/index.xml⟩

### 0.4.3 Tools for analysing corpora

A corpus by itself is simply an inert archive. However, it can be "interrogated" using dedicated software. The most important interrogation tools include, first of all, the *concordancer*, then calculators of *frequency*, *keyness*, *clusters* and *dispersion*. McEnery and Hardie have argued (2011, Chapter 2) that there has been relatively little change in the central functions of corpus linguistics tools even as the software has moved through several stages of development, although not everyone would necessarily agree with this. What has perhaps changed more, is the range of ways that linguists are making use of these corpus tools, as we will explore through our case studies.

The concordancer extracts as many examples as the analyst wishes of the word or expression under analysis – usually known as the searchword or search-item or node – and arranges them in a concordance, that is, a list of unconnected lines of text that have been summoned by the concordance program from a computer corpus, with the search-item located at the centre of each line. The rest of the line contains the immediate co-text to the left and right of the search-item. (The concordance is defined more technically by Sinclair as "a collection of the occurrences of a wordform, each in its own textual environment." [1991: 32]). It is generally possible to specify the number of characters of co-text from around, say, 40 to, realistically, around 600 on each side. Figure 0.1 is an example of a concordance with 40 characters of co-text on each side, which fits conveniently on the page of a book:

```
 1 tles are as enigmatic as they are fraught with a bemused paranoia: I Was Overcom
 2 instanley's exploration of images fraught with a sense of millennial angst, but
 3 f the work, one of gay detachment fraught with a sense of destiny, as is everyth
 4 , the reality of being a child is fraught with absurdities. Children are the onl
 5 ment of ways forward in a society fraught with alarm and confusion over unruly y
 6 hasing a property overseas can be fraught with all kinds of problems. Look for a
 7 ur total reliance on computers is fraught with all kinds of dangers. 31 July 200
 8 n gnome was a totem of our times, fraught with all kinds of symbolism: economic
 9 he whole business of nicknames is fraught with ambiguity. At their best, nicknam
10 e baby-naming process can also be fraught with anguish. Catherine, 32, a design
11 er personal experience, are often fraught with animosity and conflict. It's a pi
12 is Davis Cup debut on an occasion fraught with anxiety, not least because politi
13 ture husband. Our wedding day was fraught with anxiety, my mother saying she was
14 ensive purchases and decisions is fraught with anxiety. No wonder so many of us
15 dustry, blighted by urban sprawl, fraught with appalling social problems? Or was
16 hird Reich). The 20th century was fraught with atrocity. The atomic holocaust of
```

A concordance of the first 16 lines of expression *fraught with* from SiBol 05, aligned first word to the right, or R1).

Such a list enables the analyst to look for eventual patterns in the surrounding co-text, which proffer clues to the use of the search-item. In the example given above it can be seen how the expression *fraught with* very generally premodifies something bad, especially of three semantic categories, namely, danger, problems and anxiety (but counterexamples are possible, as in line 3). When an item displays a tendency to co-occur with items from one or more particular categories in this way, a very frequent phenomenon it is said to display a *semantic preference* for them (Sinclair 1996, 1998; both reprinted in Sinclair 2004). In studies of lexical grammar, concordances are generally used to discover patterns of *collocation*, that is, how a particular word or expression cooccurs with other words or sequences of words with particular frequency. These patterns are often not available to unassisted introspection. For studying features of discourse, lists of longer concordance lines of several hundred characters (equivalent to text extracts) are very generally employed since a wider context is needed to know what is actually being communicated interactively by the use of the word or expression being examined.

The frequency – often called the word-list – calculator supplies a list of the words in the corpus in order of frequency. The frequency lists of two or more corpora can also be compared using the *Keyword* facility to show up *relative* frequency, or *key*-ness of vocabulary in a corpus. In practice, this tool produces lists (one alphabetical and one ordered by significance) of all words which are significantly *more* frequent in the first corpus (known as the *study* or *target* corpus) than the second (the *reference* corpus) and also of those which are significantly *less* frequent.[3] The frequency word list thus gives an indication of absolute frequency of lexis in a corpus, whilst the keyword list indicates relative frequency. They can both provide considerable information about both the particular grammatical and lexical items found in the kind of discourse contained in the corpus and the sort of topics dealt with therein.

Clusters, are multi-word units, that is, sequences or strings of words which "are found repeatedly together in each others company" in sequence (Scott 2010). They are also known more technically as n-grams, where n stands for the number of words in the string, thus, a 3-gram would be a three word string. Biber and colleagues refer to a very similar phenomenon as *lexical bundles* (Biber et al. 1999; Biber & Conrad 1999). The software user can specify the length of the string s/he is interested in, generally from two to, realistically, ten words. They are a kind of extremely tight "extended collocation", and they stand in an interesting and complex relation to what are normally recognised as grammatical constructions. Table 0.2 is a list of the most common 4-word clusters found in a 500,000 corpus of UK newspaper editorials (from Partington & Morley 2004):

3. It should, however, be noted that there is currently some debate as to the most appropriate metric for measuring keyness, see Gabrielatos and Marchi 2011.

**Table 0.2.** The most common 4-word clusters in a corpus of UK newspaper editorials

| N⁰ | Cluster | Frequency |
|---|---|---|
| 1 | THE HOUSE OF COMMONS | 49 |
| 2 | THE HOUSE OF LORDS | 47 |
| 3 | THE END OF THE | 43 |
| 4 | THE REST OF THE | 38 |
| 5 | AT THE HEART OF | 29 |
| 6 | OF THE HOUSE OF | 29 |
| 7 | PER CENT OF THE | 29 |
| 8 | AT A TIME WHEN | 27 |
| 9 | AT THE END OF | 27 |
| 10 | IT IS HARD TO | 26 |

Some clusters are simply titles like *The House of Commons, The President of the United States,* or fixed phrases such as *on the one hand, by all means, never a dull moment,* and so on, but it must be born in mind that phrases which have any kind of internal variability (including the kind of phrase templates discussed in the next chapter and elsewhere) are much less likely to appear in a cluster list, unless the corpus has been lemmatised first (that is all grammatical variants of a word grouped as one). Others have a definite phrase-like quality, for example, *the rest of the, at the heart of, at a time when* and it was with this type of cluster in mind that Partington and Morley suggest they might possibly "constitute 'missing links' on the chain or cline from the linguistic morass to the abstraction we call grammar" (2004: 191). In discourse terms, they reveal typical ways of saying things and therefore typical author/speaker messages. As Biber points out, many clusters, especially lengthier ones, are very obviously discourse-type specific, as illustrated by these 6-grams from White House press briefings: *I'm not going to get into, I think it's important to understand, the American people expect us to,* which are clearly parts of stock responses by the spokesperson. The study of clusters can thus tell us a great deal about how speakers and writers go about the construction of particular kinds of discourse.

The software suite we employ for clustering in this work, namely the *WordSmith Tools Version 5.0* (Scott 2008), also permits the user to compile key-cluster lists. Lists of clusters of the required length from different corpora are first compiled by the word-list tool which allows the user to specify cluster length and these are then compared in the normal way by the keywords software. This procedure can produce interesting insights but generally only when very large corpora are being examined.

An important variation on the cluster list is the concgram (see Cheng et al. 2006 for discussion or Greaves 2009 for the software), which is also available in Wordsmith Tools Version 5. The concgram looks for sequences of words, in a similar way to clusters or n-grams, but can handle empty slots in the sequence.

Finally, the dispersion tool plots where an item occurs within a text. It can display in graphic fashion where an item or set of items typically occur in a large number of texts. One may wish, for instance, to discover whether editorial exhortative modals like *should* or ought to generally appear at the beginning middle or end of newspaper editorials or at which point during press briefings particular issues (for example *taxes*, *jobs*, *Middle East*) tend to be discussed, which may well reflect the relative degree of importance the participants endow them with. An example of a dispersion plot can be found in Chapter 5.

Other software tools will be discussed where relevant and Appendix 1 contains a list of useful resources.

## 0.5 Guide to the contents of this book

As stated earlier, the present volume has a similar format and progression to that of its predecessor, *Patterns and Meanings*, though the topics treated are very different.

Following this Introduction, Chapter 1 takes a fresh look at how discourse is organised both productively and receptively and contextualises within a cognitive framework one of the fundamental pillars of Sinclairian lexical grammar – that discourse works by the interaction of two very general principles, that is, the idiom and the open-choice principles. We argue that the two principles are an expression of two fundamental mental processes. The idiom principle can be interpreted as a special case of the application of *schema* (also known as *script*) recall, whilst open-choice language interpretation is a special case of inductive, rule-driven reasoning.

We attempt to demonstrate first of all, then, that communicative discourse is organised along similar lines – exploiting the two fundamental processes – at the micro or phrase level but also, importantly for the theme of this book, at a more macro discourse level. We go on to argue that human language behaviour follows much the same dual principles as other forms of social behaviour, that is, *recall* – with adaptation – of familiar routines and *induction* from what we (presume to) know about the world (including the grammatical rules of language).

In Chapter 2 we examine how evaluation functions in extended discourse. Most work in this area has tended to concentrate on relatively limited segments, but here we see how evaluative meanings "hunt in packs" within a discourse to the extent of contributing very greatly to textual cohesion. Concordance evidence is used to shed light on particularly complicated instances, for example, when the evaluative polarity (good or bad) may not be immediately obvious to the naked eye, that is, cases of evaluative (or semantic) prosody. In passing we attempt a rough categorisation of different types of evaluative lexis.

Chapter 3 continues with the theme of evaluation and investigates some instantiations of evaluation in communicative discourse which flow from the application of general psychological principles. Prominent among these is that of being or not being in control of our environment and what goes on inside it, the former being very generally construed as a good thing, the latter very often as highly negative. We look at examples in context where a semantic feature of control can be identified and the evaluative polarity depends on the point of view of who is in control, whether control is being lost, fought for, used against others, and so on.

Other possible general psychological principles which may affect evaluation, and which can be studied through the lexical-grammatical trace they leave in discourse include: apprehensions about change; presence (including having) or absence (including not having) and the (attempted) achievement of goals. All of these can interact with the in control – not in control principle.

Chapters 4 and 5 are concerned with two different rhetorical figures, namely irony and metaphor respectively. Chapter 4 describes three corpus-assisted investigations into the nature and functions of irony in both spoken interaction and written texts. In the first two case studies we examine utterance (or propositional) irony, to ascertain how both explicit and implicit ironic utterances operate. In the third we describe the phenomenon of phrasal irony and describe instances where ironic exploitation can become a conventionalised usage. The dual aims of these studies are, first, to see whether an examination of corpus-based real-life data can both paint a detailed picture of how irony operates in practice and second to shed light on some of the important theoretical controversies in irony studies.

Chapter 5 relates two complementary case studies, the first into conventional metaphors, in this case, those typically used to convey messages around *anti-Americanism*, and the second into novel or "nonce" metaphors, created for a specific purpose on a specific occasion. We thus investigate how a corpus-assisted approach can allow us to examine the two different functions of metaphor: in the first, metaphor is used to make the abstract and unfamiliar more tangible and comprehensible, and in the second, metaphor is employed to make the mundane and familiar appear novel, interesting and entertaining.

All the case studies in these two chapters reveal how both figures, irony and metaphor, have an overriding function of expressing evaluations and of inviting an audience to share these evaluations. Indeed to evaluate is the very reason they exist. Irony functions by reversing a surface evaluation to an underlying one – usually from positive to negative – and is generally of course, used to criticise. But it is also often employed as an attempt to win audience affiliation. The evaluations driving metaphors can be either positive ("Juliet is the sun") or negative ("fanning the flames of anti-Americanism"), and although some metaphors when not in context can seem neutral ("the march of ..."), rare is the metaphor which is not used in real-life discourse one way or the other evaluatively ("the march of democracy"; "the march of the disease" [SiBol 05]).

Chapter 6 contains a case study in corpus-assisted stylistics, that is, the use of corpus techniques combined and integrated with more traditional study methods from discourse analysis and literary criticism with the aim of identifying and describing the distinctive characteristics of a particular authorial style. The subject of the case study is the comic prose of P.G Wodehouse, the starting point of which is the compilation of a corpus of his work and, since stylistic studies are by their nature comparative, the particular characteristics of one author or set of authors only being evident and available for evaluation when their work is compared to that of others, of another two corpora of contemporary prose for the purpose of statistical comparison. The conclusion of the chapter consists of a discussion of what both corpus techniques and close reading can and cannot do by themselves, and what advantages can ensue from combining the two.

Chapter 7 contains a cross-linguistic case study in which the methods of CADS are used to analyse how racism and xenophobia are represented and discussed in the Italian and UK press. In addition to the cross-linguistic analysis, another methodological technique illustrated in this chapter is the integration of extra-corpus statistical information in the research process. We start by surveying some previous research in this area and then move on to the case study, which is divided into three main phases. In the first phase, Section 7.4, terms referring to racism and xenophobia were concordanced to investigate how the newspapers presented and used these terms. In the second phase, we focus on the terms *refugees, asylum seekers, immigrants, migrants* (and Italian equivalents) and the various nationalities associated with these terms were identified. This information is then compared to "real-world" statistical data in order to identify any mis-match between the estimated numbers of migrants from a given country and the amount of attention that they receive in the media. This simple comparison of estimated populations and media visibility aids in identifying groups which are foregrounded and which would then be objectively identified groups for subsequent analysis.

Chapter 8 and Chapter 9 concentrate on spoken discourse. The first begins with reflections on the nature of spoken language and how corpora have been and might be used to study it. We then present a comparative case study of what we call *forced priming*, that is, the deliberate attempt to impose a particular interpretation of language, in two interactive institutional discourse types, press briefings and judicial inquiry, where there is competition among participants to have a particular version of events generally accepted. We observe how the strategies employed by different institutional players in the attempt to have their particular messages adopted by other parties, including an adjudicating audience, can be very different.

Chapter 9 is concerned with im/politeness and starts with an overview of the types of research in this area. It then presents a case study in order to investigate what, in practice, a corpus approach to im/politeness may involve. The study examines the use of conventional markers of respect such as *with respect* or *sir* and challenges the blunt assumption that a polite form will necessarily be doing politeness work. Using corpus evidence, we demonstrate that the use of such forms can perform a number of different functions in discourse other than respecting an interlocutor's face. Indeed, they are sometimes used as a deliberate ploy to attack it. In the first stage of the case study, we illustrate how corpora may be employed to identify sites of potential impoliteness in a systematic and replicable way and in the second stage, we use the corpora to examine occurrences of the markers of conventional negative politeness and identify patterns of usage within different discourse types.

Chapter 10 presents firstly an overview and then a case study in the novel discipline of modern diachronic corpus-assisted discourse studies (MD-CADS). We employ three relatively large corpora, namely the SiBol and Port corpora of circa 100–150 million words respectively, sister corpora of similar structure and content containing UK broadsheet newspapers texts from 1993, 2005 and 2010 (see 0.4.1), with the aim of studying changes over recent time in the language of news reporting and comment. Since newspaper language consists of a wide variety of discourse types, it is felt that our observations may have some validity – with all due caveats – for British English as a whole.

Chapter 11, instead, employs data from the SiBol and Port 2010 corpora to compare earlier with more recent attitudes to certain social, cultural and political phenomenon, as construed and projected by the mainstream UK quality press. The first case study analyses differences in the way antisemitism is discussed. A comparison of the 1993 data with more recent datasets indicates how the loci of reported antisemitism have shifted both in place and time. In the earlier dataset it was discussed largely in terms of Eastern Europe and Russia, or Nazi Germany, and as belonging to past times. In the most recent data, however, it is discussed more as a current phenomenon, interesting the UK and Western Europe much more closely.

In the second section to the chapter, we focus on the importance of searching for sameness as well as difference. A range of methods and approaches for addressing similarity are identified and then we use a case study to illustrate the approaches and examine what a search for similarity might tell us about our data. This case study concentrates on the use of the lemmas BOY and GIRL in the broadsheet newspapers and, in particular, looks at the patterns that have remained stable over the seventeen-year time period.

Several of the case studies outlined in this volume are intended as investigations of areas which have sometimes been thought to represent particular problems for corpus linguistics approaches. Metaphor, irony, politeness, spoken interaction, and searching for similarity rather than difference are all challenges for approaches which rely wholly or mainly on quantitative techniques of searching for lexical strings. For instance, there is no special language for metaphor or irony; any piece of language used metaphorically or ironically could be used non-metaphorically or non-ironically and only the human mind can infer which use was intended in a particular context. However corpus techniques can, by revealing significant *patterns*, guide and inform research in these areas and help shed light on non-obvious *meanings*.

CHAPTER 1

# The two principles of discourse organisation

## Chunk recall and inductive reasoning

### 1.1 Introduction

Sinclair (1987a) describes two basic principles of language organisation at the phrase level. The first is the *idiom* or *collocational* principle, which sees a text as largely composed of preconstituted blocks of language whilst the other, the *open-choice* principle of language, sees a text as "the result of a very large number of complex choices", largely word by word (1987a: 319). In Sinclair (1996, 2004) these two principles are also referred to as the *phraseological tendency* (equivalent to the *idiom*), "the tendency of a speaker/writer to choose several words at a time" and the *terminological tendency* (equivalent to the *open-choice*), "the tendency of language users to protect the meaning of a word or phrase so that every time it is used it guarantees delivery of a known meaning" (2004: 170). The sense of *term* (in "*term*inological") here is that commonly implied in the sciences, that a word or phrase carries a fixed meaning, and so the terminological tendency is the tendency to use words as if they were technical terms, interpretable in a consistent manner.

The two principles do not operate in isolation from each other: "the preponderance of usage lies between the two. Some features of language patterning tend to favour one, some the other" (Sinclair 2004: 29). In other words, although both principles contribute to producing a discourse, at any particular moment of the production, according to Sinclair, one or the other will be predominantly in play.

In this chapter it is argued that the two principles are an expression of two fundamental mental processes. The idiom principle can be interpreted as a special case of the application of schema- or script-based processing, whilst open-choice language interpretation is a special case of inductive, rule-driven reasoning. In Sections 2 and 3, we will investigate the analogy between the two dualities.

Sinclair's corpus observations derive from the *Bank of English*. The work here uses the *SiBol* corpus of British broadsheet newspaper texts (see 0.4.1).

## 1.2 Grammatical organisation

### 1.2.1 Open choice

Open choice has been the traditional way of describing grammatical organisation, just as, before research into scripts and schemata began, studies of how the mind worked, from Aristotle to Hume to Russell tended to privilege the view of mental processing in terms of inferential reasoning, of inductive logic (induction is in fact the latinisation of ἐπαγωγή, first used in this sense by Aristotle): analytical for understanding concepts, synthetical for proposing, elaborating them. If we take the syllogism as an example (normally associated with deductive logic rather than inductive, but the point is the same), whoever devises it has to apply a set of logical rules (synthetically in the sense of "build up", "combine"); whoever then has to interpret it has to apply those rules to analyse it.

Open choice – at its simplest – describes language production as a continuous series of open-ended choices, each an individual unit of meaning, "a series of slots which have to be filled from a lexicon" (Sinclair 1987a: 320), the restraints being the application of the rules of the syntax of the language in question, that is, that only items from certain word classes may appear in a given slot. Thus an utterance like *the cat sat on the mat* is first prepared or analysed as:

(1) Noun Phrase *followed by* Verb Phrase *followed by* Prepositional Phrase.

The production and processing of this sequence is further broken down as follows. The noun phrase opens with a determiner *the*. One of the classes of items that can "legally" follow a determiner is a noun, so we can insert *cat*. A noun phrase Subject must (sooner or later) be followed by a verb phrase and we choose *SIT* + *past tense* i.e. *sat*. Our knowledge of English grammar tells us that *sat* (belonging to the class of so-called intransitive verbs) can be followed either by nothing (thus ending the phrase: *the cat sat*), or by an adverbial e.g. *the cat sat down*, or by a preposition as, here, *on*, in which case a noun phrase must follow. Whether or not this is the actual psychological procedure followed by the human mind in the synthesis of utterance construction or the analysis of utterance interpretation, or whether it is rather an explanatory model was one of the burning questions of traditional grammarians' debate (although, as Hoey stresses, it must all follow upon an initial *desire* to communicate, upon "the initial impulsion to inform, contradict, praise, and so on" (2005: 163).

### 1.2.2 The idiom principle and coselection

The *idiom* or *collocational* or *phraseological* principle, on the other hand, sees normal discourse as largely composed of preconstituted or semi-preconstituted blocks of language (including prefabs [Bolinger 1976], multi-word units [Zgusta 1967;

Baker & McCarthy 1990], schemas/schemata [Barlow & Kemmer 1994; Moon 1998; Stubbs 2000], templates [Morley & Partington 2009] and extended lexical units [Sinclair 2004]). Thus, "the language user has available to him a large number of preconstructed or semi-preconstructed phrases that constitute single choices, even though they appear to be analysable into segments" (Sinclair 1987a: 320). The underlying principle, in Sinclair's terms, is that of *coselection*, that items are not always inserted in discourse one by one but often in pre-packaged or semi pre-packaged lots. These include simple collocations, such as *roaring fire*, proper names, *the Houses of Parliament*, set phrases *as a matter of fact, by all means*, idioms *never a dull moment*, semi-idiomatic templates, for instance, LIVE *to a* [*ripe/grand*] *old age* (Stubbs 2000), templates containing fixed parts but also elements of considerable variability, for example, (Locality A) BE *a* number + time-word + vehicle + (*journey, trip, voyage, flight* etc.) *from* (Locality B), which can be realised as *a twenty-minute bus ride from, a two-hour train journey from, a five-day bike-hike from*, and so on (Hoey 2005: 16–17), and also other abstract items which have what we might call lexical-grammatical satellites orbiting around them, such as *brook* + negative + modal, which can be realised in a wide variety of ways *will brook no…, determined not to brook*, and so on (Sinclair 2004: 36–37). Sinclair maintains that the idiom or phraseological principle of language is more frequently in play than has often been appreciated, both in *producing* and *interpreting* discourse. We make use of coselection, from prefabs to schema templates, because we rarely recount experiences which are entirely novel and, even if we did, we would talk of them in ways that related them to previously acquired knowledge. Listeners also rely on them heavily in *interpreting* discourse, because phraseological recall requires less time and effort than constant rule-driven synthesis since it helps them to relate what is being said to what they already know and also, simply, because it is the way the hearer expects the discourse to be organised.

Sinclair illustrates the principle by means of the common phrase *out of the corner of my eye*, as found in *but I'm watching out of the corner of my eye*. "There are seven words in the phrase," he says, "and they all simultaneously choose one unit of meaning, to do with peripheral vision" (2004: 171). There is some room for internal variation: *my* can be a different possessive depending on the owner of the eye, and *out of* can occasionally cede its place to *from*. "So here we have a seven-word phrase which realizes one overall choice and at most two subsidiary choices" (2004: 171). The description is replicated and largely corroborated by the following selection of sentence concordance lines from the *SiBol 93* corpus:

1. Seeing the movement out of the corner of his eye, Faldo was distracted.
2. […] tricks of the trade that can win or lose a show, he says, observing the judges out of the corner of his eye.
3. He could appear to be dozing but was always peeping out of the corner of his eye.

4. Out of the corner of his eye the scrum-half sees a black shirt and instinctively goes the other way.
5. Out of the corner of my eye I could see the sales assistant spraying and polishing.
6. A widowed father, who lives happily with his daughter, watches out of the corner of his eye as she seems to be pushing past the best age for marriage.

In all, there were 28 occurrences in the corpus, of which only two were not accompanied by a verb of seeing and thus referred to the physical eye itself rather than the more abstract concept of vision (one, from a boxing report, refers to a cut at the corner of the eye, whilst in another, someone wipes away a tear from the corner of her eye). When the verb preceded the expression it took a variety of forms, for example, SEE, WATCH, OBSERVE, NOTICE. But when it came after, in all cases but one it was a form of SEE. The "seeing" is usually actual physical sight but, as the last example in the above list shows, figurative uses are possible, the vision in this case referring to a more metaphorical kind of vision, into the future or into hypothetical situations.

We can now represent the expression notationally as: {SEE} + [*out of*/*from*] *the corner of* [possessive] *eye*, where the curly brackets indicate (roughly speaking) a semantic set, whilst the parts inside the square brackets are variable and the parts outside brackets are invariable. Such a phrase cannot simply be dismissed as "idiom" and therefore "anomalous", not subject to the normal working of language and so irrelevant. If it is argued that *corner* in *corner of the eye* is figurative, then there is little of language which is not figurative. This is, of course, precisely the case. Consider the vast array of other anatomical expressions like *the rib cage*, *the roof of her mouth*, *the bridge of his nose*; physics could not exist without metaphor: *particle spin*, *quantum field*; nor indeed could linguistics: *lexical chain*, *fossilization*, and so on. In systemic terms we might say language is *analogous*, that is, complex concepts are described by analogy to other, often simpler and frequently more concrete ones.

Authors in the area of lexical grammar have provided similar illustrations of the idiom/phraseological principle. Pawley and Syder (1983) talk of *lexicalized sentence stems*, whilst, most revealingly for the purposes of this work, Barlow and Kemmer (Barlow & Kemmer 1994; Barlow 1996) employ the similar notion of the linguistic *schema*. The use of this term – also adopted by Moon ("idiom schema"; 1998) and Stubbs ("semantic schema"; 2000) – consciously or unconsciously recalls Bartlett's work on the role of schemata in learning in general, recalled by Koestler:

> We learn by assimilating experiences and grouping them into ordered schemata, into stable patterns of unity in variety. They enable us to cope with events and situations by applying the rules of the game appropriate to them. (1964:44)

Biber et al. provide some statistical data on the extreme frequency and pervasiveness of a related phenomenon, what they term "lexical bundles", that is, "sequences of word forms which commonly go together in natural discourse" (1999: 990). In the Longman Spoken and Written English Corpus (LSWE), they found that bundles were extremely common in both conversation and academic prose, that is to say in both the least and most formal of the registers they study. They discovered that three-word bundles occur over 80,000 times per million words in conversation and over 60,000 times per million words in academic prose and that four-word bundles occur over 8,500 times per million words in conversation and over 5,000 times in academic prose. Given that a three or four word bundle was only counted if it occurred at least ten times per million words, thus severely limiting the number of sequences taken into consideration, it is immediately clear just how much of communication consists of fixed strings of words. They find that five-word bundles are ten times less frequent than four-word bundles, six-word bundles ten times less frequent than five-word strings, and so on, but, since they counted only entirely fixed strings (much easier to locate using their corpus-searching software), templates, that is sequences with a degree of internal variation, did not show up. If these were included then the proportion of language in use consisting of fixed and semi-fixed word groups would be still greater. A further finding was that the kind of bundles predominant in conversation were clausal (that is containing a verb), such as *do you want*, *I don't know what*, whilst there was a greater tendency for those in academic writing to be nominal (an incomplete noun phrase), such as *the nature of* and *as a result of*. That conversation, given the time constraints in both production and reception should consist heavily of ready-made chunks is perhaps not surprising. We might speculate that the fact that text-chunks are also so frequently employed in academic prose, where time constraint is not a problem, is because they also contribute to clarity of message by standardising the means of communication. We can infer that habit plays a much more important part in language than was previously imagined.

### 1.2.3 Issues with idioms

Having noted all the above, it must also be underlined that, although the existence of prefabs/bundles/templates, and so on, has long been recognised in the field of corpus-assisted lexical grammar, what was missing until recently was a coherent account of how they come into existence, in other words, what are the linguistic and psycholinguistic forces which bring them into being. Hoey's theory of lexical priming (2005), to which we turn in Section 1.5.2, addresses this lacuna.

There are a couple of other issues concerning the idiom principle. Firstly, it is often hard to know the limits of an extended lexical item, to know just what it includes. To take a couple of examples from the literature, is the lexical item *smelling of roses* or is it [come up] *smelling of roses* or, given that it is normally found with negative polarity, is it *not* + [come up] *smelling of roses* (Stubbs 2009: 23–24)? Is *the naked eye* the full lexical item or is it [visible] *to the naked eye* or, once again, given the frequent negative polarity, [invisible] *to the naked eye* (Sinclair 2004: 31–47; Morley 2004a). This issue of what precisely is the extent of a lexical item becomes a vital one in considering which evaluative (or semantic) prosody (see Chapter 2) it helps express. For instance if the item is *smelling of roses*, the prosody is positive, because someone is being described as morally irreprehensible, but if it is *not* + [come up] *smelling of roses*, then the prosody is clearly negative.

Secondly, some items have a highly abstract form or template which normal corpus analysis technology finds hard to handle. As Stubbs notes, the apparent unit *can't stand the smell*, which can be picked up by an n-gram (cluster) search, is actually a variant of a wider model CAN + *not* (*stand/bear/tolerate* etc.) the (*heat, sight, smell, thought* etc.), which cannot be detected by n-gram search. Similarly, the template BE *a* number + time-word + vehicle + (*journey, trip, voyage, flight* etc.) *from* has no invariant elements at all (apart from *a* and *from*) and can have innumerable realisations which corpus technology would find hard to relate together. Lexical priming theory (1.5.2) also attempts to get to grips with both of these issues, namely, the limits of the item and this variability of realisation.

The next section here (1.3) provides an account of the theory of scripts, the historical development of Barlett's work, in order to examine the link, or analogy, between it and the idiom principle, that is, between cognitive processing using scripts and language processing using linguistic schemata (or preconstructed phrases, or templates, or extended units of meaning). Any attempt to settle the ancient debate over whether language processing is a form of cognitive processing or whether the two are of distinct types is, of course, well beyond the scope of this book. What we are intending is to test the hypothesis that some of the processes involved in cognitive and language processing are similar.

This is followed (Section 1.4) by an overview of the second general tendency of cognitive processing, inferencing from general knowledge and context, with the aim of appraising its potential relation to the other language-organising principle, that of open choice.

## 1.3 Script theory

### 1.3.1 Learning and memory

The closely related schema (Bartlett 1932), frame (Minsky 1975) and script theories (Schank & Abelson 1977; Schank 1986, 1991) are theories first and foremost of learning and memory. Bartlett's seminal work is entitled *Remembering* whilst Schank and Abelson state plainly that their book is, "in a sense, entirely about memory [...] human memory organization" (Schank & Abelson 1977: 17). These theories are obviously mentalist in character, in that they take for granted the existence of mind:

> American social psychology had its roots in Gestalt psychology and therefore did not succumb to the excesses of behaviorism the way human experimental psychology did. The phenomenology of mental life maintained a central role. (Schank & Abelson 1977: 10)

At the core of these theories is the argument that the mind plays an *active* role in the organisation of memory.

Schank and Abelson argue that many of the experiences, or "sequences of events" that humans encounter are similar to or reminiscent of others, that is to say, much of life consists of meeting with roughly comparable experiences. It is reasonable to assume, they continue, that human memory must include the capability of recognising repeated or similar sequences of events. When sufficient experiences of a certain type have been met, the memory "as an economy measure" stores the sequences of events as a "standardized generalized episode which we will call a script" (1977: 19). The script contains an outline description of the typical events in their proper sequence. Thus, after having eaten in restaurants (Schank & Abelson's recurrent example) a number of times, an individual's memory will have constructed a *restaurant script* (**$RESTAURANT** in their notation) of how the events contingent upon a visit to a restaurant normally unfold (arrive, enter, allow the waiter/waitress to show you to a table, etc.) and for each subsequent visit to a restaurant "rather than list the details of what happened [...] memory simply stores the items in this particular episode that were significantly different from the standard script as the only items specifically in the description of that episode" (1977: 19). A script then "is a structure that describes appropriate sequences of events in a particular context" and consists of "slots and requirements about what can fill those slots". "Slot-fillers" can be particular events or sequences of events, i.e. (sub)scripts (e.g. choosing what to eat and drink). Scripts are thus described as syntagms in many ways analogous to the linguistic schema or phrase template which, as we have seen, have some invariable parts and some other segments which vary according to context on individual instantiation.

A script differs from a *concept* in that it must unfold ("be written" 1977: 42) from one particular role's point of view – the restaurant script for the customer is different from that of the waiter. One participant's script interacts with those of others in an event, just as speakers' contributions interaction in a language event (conversation, interview, and so on).

### 1.3.2 Understanding discourse

Scripts were earlier defined in terms of their contribution to memory, but script theory has aroused the greatest interest in those fields which attempt to explain human *understanding* including, indeed especially, that of processing natural discourse. Script theory was elaborated in the domain of Artificial Intelligence as an attempt to solve some of the problems researchers encountered in trying to teach machines to understand human communication, in particular the problem of how "the appropriate ingredients for extracting the meaning of a sentence [...] are often nowhere to be found within the sentence" (Schank & Abelson 1977: 9). The researchers recognized that acquired background knowledge of both situation and texts/discourses was of overwhelming importance in interpreting the simplest utterances, for instance:

(2) I went to three drugstores this morning.

usually implies that the speaker did not find what they were looking for in the first two. The problem is the same as that which interests Grice, who asserts that with the utterance:

(3) [Mr] X is meeting a woman this evening.

the speaker is normally implying (or "implicating") that "the person to be met was someone other than Mr X's wife, mother, sister or perhaps even close Platonic friend" (Grice 1975: 50).

In analogy with preconstructed phrases, preconstructed scripts are used to "*interpret* and *participate in* (our emphasis) events we have been through many times" (Schank & Abelson 1977: 37). Although the interpretation of a situation is of course frequently the prelude to participation in it, most of Schank and Abelson's discussion concentrates on the first of these and examines the ways subjects understand stories, sequential narratives, and so on.

For Schank and Abelson, proof that humans use scripts comes in the form of what they call *causal chains*. In speaking and writing, people consistently leave out information that they feel can easily be recovered by the listener or reader because it is contained within the prefabricated script (Schank & Abelson 1977: 22). In particular in a context where A causes B and B causes C, when the path is "obvious", humans communicate "A, then C". For example, compare the utterances:

(4) John burned his hand because he touched the stove.

(5) John burned his hand because he forgot the stove was on.

The first means what it says causally, but in the second, "forgetting" does not cause "burning" except by a missing process – that of absent-mindedly touching the stove. The following:

(6) John cried because Mary said she loved Bill.

"is a meaningful, well-constructed sentence [...] Yet, it is literally quite silly". And though such sentences do not generally cause problems in human communication, "in designing a theory of understanding, there is a great deal to worry about" (Schank & Abelson 1977:23). The only explanation of how humans cope so effortlessly with this kind of utterance is that they have the necessary interpretative information, especially the missing links, already stored away, largely in the form of preconstructed scripts. In practice, speakers tend to concentrate on what cannot be assumed, the deviations from the default script, which will, of course, generally be the *point* of the narration. Hearers will expect the same, will expect not to be burdened with information they can safely assume and indeed, if assumable procedures are explicitly mentioned (e.g. "the food was eaten"), they are liable to cast around for the special significance of its inclusion. All this is in accord with Sperber and Wilson's (1995) general communicative principle of *relevance* which states that, in normal circumstances, speakers attempt to achieve *optimal relevance*, that is, they try to communicate meaning at the lowest possible processing cost to the hearer. This implies that, from the hearer's point of view, they will presume that any apparent extra demands on them are being made because extra information is being conveyed.

In close analogy, in linguistic terms at the phrase level, the employment of preconstructed phrases entails the leaving out and taking for granted of a considerable degree of shared information. The meaning of most lexical phrases is not self-explanatory as Sinclair notes in his detailed discussion of the expression *naked eye* (which is also "literally quite silly"): "there is no useful interpretation for this phrase based on the core meaning of the two words, e.g. 'unclothed organ of sight'" (2004:31). Both speaker and listener need to share knowledge of conventional meanings which thus have no need to be spelled out. We might even presume that many preconstructed phrases, like scripts, have the precise purpose of concentrating as much information as possible in a brief unit (see 1.5.2 below on the productive template already mentioned: BE *a* number + time-word + vehicle + (*journey*, *trip*, *voyage*, *flight* etc.) *from*).

There remain, however, a number of fundamental questions to consider. For example, how many times does one have to have experience of a situation to internalise its features into a script? Or consider the following set of related issues. How can anyone do anything for the first time (say, buy a car)? How can people have a hearsay script, that is, one you have not experienced yourself but have been told about or even explicitly taught? How do these differ from the standard experiential scripts? Similarly, what is the status of scripts in fiction, that is, event sequences that never actually happened, and, more outlandishly still, do we have "unreal scripts", that is, stereotypical information about events that could never happen?

These questions have their correlates with regard to language at the phrase level. For example, how are linguistic templates built up and memorised by an individual by exposure to language and interaction with others? How do people deal with language constructions never before heard, and how do we actively produce novel and creative language forms? Hoey, in formulating the theory of lexical priming (1.5.2), grapples with such questions, as we begin to in the next section.

## 1.4 Inductive knowledge-driven reasoning

Throughout this chapter, the term *induction* is used in its technical sense as the most important form of *inference* (itself intended to mean something rather more precise than its day-to-day usage [labelled by *Webster's* as "loose"] as "guessing") and refers to the mental process of "the forming of a conclusion from data or premisses […]; reasoning from something known or assumed to something else which follows from it" (*OED*). It is the process by which new knowledge (or as the epistemological philosopher Hume would have it, *beliefs*) is formed from pre-existing knowledge/beliefs, the important point being that the new knowledge/beliefs goes beyond anything that we perceive or remember (see for instance Example 7 below). We place it in contraposition to wholesale script evocation and recall which involves much less or no real-time induction or deduction.

### 1.4.1 Needs, goals and plans

There is one important part of Schank and Abelson's theory which is frequently overlooked, namely their description of how understanding occurs when an actor has no script for a particular situation. The answer, they contend, is that human beings also, according to Schank and Abelson, make use of another type of knowledge. The kind of information contained in scripts is described as *specific* knowledge, but we also have access to what they call *general* knowledge which:

> enables a person to understand and interpret another person's actions simply because the other person is a human being with certain standard needs who lives in a world which has certain standard methods of getting those needs fulfilled.
> (Schank & Abelson 1977: 37)

Because we inhabit the same sort of bodies in the same sort of world, we share many similar needs with our fellow human animals, thus "if someone asks you for a glass of water, you need not ask why he wants it" (Schank & Abelson 1977: 37). It is this general sort of knowledge of the rules and regularities which generally drive human behaviour that allows us – by a process of inductive reasoning – to begin to interpret novel situations in the first place and then go on to construct scripts from our experiences.

More particularly, we readily assume (sometimes erroneously) that our fellows will have much the same goals as we do or at least that we can envisage having. Thus we are able to interpret "John cried because Mary said she loved Bill" partly because we know human males often desire the exclusive affection of a particular female and, on discovering that they do not possess it, are liable to feel pain. Furthermore, we also assume (sometimes just as erroneously) that our fellows are rational, in the sense of being goal-oriented and likely to follow some kind of reasonable plan to achieve those goals. We use this knowledge of plan-making, say Schank and Abelson, to interpret even the most seemingly disconnected sentences:

(7) John knew that his wife's operation would be very expensive.
There was always Uncle Harry...
He reached for the suburban phone book.

even when this is our very first experience of sick wives and rich uncles.

Thus, we make use of inductive reasoning in order both to build scripts in the first place and also to make sense of novel situations.

Note that, although the logical inductive inferencing of goals and plans constitute "the mechanisms that underlie scripts", that is, it constitutes the main means by which we construct our scripts, understanding via scripts tends to have priority. If we can interpret an event by finding a script, then we will do so, since it saves much processing time and effort. Only if we fail to interpret it do we fall back on general knowledge induction. The first is "quick and dirty" whilst the second requires the deliberate inductive construction of a *mental model* (Johnson-Laird 1981a, 1981b, 1983) that will fit the data. As we shall see, this too has its parallel in real-time language organisation.

Such issues are not just of academic interest. Power in many types of institutional interaction can be explained in terms of superior script-awareness. Often the powerful participant is one who has experience of the script, can guide or exploit less experienced participants to his/her own advantage, for example, barristers, police interrogators and journalists.

## 1.5 Parallels

### 1.5.1 Open choice and logical induction: *Rule-driven* behaviour

The parallels between the open-choice principle and induction from first basics is thus very close. As we have seen, general-knowledge driven induction enables a hearer to build up a model of what is happening at any particular juncture by applying a *set of rules* deriving from what the individual knows of the normal behaviour of people and objects. Similarly, in linguistic terms, when interpreting novel utterances, hearers check whether the input they are receiving is decipherable by applying a *set of rules* deriving from what that individual knows of the normal behaviour and interaction of lexical items, that is, their internalised lexical grammar of the language.

Even if the input is defective, a best model can still be put together. The parallel between cognitive and grammatical rule-driven procedures for model-building is strongly supported by the observations from many parts that a great deal of real-life language, especially spoken language, is not entirely grammatically well-formed but nevertheless interpretable. Just as "this book fills a much needed gap" – again, "literally quite silly" as it stands – was still found to be cognitively meaningful (Johnson-Laird 1981a), at the lexical-grammatical level, lapses, false starts, interruptions, failure to finish phrases are all commonplace (as in the following examples taken from White House press briefings, Partington 2003):

(8) You talked yesterday about Senator Byrd had a valid point when he talked about [...]

(9) No, but neither is he someone that's easy to control or to tell him what to say.

as are utterances containing lexical items used idiosyncratically (our emphasis):

(10) The enemy understands a free Iraq will be a major defeat in their ideology of hatred. That's why they're fighting so *vociferously*.
(George W. Bush, Presidential Debate, University of Miami, 2005)

Nevertheless, except in extreme cases, discourse interaction is not impeded, participants carry on regardless. The simplest explanation, as we noted earlier, is that we develop a best inductive inference of what the "imperfect" utterance must have been, a mental model of what the other person meant to say, deriving from both our knowledge of the lexical grammar of the language and our experience of human interaction, including which mistakes or inadequacies are most likely to occur.

### 1.5.2 The idiom and the script principles: Lexical priming

The analogy between the idiom and script principles is equally close. To highlight the parallel between how we learn to behave in social interaction and how we learn a language, we can profitably examine Hoey's (2005) notion of *lexical priming*. Lexical priming is a self-reproducing *mental* phenomenon whereby the normal language user learns, by repeated acquaintance with a lexical item and by processes of analogy with other similar items, the typical behaviour of that item in interaction. In particular, we learn which other lexical items it co-occurs with regularly (*collocation*), which semantic sets it occurs with (*semantic association*; other authors would favour the term *semantic preference*; see Sinclair 2004: 32–33, 142; Partington 2004b), which grammatical categories it co-occurs with or avoids and which grammatical positions it favours or disfavours (*colligation*), which positions in an utterance or sentence or paragraph or entire text it tends to prefer or to avoid occurring in (*textual colligation*) and whether it tends to participate in cohesion or not.

The user then reproduces this behaviour in their own linguistic performance. By metaphorical extension (a process common to all descriptions of grammar: for instance, when we declare that "x is a noun", this is a metaphorical statement whose literal meaning is that "x is generally employed by speakers to fulfil a set of functions conventionally associated with the set of items we denominate *nouns*"), the lexical item itself is said to be primed to behave in these particular ways, and so lexical priming is also regarded as a *textual* phenomenon. Thus, for example, the item *winter* is said to be primed to collocate with *in*, *that*, *during the*, etc. As regards colligational behaviour, the expression *in winter* is primed to occur with verbs in the present tense in clauses expressing relational processes, and it displays a semantic preference to occur with expressions of "timeless truths" e.g.: "In winter, Hammerfest is a thirty-hour ride by bus from Oslo [...]". In terms of textual colligation, in some kinds of discourse (e.g. travel writing) *in winter* is weakly primed to appear at the beginning of a sentence, as above. It is only weakly primed to occur in cohesive chains. Finally, as suggested earlier, the fact that *winter* is normally classified as a nominal, a noun, is entirely a result of its set of combinational primings (2005: 154–155, 166). In other words, its priming profile fits what we expect of items we have decided to call "nouns" (although every single noun will have a different profile, and some items fit the expectations associated with its word class closer than others).

Hoey's theory also begins to explain, for perhaps the first time, how prefabricated phrases and phrase templates come to exist at all. They are a simple logical consequence of how learners learn to compose text(s) synthetically. As we noted above, they are gradually primed to know the set of phonological and morphological units a particular unit – whether it be *it*, *was*, *the*, *-ing*, *-ly*, – normally colligates with and in what positions it normally appears in (and which it does not). At the same time, by exposure to instances of use, they learn which other set of items it normally, to use Hoey's terminology, *nests within* (and which it does not) to form his/her knowledge of word formation and of lexical item formation from prefabs like *as a matter of fact* to phrase templates such as BE *a* number + time-word + vehicle + (*journey*, *trip*, *voyage*, *flight* etc.) *from*, and the like. They are further primed to recognise and reproduce grammatical and then textual regularities (where, of course, the width of choice is infinitely wider, but speakers still have primed expectations for which positions in a text an item will appear in or avoid). Of course, in actual speech or language this synthesis is not the only process at work; as Hoey himself stresses, an act of communication actually begins top-down with the impetus to communicate something, advice, warning, encouragement, and so on, even before the bottom-up processes kick in (2005: 163).

Hoey offers a very practical illustration of how the twin processes of colligation and (in)nesting function to produce the kind of (semi)preconstructed phrases and phrase templates that have been the subject of attention in this chapter, namely the above-mentioned:

> BE *a* number + time-word + vehicle + (*journey, trip, voyage, flight* etc.) *from*

The template colligates the lexical items *journey* or *ride* with other items from three lexical classes – a number, a time expression and a vehicle – for example:

(11) a three-hour *car* journey
a five-hour *coach* ride
a half-hour *train* journey
a two-hour ride by *four wheel drive vehicle*

Such processes were discussed earlier in terms of semantic preference, that is, as we said, the tendency of a lexical item to co-occur with other items from a particular semantic field.

By steady acquaintance with the template, speakers are primed to both recognise similar phrases they have heard before but can also interpret novel, fresh ones like, say, "a 27-hour meander by sledge" (2005: 17). We saw that script use is an *active* mental process which helps us make sense of new situations by reference to old familiar ones. Hoey's theory of lexical priming, especially semantic preference, explains how the same is true in language reception at the phraseological level.

It must be stressed that lexical priming does not imply that language is entirely deterministic. Hoey is, in fact, at great pains to stress that normal priming prosodies can always be overridden by users, as in the example he provides: "The expedition returns to England, having rescued the men left to *winter* on Elephant Island…" (2005: 155), where an item – *winter* – normally primed for use as a noun, is employed as a verb. Creativity with language is largely a process of overriding or exploiting normal primings (see Chapters 5 and 6).

The analogy of linguistic schemata with knowledge schemata or scripts, then, seems clear. Of scripts we have already said that they too are templates consisting of some fixed routines and some variable ones, and that they too can often accommodate insertions and be adapted to new circumstances. Just as scripts are typically made up of other scripts and go on themselves to compose larger ones, lexical-semantic templates too tend to *nest*, to use Hoey's term. For instance, in the template we discussed above, BE *a* number + time-word + vehicle + (*journey, trip, voyage, flight* etc.) *from* is primed to nest within another template [Locality A] BE *a* number + time-word + vehicle + (*journey, trip, voyage, flight* etc.) *from* [Locality B], as in the example already cited: "In winter, Hammerfest is a thirty-hour ride by bus from Oslo [...]". And having heard such a template once or twice, one has little problem interpreting, say, "Ferrara is a seventy-minute train journey from Venice". Hoey also notes still more subtle textual colligational effects. In travel writing it is usually the lesser known of the two locations which is placed in sentence initial position (in conversation things may well be more dependent on actual context – where the speakers are for example).

Not least of the analogy between linguistic and knowledge schemata/scripts is that they serve similar purposes, namely, to save mental processing time and effort. There is, however, a trade-off involved. If it is the case that the language user needs to store in their memory *both* the single vocabulary items *and* a lexicon of lexical-semantic templates, the number of which is probably in excess of the number of vocabulary items used productively by the individual, then it would seem counterproductive to store linguistic information in this way. The reason why this happens must be that the effort saved by making far fewer slot-filling choices in *real-time* – i.e. in the process of communication – easily outweighs the disadvantages of unwieldy storage:

> In formulating performance models of language processing, researchers endeavour to offer direct descriptions of psychological categories and processes, attempting to describe languages in terms of how they are perceived, stored, remembered and produced. These researchers feel that the storage capacity of memory is vast, but that the speed for processing those memories is not (Crick 1979: 219), so that we must learn short cuts for making efficient use of this processing time. (Nattinger & DeCarrico 1992: 31)

Principal among these short cuts is coselection, that is, the use of schema templates/ extended lexical units.

A still more powerful reason for the employment of such units probably lies in the way it facilitates communication processing on the part of the hearer. Language consisting of a relatively high number of (semi-)fixed phrases is generally more predictable than that which is not. In real-time language decoding, hearers need all the help they can get. Redundancy in communication is often explained in this way and the idiom principle probably has the same functional origins.

To complete the analogies between the script recall-inferencing duality in cognition and idiom-open choice in language, just as Schank and Abelson claim that script-based understanding is the hearer's default approach, that, in simple terms, script recall is more frequently employed than inferencing, Sinclair argues that production and interpretation at utterance level are also dominated by schemata, even suggesting a proportion: "early estimates were that up to 80 per cent of the occurrence of words could be through coselections, which would leave, of course, only 20 per cent for the sort of independent paradigmatic choices of the grammar" (2004: 171). However such a calculation is necessarily subjective since the same string of words will strike one observer as idiomatic, another as not. Much will depend on their personal language primings. There have also been "within modern computer-assisted corpus studies many attempts to automatically extract recurrent phrasal units from large corpora" (Stubbs 2009: 16, and see Section 1.2.2), but the extreme variability of realisation of many phrase templates as mentioned in Section 1.2.3 means that only a proportion will be recovered.

Finally here, Hoey elsewhere (2009) warns against the danger of assuming that grammatical choices are only relevant when the open-choice principle is in play and that grammar no longer applies to idioms. He demonstrates how lexical chunks such as (*the*) *naked eye* and *dry up* have their own lexical primings, including for typical collocational, colligational, text-colligational and semantic behaviours. We might add that most prefabs which are not entirely preconstructed, and certainly all phrase templates, are also internally subject to the rules of syntax, including to the effects of number, gender, and so on.

Hoey's definition of grammar is all-encompassing, describing language (and users') behaviour from morphology to textual colligation, and so it reduces somewhat the net distinction between idiom and open choice envisaged by Sinclair. Nevertheless it in no way undermines the concept of coselection, and the particular primings of an idiom become active upon the result of initial coselection (including nestings), in other words, upon the set phrase, the coselected unit. And the primings of this resulting unit, as Hoey himself stresses, are different from those of the original constituent items. Once we accept the notion of coselection we do not need to discard the idea of idiom and open-choice as two principles of text production and reception, even if we recognise that they are both subject to the rules and regularities of lexical grammar.

## 1.6 Conclusion

It ought not perhaps to come as a surprise firstly that language is organised using similar principles at both the micro or phrase level and at a more macro discourse level, secondly that human language behaviour should follow much the same dual principles as other forms of social behaviour, that is, *recall* – with adaptation – of familiar routines and *induction* from what we (presume to) know about the world (including the grammatical rules of language) and thirdly that in consequence the learning of language should bear a close resemblance to learning in general.

Having said this, historically, models have tended to privilege quite markedly one half of the picture. As regards cognition, studies of the rules of logic (inference, induction, deduction) predominate over and far predate those into schemata (Barlett 1932) or scripts (Schank & Abelson 1977). In terms of grammar, early models privileged the open-choice/paradigmatic principle to the detriment, sometimes almost exclusion, of the idiom/phraseological/syntagmatic tendency: "it is the idiom principle that has traditionally been under-described and to which the notion of phraseology is most important" (Hunston 2000: 234; also Sinclair 2004: 140–141, 168–170). The principal reason for this near-blindness to the phraseological tendency was that, as Sinclair (1991: 1) puts it, in pre-corpora days linguistics was relatively "starved of data" and it is very largely corpus analysis, the ability to look at very large samples of language which has revealed the high degree of repetitiousness – of "chunkiness" – of the majority of discourse types. Modern corpus-based techniques would seem to have a privileged role to play in redressing the descriptive imbalance and allowing the idiom-phraseology principle to receive the attention it undoubtedly deserves.

CHAPTER 2

# Evaluation in discourse communication

## 2.1 For good and for bad, for better and for worse

The two language principles discussed in Chapter 1 tell us how natural language communication is organised but they do not tell us what is communicated or why a speaker should wish to communicate any particular message. For the *what* and, especially, the *why* of communication, we need to look at another behavioural phenomenon, namely, *evaluation*.

Although extremely complex in its application in real-life communicative contexts (Hunston 2010: 10–24), evaluation is intended here in the essentialist dualistic, bi-dimensional sense defined by Hunston as "the indication that something is good or bad" (2004: 157) and restricting the term to something like "desirable or undesirable" also has the advantage of emphasising "areas of agreement" among various differing but overlapping theories (Hunston 2010: 13). The goodness and the badness can, of course, come in many forms. In this volume, therefore we will adopt a two-term Linnaean-style binomial notation in describing evaluation, for example, (good: pleasurable), (good: profitable), (good: being in control), [bad: dangerous], [bad: difficult], [bad: not being in control], and so on, where the colon is to be read "because" (here and throughout, round brackets will be used to annotate positive evaluation, square brackets for negative evaluation).

Some writers adopt a wider definition and include a number of other parameters such as certainty/uncertainty, expectedness/unexpectedness and importance. These are all, in practice, interrelated with and dependent on good-bad evaluation, (Thompson & Hunston 2000; Hunston 2000), which is the driving force of almost all communication, indeed, of most behaviour. In any case "the most basic parameter, the one to which the others can be seen to relate, is the good-bad parameter" (Thompson & Hunston 2000: 25).

Until relatively recently, models of how language functions tended to concentrate on the descriptive, also known as ideational, conceptual or denotational, meaning as the primary form and connotational meaning, including evaluative meaning, as "the vaguer associations of a word for a group or individual" (Cook 1992: 8), or the "secondary implications" of an item (Lyons 1977: 278). In traditional semantics, connotation was often seen as "lying outside the core meaning" (Backhouse 1992: 297).

More recent research, however, has led to a re-appraisal of the importance of evaluation and evaluative prosody. Evaluation is pervasive in practically all forms of linguistic communication. Apart from the simplest transactions ("When is the next train to Dublin?": "In 25 minutes"), very few discourses are merely purely ideational and in all normal circumstances speakers/writers both give experiential messages about the world and simultaneously express their own evaluative attitude to it, approving or critical. On many occasions the evaluative attitude is in fact the core information communicated ("What did you think of Michael's talk?": "It was both well thought-out and entertaining"). As Stubbs puts it: "the whole point of an utterance may be to express the speaker's attitude, evaluation and point of view" (2001: 198). Evaluation sits somewhere between the ideational and interpersonal metafunctions of language or, rather, bestrides them and is cohesive of the two, since it can act simultaneously as both topic and comment on the topic (the terminology here – *ideational*, *experiential* and *interpersonal* – is that generally employed in functional grammar, Halliday & Matthiessen 2004).

Evaluation, Thompson and Hunston inform us, can be expressed overtly or covertly. Overt markers can be (i) lexical, e.g. *splendid*, *untrue*, *happily*, *unfortunately*, *success*, *failure*, *win*, *lose* or (ii) grammatical, for instance, comparatives, e.g. *better*, *more*, *newer* (the polarity they express will often depend on context), the use of past tense to indicate remoteness, the thematised *it* structure (*it is frightening to think that…*)[1] or (iii) textual, for example, final paragraphs of newspaper editorials tend to indicate favoured solutions to problems proposed in the previous parts of the text (Morley 2004b); in fact Labov (1972) asserts that evaluation tells the reader the "point" of the narrative and editorials tend to "make their point" at the end. Transitivity, which tells us who does what to whom largely by, in English, placing participants in a particular order in an utterance and thus assigning responsibility – and therefore often praise (good) or blame [bad] – for an action, can generally be seen as combining grammatical and textual evaluation.

1. Thompson argues that "evaluation does not have structures of its own: it is […] parasitic on other structural elements" (1997: 65). In other words, since it is everywhere, it can be expressed by all structures. Nevertheless Hunston (2004), using corpus evidence, discusses a number of constructions with marked evaluative leanings, such as *there is something* [adjective] *about* and [adjective] *to the point of* [Noun Phrase].

Assigning responsibility, praise and blame is also very much the "point" of many narratives.[2]

However, evaluation can also be implicit or "conceptual", with no obvious linguistic clues, exploiting systems of shared values and the audience's ability to recognise a good or bad thing when they see it. Thompson and Hunston argue, for instance, that what is good or bad is frequently construed in terms of goal achievement, things which are deemed good help someone to achieve their objective, those evaluated as bad are whatever hampers or thwarts the achievement of their goal (2000: 14). And so all the actions in a narrative are meant to be evaluated in reference to an explicit or implicit goal (such as, say, "the hero's survival" or "getting the girl/boy").

Although rarely expressed in such a way, evaluation can be seen as a fundamental socio-biological or ethological impulse (which also has fundamental implications for the psychology of discourse). In evolutionary terms, it is of extreme importance for an organism to judge whether an incoming stimulus, a change in its environment, is likely to bode well or ill (and of course *how* well or ill) because such evaluations are the basis for action, for the decision whether to flee or fight or do nothing and save energy resources. Indifference can set in at a later moment, but the initial process of evaluation is bi-dimensional: is it dangerous? (yes = bad, no = good); can I eat it? (yes = good, no = bad).

Other forms of appraisal are, in origin, largely instrumental to good-bad evaluation because it is only this latter which informs decision-making directly. For instance, the assessment of how likely or how true an event is, which subsumes a large proportion of modality (probability, ability, certainty, doubt etc.), is only important in phylogenetic terms if the event itself is of survival relevance, that is, is beneficial or harmful to the organism. The degree of *truth* or *certainty* which can be attributed to the report of, say, a new food source two days' journey away only really matters, in evolutionary survival terms, because a new food source is intrinsically and a priori evaluated as a good thing. Judgements on how *necessary* an action is are, still more transparently, factors in deciding whether to commit oneself to action which will bring some benefit. In short, human (and animal) perception is decision-driven and decisions are essentially dual: one can either

2. Compare, say:

> William and Mary got a divorce;
> William divorced his wife, Mary;
> Mary was divorced by William;
> William got a divorce.

do or not do something on the basis of a prior evaluation of global advantage or disadvantage.

It might be argued that evaluation is too individualistic, too solipsistic to form the basis of a theory of language use. But there is a social as well as a psychological motivation to evaluation. Evaluations may seem at first blush to be personal judgements, but speakers also communicate their evaluative opinions incessantly. Signalling one's evaluation has two major functions. First of all, it expresses group belonging by (seemingly) offering a potential service to the group by warning of bad things and advertising good ones. Moreover, it can assure an audience that the speaker/writer shares its same value system. In this way it helps "to construct and maintain relations between the speaker or writer and hearer or reader" (Thompson & Hunston 2000: 6). Darwin explains the fundamental human desire to fit into one's society, to be approved of and praised (good) and to shun disapproval and blame [because bad]:

> We may therefore conclude that primeval man, at a very remote period, was influenced by the praise and blame of his fellows. It is obvious, that the members of the same tribe would approve of conduct which appeared to them to be for the general good, and would reprobate that which appeared evil [...]
>
> It is, therefore, hardly possible to exaggerate the importance during rude times of the love of praise and the dread of blame. (1901 [1874]: 202)

It must be stressed that each individual in a community of speakers is likely to have acquired not only linguistic primings (as discussed in Chapter 1) but value primings too from previous contacts with other members, especially when these have high status or affective significance; value primings are at least as important as language primings in an individual's ability to interact with the in-group, in the process of socialisation; in any case they function in tandem through the expression of evaluation.

Secondly, signalling evaluations both explicitly and implicitly, can be used to direct, control and even manipulate the behaviour of others, generally to the advantage of the individual performing the evaluation (and this is where the social and individual functions of evaluation combine). Evaluation is the engine of persuasion. Speakers employ it to convince an audience of what should be seen as right and proper and what not and that therefore the audience should conduct itself in a manner appropriate to the goal of achieving the former and eschewing the latter. Thus, as well as reflect, it can impose, overtly or covertly, a value system.

## 2.2 Point of view

Finally, here, a general word needs to be spent on evaluation and point of view. In conversation, the default point of view, the standpoint taken unless another is specified or implicit, is that of the speaker or of some group to which the speaker projects him/herself as belonging (frequently "everybody" or "all right-thinking people" or "*Times* readers", and so on). It is reasonable, then, when defining the polarity of the evaluative priming associated with any item, to assume the default point of view is the speaker's, in other words, that whatever is projected as good or bad by the use of the item is good or bad for the speaker. When the item is instantiated in discourse and interacts with the contextual features, including other participants, then things of course may well change. Speakers and writers freely and frequently adopt the points of view of others. For example, in "the space shuttle Discovery lands in Florida after a mission fraught with difficulties" (SiBol 05), the writer adopts the perspective of another party, namely, the crew and the controllers and empathises with the goals they are trying to achieve. If the third party is one to which the observer is actually hostile, the overall evaluation implicitly expressed is, of course, bad for that party but good for the observer. In the following example, Labour, whose perspective is originally taken ("Labour believes"), is presumably delighted that John Major, Conservative Prime Minister, might be on the path *fraught with* the danger of political embarrassment:

(1) [...] a series of hurdles remain, followed by an end-game which Labour believes will be **fraught with** danger for John Major [...] If Ms Boothroyd [Speaker of the House of Commons] decides to allow a vote on this amendment, the Government would certainly suffer a humiliating defeat. (SiBol 93)

Readers and listeners normally have no trouble at all interpreting the communicative intent behind such plays with point of view. However, just because things in these particular circumstances are good for the party whose perspective is taken, which we will henceforth call the *adopted perspective*, the items *fraught with* and *difficulties* have not suddenly acquired positive polarity. This may seem hardly worth saying but it has sometimes been forgotten in discussions of evaluative prosodies, that is, of items whose evaluative polarity is not immediately obvious to the naked eye (see 2.7).

## 2.3 Evaluation working in discourse

We can now put the notion that evaluation is both centrally significant and pervasive in communicative discourse to a practical test by examining the evaluative function of lexical units in an authentic text. Given the focus of the present volume on the value of corpus techniques in studying discourse, it is particularly appropriate to look at a naturally occurring stretch of text, in which we combine the qualitative study (close reading) traditional to discourse studies with quantitative corpus analyses. In this instance we also illustrate the lesser-used methodology of starting with a single text, and then moving to the corpus in order to describe it more fully. The following is the opening part of a book review from the *Guardian* newspaper:[3]

> ***How Whitehall Helped Hitler***
> (BY MARTIN GILBERT)
>
> The Unnecessary War, by Patricia Meehan (Sinclair-Stevenson, £18.95)
>
> 1 This book delves into one of the murky corners of recent history, the official British response to the German
> 2 opposition to Hitler. Even before the outbreak of the second world war, individual Germans of some
> 3 stature had asked the British government for moral support in their opposition to Hitler, and these
> 4 approaches continued throughout the war. Most of those who made them were eventually killed by
> 5 the Gestapo after the Hitler bomb plot in 1944. This book is the fullest attempt yet to examine who
> 6 these Germans were, how serious and sustained their approaches to the British had been, and how,
> 7 almost without exception, their efforts to enlist British support were dismissed and belittled.

The extract contains a number of lexical items with in-built evaluation, that is, a major, principal even, part of their function in this and any text is to express a favourable or unfavourable appraisal. As regards the former (good) we find *of some stature/standing* (line 2–3) and *moral support* (line 3).We will analyse the seemingly favourable *the fullest attempt yet* (line 5) in detail below. As regards the latter [bad] we have *murky* (line 1), BE *killed* (line 4) *dismissed* and *belittled* (line 7). *Murky* (line 1) co-occurs with *corners* – a combination found six times in the two SiBol corpora, four of which are, as here, used metaphorically. A *murky corner*, of course, is not a congenial place to find oneself.

The opening to the first sentence constitutes an interesting example of a phenomenon we may refer to as *evaluative embedding*, namely: "This book delves into one of the murky corners of recent history", that is, where evaluation of one type is found embedded within that of another. The SiBol concordance evidence indicates how *delve* (*deep*) [*into/down/through* etc.] generally collocates, as here, with mysteries, complex situations, often from the past and often unpleasant, but very frequently light is successfully shed and the delving is very generally seen as a laudable, often courageous, activity:

3. *The Guardian*, 23rd July 1992. This article achieved a degree of fame when it was cited in a U.S. Senate tribute to Baron Von Kleist. The full text of the article can be retrieved from the Library of Congress by typing the headline into a research engine.

1. [...] she has the courage to **delve into** areas of life that most people shy away from. (SiBol 93)
2. One of the glories of Radio 4 is its disparateness. Barred from padding its schedules with music or sport it must willy-nilly **delve into** the obscure corners of culture, history, science and the human heart. (SiBol 05)
3. Instead they should **delve into** the financials and have a cold hard look at the cash flow – because this company is haemorrhaging the stuff. (SiBol 05)

Thus if we combine sentence grammar and phraseology we have an outline form: someone (successfully) *delves into* something bad or problematic and comes up with new information. A goal has been achieved. The overall appraisal is good. We can annotate the relation thus (where round brackets indicate favourable evaluation and square brackets unfavourable): (*delve into* [*murky corner*]).

We find a similar but reversed instance of embedded evaluation at the end of the final sentence, line 7: "their efforts to enlist British support were dismissed and belittled". The SiBol concordance evidence indicates that the expression *efforts to/at* displays, not surprisingly, a strong semantic preference (Chapter 0.4.2) for problems and troubles. However, *efforts to* bring about *x* (where *x* tends to be something good for someone – a *solution* or *peace*, for instance or, in the text above, enlisting someone's support) tend to be fraught with difficulties and frustrations and are frequently crowned with failure or dissatisfaction, as these examples show:

1. But the leak of the Camilla tape also raises the question of whether **efforts to** protect the future king were adequate, or were deliberately slackened. (SiBol 93)
2. Scientists made superhuman **efforts to** get it up and running again [...] But it had only travelled 21 feet when a fibre-optic nerve was severed [...] and the mission had to be aborted. (SiBol 93)
3. Despite my best **efforts to** avoid quacks and oddballs in cyberspace, I have acquired an Internet stalker. (SiBol 05)

In such cases, the evaluation is again embedded: the doers are – from someone's perspective – to be praised (good) but the failure of the doing is lamented [bad]. Thus the overall evaluation is adverse, their goal has not been achieved (co-incidentally Sinclair also discusses the negative prosody of *efforts to* and the very similar *attempts to* [2004: 175–176]). We might represent this notationally as [failure of/frustration at (*efforts to* bring about *x*)], where once again round brackets indicate favourable evaluation and square brackets unfavourable.[4]

4. It needs to be said that the [failure of/dissatisfaction at (*efforts to* bring about *x*)] template is by no means the only way *efforts to* is used. The outcome or effect of the *efforts* is

In both the phrases we have considered ("This book … history" and "their efforts … belittled") the overall evaluation is set by the first evaluating element which thus, in these cases, constitutes the outermost and deciding layer of the evaluation embedding. This is the general case.

Returning to the opening segment of our test passage, the final lexical unit – *of/in + recent history* (line 1) – is, here, entirely denotational, or perhaps we might call it *deictic* in that it anchors the preceding (rather mixed) metaphor – "murky corners of recent history" – in real-world time and space. Other denotational/deictic phrases in the text include *this book* and *the British* (*government*) (see point 4 in Section 2.4 below).

The second sentence in our text contains the item [*an*/*the*] *outbreak of* (line 2). *Outbreak* has the denotation "a sudden and active manifestation" (*Webster's Encyclopedic Dictionary*), but, in evaluative or connotational terms, it collocates very generally with unpleasant events and entities – violence, diseases, corruption, and so on (when found with the definite article – *the outbreak of* – the most common co-occurring item in the SiBol corpora is, as here, *war*). On the rare occasions it occurs with something apparently neutral, or even positive, for example:

(2) So, what hope is there for an outbreak of honesty among Italian journalists? (SiBol 93)

(3) What we need now is an outbreak of realism among European governments. (SiBol 93)

---

often projected as unknown with their success or failure still in the balance (all examples from SiBol):

1. The first tentative **efforts to** touch on what is perceived as a hyper-sensitive political issue will be made today at the opening meeting of Labour's joint shadow cabinet.
2. "… The police will continue their **efforts to** target the anti-social activities of a selfish minority of motorists during 1993." Roads minister Kenneth Carlisle […]

On other occasions, the *x* the *efforts* are meant to bring about are not seen as good at all:

"Every legal manoeuvre, effort, caprice and effrontery was attempted on behalf of Alger Hiss, and always these **efforts to** turn history around came to naught […]"

Nevertheless, the preference of *efforts to* with difficulties is so strong that it can often be only implied and employed for humorous or ironic effects:

1. Church dignitaries lost capes, spectacles and decorum in their **efforts to** follow him.
2. In strenuous **efforts to** describe what they were talking about without actually showing it, The Good Sex Guide leaned heavily on innuendo and metaphor. It was like covering soccer with no goals.

the writer's use of *outbreak* projects the expectation of negativity from the item to the context to effect an implicit unflattering appraisal of some entity in the discourse, *Italian journalists* and *European governments* respectively, the implication being that the first are unused to honesty, the second to realism (a classic example of both ironic reversal of evaluation and the overriding of a normal priming, see Chapter 4 on phrasal irony).

The passage also contains a number of other lexical units or templates including *almost without exception*, *the *est* [noun] *yet*, *the official* [adjective] *response*, *serious* and *sustained*. Can the corpus evidence tell us whether and in what way these contribute to the organisation of the evaluative interplay within the text?

In our passage, *almost without exception* (line 7) is used in a highly unfavourable context and in SiBol we also find: (conferences) *almost without exception,* [are] *a complete waste of time* / (political conference speakers) *almost without exception, are dreadful*. But there are as many favourable uses: (Hong Kong pupils) *are almost without exception, outstanding* and *Turks, almost without exception, love children*. In others, whatever the writer's stance, the perlocutionary evaluative effect would seem to depend entirely on the readers' individual mindset, for example:

(4) San was about to employ his first woman programmer, but, **almost without exception**, creative staff are young men. (SiBol 93)

is music to the ears of male chauvinist readers, but not for more civilised society. We might call this *receiver-onus* evaluation. The overall purpose of the unit *almost without exception* is to intensify, as the above examples illustrate, but the matter to be intensified can be either a good or a bad one.

Instantiations of *the *est* [noun] *yet* (line 5) schema can also evaluate either way, depending on the nature of the superlative and noun. In our text, the choice of *fullest* renders the phrase favourable. SiBol gives us *the best try yet to bridge the gap, the fullest account yet written of…, the biggest breakthrough yet*, but in SiBol we also find *the biggest blow yet to his plans to reform…the blackest day yet in….* Favourable cases seem to outweigh unfavourable ones by about four to one in the SiBol data.

An *official response* (line 1), too, can be viewed either way, as firm and authoritative (good), for instance: *the toughest official response to one of the cruellest practices in the country*, or as unsatisfactory, evasive, or very often, simply missing [bad]: *unimpressed with the official response, frustrated by the lack of an official response, the official response is to close more beds, but the official government response is still in the Home Secretary's in-tray*. Unfavourable uses outweigh favourable ones in the SiBol corpora (to which we add the instance in our text) but this may well be due in part to the critical function that newspapers generally perform.

Turning to the intensifiers *serious* and *sustained* (line 6), the first collocates, predictably, with many unpleasant items like *accident*, *allegation*, *blunder*, *danger*, *fraud*, and so on, but serious *talks*, *discussions*, *efforts* are, by implication, better than non-serious ones, and when a person is described as *serious* – *a serious artist/academic/contender* etc. – it is a compliment. There were several instances of *serious approach*, but only one of *serious approaches* (namely, *he has received no serious approaches from buyers*, where from "his" point of view, serious approaches would be positive). Things which are *sustained* are generally beneficial, at least in newspapers: *growth*, *recovery*, *success*, *attempts*. The combination in our text, *serious and sustained approaches*, represents a good thing in itself but, since the approaches in question are snubbed, the segment is embedded in an overall adverse context, which we can annotate [(serious and sustained approaches) were dismissed and belittled].

We are still left with a couple of items with clear evaluative content, namely *helped* (headline) and *bomb plot* (line 5). The first, of course, has a highly benevolent evaluation, whilst the second is normally very bad and its collocates in SiBol include *terrorists*, *hatched* and *foiled* (interestingly, six out of the 32 occurrences in SiBol 93 refer to this very plan to rid the world of the Nazi leader). In both cases however, the usual evaluation gets reversed by the context – helping *Hitler* becoming a thoroughly reprehensible thing to do, whilst a plot to blow him up becomes a jolly good idea. Whenever evaluation is calculated in individual instances, context – which includes shared cultural values – is paramount.

## 2.4 Categories of evaluative lexis

As a result of this detailed examination of the interplay of evaluation in a text, we can perhaps attempt an outline categorisation of lexical units as regards their evaluative potential. There seem to be the following overall categories:

1. Items whose evaluative weight is intrinsic, is in-built, whose evaluation is a major if not predominant part of their function. As Hunston puts it "some evaluative meaning is very easily identified, as it is signalled by evaluative lexical items such as *wonderful* or *terrible*" (2004: 157).
2. Items with a predominantly good or bad evaluative function but where this is not obvious to the naked eye, is not part of the immediate semantics of the item but becomes apparent in its interaction with other items of a particular polarity. Corpus study can be an invaluable tool in bringing such "non-obvious" meaning(s) to the light of day (see *inter alia* Louw 1993; Stubbs 1996; Hunston & Sinclair 2000). This is the kind of lexis which is usually examined

in studies of evaluative (also known as *semantic*) prosody (see 2.7 for further description and examples).

3. Items which do not appear to have any strong inherent evaluative leaning, but which, in different contexts, may be observed to express favourable or unfavourable evaluations. The unit *almost without exception* would seem to fall into this category.
4. A sub-category of (3) might be lexis which is predominantly denotational or deictic and is generally evaluatively neutral, at least at first sight and when free of context. In the above text, *book*, *recent history* and *British government* might fall into this category. Nevertheless even these items, unless being used in one of the rare discourse types where evaluation is suppressed, tend to acquire evaluative "content", especially if repeated or part of a cohesive chain. Hunston (2010) stresses how evaluation is cumulative in authentic discourse. For instance, in the course of our book review, *the British government* with its suspicious and mean-spirited response to anti-Nazi Germans gradually receives a highly unfavourable appraisal, whilst *this book* (that is the book being reviewed) is gradually much praised. (By suppressed evaluation or even *de*-evaluated discourse, we intend those types, including, say, lists, didactic description ["Liverpool is a city in the north-west of England, with a population of…."] and so on, where the communicative purpose is strictly limited, or where language is being "mentioned" rather than "used" (for example "why did you call him 'a stupid ass'?"), in Quine's [1940] and Sperber and Wilson's [1995] celebrated distinction).

This leaves us with one final observation arising from the text which is vital in the context of the present chapter. The article was intended for a British audience and many British people are primed to have a number of internalised scripts regarding the Second World War (nowadays largely second-hand, hearsay and fictional), which, almost without exception, are associated with the evaluations British = good and Germans = bad. Both the article and the book it reviews reverse this opposition; the British, especially the authorities, are here the villains, whilst a group of honest, courageous but ill-fated Germans are the good guys. Thus the analogy between language schemata and cognitive-behavioural scripts, as described in Chapter 1 is almost complete. We have discussed at some length the evaluative import of the former and there is much evidence that scripts too have associated evaluative content. Louw, for example, mentions the different "prosodies", as he calls them, for most people of the scripts for attending a wedding and attending a funeral (2000: 50–51). Here, in our short *Whitehall* text, we also see that, just as phraseological evaluation and evaluative prosodies can be overturned for particular rhetorical effect, script evaluations, such as British = good and Germans = bad, can also be reversed for special argumentative purposes. Both phenomena can be described as "normal priming reversal".

## 2.5 Note: The evaluator and evaluative voices

Ultimately, of course, all the conscious, explicit evaluations expressed in a text are being performed by the author (there may, of course, be all sorts of unconscious evaluations, as authors from Wimsatt and Beardsley [1946] to Louw [1993] have pointed out). Even direct quotations of other speakers/writers are very generally deliberately chosen by the author and are therefore ultimately his or her responsibility (even when introduced to be argued against they still play a part in the speaker's/writer's web of evaluation). Nevertheless, a useful distinction has been made between evaluations which are *averred*, that is, which are affirmed by the author/speaker as his/her own, and those which are *attributed*, that is, where the author/speaker assigns evaluations to other voices (Sinclair 1988; Tadros 1993). It can often be important to determine who is projected by an author as performing an evaluation, in other words, who is projected as the "principal" (Goffman 1981) or the "responsible" or "motivator" (Levinson 1988) of the evaluation, that is, the supposed evaluator.

In our short text, most of the evaluation is expressed openly, is averred by the author, in other words he takes responsibility for it. In the last sentence, though, he attributes to the British authorities an unfavourable evaluation of the dissident Germans' overtures.

Attributed evaluation, the play of evaluative "voices" in a text can become quite complex. Consider the following newspaper extract:

(5) "The [Conservative] party overwhelmingly selects white, heterosexual, middle-aged, male, professional people as its Parliamentary candidates, and the people doing the selecting are likely to be female and more than 50," he says. "It's always been the great irony that it's women who select the men and who say to the women "What will your husband do if you're not there to make his dinner?"[…] This is something we have to deal with." (SiBol 93)

The speaker being quoted by the journalist is saying that Conservative selectors disfavour women as candidates and, second, that the selectors themselves are women. This is presented as a paradoxical irony: the readers have to avail themselves of some general implied expectation such as "one might normally expect people to have the goal of electing other people who are similar to themselves". But there is also an underlying unfavourable evaluation of how the selectors act. Indeed, the last phrase signals explicitly the situation as a "problem" ("something we have to deal with"); the speaker is presenting the situation not just as paradoxical but perverse. But not only is the selection procedure, that is, the evaluations performed by the women, evaluated badly, with the speaker reversing their evaluation (choosing women becoming a good thing), but so are the women themselves. Finally, since the speaker being quoted in the newspaper is the chairman of the political party in question, and therefore perhaps in a position to remedy things, there may even be an implicit unfavourable evaluation of the speaker on the part of the author of the article. Hunston talks of the "layering" or "embedding" of voices (2010: 18–19).

## 2.6 Evaluation and cohesion; evaluative consistency or *harmony*

One advantage of considering how evaluation functions in a stretch of text is that it highlights the particular cohesive function that evaluation plays in discourse. In the first sentence of the text, the phrase "one of the murky corners of recent history" is a cataphoric (forward-looking) reference to "the official British response to the German opposition to Hitler". But it also quite clearly communicates an instruction which prepares the reader to view the referent, the British reaction, in a negative way, even though there is nothing inherently negative in the item *response*.

In the second sentence of our sample text:

> Even before the outbreak of the second world war, individual Germans of some stature had asked the British government for moral support in their opposition to Hitler, and these approaches continued throughout the war.

*the outbreak of* normally co-occurs as we have seen with negative items, often as here, with *war* and in this way consistency of evaluation within the phrase is maintained. Consistency of evaluation at local points in the text helps maintain comprehensibility for the listener, since it meets rather than upsets primed expectations (such expectations can of course be intentionally overridden for rhetorical effect, Hoey [2005: 173–177] and see Chapter 4). There may also be an aesthetic impulse to choose meanings which "sound well" together (Gavioli 2005: 46) and so we might go so far as to talk of this consistency of evaluation as *evaluative harmony*.

The rest of the second sentence contains two positively evaluated expressions, "individual Germans *of some standing*" and "moral support", which combine to instruct the reader that something to commend is being described. But, of course, we have been fore-warned by the first sentence that the response will not be satisfactory; the evaluative cohesion spreads across the two sentences.

In the third sentence the negative expectations previously constructed in the text are fulfilled when we learn that "most of those" – anaphoric (backward-looking) reference to the "Germans of some standing" – people we had been instructed to commend, were "killed".

The fourth and final sentence begins with "This book", which repeats and links to the opening item of the article and reminds us that the text is a book review. However it also now receives an explicit positive evaluation "is the fullest attempt yet to examine …". The sentence also contains the final two items in a cohesive chain of four elements which begins in the second sentence: "had asked … these approaches … their approaches … their efforts". The first two links are not openly evaluated but in the third case "their approaches" are described, positively as "serious and sustained" and the fate "their efforts" eventually met is expressed by the highly and explicitly negative evaluation "dismissed and belittled". The reference to "efforts to enlist *British* support" constitutes a concluding cohesive link to "the official *British* response" of the first sentence, which is now finally explicitly explained and evaluated in this negative way. All of which, of course, had been hinted at cataphorically by the implicit negative evaluation in the article title "How Whitehall Helped Hitler", *Whitehall* being an elegant metonymic variation and cohesive link to "the British (government)"; the reader is pre-alerted that, and their curiosity is being aroused as to why, "the British" are not going to come out of this text with a favourable evaluation.

The role of evaluation in cohesion becomes especially interesting when radically differing points of view are being presented in the same text and especially where the goals of participants are in conflict. The following is the opening to an essay article on the current work of charities, including Oxfam, in the UK.

> 1 Oxfam was founded in 1942 to bring aid to the oppressed of Nazi Europe, a cause that did not
> 2 make it popular with the Churchill government. After the Germans occupied Greece, the Royal
> 3 Navy blocked the shipping lanes. Famine spread across the mainland and the islands. Lifting the
> 4 blockade might have helped the starving, but Whitehall wondered whether food meant for the
> 5 hungry would end up in the bellies of German troops instead, and gazed with some disdain on the
> 6 new lobbyists.
>
> Nick Cohen, *New Statesman*, May 2007.

There are two separate but co-existing narrative points of view expressed in the text, a dominant one, that of Oxfam, the writer and presumed "right-thinking readers" and a subordinate one, that of the British government.

The extract begins by describing the reason why the charity was founded "to bring aid to the oppressed", notationally (to bring aid to [the oppressed]), with overall clear positive evaluation of those laudable aims. The dominance of

Oxfam's viewpoint is established by the situation being presented with its intentions foregrounded. But in the second part of the sentence the point of view shifts abruptly to that of the wartime government, which views these aims negatively. The opposing points of view remain in creative tension throughout the extract, a not uncommon form of textual macro-structure, a kind of macro contrasting pair. For instance "lifting the blockade might have helped the starving" appears good from Oxfam's, the writer's and the readers' point of view, but bad from the government's. From the point of view of "Whitehall" (here again linking cohesively to "the Churchill [that is, British] government"), the fear is that food will "*end up* in the bellies of German troops". The expression *end up* + [preposition] + somewhere is primed for negative meaning, largely because something has gone to a place which the adopted perspective does not intend; it has passed out of their control (see the next chapter on the interconnection of control and evaluation and specifically 3.3.8). The SiBol corpus provides the following somewhat similar instance (italics added):

(6) The challenge for the future is to increase yields on marginal lands where much of the crop *ends up in the bellies of* insects or is devastated by drought or disease. (SiBol 05)

What is interesting is how, at this point in the text, the author of the extract chooses to employ an evaluative prosody (bad) consistent with the adopted perspective (the government), not his own. Similarly, the choice of the item *lobbyists* to describe Oxfam is made from the government's perspective; very likely Oxfam would have chosen a more favourable term to describe themselves.

The dominant evaluative reading however reasserts itself in the description of the government's "gazed with some disdain" on Oxfam. According to the SiBol evidence, alleging that someone is acting with *disdain* is generally a means of portraying them unsympathetically, for instance:

(7) When I'm with my childless friends, I feel that they're looking at me with disdain and judging my kid's behaviour. (SiBol 05)

(although there can be exceptions, mainly when the adopted perspective is in control of the expression of disdain). What we should stress is that readers have no trouble keeping the two narrative readings apart, despite the complexity of their interaction, having learned or been primed to do so by previous encounters with the contrasting-pair macro-structure.

Finally we might also note the existence in the passage of evaluative cohesive links between "bring aid", "helped" and "lifting the blockade" (good) and "the oppressed" and "the starving" [bad].

## 2.7 Evaluative prosody

We saw in the previous section by looking at how evaluation functions in authentic texts, how evaluative meaning is achieved by the cumulative interplay of items. One particular type of interplay of item with discourse environment, namely evaluative prosody, has received considerable attention (also known as "semantic prosody" Sinclair 1987b, 1991; Louw 1993, 2000; Stewart 2010, among others, and occasionally as "discourse prosody" Tognini-Bonelli 2001; Stubbs 2001). The term *prosody*, borrowed from phonology, is used to describe a language phenomenon expressed over more than a single linguistic unit.

The simplest kind of evaluative prosody is seen in collocational relations. A writer who wishes to describe a situation as dangerous may well describe it as *fraught with* danger (rather than say *brimming with* which normally co-occurs with positive items), since *fraught with* is normally found in the company of negative items and displays a semantic preference for items from the field of "danger" (and also for three other fields: "difficulty-problems", "complications" and "anxiety", see the concordance in Chapter 0.4.2). In SiBol 05 *fraught with* (326 occurrences in all) is indeed followed by *danger/s* (67), *risk/s* (21), *peril* (10) and *hazards* (2).

(8) How Bamse and his friend Anton take on new roles, moving from adventure games to adventures **fraught with** real danger, is brilliantly told. (SiBol 05)

(9) The other route to a ticket – the black market – is likely to be **fraught with** risk. (SiBol 05)

Not all evaluative prosody is effected by immediate collocational co-occurrence. For instance, the item *par for the course* tends to link with negative elements (Channell 2000:47–50), sometimes entire stretches of text, in its wider cotext, even across clause or sentence boundaries:

(10) *Horse wrestling, spilt drinks* and *irate car owners* are all **par for the course** when you're travelling around Ireland in a horse and cart. (SiBol 05)

(11) George Bush is talking again and I don't have a clue what he's saying. It's not that he's *mangling his syntax*. That's **par for the course**. (SiBol 05)

In any case, the array of items which combine to create evaluative harmony can spread quite widely, as we have seen in the texts in 2.3 and 2.6 and as witnessed in the following (the negatively evaluating items are italicised, some are intrinsically negative, some become bad in the context):

(12) The seven-year journey from that dazzling sales pitch in the Far East to the reality of 2012 will be *complicated* and *arduous*, and after Thursday we must *fear* it will be **fraught with** the *rawest of hazards* for ordinary citizens. (SiBol 05)

(13) But *appearances can be deceptive* – these funds can be **fraught with** *danger*. The managers buy *riskier* bonds to add to the mix to boost the income. (SiBol 05)

In the second sentence of the following we encounter the cohesion by contrast we also noted in the previous section:

(14) The simple act of buying and selling a house in England and Wales is so **fraught with** *hazards* that it is a *notorious minefield*. Despite a succession of governments promising to make the process *easier*, *cheaper*, *safer* and *faster*, the entire process remains *complex*, *expensive*, *difficult* and *time-consuming*. (SiBol 05)

where the string *easier*, *cheaper*, *safer* and *faster* coheres by contrast with *complex*, *expensive*, *difficult* and *time-consuming*.

Finally, a steady crescendo of evaluative harmony can be built for rhetorical effect; in the following for sarcasm at the expense of the council in question:

(15) The council decided that a stroll in rural England was **fraught with** *danger* and that a *risk* assessment form should be completed before it could take place. Possible *pitfalls* to be identified were *rabbit holes*, *barbed wire* and *rogue cows* along the way. (SiBol 05)

Discussions on evaluative prosody generally revolve around items whose evaluation is not seemingly inherent in its semantics as is the case with, say, *wonderful*, *ridiculous*, *sadist*, and so on, but whose evaluative potential is realised when interacting with other items in discourse (see Section 2.4, point 2). We have so far come across a couple of examples:

[an/the] *outbreak of*
*end up* + [preposition] [somewhere]

A fair number of other items have been discussed in the literature, including: *set in*, *happen*, *bent on*, *bordering on*, (not) *budge*, *dealings*, *potentially*, *sit through*, *orchestrate*, *fraught with*, *true feelings*, *par for the course*, all of which have been claimed to participate in negative evaluation, and *flexible*, *provide*, *my place*, *make a difference* and *brimming with*, which are said to help express positive evaluation. It has been noted that there seem to be more items of negative than of positive prosodic priming. It may simply be that speakers generally feel the need to talk more about the negative than the positive aspects of the world

(Louw 2000: 52). Alternatively, it may be that positive evaluation is generally more obviously inherent, more explicit in the semantics of lexical items; compare, say, the two intensifiers *utterly* and *perfectly*, the first of which tends to co-occur with negative items, the second, more predictably, with good ones (Partington 2004b).

The term evaluative prosody is variously applied and can be viewed in at least four ways. Firstly it is used to describe an item's inherent potential to behave in evaluative interactions, thus items are sometimes described as *having* or *possessing* or *being primed with* a positive or negative prosody (the lexical description).

Secondly it is used to describe the interaction of the item with others of particular polarity as witnessed within a certain text, thus evaluative prosody is sometimes said to describe the spreading of a particular evaluation over a stretch of text in order to maintain evaluative harmony (the textual description).

Thirdly it can refer to a community of speakers' shared primed intuitive knowledge of how to use a particular item in conjunction with others of a particularly polarity in order to maintain evaluative harmony when speaking or writing (the psychological description).

Fourthly, the community of speakers has acquired this shared primed knowledge by repeatedly encountering an item in co-occurrence with other items of a certain polarity. In other words it so co-occurs much more often than is to be expected by random probability (the statistical description).

Finally, several authors including Louw, Stubbs, Hunston and Morley and Partington, note that evaluative prosodies are not always invariant across different usages; they can change depending on syntax, the discourse type it is found in and whether or not it is being employed metaphorically or non-metaphorically.

Regarding syntax, Louw observes that when the item *build up* is used transitively with a human subject "the prosody is uniformly good. People *build up organisations, better understanding* and so on". But "[w]here things or forces such as *cholesterol, toxins*, and *armaments build up* intransitively [...] they are uniformly bad" (1993: 171).

As regards discourse types, Stubbs notes how the item *lavish* in newspaper reporting, especially crime reporting, has a prosody of [bad: excessive wastefulness] (2001: 106). The SiBol corpus evidence demonstrates, however, that in fields or discourse types other than news reporting – arts reviews for instance – *lavish* displays a prosody of (good: generous, pleasantly decorated). In general, lexical items have different primings in different discourse types, even in different fields of human experience:

> in the "lexi-grammar" of newspaper reporting, the item LAVISH is accompanied by an indication that "this word is often used to express disapproval", whereas in the lexi-grammar of, say, normal British conversation, the entry for LAVISH would

> contain no such indication. All of this also implies, as Hoey [2005] himself argues, that the process by which items are primed in the mind is highly contextually dependent. (Partington 2004b: 153)

Lastly, regarding metaphorical usage, Hunston notes how *pay…price* can be purely descriptive, but when used figuratively, a situation is being evaluated as highly negative for someone: "the British are *paying a price* for their obstinacy" (2010: 60–61). The verb *orchestrate*, when used literally to refer to music arrangement, is seen, predictably, as a good thing. When used semi-metaphorically to refer to the harmonisation of a sports team, it remains positive. However, when used metaphorically in politics and current affairs, on the other hand, the verb forms of *orchestrat** co-occur with *attacks, threats, violence, fraud* and suchlike, and are most frequently found in combination with other indications of bad evaluation: *found guilty of orchestrating a …*(10 occurrences), *the Ottoman authorities orchestrated the killing of 1.5 million Armenians, … a campaign is being orchestrated to destroy the credibility of…, pandering to the climate of fear orchestrated by populist politicians* (Morley & Partington 2009; Chapter 3.3.12).

## 2.8 Embedding and nesting

Returning to the concept of embedded evaluation illustrated and discussed in relation to the "How Whitehall Helped Hitler" text, it can help resolve one of the issues concerning evaluative prosody apparent in Stubbs (2001) and discussed in Partington (2004b), Whitsitt (2005) and Stewart (2010). To illustrate, the item *exacerbate* displays a very obvious unfavourable evaluative priming, co-occurring in SiBol with such items as *anxieties, conflicts, problems* and *tensions*. But what of items like, say, *alleviate, heal, repair* or *reform*? They too collocate regularly with unfavourable items (*alleviate*, in fact, collocates with many of the same items as *exacerbate*, including, *poverty, pressures* and *problems*). If we adopt a simple definition that the evaluative potential of an item is a simple reflection of the nature of its collocates, then these too would have to be classified as of negative prosodic priming. This, however, would seem counterintuitive. The relationship between the node and its collocates needs to be contemplated in the definition. As Partington points out:

> the logical relationship of an item to its collocates is a vital consideration. Simply being primed to appear in the environment of collocates of a certain evaluative sense, good or bad, is not a sufficient condition for an item to acquire the same sense. If the relationship between the item and its collocates is one of opposition or detraction, then the combination does not acquire the evaluative sense of the collocates. (2004b: 154–155)

The different states of affairs can be represented notationally as [*exacerbate* [a problem]] and (*alleviate* [a problem]), where one evaluation is embedded within another and where the outer bracketing indicates the overall evaluation and the evaluative polarity of the key item.

Given that the focus of this volume is discourse, we might consider a few cases in context in authentic discourses. As we have already seen it is quite normal to encounter items of intrinsically favourable evaluation which are found embedded in expressions of overall unfavourability. This occurs frequently in the discourses of the social sciences. Tucker (2006), utilising the Cobuild corpus, discusses the lexical grammar of the item *representation* in its political sense, which in itself is a good thing and which people generally desire *more of*. However, in examining its wider context, he found that the item tends to be embedded in expressions of unfavourable meaning, in environments where representation is lacking, inadequate, unsatisfactory. He lists, for instance, the process verbs of which *representation* functions as complement, which appear to fall into three overall categories, "struggle to achieve": *battle for, fight for, try to get, seek, demand*; "find lacking" *need, want, lack, lose* and "need to foster or improve": *redress, strengthen, boost, encourage, promote*. Concordance lines include:

1. The faction has consistently argued it is under-represented in Cabinet and plans to **fight for** increased **representation** in reshuffle. (Cobuild)
2. Members of Poland's fringe Bald People's Party have launched a hunger strike to **demand representation** in the country's top echelons of power. (Cobuild)
3. The present Parliament in Poland elected in September 1993, is lopsided as it **lacks representation** of the Right. (Cobuild)

Bayley (2006), instead, looks at the items *accountable/accountability*, another generally favourable item, in a corpus of Hansard/House of Commons speeches. Fairly typical phraseologies include: *should/ought to be held more accountable, make* [someone] *more accountable, lack of accountability* and *need for greater accountability*. Thus, in the case of both *representation* and *accountability*, though good things in themselves, their appearance in the discourse often flags a problem or a regrettable shortcoming; they are often, that is, embedded in a discourse of adversity.

In the previous chapter (Section 1.4.2) we discussed the phenomenon of *nesting*, as elaborated by Hoey (2005), which we might usefully compare to and contrast with embedding. What he terms "word sequences", including extended lexical items, consist of words and other smaller word sequences, for example:

> The word *word* collocates with *say*, *say a word* in turn collocates with *against*, and *say a word against* collocates with *won't* [...] In this way, lexical items (Sinclair 1998, 2004) and bundles (Biber et al. 1999) are created. (Hoey 2005: 11)

It is generally the case, he stresses, that "the product of a priming becomes itself primed in ways that do not apply to the individual words making up the combination" (2005: 8), in other words, *say* and *say a word* and *won't say a word against* all behave as different items. We need to investigate whether this behaviour applies as much to evaluative meaning as it does to other forms of meaning.

If we concordance, as an example, the item *daylight* in the SiBol corpora, we discover, unsurprisingly, that it has a generally favourable evaluation – people like it in their houses and we want more of it in the day. However the sequence or extended lexical unit *in broad daylight* (along with the possibly related *daylight robbery*) is very generally associated with bad events, particularly crime and violence (Baker in Hoey 2005: 19), presumably because it plays on a script assumption that evil deeds are normally carried out with some semblance of an attempt to hide them. The point is that, although *daylight* nests within the new phrase, to all intents and purposes, its original evaluative potential is totally subsumed and superseded by that of the new larger construction. Similarly, the adjective *naked* displays an unfavourable prosody, redolent at times of vulnerability and sometimes of bare and perhaps shameless aggressivity (e.g. *naked materialism*, *naked ambition*). But if something is *visible to the naked eye*, the evaluation is often good (for instance, from the point of view of the impecunious amateur astronomer).

The distinction between embedding and nesting then is important. One lexical item can find itself *embedded* within another of opposing evaluation but it retains its original evaluative polarity (as well as other elements of its meaning) even though the overall evaluation of the segment is the opposite. Thus, *poverty* and *disease* remain bad things even when embedded within *alleviate*, and *murky corner* is still an uncongenial place even when being *delved into*. In contrast, if a word or sequence *nests* within another, it loses its independent primings, including its original evaluation. Embedding occurs when two lexical items interact, nesting when one is subsumed within another. We can, in consequence, use bracketing to represent embedding but it becomes irrelevant for nesting.

## 2.9 Conclusion

Linguistics has developed considerably since the 1950s and Chomsky's attempt to describe the syntactic structures of language without any recourse to meaning (Chomsky 1957). Even after the failure of this project, much of linguistics regarded conceptual, also known as ideational or denotational, meaning as the primary form and connotational meaning, including evaluative meaning, as secondary. This stance too has now been widely questioned: "[a]s linguistic study moves away from truth-value and towards a focus on the interactive, the importance of this aspect [expressing evaluation and negotiating alignment between speakers] has become more apparent" (Hunston 2010: 3).

In this chapter we have argued that evaluation pervades all forms of communicative discourses (with the sole exception of de-evaluated discourses, such as lists or, sometimes, the language of instruction), that it is not secondary to conceptual or ideational meaning or even divorced from it, since it is often itself the core information being requested or provided, and that it runs through stretches of authentic discourses providing cohesion to the arguments presented. We might recall Labov who refers to it as *the point* of a stretch of discourse, whilst Sinclair (2004: 34, 114) defines the prosody of a lexical unit as its function in the discourse, as what it is *for*.

At the level of lexical grammar and within the field of corpus-assisted research into phraseology, the reappraisal of evaluation finds its most rigorous expression in the work of Hunston (Hunston & Thompson (eds) 2000; Hunston 2004; Hunston 2010, amongst others) of Martin and White (2005) and of Biber (Biber et al. 1999, Chapter 12; Conrad & Biber 2000). It finds perhaps its strongest expression in Sinclair's argument that prosody is no longer to be seen as an adjunct to the phrase but one of its two indispensable elements along with the "core" or topic (Sinclair 2004: 141). Others have felt this to be an overstatement (Stubbs 2001: 107) which ignores the fact that purely ideational, intrinsically non-evaluative and non-attitudinal terms do exist. However, as we saw with "this book" and "the British" in our first test text, even denotational items often take on positive or negative force in context in authentic communication.

Finally, as regards language acquisition, we can hypothesise that the child internalises the evaluative tendencies or primings of lexical items at the same time as s/he learns their form and combinatorial primings, as well as how these tendencies vary in different discourse types (and perhaps a little later in her/his development how they can be exploited for particular effects, such as irony). These tendencies are something which large-scale comparative corpus studies help us study.

## Suggestions for further Research

1. Choose two paragraphs or so (100–150 words) from a film/music/book etc. review, or from a political comment piece in a newspaper and subject it to the same kind of analysis of the expression of evaluation we conducted in the passages to be found in Sections 2.3 and 2.6. Look out for instances of embedded evaluations (2.8).

2. In Section 2.7 a number of items were listed which have been discussed in the literature on evaluative prosody including: *set in*, *happen*, *bent on*, *bordering on*, (not) *budge*, *dealings*, *potentially*, *sit through*, *orchestrate*, *fraught with*, *true feelings*, *par for the course*, all of which have been claimed to participate in negative evaluation, and *flexible*, *provide*, *my place*, *make a difference* and *brimming with*, which are said to help express positive evaluation. We also saw, in discussing *fraught with* that it co-occurs with items from particular semantic domains of "badness", namely, "danger, "difficulty-problems", "complications" and "anxiety". We represented this notationally as *fraught with* [bad: dangerous/difficult/complicated/anxiety-provoking].

   Concordance some of the items in these lists and try to identify what particular kinds of "badness" and "goodness" they tend to express.

CHAPTER 3

# Evaluation and control

In the last chapter we discussed briefly how evaluation can be viewed phylogenetically as a vital survival construct in species psychology. In this chapter we consider another highly important functional psychological construct shaping both the form of language and linguistic interaction, that of control or, more precisely, of being or not being in control of events and of one's environment.

Firstly we will illustrate the importance of the notion of control for speakers and how it is inseparably bound up with evaluation. We will then go on to show how it can help some of the questions and difficulties which authors have identified in evaluation theory, in particular, problems in the description of evaluative (semantic) prosodies (Chapter 2.7).

## 3.1 Control: The linguistic unit

To begin we look at the word *control* itself as used in context by consulting the SiBol newspaper corpus (described in 0.4.1) to get an idea of the range of meaning potential in the term. Where *control* as a lexical item does occur in corpus data it appears to indicate a battleground. When we look at its frequent collocates, (*seize, relinquish, regain, wrest, take, lose, retain, cede, greater, tighter, effective* or *insufficient)* it seems that it is something people would, in general, rather have than not have, and the more of it the better:

(1) In his determination to deliver some form of **tight control over** the press he is blind to the idea that newspapers have to operate independently of the state. (*Times* 2005)

(2) In these circumstances, Mr Byers deserves to take the rap for telling untruths to MPs, though he also deserves praise for the decisive way he **wrested control** of the railways **away from** a private management that had simply lost its way. (*Guardian* 2005)

(3) There were also renewed fears that Ethiopia and Eritrea may be about to embark on a new round in their bloody **battle for control** of disputed areas along their border. (*Times* 2005)

Corpus-based dictionaries give a similar picture. The Macmillan *Online Dictionary* gives the following collocates of *control* as a noun: *assume, exercise, exert, gain, have, keep, lose, maintain, regain, relinquish, retain, seize, take, tighten, wrest.* Control can either be expressed in terms of a polarity, as indicated by the collocating items *seizing, wresting, losing, gaining,* having or not having, getting or losing, as illustrated in Examples (1) to (3) above, or it can be used with expressions which indicate a notional cline of control. For this we find examples which suggest that the extent of the control, and how rigid the control is, are also important for evaluation, with collocates like *tight, tighter, complete, effective*, as illustrated in Examples (4) to (6):

(4) Given that initial premise, it's not surprising that most managers respond to any performance challenge by **tightening control, not loosening it**. (*Observer* 2005)

(5) Formal trading contracts were needed for key clients. Computerised estimating and work tracking systems were required for **effective control**. (*Sunday Times* 2005)

(6) Stubbs seemed to understand that the mastery of horses is a delicate balance of power and submission, which depends on human beings accepting that they are **never in complete control**. (*Observer* 2005)

Moreover, the question is often raised, explicitly or implicitly of whether or not those who are in control have other parties' best interests at heart:

(7) There is great concern among scientists and liberals here about the effects of global warming. Our problem is that the Bush Administration and its selfish supporters are in **control** and they do not care. (*Observer* 2005)

To interpret these questions, attention needs to be paid to whose point of view is being expressed and what relationships prevail among the protagonists involved (see Chapter 2 for more on point of view). Political figures – predictably – do not like the other side to be in control. In Example (7) the Bush Administration being in control is seen by an observer (the writer) as a problem (that is to say something bad) rather than, as one would normally expect, a positive characteristic for an administration. The situation is being presented and negatively evaluated by the observer from the point of view of outsiders of the Administration, the "liberals and scientists" reportedly greatly concerned about the effects of climate change. In the following too, control in the hands of someone with asymmetric power is definitely not positive:

(8) Men who are in **control** most of the time, who maybe go around humiliating and degrading other people, sometimes like to be on the receiving end of it, like the high-powered executives who dress up in baby

clothes. The illusion of not being in **control** can be a bit of a relief. But he is still in **control**. If you're with a prostitute, it's not on a consensual basis. That person is not there because of any enjoyment. Once you're paying, you call the shots. Everything a man like this does is about being in **control**. (*Guardian* 2005)

An accumulation of negative evaluation (*humiliating, degrading, not consensual, not any enjoyment*) depicts the point of view of being under the control of someone else in an asymmetric relationship where control is exerted by virtue of superior strength or socio-economic power rendering the other person unable either to resist or consent in any real sense, and without the best interests of the person at heart.

However, leaving others in control is not always a bad thing:

(9) As long as players understand you are in **control** they are happy to work with you. For the players it's a tough game and it's the same for the referee. In the main, players respect that. (*Guardian* 2005)

Here referee and players are joined in a collaborative activity where both contributions are necessary and the needs of the game demand a neutral figure to take control and have jurisdiction over the two teams. Control here is seen as being a good thing even when it is in the hands of another.

In (8) we saw how an illusory relinquishing of control could be seen as very bad, but letting go of control is not necessarily portrayed as negative, especially when it is a voluntary decision:

(10) Storytelling is built into the fabric of the brain and if it's not our own story we are attending to we readily latch on to others. You are doing it now, reading these words. My reason for writing them is precisely to take charge of the little voice in your head. You **happily relinquish control**. It feels satisfying to submit to the guidance of another voice. Think of a green giraffe. See, it's irresistible. (*Times* 2005)

Where the issue is one of self-control, sometimes too little control or an inability to keep control is negative or has negative effects and is often connotated with danger as in the following examples:

(10) It's also about **control**. Dr Joan Harvey, a psychologist researching risk attitudes at Newcastle University, believes that high-risk behaviours such as driving fast and smoking don't bother us because our fate is in our own hands. But being driven by someone else, or being subjected to the unexpected on daily routines, can be a lot scarier. "I think what's panicking people at the moment is the lack of **control** we feel on a public transport system," she says. (*Times* 2005)

(11) Phobics live in constant fear of the **loss of control** and danger associated with that which they avoid. (*Observer* 2005)

(12) Wilkinson's message is that social environment can be more toxic than any pollutant. Low status and **lack of control** over one's life is a destroyer of human health and happiness. (*Guardian* 2005)

When entities are out of control they *career, spin, spiral, veer, slide, slip* and *escalate*; that is to say, speakers employ metaphors of movement to indicate that the direction and pace of some event are no longer being decided by the protagonist whose point of view is taken, and that, metaphorically, gravity and speed have taken over control.

On the other hand too much control is also negative; expressions such as *control freakery, micro-management, obsessive compulsive behaviour* express a negative evaluation of a perceived excess of control or of the inability to let go of control, as we can see from the following examples:

(13) Behind the scenes senior Tories offer dark warnings about their bothersome Ken. Harmful egomaniac, apparently. Impossible to work with. Complete **control freak**. (*Times* 2005)

(14) It lambasts Blair as a vain, shallow, hairspray- and legacy-obsessed **control freak**, who avoids collective consultation. (*Guardian* 2005)

(15) Peter Moffat picks up on the testosterone-laden, **control-freak** machismo of a top restaurant kitchen as a backdrop. (*Times* 2005)

Again we see how political differences can construe control negatively as excessive. In Example (15), although "top" is good, the use of the term *control freak* is negative and the expressions *testosterone-laden* and *machismo* are distancing, over-the-fence terms, usually applied to someone else, not oneself.

The related concept of micro-management usually carries negative evaluation though it may have had its origins as a descriptive term or even one denoting good practice. In SiBol 05 there are 51 examples to be found using the search term *micro-manag** (divided more or less equally between *The Times* and the *Guardian*), which provide us with an idea of the profile of its use, that is to say, the sum of the variations and patterns of semantic preferences, collocations and contexts which make up the primings of the lexical item. As a descriptive term *micro-management* seems to indicate a practice that some are beginning to abandon:

(16) The Commission for Racial Equality has been a concert master for many years, bringing together the disparate players. But with so many groups emerging, including those who prioritise religion above race, it cannot hope to **micro-manage** minority affairs in the way it has. (*Guardian* 2005)

It seems to have come to designate a practice which can be excessive and is to be avoided:

(17) But it is hard not to see that centralisation, complexity and **micro-management** are strongly related to many of these failed systems. (*Guardian* 2005)

It is also a perceived particular failing of governments who try to exert too much control:

(18) Many voters, away from the **micro-managed** public appearances and soft-lob questions, remained angry or apathetic about both main parties. (*Sunday Times* 2005)

(19) Even Whitehall now recognises that their **micro-management** went too far. (*Guardian* 2005)

A dislike of excessive control, presented by the press as unfair manipulation with negative effects, in much the same way as *orchestration* (see 3.3.12 below) may also be a strategy for avoiding detailed questions or countering accusations of not doing enough:

(20) "It is **not for me to micro-manage** athletics," Jowell said. (*Times* 2005)

(21) "[...] We don't investigate, we observe the electorate as a whole. It is **not up to us to micro-manage** the police," she said. (*Times* 2005)

The notion of "control" thus involves both questions of who has it and who has not and also how much and how tight the control is.

## 3.2 Control and power relations

Many of the situations portrayed in the concordance lines and texts in our data involve asymmetrical power relationships: management and workers, managers and players, government and the people. Relative power relationships are a decisive factor in human affairs. Being subject to another's control, and the question of having or not having power in a particular situation is listed as one of the three most important factors governing face-work (along with social distance and degree or "absolute ranking" of face-threat: Goffman 1955; Brown & Levinson 1987). Not being in control threatens our positive face, that is to say, our sense of our competence, worth and esteem, and also our negative face, more precisely, our autonomy, freedom of movement and right to personal space. Both are put at risk when we lose control, when things *break out*, *happen*, *set in*, etc. against our will or our ability to control the state of affairs. Many of the dictionary definitions of *control*, distilled from the accumulated co-texts of concordance lines, involve the terms *power* or *ability*, or variants on the theme of decision making and doing what one wants, or obtaining desired results and avoiding undesired ones, for example, goal achievement. *Macmillan Online Dictionary* provides the following glosses:

- power to make something such as a vehicle, machine or animal do what you want
- power to make decisions
- the ability to remain calm even when you are feeling upset or angry

The *Cambridge Online Dictionary* gives:

- Control (n) when you control something or someone, or the power to do this
- Control (v) to order, limit or rule something, or someone's actions or behaviour

and also provides as related concepts the following terms, which are clearly part of asymmetrical power relationships: *condition, manipulate, keep in line, ascendancy, dominance, curb, check, mastery, restraint, command.*

All of this would account for a negative evaluation of not having control. In Chapter 2 we presented a phylogenetic view of evaluation as vital for evolutionary success. Similarly, the struggle for survival involves bringing one's environment under control, having power over it and thus achieving one's goals, and avoiding being powerless to control external forces. As Hunston points out, an evaluation of power relations will depend on point of view, which involves relative status:

> Such meaning is often not reducible to a simple positive or negative. It is essentially linked to point of view so that there is often not one indisputable interpretation of attitude. (Hunston 2007: 256)

It is clear in adversarial scenarios of war, politics or sport where there are two sides, what is good for one will be bad for the other as in the following examples:

(22) Lincoln did a fine impression of Dracula last night, biting back when, at 2–0 down and with Fulham seeming comfortable, they raised their game and **took control** of the match. (*Times* 2005)

The two football teams (literally) have opposing goals. The writer here describes how one team openly ***took*** control. In other situations, events can be interpreted in terms of a control which happens behind the scenes but can still be total:

(23) According to Mr McDowell, Mr Adams and Mr McGuinness resigned from the Army Council two months ago and substituted placemen to do their bidding as part of the backroom deal surrounding the IRA's July cessation statement. But nothing has really changed. "They (Adams and McGuinness) are **in overall control** of the movement, and there is no challenge to their authority." (*Times* 2005)

Here the question is of ***covert*** control in a situation where there is no overt or apparent designated formal power.

Morley and Partington make the similar straightforward point in discussing evaluative prosody that "if a situation is *fraught with difficulties* for me, this is bad; if it is *fraught with difficulties* for my enemy, this is bad for him but good for me" (2009: 150). Thus many of the arguments in the literature (see Stewart 2010 for an overview) on the evaluative polarity of certain items such as *budge* are a consequence of differences in the speaker's situation and point of view, as we shall see below when we examine in terms of control (and lack of it) a number of items discussed in the literature on evaluative prosody. Hunston (2002), when discussing the lexical item *sit through*, notes that there are many references to imposition or constraint, *having to* or being *forced to* do something, which suggest situations where someone or some circumstance has power or control over the person whose point of view is being related. She finds that *sit through* "often follows *have to*, or an expression indicating that pressure has been exerted or an expression indicating that someone doesn't want to do something" (2002: 61–62). There may be no overt power relationships involved; we may find that socialisation has resulted in perceived obligations which encourage *self*-control and even if there is no other person to control us, a concern for others can become a form of obligation enforcing control of self. Among the synonyms provided for the noun *control* by the *Macmillan's Online Thesaurus* we find *power, authority, nomination, constriction, force, constraint, restriction, limitation*.

## 3.3 The control feature and evaluative prosody: Examples

Having provided an overview of how *control* is used, in this section, we examine some of the items which have been discussed in the literature on evaluative prosody to see whether what has been said so far about the cognitive-semantic features of control can shed any light on some of the problematic issues which have arisen.

### 3.3.1 *Set in*

Sinclair initiated what has turned into a contentious discussion when he illustrated the use in context of the item *set in*, showing that it is very generally employed in negative contexts (sometimes also in neutral but never, in his data, in positive ones), for example:

> The most striking feature of this phrasal verb is the nature of its subjects. In general, they refer to unpleasant states of affairs. (1991: 75)

He gives a list of items which collocate from his data: *rot, delay, malaise, despair, ill-will, decadence, impoverishment, infection, prejudice, rigor mortis* and states: "[n]ot one of these is conventionally desirable or attractive" (Sinclair 1991:74–75).

In terms of the concepts being discussed here, we note that once a process has *set in* we can no longer control it but have to wait for it to run its course, it represents a process once begun that cannot be interrupted; that is to say, in the data either the protagonists are unable or are obliged to move or act or they defer their freedom to do so. Of the examples of *set in* from the SiBol corpora, many instantiations contain items from the semantic field of emotions, some from the physical world, some concepts such as *reality* or *realism* where high hopes are brought down to earth (or worse in Example 24) as we can see in the following examples. In many instances, *set in* co-occurs with the modal *can* or other forms related to ability or possibility with a negative. In the examples both the search word and the negative co-textual elements are highlighted in bold:

(24) I suppose it would be nice never to have to make irreversible decisions: there would always be time to change one's mind about everything, from choice of career to that of partner. But decisions would thus cease to have any importance, and **a sense of futility** would ***set in***. While it can be hard already to discern the meaning of life, it would become quite **impossible** if life were to last for a millennium. (*Guardian* 2005)

(25) It should be the unequivocal position of the Government that rigor mortis has ***set in*** and that the constitutional corpse **cannot** be revived by a French kiss of life. (*Times* 2005)

(26) What is more depressing is that the figures suggest that there will still be a loss for many departments after the introduction of top-up fees. The reaction has ***set in***. You **can't** unbuild the lecture theatre or the halls of residence, although you can let them rot. You **can't very easily** shed tenured staff, but you can plan for a "phased reduction" in numbers, using voluntary redundancy combined with abolishing the posts of those who retire. (*Guardian* 2005)

So the prosody associated with *set in* is negative in this dataset too. However, we also came across an interesting counterexample, where *set in* is used in a positive setting:

(27) He chastised himself at St Andrews this year, saying he was far from satisfied at finishing 11th in the Open Championship. Now the Poulter brand of **determination** has **set in. He feels, like his beloved Arsenal, that better days are ahead. "I can win,"** he said. (*Sunday Telegraph* 2005)

This example lends weight to the argument that the evaluative prosody of *set in* is partly dependent on its usually expressing a lack of control over events. In this case, the protagonist's sense of *determination* restores control of events to him and this is enough, here at least, to override any negativity associated with the verb.

### 3.3.2 *Sit through*

Another item to undergo scrutiny in the literature on evaluative prosody is *sit through* (Hunston 2002). *Macmillan's Online Dictionary* gives the definition: "sit through something to stay to the end of something, especially if you are not enjoying it" but, as we shall see, such a definition does not reveal the whole story. Hunston points out that it is often preceded by *have to* or an expression indicating that pressure has been exerted and she notes that many of the concordance lines in her data include an indication of a specific length of time or by an indication that the length of time is judged to be uncomfortably long:

> SIT THROUGH might be said to "carry connotations of boredom" amassed through the typical contexts in which the phrase is used. (Hunston 2002:62)

When we have to *sit through* something, we are obliged to remain where we are until the end, unable to get up and go, even when the experience is a painful or tedious one. In other words, for some reason – external obligation or internal sense of duty – we do not have control over the decision to stay or leave. It is not the length of time that is at issue but the conflict between perceived obligation to stay to the end of the process and the quality of the experience. The co-text often contains modal verbs of obligation or necessity, in fact two thirds of the examples found in Sibol 05 have collocates such as *had to, having to, forced to, obliged to,* or as in the following example, the notion of being able to cope with an experience:

(28) I have vivid memories of watching Spongers, a Jim Allen script about a woman who has her children taken away from her. It was absolutely shattering and part of that was seeing the effect it had on my dad. I noticed my mum could **sit through** anything harrowing, but my dad couldn't. (*Observer* 2005)

or some reference to foregoing alternative choices because of some commitment:

(29) Mr Roberts, whose ever-dedicated wife managed to **sit through** the entire 48 hours of his record-breaking sermon without falling asleep, suggests a "three-point sermon" to keep the audience's attention. (*Sunday Telegraph* 2005)

or to deferred gratification:

(30) Just as the fans were accepting that sometimes you **have to sit through a tedious match in order to be part of the celebrations at the end**, and that the best thing to do in the circumstances would be to throw their celery sticks in the air, the match was awarded an emotional twist. (*Times* 2005)

or to difficulty:

(31) They even argue – the feeble retort of the morally bankrupt – that if they didn't do it, somebody else would. For all that, it is difficult to **sit through** the last in this series without feeling shop-soiled. The big excitement tonight comes when a photographer gets pictures of David Beckham standing on the balcony of his hotel before Euro 2004 wearing boxer shorts. (*Times* 2005)

In the examples the *sitting through* is described as a feat of endurance requiring dedication or personal capacity (29, 30 and 32) or the experience itself is described as tedious (31). There is an expressed obligation (*have to*) if some other advantage is to be gained (being part of the celebration at the end). Or the experience is described as difficult to achieve without unpleasant results (*feeling shop-soiled*). All the evaluations are about the whole process which is seen from beginning to end and not simply in terms of the quality of the event. We might even consider *through* as being a kind of shorthand for "all the way through to the end" as opposed to the freedom to get up and leave at any point along the way. Stewart (2010: 93, 111), who is concerned that not all the states of affairs to be *undergone* are unfavourable (discussed below), also questioned the suggested prosody of boredom for *sit through*. If we use the Morley and Partington (2009) notation presented in the previous chapter, he interprets the evaluation as being [negative: unpleasant experience] which, on the evidence here, does not apply to all cases. With reference to *sit through* he argues that there is a tendency to convert neutral looking co-occurrences into pleasant or unpleasant ones, claiming that often *sitting through* can be substituted by *watching* and that this would relieve the concordance line of the negative evaluation. We might interpret this not as [negative: boring or long], but rather as [negative: no control over freedom to get up and go]. Although it must be stressed again that this is not always the result of obvious external coercion and not always observable in the immediate co-textual window of the concordance line.

The *Macmillan's Online Dictionary* definition (if we recall: "sit through something to stay to the end of something, especially if you are not enjoying it") does not make reference to the conflicted reasons one might have for staying, but, as noted above, two-thirds of the examples found in SiBol 05 have collocates such as *had to, having to, forced to, obliged to*, conveying someone's lack of control over whether to leave.

Instead, when the co-text contains no elements of explicit negative evaluation and no expression of obligation, this is generally because no conflict exists between the staying and the alternative, so no external control or self-control is involved:

(32) The night before this interview, he took her to see Billy Elliott, and cannot quite believe that he **sat through** the musical without once thinking of his swing. (*Sunday Times* 2005)

(33) Having **sat through** the Hutton Inquiry the previous summer, and spent a lot of time wondering exactly what kind of man David Kelly had been, I was disconcerted to see him brought so palpably to life by Rylance, who, when the camera was rolling and when it was not, inhabited the scientist's bottled-up despair, and his sudden forced lightness, with unnerving intensity. (*Observer* 2005)

(34) At Digum school I also **sat through** a Grade 8 class of 56 students. Here in the top form boys and girls aged between 10 and 20 were being coached by the excellent Mr Hailay. (*Times* 2005)

Finally, the corpus material also contains an example where there is explicit positive evaluation attached to the *sitting through*:

(35) Disappointingly, however, for red-blooded males, who would doubtless appreciate the chance to see the comely Sophia in the buff, the love scenes are of the kind that you **could happily sit through** with your aunt. (*Times* 2005)

There is no constraint at play, no sense of having to yield control, in this instance. Once more we have evidence that the cognitive-semantic metafunction of control, or lack of it, is an important determining factor in the evaluative use of an item.

This is, of course, not to argue that the item *sit through* is *not* primed for negative prosody. The argument is that it is, first of all, primed for 'under obligation', or that it has a *semantic preference* for being under compulsion, and since being under obligation is generally deemed to be unpleasant in that control has been taken away from us, this builds into its negative prosody. In fact the priming for the negative prosody of *sit through* is so strong that a qualifier like *happily* is often required to override the expectation of unpleasantness.

### 3.3.3 *Undergo*

A similar meaning of enduring the completion of a process with no say or control over the experience or its outcome is expressed by the term *undergo*. *Macmillan's Online Dictionary* defines it as "to experience something, especially something that is unpleasant but necessary; undergo surgery/treatment/an operation etc.: e.g. She underwent emergency surgery for suspected appendicitis".

In the SiBol corpus the co-text often contains items with a meaning of constraint, obligation or other control factor:

(36) New followers **undergo** a two-year indoctrination course and can become a full member only when they "melt with the party". (*Sunday Times* 2005)

The constraint being expressed by the idea that followers who would like to become full members cannot, unless they undergo the course.

(37) Some members of the local party **made him undergo** a vote to deselect him last year.

(38) If ID cards really are essential, then give me one – I'll **undergo all the necessary** finger-printing without complaint – but please don't ask me to pay for it as well. (*Guardian* 2005)

Hypothesising a control feature as part of the meaning, that is [negative: no control over the process], would resolve some of the perplexities articulated by Stewart (2010). With reference to *undergo* he argues that some of the instances of use identified by others (in particular Stubbs 2001: 89–95) as being unequivocally unfavourable are in fact neutral or even positive. He also points out that most of the negative items are preceded by items such as *forced to* or *had to,* or other expressions involving coercion, and that a decision to use only base forms of the verb will result in a higher proportion of negative evaluative prosody. Using all the forms of the verb, he says, will give a different picture. However, much of his argument ignores whether the presence of a human or sentient subject is important in the prosody, and in particular the distinction between what the person undergoes, that is to say the process undergone (e.g. a surgical operation), and the eventual benefits which result from the process. He claims that we should be wary of labelling as negative something which saves lives and restores health. He rightly points out that perhaps undergoing extensive skills and fitness training is neutral rather than negative but, does not consider, when compared to undergoing emergency operations, that the person is likely to be far more in control and this will account for the neutral rather than negative prosody.

It is to be noted that we are also using more than just the list of collocates or the concordance lines in our analysis. In CADS methodology the analyst is encouraged to go into the text and this would resolve many of the problems posed by Stewart (2010) who tends to work mostly with concordance lines while simultaneously claiming that this distorts perceptions by creating an impression of what he calls group cohesion and unity.

### 3.3.4 *Budge*

Another item discussed at length in the literature on prosody is *budge* (Sinclair 1998; Stubbs 2001; Hunston 2007 and see Morley & Partington 2009 for a summary). If something will not *budge* we are unable to control its choice of position. Sinclair concludes:

> Something does not *budge* when it does not move despite attempts to move it. From the perspective of the person who wants something moved this is frustrating and irritating and these emotions may find expression because this

> is the 'semantic prosody' of the use of *budge*. [....] in the use of *budge* the user wishes to express or report frustration (or a similar emotion) at the refusal or inability of some obstacle to move, despite pressure being applied. (1998:20)

Hunston provides counterexamples to the generalisation proposed by Sinclair and warns that a positive achievement may also be expressed by a person refusing to budge or the failure of an inanimate object to move is surprising but welcome. If someone will not budge the co-text usually suggests some conflict of wills, and from that person's point of view they are in control and do not want to lose it. If the person refusing to budge is the speaker or a protagonist whose point of view is adopted by the speaker then control is being used to good effect:

(39) The chancellor **refuses to budge** from Labour's agreed campaign script despite complaints that Mr Letwin's £35bn figure is not a cut, but a reduced increase. (*Guardian* 2005)

(40) To press him on the subject would be fruitless: Adams **will not budge**. Years of interrogation by journalists – and before that, the RUC and the British army – make it unlikely he will tell you anything he doesn't mean you to hear. (*Guardian* 2005)

(41) I'm very stubborn, and if my mind's set on something, I **won't budge**. (*Sunday Times* 2005)

In these examples there are explicit references to mental will (*agreed, doesn't mean, mind set*) which would tend to suggest a positive evaluation as part of a goal/achievement script whereby protagonists are in control enough to be able to stand their ground and keep to their decisions and convictions. Even where there is no human volition explicitly mentioned, goal achievement is part of the sub-text, as in the example proposed in Hunston of a certain Mr Otis the inventor of a new kind of lift (2007:258):

(42) He chose the New York Exposition to demonstrate his device, standing on an open lift high above the ground as his assistant cut the cord supporting it. The lift **did not budge**.

Hunston says that the favourable evaluation might be described as an expression of surprise on the part of onlookers that something might be expected to happen (the lift plunges to the ground) has not happened. It seems rather that with the inventor as the theme and adopted perspective (see Chapter 2.2) of the previous sentence, it is more reasonable to describe the positive evaluation as related to Mr Otis's control of the event ("He chose").

### 3.3.5 *Persistence/Persistent*

A similar picture is presented by the items *persistence/ persistent*, discussed by Hunston (2007:256) where purpose and will are part of the sub-text. She illustrates how the noun *persistence* can be either a quality to be approved of (the examples given are [*the arrest*] *is a triumph for persistence; Pupils work with commendable persistence*) or a negative quality: [...] *can strike the wrong note with her pushy persistence*. The co-text in these cases indicates the evaluation explicitly: [positive: a triumph], [positive: commendable] and [negative: pushy] (Hunston 2007:256).

As regards the adjective form *persistent*, Hunston (2007:255–256) claims that where it is followed by a noun (attributive use), the items it co-occurs with are consistently negative in their evaluation (*persistent errors, persistent offenders*); where this is not explicit she gives examples where the wider co-text would support the hypothesis that the noun phrase modified by *persistent* indicates something undesirable, at least from the point of view of the producer of the text.

The situation is different for *persistent* when used predicatively where the attitudinal implications are less consistently negative (for example, *But she is so persistent, that Beth- that they end up- they have a real break, a very good conversation about religion and about death, they are communicating*). Hunston concludes that precise observations of co-text and phraseology need to be made before statements about evaluation can be made and that there is often a dual point of view in terms of the participants. The quality is desirable or undesirable in terms of the different goals of the participants, that is, it is positive when the goals of the adopted perspective are achieved or negative when the goals of the adopted perspective are not achieved. The next two examples, from SiBol 05, clearly show how goal achievement is a key factor in the evaluation:

(43) With the **persistent** consumer downturn meaning that growth is falling far short of the Chancellor's expectations, the IMF expects borrowing to reach 3.2 per cent of GDP in 2005 and 3.4 per cent in 2006. (*Times* 2005)

(44) Further gains for Asian bourses and the rekindling of **persistent** bid speculation gave Standard Chartered the best blue-chip rise as the FTSE 100 hit a new four-year high. (*Times* 2005)

In the first the overall evaluation is negative, in the second positive. The evaluation depends on who is in control and whose point of view is being recounted; in (44) the situation is negative from the adopted perspective (the Chancellor) who is not in control (or has lost control) of the behaviour of others (consumers), whilst in (45) it is positive from the point of view of Standard Chartered, whose plans are bearing fruit. In our data we see that where the participant's goals are achieved even a negative co-text will not affect the evaluation, it is the goal achievement which counts and makes persistence a good thing. In the following examples *persistent*, though linked with painful effort or as part of a lengthy process, has a positive evaluation:

(45) This is a sound and significant observation. It has been arrived at after eight years of **persistent** and often painful effort. (*Times* 2005)

(46) "Never give up," Convey says. The first "no" is just the start of a lengthy process: "You have to be **persistent** and persuasive." But not pushy; keep the door open rather than have it slammed in your irritating little face. (*Times* 2005)

As Hunston points out, phraseology is an important consideration. We found, for example, that a human subject (and particularly personal pronouns), as in (46) will often signal a situation where a person is in control and we will observe this again in the next section.

### 3.3.6 *Break out*

The lexical item *break out* has been used as an example of evaluative prosody and the claim is made that undesirable things or states of affairs will be found in its environment, especially with regard to the subject (Sinclair 1994). This claim can be investigated in the light of the current theme of control. When something has *broken out*, in particular impersonal or non-human entities, it has passed beyond a restraint of some sort and is out of control with negative consequences (that is [negative: out of control]):

(47) Americans are facing queues at the petrol pumps for the first time since the 1970s as shortages and panic hit parts of the country. Fist fights **broke out** at some petrol stations as motorists waited in long queues for fuel for the upcoming Labor Day holiday weekend, when millions hit the road. (*Times* 2005)

(48) Then we left and went to Sri Lanka and got evacuated when a civil war **broke out** – the flashpoint was right where we were living. (*Times* 2005)

(49) The worst flu pandemic, which **broke out** in 1918, killed more than 40 million people. (*Times* 2005)

In these three examples the subject of the verb – whatever *breaks out* – is itself negative, not just the consequences. There are occasional instances where positive entities break out such as *laughter, cheers, applause, dancing*, which relate to situations in which strong positive emotions overcome some form of restraint, but these are a minority.

When, on the other hand, the point of view is that of a person who has broken out of something or somewhere constraining, there is a positive aura of having escaped the control of others and of regaining one's own control (i.e. positive: [control regained]). This can even be portrayed as heroic in the case of Jake the Muscovy duck in Example (53):

(50) "[…] I have absolutely no regrets," says Geldof. "The Rats were a fantastic band, there's no question about that. We sold millions of records and played vast gigs: in very hostile times at home and abroad we **broke out** and got there. (*Sunday Times* 2005)

(51) "One flat had no heating," says Fallon, "and we'd go to the pub and buy a pint each to last all night, just to stay warm. Ricky and I were the most unambitious people ever." She **broke out** first, as a script editor on EastEnders. Then Gervais lucked into a job as "head of speech" at Xfm, the London radio station. He was 36. (*Sunday Times* 2005)

(52) "But my mother was strict, and anything not serious was forbidden. I was always dreaming, though. And when I was 15, I **broke out**. I started looking for things that were inappropriate." Prada realised that choosing the inappropriate is what moves creativity forward. (*Sunday Times* 2005)

(53) Within a week of moving from Kentisbury Grange Country Park, near Lynton, North Devon, to a farm at Burridge, near Barnstaple, he **broke out** and headed home. He could not live without his mate, who had already hatched 16 of his offspring, Roy Shindler, his owner, said. Muscovy ducks are not good fliers because they are too heavy for take-off. Jake usually waddles at leisurely pace, but in his four week love trek he braved snowstorms, crossed the busy Barnstaple-Ilfracombe road and swam the River Yeo. (*Times* 2005)

Whether these two usages, with their two distinct phraseological patterns, are different but related lexical items or different senses of the same item is a moot point. What is certain is that the overall difference in meaning is one which involves human or at least sentient perceptions of being able or unable to control events, and whether that control is a good thing or a bad thing.

### 3.3.7 *Outbreak*

The expression *an outbreak of* is very generally followed by something bad. *Macmillan's Online Dictionary* tells us it means "the sudden start of war violence, disease etc." which suggests it is also probably primed for the evaluation [negative: out of control] since all these entities tend to be undesirable and their outbreak indicates the breaking of constraints as a loss of control. Collocates indicating violence disease or conflict are prevalent in the SiBol 05 corpus:

| N | Concordance | | |
|---|---|---|---|
| 1 | with strangers. ELDER ABUSE Brace yourself for: An | outbreak of | ageism among your offspring, who will also |
| 2 | the French Interior Minister, ill-advisedly referred to at the | outbreak of | anarchy last month. Before kick-off, all was |
| 3 | Some people have all the luck. I suspect that a selective | outbreak of | arson, featuring several hundred distinctive |
| 4 | during the party conference season, has suffered an | outbreak of | bed bugs. Blood-sucking parasites at a party |
| 5 | of Scotland are becoming concerned about an apparent | outbreak of | folie de grandeur from the bank whose chief |
| 6 | new cases of E. coli were confirmed in the South Wales | outbreak of | food poisoning, bringing the total to 117. It was |
| 7 | the September 11, 2001 terrorist attacks and the | outbreak of | foot and mouth disease. Recent acquisitions |
| 8 | is exactly what the German Left perceive. The feral | outbreak of | greed and violence in New Orleans is likely to |
| 9 | and mussels as she speaks, with no break or discernible | outbreak of | ill humour. The director of the new film, Curtis |
| 10 | visitors to the National Theatre have been hit with an | outbreak of | spamming. Someone is launching malicious |
| 11 | the quality of life of many asthma sufferers, and warns an | outbreak of | 'steroid phobia' should be avoided." Health |
| 12 | has gone down by 15 per cent. The problem is not an | outbreak of | surly service or a sudden rise in prices these |
| 13 | Force, George Francis Rice was called up at the | outbreak of | the Great War in August 1914. He was a |
| 14 | new property developments in the Square Mile, after an | outbreak of | theft, and five men have been arrested and |
| 15 | on top of David Blunkett's second resignation and an | outbreak of | unprecedented Cabinet indiscipline, the defeat |
| 16 | his third television appearance last night since the | outbreak of | unrest on October 27, appealing for calm and |
| 17 | criticised for taking a low profile during France's biggest | outbreak of | urban violence since the 1960s. His speech |
| 18 | half of some repute and a member of the RAFVR. On the | outbreak of | war he presented himself to the RAF but was |

However, speakers and writers sometimes consciously reverse the evaluative polarity of *an outbreak of* for rhetorical effect, either for emphasis or irony (see Chapter 4.11). In these cases the meaning expressed is that of a breaking out where the escape from control is beneficial to some protagonist or observer:

(54) A committee is apparently looking at such a step to prevent further damage to Aim's reputation. That sounds like an **outbreak** of common sense, but it is hard to see how the exchange can interfere very far with a system that is meant to be self-policing. (*Guardian* 2005)

(55) The confessions grow ever more suggestive, while her revelations about her husband suggest danger. Or is it all just some elaborate sexual game she's playing? Leavened by a sly, dry sense of mischief and a delightful **outbreak** of loose-hipped dancing from the lonely lawyer that pleasingly evokes the earlier film, this is very good. (*Sunday Times* 2005)

(56) Brussels prefers to keep reality away from the EU project, but this week there was **an outbreak of** sanity (*Times* 2005)

(57) Not for the first time there has been **an outbreak of** candour at the Home Office shortly after an election. (*Times* 2005)

Here we are faced with the connotation of an excessive amount of control as opposed to a proper amount, which provides the evaluation. The evaluation being in these cases [positive: *excessive* control broken]. In the following chapter we will see how the expectations of a certain evaluation allows for ironic meanings when the expectation in thwarted.

### 3.3.8 *End up*

When we *end up* (Louw 2000; Morley & Partington 2009) being or doing something, whatever we have ended up being or doing was not according to the original plan but has gone off programme in some way, and is no longer subject to our cognitive control. Frequently *end up* is associated with negative outcomes and human impotence and inability to control the outcomes:

(58) The virus causes high fevers, followed by convulsions and coma. An estimated three quarters of survivors **end up** with some form of physical or mental disability. (*Times* 2005)

(59) The second-half incident had the same ingredients for what would **end up** becoming "mayhem" in the inflammable Old Firm arena. (*Times* 2005)

(60) You never want to **end up** as a patient in Casualty. (*Times* 2005)

However, when the speaker appears not to fear letting go and is able to take the risk of unplanned events and where there is a lack of anxiety about loss of control it can be positive:

(61) The menu features a fairly unintelligible (to Western eyes at least) list of dishes, so let Tobia's enthusiastic owner, Sophie Sirak-Kebede, choose for you. You'll probably **end up** with a huge tray of assorted stews and salads dotted on top of a vast expanse of injera, the fermented bread used to pick up a pinch of the food and convey it to the mouth. It's not for everyone, but if you're willing to go with the flow, it's a fun evening out. (*Times* 2005)

(62) Although made from leather, only vegetable dyes are used and the soles are made from recycled rubber and cork. That said, my bet is that the pair you **end up** drooling over won't carry any emblems of ethical manufacture. In which case -and I'm whispering now -unless you are certain they are made from the skin of the last surviving animal of its kind, I wouldn't hold back. (*Times* 2005)

### 3.3.9 *Cause*

Another item much discussed in the literature (Stubbs 1995; Hunston 2007; Partington 2004b, Stewart 2010) is *cause*. There has been much debate about whether it is generally used in contexts to express a negative evaluative prosody. Among its collocates in the SiBol corpus we find *trouble, damage, death, mayhem, cancer, problems offence, outrage, serious, grievous*. These tend to be illustrating cases where planning, forethought and prevention and conscious will are not part of the process:

(63) Experts are warning that it poses a severe environmental threat. As it silts up and ceases to work it could well **cause** catastrophic flooding. (*Times* 2005)

(64) Sprays are suspected to **cause** asthma, allergies, rashes and liver complaints. (*Times* 2005)

(65) Mr McConnell, who has made the Scottish smoking ban a flagship policy of his devolved administration, told a radio phone-in programme last night that while he saw the attractions of compromise, the legislation planned for England would **cause** problems. (*Times* 2005)

In the terms we are using in this chapter, when things have been *caused* they have very generally come about as a result of other factors than our will and planning and to this extent they are not under our control. In the first example we see an amount of debris silting up and accumulating beyond the ability to control it. In the second, side effects of *sprays*, that is, unintended consequences of their use, are the cause of a number of pathologies, while in the fourth the problematic effects of a *compromise* are envisaged as being a triggering factor for undesirable consequences.

It has also been argued that evaluative function of *cause* depends on discourse-type or sector-specific factors (Hunston 2007: 252, 263–265). Hunston suggests *cause* loses its negative evaluation when it occurs in "scientific" registers positing the argument that the attitudinal meaning applies only when "the caused entity concerns animate beings, their activities and their goals" (2007: 263). Strict cause and effect relationships, resulting from the forces of nature, reported in scientific work would not trigger the evaluation because of the textual/pragmatic priming.

However, we do find some counterexamples to the negative evaluation posited by Sinclair and Stubbs for *cause*. They seem to occur in situations where some kind of cognitive control is being exerted by a party whose point of view is being adopted. For instance, if an experiment is being performed which causes a particular outcome, then control and preplanning will have been a part of the process, and similarly if a policy, tactic, strategy or creative decision is indicated. In the following examples, some kind of conscious controlled decision has been taken and the evaluation is not negative:

(66) "[…] As it vastly reduces heating requirements, too, straw-bale buildings can actually **cause** a net decrease in greenhouse gas emissions. And there's no reason why they shouldn't last for at least 100 years." (*Sunday Telegraph* 2005)

(67) The cyclist in me knows that the authorities would not have to go very far down this road to **cause** a step-change in the behaviour of cyclists. (*Sunday Telegraph* 2005)

Macmillan's dictionary tells us that a *step change* involves "a noticeable improvement in something" so the hypothesised policy in (68) is presented as having a positive outcome.

(68) But the real reason Mimi is **causing** such a stir is that the songs make the most of Carey's magnificent voice. Gone is the girly whispering that made Glitter such a stinker. (*Times* 2005)

Here the creative decisions in the choice of songs has positive effects in terms of impact for a singer. Often however we need to make an effort to unpack the reason why the evaluation could be considered positive. In Example (69) you need to know that firm skin, achieved by the tightening, is considered desirable as the end result of a skin product:

(69) This deep, uniform "volumetric" heating action **causes** the collagen and elastin in your skin to contract immediately, thereby producing a tightening effect. This does not affect the epidermis (the top layer of skin). (*Times* 2005)

In (70) and (71) we also find illustrations of how conflicting goals make the balance of control good for one party and bad for the other:

(70) I thought we were brilliant in the first half – the playing surface was good and it suited us. We **caused** them numerous problems and I actually think that maybe we should have been more in front than we were at the break. (*Times* 2005)

(71) Off-shoring – sending business abroad – is **causing** optimism and pessimism in equal quantities. Either way you'd better get used to it because we are likely to see more work go to more countries – Russia, the Philippines and Latin America are already jostling for a cut of the action. (*Times* 2005)

### 3.3.10 *Fuel*

*Macmillan's Online Dictionary* tells us that the verb *fuel* is used mainly in journalism with the meaning: "To make something increase or become worse, especially something unpleasant". However, in economic discourse it can have positive evaluation (Taylor 2005). As Nelson (2006) points out, words become more collocationally fixed in specific linguistic environments. A positive evaluation is expressed by collocates such as *growth* and *value* in the SiBol 05 data, which are *fuelled* as part of someone's plan:

(72) Tesco has provided some personal data held by Clubcard, the loyalty scheme that monitors members' shopping and which has been credited with **fuelling** the supermarket group's astronomical growth in the past decade. (*Guardian* 2005)

(73) Pipeline gas has **fuelled** export growth in recent years but LNG is poised for healthy expansion as Spanish companies embark on Algeria's first integrated LNG project – the Gassi Touil. (*Times* 2005)

(74) This increase in invested capital, combined with a margin-driven increase in returns, helped to **fuel** an increase in the economic value of Granada, which was also boosted by a lower discount rate as interest rates fell. (*Times* 2005)

After the 2008 economic crisis, it often carries a decidedly more negative evaluation, as in these examples from the *Guardian* in 2009:

(75) Of course it was economically unsustainable, but the difference between us and them is one of degree rather than kind. Their boom was **fuelled by** rising property prices that nobody thought would ever fall, and by cheap money that kept flowing through the tap marked low interest rates. (*Guardian* 2009)

(76) In the illusory days before the crash there were only three engines of growth in this country – financial and business services, consumption **fuelled** by property speculation, and public spending. In the long term, a recovery based on the return of business as usual is no recovery at all. (*Guardian* 2009)

(77) Despite claims that the macho culture at the top of UK companies **fuelled** the credit crunch, of the 156 appointments to top boardrooms last year only 23, or just 14.7%, were women. (*Guardian* 2009)

In each case, the negative consequences were not planned. The term *fuel* then would seem to express evaluations which depend on a tension between the positive, in the sense of nourishing and helping growth, and the negative, in the sense of an incendiary action out of control. We see the former also in contexts around *fuel* where efforts, creativity or emotions are being nourished in some way and encouraged to grow, perhaps because initially fragile, as in the following examples:

(78) " [...] The clubs that really **fuel** the music are unfunded and almost off the radar as far as the official bodies are concerned." Be optimistic rather than resigned and pessimistic. Optimism **fuels** motivation, stamina and creativity. (*Times* 2005)

(79) Apparently economic development **fuels** good music, which is why Austrian composers were all the rage in the 18th century, American jazz musicians in the 20th, and so forth. (*Observer* 2005)

while negative emotions can be presented as being out of control and needing to be damped down:

(80) Maximising investment returns may top university agendas, but Campaign Against Arms Trade (CAAT) argues that these institutions need to consider their image, particularly with overseas students, because they are funding "a trade that **fuels** international tensions". (*Times* 2005)

(81) I can understand that your daughter's behaviour is distressing, but the anxiety generated among the adults will only be **fuelling** her screams and tears. (*Times* 2005)

### 3.3.11 *Fickle* and *flexible*

The distinction between *flexible* and *fickle*, made by Tognini-Bonelli (2001) and discussed by Stewart (2010: 115–116) is that, although they both have a core semantic element of "changeability", they express very different evaluative meanings, as can be seen in their very different collocational patterns. Tognini-Bonelli uses the distinction to highlight the usefulness of corpus work in foregrounding distinctions by showing different patterns. She found that *fickle* was used with themes such as human subjects or the vagaries of fortune or ephemeral fashions and was often found with a human actor, that is, to denote unreliable people; while *flexible*, on the other hand, rarely had a human subject and was used to describe abstract notions and entities such as markets. In the SiBol 05 corpus we find that *fickle* has, among its more frequent collocates, human subjects including *friends* and *fans*, and inanimate subjects such as *weather, winds, media, fortune*:

(82) Well, fashion always was a **fickle** lady and hard to suss. You wouldn't want it to be that simple, would you? (*Times* 2005)

(83) Tesco, the supermarket chain, is the latest company to fall foul of **fickle** British public opinion. (*Times* 2005)

(84) A sequence of three matches that starts away to Wolverhampton Wanderers tomorrow night and culminates with the steel city derby against Sheffield Wednesday is testing enough for United's resolve and their **fickle** supporters. (*Times* 2005)

while flexible has collocates which tend to indicate approaches, options, policies or market-related phenomena: *working hours, learning, exchange, systems, workforce, rents*, and so on. All of which presuppose some prevision or prediction and thus the result of someone's cognitive control:

(85) The Department of Trade and Industry yesterday challenged the report's figures, saying government statistics showed that almost 40% of all employees – 9.7 million – already have some kind of flexible arrangement. A spokesman said latest figures showed only 11% of **flexible** working requests are being turned down, compared with 20% before the right to request was introduced. (*Guardian* 2005)

(86) the company's intranet is one of the largest in Europe; and its **flexible** approach to working hours may explain why 99 per cent of employees who take maternity leave return to work once they have given birth. Employee retention is high, with a turnover of 3 per cent a year. (*Times* 2005)

(87) All of this is creating a credit market that is **flexible** and open to rapid lending growth. It is also creating a wealth effect within the wider economy. (*Times* 2005)

Concordancing of the two items illustrates the usefulness of corpus work in teasing out differences in meanings resulting from semantic preferences. Here we observe that the main factor in accounting for the distinction in evaluative polarity between these two items is the different nature of the control over circumstances they express. It depends mainly, that is, on the speaker's (or the adopted perspective's) ability to control the situation, the entity or the person they are confronted with, which is *flexible* when it bends to our needs [positive: under our control] but *fickle* if it depends on the other's control and our needs are ignored [negative: out of our control]. Here we see *market* and *business* being called both *fickle* and *flexible*:

(88) Alan Greenspan, Chairman of the US Federal Reserve, sent share prices up after he said that the US economy was surviving the oil price shock because of its **flexible** markets. (*Times* 2005)

(89) Chief information officers (CIOs) can also use them to help plan and budget, while still being able to respond to the changing demands of a **flexible** business. (*Times* 2005)

(90) The market for digital cameras may be **fickle** but the need for plumbing is constant. (Times 2005)

(91) Only latterly has Rossignol moved into skiwear, the **fickle** business that Quiksilver has so successfully mastered. (*Times* 2005)

The differences being in terms of *flexible* choice in variation and extension of markets and the ability to predict and respond to change, all of which are indicators of control contrasting with the difficulties of dealing with *fickle* unpredictable or unforeseen change which indicate a lack of control.

### 3.3.12 *Orchestrate*

Attempts to control carefully and coordinate what is normally spontaneous can also be viewed negatively, as we saw with the example of *micro-management* above. In the literature on evaluative prosody, Morley and Partington (2009) discuss the word *orchestrate*. First of all they point out that its definition in the *OED* is to "combine harmoniously like instruments in an orchestra" which would appear to be positive in its evaluation. However, they go on to show, using SiBol data, how it is often used, by metaphorical extension, to express a highly negative concept of covert, secretive engineering of something apparently spontaneous for strategic purposes:

(92) [...] warned that Sinn Fein and the IRA might **orchestrate** violence so they could then try to claim advantage. (*Guardian* 2005)

(93) Employment law experts said if BA could prove the TGWU helped to **orchestrate** the action, it could sue. (*Sunday Times* 2005)

This can be further contrasted with another sort of control, with *openly acknowledged* organisation for, say, economic and especially sporting advantage, which does not have this negative evaluation, which in fact is often seen as admirable, for example:

(94) he occupies the pivotal role at No. 3, where a top batsman can **orchestrate** the innings, assessing the potential in a pitch and dictating the pace of play. (*Guardian* 2005)

(95) Some can control the game and field position with the boot, while others **orchestrate** with their running and distribution. (*Sunday Telegraph* 2005)

(96) Instead he is aiming to **orchestrate** a smooth move into the new Terminal 5 building at Heathrow and commit himself to the profitability targets set by his predecessor Sir Rod Eddington. (*Guardian* 2005)

Although such cases are still metaphorical (there is no literal orchestra involved), they are closer to the original literal sense of "combine harmoniously" various disparate elements of a complex organisation such as a business or a team. Particular sorts of metaphorical extensions can thus be more typical in certain fields (here, the negative sort in politics, the positive in sport) and what might be seen as the same lexical item used metaphorically can exert a very different evaluative effect depending on the field of context.

Metaphorical extensions are almost always created to perform evaluations (Partington & Taylor 2010: 86–107) and we can see from these examples that the interaction of text and environment illustrates the negative evaluation of orchestration, which is harmonious if done openly and for all to see but sinister if seen as trying exert control in secret to gain some hidden advantage.

### 3.3.13 *True feelings*

Another item discussed in the literature on evaluative prosody is *true feelings*. Sinclair reports that it displays a semantic preference for expression (presumably reporting verbs) and a prosody of [negative: reluctance] or [negative: inability] (2004: 35):

(97) A private man behind the public banter, he hid his **true feelings**, an act of heroic modesty considering his huge potential influence. (*Guardian* 2005)

(98) It could be they're keeping their heads down, anonymously executing the template and subverting their voices to the greater personality of the title. Then maybe they go home and vent their **true feelings** via, say, their own blog. (*Guardian* 2005)

A more significant generalisation can be made if we once again posit control as the key feature determining the evaluative function of this item. The co-text nearly always contains items describing and delineating issues regarding the right to control one's own private space, including and especially, the freedom to express oneself. Constraints on this right infringe our personal autonomy; in Brown and Levinson's (1987) terms, they are threats to our negative face. If the speaker controls the right to express his/her *true feelings*, then the overall evaluation of the situation is liable to be positive. If, on the other hand, s/he suffers some constraint or obligation to reveal *true feelings* – that is, s/he has lost control – then the evaluation tends to be negative. In some instances, the ability of others to gain access to private space is an issue and, in these cases, the relationship with the other person is all-important since, if they are not perceived to be sympathetic, this will generally be a particularly face-threatening experience.

There are four general categories of scenario, the first two where the subject is in control and the evaluations are positive or neutral, and two where s/he is not in control and the evaluations are much more likely to be evaluated negatively:

When the subject is in control:

i. s/he can hide true feelings when s/he wants (the co-text contains items such as *conceal, hide, cover up, suppress, mask, disguise, bury, rein in*), for example:

(99) A private man behind the public banter, he hid his true feelings, an act of heroic modesty considering his huge potential influence. (*Guardian* 2005)

ii. s/he can reveal them when s/he wants (the co-text contains items such as *give rein to, show, communicate, share, convey*), for example:

(100) Pasternak conveyed his true feelings. Foreign publishers, he said, "must not hold back from publishing for fear of harming me. I wrote the novel to be published and read. That remains my only wish".

When the subject is *not* in control then either:

iii. s/he might reveal them involuntarily: in these cases the co-text contains expressions such as *betray, expose, emerged, evidence of, give away*:

(101) it is the involuntary tics that betray our true feelings. (*Telegraph* 2005)

(102) true feelings emerged in one bleak, rhetorical question. (*Telegraph* 2005)

iv. others find them out when s/he does not intend them to. In this case, since other people do not often get to know a person's feelings without either voluntary or involuntary participation of the person concerned, the co-text is less likely to contain expressions of uncovering or suppression of some kind or of the right to know another's true feelings, for example, *the people are entitled to know*:

(103) The people are entitled to know her true feelings about John Major and other leading Tories. (*Telegraph* 2005)

(104) her true feelings about the case can perhaps be surmised by the fact that she omits the case entirely from the final volume of her memoirs. (*Guardian* 2005)

In reality, of course, *true feelings* are something only a first person account or an omniscient author can reliably tell us about, although they can be speculated upon, as witnessed in the newspaper data considered so far. We turn our attention explicitly to some of the features of literary discourse later in this volume (Chapter 5) but, as a foretaste, we might mention how the study of the interrelation of control/lack of control and evaluation is highly relevant in literary works. Römer (2006) illustrates the use of a corpus approach to investigate the collocates and semantic prosodies of words in a corpus of Jane Austen's novels, contrasting these features with those contained in a reference corpus of novels of the same period. She gives an example of Austen's use of the word *recover* as an example of deviation from a norm of eighteenth-century novel writing where the item would be used to express a change from a negative state of affairs to a neutral one. Her examples, from her reference corpus, all exhibit contexts where the initial state involves something unpleasant. Römer tells us:

> While recover is normally used in rather negative contexts with unfavourable semantic prosodies by Austen's contemporaries ... – just as it is used in 'general' English today (people usually recover from something unpleasant) Austen uses collocations such as, "the agitating happiness of success", "the flutter of pleasure", or "a fit of good humour" in the context of *recover*, collocations that run counter the general negative pattern and thus create ironic or humorous effects.
>
> (Römer 2006: 99)

Her concordance examples from the reference corpus show collocates like *shock, depression, horror, uneasiness, agony, hysterics*. These, and the Austen examples all seem to have a semantic preference for emotions and affect. Römer claims that the positive prosody of *good humour, happiness of success, pleasure* are examples of ironic reversal (as in the examples of *outbreak* above and Chapter 5). However, Römer's data can be interpreted in another way. If we look more closely at the contexts, bearing in mind the issues of control discussed in this chapter, these collocates can still be construed as negative because they express a meaning of "loss of self control" in the phraseology (*agitating, flutter, fit, surprise*) that is, "emotional leakage" (Brown & Levinson 1987: 67–68), not a praiseworthy trait in upper-class eighteenth century England where rationality was highly prized. Indeed the emotions in general, and love in particular, are treated as pathological, as excessive or dangerous loss of reason, sharing the collocation *recover* with physical illnesses, and expressing the idea that a return to a natural and steady state from an unnatural unsteady one is what recovery brings:

(105) It was long before Fanny could **recover** from the agitating happiness of such an hour as was formed by the last thirty minutes of expectation, and the first of fruition. (*Mansfield Park*)

(106) Emma understood him; and as soon as she could **recover** from the flutter of pleasure, excited by such tender consideration, replied. (*Emma*)

(107) She paused a moment to **recover** from the emotion of hearing herself so spoken of. The other two warmly agreed with what he said, and she then appeared. (*Persuasion*)

(108) The sounds were retreating, and Anne distinguished no more. Her own emotions still kept her fixed. She had much to **recover** from, before she could move. (*Persuasion*)

(109) Mrs. Bennet was restored to her usual querulous serenity; and, by the middle of June, Kitty was so much **recovered** as to be able to enter Meryton without tears. (*Pride and Prejudice*)

(110) And knowing, as she did, the favourable state of mind of each at this period, it struck her the more. He was wishing to get the better of his attachment to herself, she just **recovering** from her mania for Mr. Elton. (*Emma*)

Significantly the word is used also with words relating not so much to expression but to the visibility (or audibility of feelings) to others:

(111) Miss Crawford, rallying her spirits, and **recovering her complexion**, replied only, "If I had known this before, I would have spoken of the cloth with more respect," and turned the subject. (*Mansfield Park*)

(112) "It is a great relief to me – what Elinor told me this morning – I have now heard exactly what I wished to hear" – For some **moments her voice was lost; but recovering herself**, she added, and with greater calmness than before. (*Sense and Sensibility*)

(113) Their eyes instantly met, and the cheeks of both were overspread with the **deepest blush**. He absolutely started, and for a moment seemed immovable from surprise; but shortly **recovering himself**, advanced towards the party, and spoke to Elizabeth, if not in terms of perfect composure, at least of perfect civility. (*Pride and Prejudice*)

(114) "Is this," thought Elizabeth, "meant for me?" and she coloured at the idea; but, **recovering** herself, said in a lively tone, "And pray, what is the usual price of an earl's younger son? (*Pride and Prejudice*)

The leakage of *true feelings* to others is a key theme in Austen's works and control and loss of control of one's emotions is frequently dealt with contrastively. In *Sense and Sensibility* in particular Romantic sensibilities are parodied and self control shown to be a desirable attribute. Thus rather than ironic reversal of expectation (that is, expecting recovery from something bad but finding our characters recovering from something good), the *recovery* always expresses the movement from loss of self-control [bad] to restored self-control, "normal service resumed" (good).

## 3.4 Conclusions

The notion of control or lack of control over events or one's environment is associated very frequently with evaluation even when the lexical item *control* or a synonym does not appear overtly in the co-text. We have seen how a positive or negative evaluation will be found according to the extent to which the speaker or writer is in control of events or constrained or obliged to act against his or her will. Being – or rather the feeling, the conviction of being or not being – in control is fundamental to very many aspects of human behaviour. The association of linguistic expressions of the former (being in control) with positive evaluation and the latter (not being in control) with negative would therefore seem natural but, in addition, their meaning potentials as positive or negative are realised in the actual discourse we participate in frequently enough for them to have become conventionalised. In other words, the encounters we have had with lexical items which convey control/lack of control have reinforced the original expectations we have in terms of collocation and evaluation so much that an evaluative prosody has become part of the item's primings. From the evidence presented here, the notion of control/lack of control appears to resolve some of the problems which have been debated in the literature on evaluative prosody. We have, in passing, also seen how important is the normal CADS practice of accessing more of the text than the artificial window of a short concordance line since often the relevant information on how evaluations are expressed lies in the wider co-text.

In the next chapter we continue with the theme of evaluation and look at one of the principal ways in which speakers and writers play with evaluations for rhetorical effect, namely, irony.

CHAPTER 4

# Investigating rhetoric in discourse 1

## Irony

This chapter describes three corpus-assisted investigations into the nature and functions of irony in both spoken interaction and written texts. Until recently, very many linguistic studies into irony have been conducted with little recourse to contextualised episodes in real-life use, often preferring to study examples invented by the researcher, and there are particularly few which examine irony in interactive multi-party discourse. When they have used authentic data they have relied on a comparatively small number of examples. Moreover, the instances examined are generally described as ironic on the simple basis that the researcher deems them so. The principal aim of the studies in this chapter is to see whether an examination of real-life data contained in corpora can both paint a detailed picture of how irony operates in practice and also shed light on some of the important theoretical controversies in irony studies. In the first two case studies we will examine utterance – also known as propositional – irony, how both explicit and implicit ironic utterances operate. In the third we shall describe the phenomenon of phrasal irony and look at examples of how ironic exploitation can become a conventionalised usage.

### Utterance irony

### 4.1 Irony explicit and implicit

Ironic utterances can be either explicit or implicit, the first difference being that the former is characterised by the presence in the text of an explicit lexical marker of irony: *ironically, the irony is*, and so on.

The following is a straightforward instance of an explicitly ironic statement or proposition

(1) **It is ironic** that the majority of Quebecers favor constitutional recognition of their special and unique heritage, yet have failed and continue to fail to treat native North American Indians with any special respect due to their unique heritage. (*Chicago Tribune* 9/3/1990) (Barbe 1993: 584)

in which the writer juxtaposes two narratives which are felt to be incongruous:

Narrative 1: Quebecers demand recognition of their own special heritage.
Narrative 2: Quebecers deny recognition of the special heritage of native Americans.

In implicit irony, on the other hand, only one of the narratives is present in the text (the *dictum*), whilst the other (the *implicatum*) remains unspoken and has to be (re-)constructed by the audience, as in the much-debated instance (Gibbs & O'Brien 1991; Hamamoto 1998; Sperber & Wilson 1998):

(2) Mother (on entering her child's untidy room): I love children who keep their rooms clean.

where the *implicatum* is that she is less keen on children (particularly the one in question) who do not keep their rooms clean.

Implicit irony is often humorous in intent whilst explicit irony is rarely so. Because they include a lexical marker, instances of explicit irony can be obtained by a straightforward concordance search (using *irony* and *ironic**); matters are more complex when looking for implicit irony.

We consider, then, from an examination of concordance data, firstly, how explicit irony operates and then from this whether there might be a more objective way of identifying and defining episodes of implicit irony than simple reliance on the researcher's unsupported intuition. Potential sites of implicit irony are then examined in the data to see how and why speakers and writers employ it and how hearers and audiences respond.

Several corpora were employed, two of semi-spontaneous interactive spoken discourse and one of written texts. WHB contains circa 250,000 words of White House press briefings in transcription from the Clinton administration. WH-Reps (Republicans) contains circa six million words of White House press briefings in transcription from 2001–2004. Ints consists of 250,000 words of transcribed televised UK political interviews and SiBol 93 and SiBol 05 are respectively 100 million-word and 150 million-word corpora of UK broadsheet newspaper texts (Introduction 0.4.1).

## 4.2 Suitability of data

Irony has of course, been studied since classical times. Most modern studies of irony, however, whether literary, linguistic, stylistic or psychological, tend to take the object of study for granted. The question of what kind of data is appropriate in irony research, for instance, is seldom discussed explicitly and until recently irony has rarely been studied in its authentic discourse context, as Kotthoff notes: "irony has seldom been studied in live interaction" (2003: 1392). Moreover, as noted above, the examples discussed, whether invented or selected, are often taken for granted as being ironic for no other reason than the author intuitively feels them to be so. Any discussion of irony based upon data which has not been previously validated as ironic runs the risk of being both over-subjective and circular.

## 4.3 Case study 1: Explicit irony

### 4.3.1 What is irony? Ask the people

In the following sections we will look at explicit markers of irony as they are used in WHB, Ints and the SiBol corpora in an attempt to determine what language users actually intend when they overtly signal a certain statement, situation or state-of-affairs as *ironic*. What do people actually label as ironic?

Using *WordSmith Tools* to examine the collocates within a 3L, 3R span of *irony, ironic* in the combined SiBol corpora proved to be quite revealing. One set of collocates reveals an association of irony with language, and especially with the spoken language. These include among many others: *say-says-said* (186), *hint* (58), *comment(s)* (34), *word(s)* (25), *story* (23), *voice* (17), *commentary* (16), *remark(s)* (11), *phrase* (9), *question* (8), *quotation* (8), *dialogue* (6), *narrative* (6). Its connectionn with humour was also confirmed since the list included *humour* (69), *wit* (33), and *witty* (20), *smile* (22), *joke(s)* (18), *comedy* (13) and *comic* (9), *laugh(s)* (10) and *funny* (7). Of especial interest too was the semantic group *twist* (47), *reversal* (9), *juxtaposition* (7) and *turn* (6), evidence of how it is commonly felt that there are two elements involved in irony and that something is being radically transformed or reversed.

Very noticeable was the number of adverbial intensifiers found in the company of *irony* and *ironic*, including: *deeply, particularly, especially, indeed, certainly, doubly, genuinely, bitterly* and *supremely*. Seto also lists a good many similar adverbs. He argues that speakers regularly intensify or exaggerate the "surface meaning" as a signal to the hearer to "reverse the polarity" (usually from positive to negative) (1998: 244–246). Several other authors have noted the connection with hyperbole (Kreuz & Roberts 1995; Colston & Keller 1998; Attardo 2000).

Finally, there was a large number of overtly evaluative vocabulary, both positive and negative, including *bitter* (72), *cruel* (61), *delicious* (52) *tragic* (43), *grim* (19), *savage* (12), *painful* (12), *wonderful* (11), *horrible* (9) and *glorious* (8). These are generally expressive of very strong emotions, another form of intensification.

The next step was to examine the use of explicit irony markers in running spoken discourse by using *WordSmith Tools* to produce concordances of the items *irony, ironic, ironical* and *ironically* in the spoken corpora, WHB and Ints. Surprisingly, our keywords – *irony, ironic, ironical* and *ironically* – were employed just nine times in the circa six million words of briefings but nine times in the 250,000 words of the interviews. These are fairly erudite words and this disproportion reflects the greater formality of the interviews. For comparison purposes, the combined SiBol corpora contain 10,856 occurrences in its c.250 million words (uses of the item *irony* where it is the topic of discourse, as in, say, theatre reviews, were excluded). Table 4.1 displays the comparative frequency of these items across the corpora.

**Table 4.1.** The incidence of the items *irony, ironic, ironical* and *ironically* in the three main corpora

| Corpus | Per thousand words | One every x words |
|---|---|---|
| *WHB* | 0.0015 | x = 666,666 |
| *Ints* | 0.0360 | x = 27,777 |
| *SiBol 93 & SiBol 05* | 0.0424 | x = 23,606 |

On closer analysis of the interactive spoken data (briefings and interviews), the most immediate observation was that the explicit irony markers in such structures were not simply metalinguistic flags, noting and bringing to the readers' attention some ironic potential pre-existing in the discourse at some particular point. Instead these structures, rhetorical figures in fact, were used far more creatively to construct an argument with a specific critical message. First of all, explicitly marked irony can be employed to accuse a person or group of people of having contradicted themselves, either wilfully or otherwise. When the implication is of deliberate self-contradiction, there is generally an ulterior imputation of dishonesty, double-dealing or deceit, sometimes openly expressed (my emphases):

(3) Q: […] You cited two precedents: one, the Kosovo situation and the other, the second is Desert Fox. Both of those were actions taken under the Clinton administration. The President […] was very critical and even disdainful of the foreign policy of that administration. Is that not somewhat **ironic** and even a little *hypocritical* that you're citing […] (WH-Reps)

(4) Q: Ari, can I go back to […] Bill's question about the French role, especially the Russian role. These are countries that fought [UN] sanctions in the past, and now seem to want to keep them. Do you not see something, at least **ironic**, and maybe *cynical*, about this? (WH-Reps)

The first of these can be paraphrased in terms of a pair of allegedly conflicting narratives:

N1: The President, before he came to office, said military intervention was bad.
N2: The President is now saying military intervention is good.

In other words, the President has reversed his own evaluation to suit his purposes. The strategic discursive or rhetorical function or point (the term is borrowed from Labov 1972) is to accuse the President of inconsistency or double standards.

Example, (4), can be similarly analysed into contrasting narratives:

N1: The French and Russians first fought sanctions.
N2: They now support them.

The French and Russians too have reversed an evaluation (sanctions going from *bad* to *good*). Again, the point of the utterance is to accuse them of duplicity.

On other occasions, *irony/ironic* appears in the reply to a question and is used to imply that it contains unfair allegations or presuppositions:

(5) Q: [...] what does he say to his critics [...] who say that the government has succumbed to protectionist pressures [...] ?

MR. FLEISCHER: I think that's kind of an **ironic** statement for people to make, given the fact that this is one of the most free-trading Presidents we've seen. (WH-Reps)

(6) DAVID FROST: What about what Gordon Brown said yesterday [...] that state schools provide 67 per cent of suitably qualified leaders but only 52 per cent of places at Britain's five leading universities?

JOHN STEIN: I think that's incredibly **ironic** because I pointed that out in a seminar in the House of Commons three years ago [...] the steps that we were taking in Oxford to widen access [...] (Ints)

In both episodes evaluations are reversed by the respondent. The President is no protectionist (bad), he's a free-trader (good). We are not elitist (bad), we are widening access for the less well-off to the top Universities (good).

Note the presence of intensifying elements *one of the most* and *incredibly*. We need to stress once more that explicit irony is not just a way of pointing out some pre-existing irony in a certain situation. Instead, the ironist adopts a particular stance, marshals particular information, highlighting contrast and often intensifying elements of the context, so as to express criticism of the object of his or her attention.

### 4.3.2 The evaluator

Having isolated reversal of evaluation as a key element in irony, the next step is to determine who is projected by the speaker as performing the evaluation, that is, who is said, to be the *principal* (the party responsible for the sentiment, Goffman 1981) of the evaluation. In (3) and (4), the questioners attribute the (contradictory) evaluations to another party; the President and foreigners, respectively, are projected as the evaluators. Very often, however, the speaker takes responsibility for the evaluation:

(7) Because **ironically** although the Euro is the subject about which people get most neurotic in British politics at the moment, the fact is we all talk about wait and see, I and people in Britain and Europe say we're waiting until the economic conditions come right and then we'll have a referendum [...]. (Ints)

This is analysable as:

N1: (I assert that) people "get neurotic" about – that is, there is a lot of argument regarding – Britain joining the Euro.
N2: (I assert that) people (*we*) are in basic agreement that the correct policy is to wait and see.

The contrast in evaluation is quite subtle and evokes an implied value system underlying the discourse. In the wide world, we are meant to understand that argument (in N1) is generally a bad thing (note both the negativity and the hyperbole of "neurotic"), whilst agreement (in N2) is, conversely, a good thing.

The episodes we have seen so far would seem to be instances of what Barbe (1993) calls "strong" irony, that is, irony where the evaluators in each case are the same person or group in both narratives, as are the narrative protagonists. However, the data throws up a number of cases of varying degrees of what Barbe calls "weak" irony – where the evaluators in the two narratives are different parties – for instance (the context is the 1999 Seattle protests against the World Trade Organization):

(8) CLARE SHORT. [...] So the [protesters'] broad intent was right but it was very misinformed [...] whereas actually it was the most democratic forum we've ever had for trade negotiations... **ironically**. (Ints)

in which:

N1: People protested against the forum (*they* evaluated it as bad).
N2: (I assert that) it was the most democratic forum we have had (*I* evaluate it as good).

If the projected evaluators are different, can the relationship between the narratives still be described as ironic? It is in fact irony of a different type, an example of what we might call *paradoxical* irony, in which the speaker suggests that, *of all* the forums possible, they had to protest against *this one*. The point of paradoxical irony, like other forms, is generally to criticise, but there is often an additional wry or sardonic sense of the irony of fate.

On occasion, any irony in the situation illustrated seems very faint indeed:

(9) [...] could I just say how saddened I was to hear of the, yesterday, of the death of my good friend and colleague Bernie Grant who was someone who'd always spoken up for Londoners [...] always said what he thought and **ironically** I was supposed to be appearing on a platform with him this afternoon. (Ints)

There hardly seems to be a contrast here at all, and a better choice of word might well have been *coincidentally*, but *ironically*, being more erudite, adds gravitas to a sad moment. Nevertheless, one individual just calling a particular situation "ironic" does not necessarily make it so.

It must also not be forgotten that ironic criticism is, superficially at least, indirect. This is the essence of the rhetorical effect of using a form with no personal actor in subject position: *it* is ironic that..., *there* is an irony in ..., ironically..., and so on. The subject is not usually accused or blamed entirely openly, we are told instead that a state of affairs happens to exist. The degree of blame and the level to which it is hidden can vary considerably, as we have seen. In (4) the French and Russians are accused explicitly, but in other cases further linguistic signals are required to assist us, such as *neurotic* (7) and *misinformed* (8). This very indirectness makes these formulae a useful tool when it is prudent to be polite in answering criticism and one's critics, as in (6), or when it is politic not to be too harsh on someone, such as the misguided-but-well-meaning demonstrators in (8). Analysing real-life episodes in discourse context, rather than invented or decontextualized examples commonly found in irony studies, helps us appreciate the creative impetus of irony, its essentially imaginative, even ingenious raison d'être.

### 4.3.3 Reversal of evaluation

As we have stressed then, an implied reversal of evaluation appears to be a dominant factor in all the examples of explicit irony in the interactive data examined here.

However, reversal of evaluation by itself is too wide a definition. The reversal must be signalled as marked in some way, as being out of the ordinary and therefore worthy of notice, debate or scandal. As has been noted, the reversal is often painstakingly emphasised, grammatically, lexically and phonologically. It is not sufficient to say, for example, "{A asserts that} X did well but {B asserts that} Y did badly" (where A and B may or may not be the same party). The contrast in evaluation needs to be intensified, especially when protagonists or evaluators in the two narratives are different parties or when in actual fact the contrast might appear a little weak, and has to be expressed as "it is ironic that, whereas X did extraordinarily well, Y did remarkably badly":

(10) **Ironically**, whereas Agassi *confounded the sceptics* by *slipping through with little cause for alarm*, the No. 3 seed Stefan Edberg had a *monumental struggle* with a Canadian qualifier, Greg Rusedski. (SiBol 93)

(11) The *cruellest* **irony** is that while publishers *turn up their noses* at the thought of Lamont's bitter reminiscences, the diaries of another former Conservative minister, Alan Clark, are about to become *the best-selling* political memoirs *for decades*. (SiBol 93)

Note the liberal sprinkling of emphasising or overtly evaluative expressions (highlighted). It will be remembered that the list of collocates of *irony/ironic* in the SiBol corpora contained a large number of intensifiers and emotive items. These two examples have a very clear dual-narrative form whereby the relationship is introduced by *ironic/irony/ironically* followed by a contrastive conjunction *while/whilst/whereas*. Given that *WordSmith Tools* found 109 instances of this structure in the two SiBol corpora, it appears to be relatively common, at least in newspaper prose.

Similarly, as we have already mentioned, simple defeat of positive expectations is not a sufficient condition for irony. Again, we must note that irony does not somehow exist in a situation but has to be construed by the ironist. As regards the example we used earlier: "I really thought I would pass my exams but I didn't" is not, as it stands, ironic. Expressed in terms of its underlying narratives this would be:

N1: I worked very hard for this exam thus having a reasonable expectation of passing.
N2: I didn't pass.

which is just a hard-luck story. Irony can be construed into the situation by presenting it as a paradox along the following lines: "I failed my exam. *The irony is* I worked harder for this one than all the others put together", in which:

N1: I didn't work hard for other exams but passed.
N2: I worked very hard for this exam (thus having a reasonable expectation of passing) but didn't pass.

The relation between the two narratives is now inversion (accompanied by good to bad evaluation reversal) and involves a combination of paradoxical irony and irony of fate.

In espousing evaluation reversal as the basis of irony we begin to comprehend why speakers should wish to employ it, why it is so popular. Given the "element of surprise" inherent in reversal, it enables speakers/writers to project themselves as interesting and dramatic. Irony allows one to be both suspenseful and sententious.

It says: Someone (you – me – a third party – the world) thought things were in such a way. Let me tell you this: they are really in quite a different fashion altogether.

## 4.4 Case study 2: Implicit irony

### 4.4.1 Using corpus techniques to find episodes of implicit irony

In this section we turn our attention to episodes of implicit irony, that is, where no explicit irony marker appears in the text. This kind of irony is also implicit in that only one of the narratives is present in the text (the *dictum*), whilst the other (the *implicatum*) remains unspoken and has to be (re-)constructed by the audience.

As we have already noted, in very many studies of implicit irony, various utterances are taken for granted as being ironic for no other reason than that the researcher deems them to be so. Here, instead, we propose a way, using corpus-search methodology, of localising candidate sites of implicit irony in interactive discourse with a greater degree of objectivity.

We adopted three processes. Firstly, in the press briefings corpora the transcribers mark explicitly episodes where laughter has occurred in the interaction. A considerable body of work, including Kreuz et al. (1991), Dews et al. (1995), Dews and Winner (1995), Gibbs (2000), Colston and O'Brien (2000), and Norrick (2003) "shows irony can elicit laughter [...] and lead to further joking" (Norrick 2003 1340–1341). A concordance with 300 words of cotext was therefore prepared of laughter episodes from one million-words of White House briefings from both the Clinton and Bush eras, consisting of 178 separate briefings. These were called the *laughter files* and contain 543 bouts.

Secondly, as we saw above, many ironical utterances are signalled by some kind of lexical or grammatical intensifier, some of which can be sought within the laughter files using the concordancer (for instance, *-ly* intensifying adverbs like *really* or *-est* superlatives) or "manually". In the examples below we highlight intensifying or emphasising items using italics.

Thirdly, given that we have already defined irony, through examination of the use of the term in authentic discourse, as involving evaluation reversal, the laughter files were analysed by eye, this time to localise laughter episodes where speakers employ some form of reversal. It is of course not possible to give precise numbers regarding the occurrence of implicit irony, as was the case for explicit irony (see Table 4.1). As we shall see below, much of the rhetorical effectiveness of implicit irony lies in its subtlety, its (apparent) subjectivity and very often, its deniability. Nevertheless, applying the above search techniques, the laughter files were found to contain not less than 110 occurrences of implicit irony. Though hardly overwhelmingly frequent, this makes it much more common than explicit irony in this discourse type.

### 4.4.2 Reversal of evaluation in implicit irony

Firstly, then, we shall examine whether and how evaluation and reversal are employed in the implicit variety of irony. Several examples of very straightforward ironic reversal were apparent, including:

(12) Q: Joe, was the President pleased or saddened that his good friend, Mayor Schmoke, and the Baltimore Orioles participated in that "glory to Comrade Fidel" rally thinly disguised as a baseball game, and denounced by so many free Cubans? And I have one follow-up. (Laughter.)
MR. LOCKHART: I *can't wait.* (Laughter.) (WHB)

where the ironic enthusiasm (good) of the dictum of the podium response ("I can't wait") implies an expectation that the follow-up will be just as tiresome (bad) as the original question.

The majority of the episodes, however, turned out in actual practice to be more complex and sophisticated, for example:

(13) MR. LOCKHART: [...] But I do understand that there are some implications 20 years down the road – I hope none of us in this room are here then. (Laughter.)
Q: Helen – (Laughter.)
MR. LOCKHART: Wolf, that was uncalled for. You should leave.
Q: God willing, she'll still be here. (WHB)

Everyone in the room knows that Helen (Foster, *UPI*) is the senior member, the eldest person present. Wolf's (Blitzer, *CNN*) naming of her is ambiguous: it could be ironic, affirming that Helen will still be here (good) and implying she certainly will not be (bad), or it could be non-ironic, meaning good old Helen has been here for as long as anyone can remember and will outlast us all. Mr Lockhart interprets it as the first and good-humouredly admonishes the questioner. Wolf retorts that he meant the second. His utterance was, of course, potentially face-threatening for Helen. The indirectness of irony, like other indirectnesses, is often used to perform face threats which, if need be, can be denied (Chapters 7 and 8).

Not dissimilar in its ambiguity is the following:

(14) MR. TOIV: Joe, we're not ready to announce Texas [...]
MR. LOCKHART: Gotcha. (Laughter.) Okay. Everything I just said about Texas – strike. That was off the record. (Laughter.) [...]

Q: Tell your C-SPAN viewers as well.
MR. LOCKHART: Yes. (Laughter.) To my C-SPAN viewers: those of you who don't like me, please stop writing. (Laughter.) I am *very* thin-skinned, and it *really* gets to me. (Laughter.) Guarantees *about 300* next week. (Laughter.) (WHB)

Mr Lockhart is able to "mean" both the dictum ("I am a sensitive sort") and the implicatum ("I couldn't care less about criticism") inherent in his "I am very thin-skinned" and to milk the rewards of both senses. The laughter which accompanies ironic utterances seems to be in recognition of a speaker's rhetorical skill. A further example:

(15) You know deadlines are a double-edged sword. On the one hand, deadlines provide a –
Q: Selling point. (Laughter.)
MR. BERGER: No. That's more cynical than I know you mean to be, Helen. (Laughter.) (WHB)

Mr Berger's backhanded compliment allows the speaker effectively to say "you aren't a cynic" while implying that "you are a cynic", with little danger of being called to account. As Brown and Levinson put it:

> Given [...] the difficulty of "knowing what is inside someone's head", and the non-recoverability of intonational or kinesic clues, even fairly blatant indirectness may be defensible as innocent – a speaker could protest that he didn't mean an irony in a sarcastic way, for example. S and H could both go away from the interaction "knowing" in their hearts that it really was sarcastic, but because face (as the word implies) is largely a matter of surface appearances, S may well get away with his Face-Threatening-Act. (1978:217)

The audience laughter seems to suggest they recognise what is going on *under* the surface of discourse. Questions too, of course, can be ironical (Section 4.4.4):

(16) Q: You believe in what reporters tell you, don't you, Ari? (Laughter.) (WHB)

where both his believing (dictum) and not believing (implicatum) are left in the air.

### 4.4.3 Verisimilar ironies: Litotes

A good number of theories in the field claim that verbal irony is necessarily the deliberate expression of insincerity (for example, Haverkate 1990), or that an ironic utterance (the dictum) must be either untrue (Grice 1975) or "non-veridical" (Kruez & Glucksberg 1989; Kreuz & Roberts 1995). In Pretense theory, (see Clift 1999), the ironist is said to dissociate him/herself from the dictum. In Sinclair's (2004) terms, s/he *attributes* it to another fictional speaker, whilst *averring* the unspoken implicatum, whilst in Goffman's terms (1981), s/he is merely the *animator* (the vehicle) of the dictum but the *principal* (responsible for the content) of the implicatum.

However, our analyses of authentic episodes have demonstrated that this is not always the case. There is a category of ironic utterances in which speakers, rather than saying the opposite of what they intend, or even dissociating themselves from the dictum, say something that corresponds to "the facts", to their apparent beliefs, or to the way things really are to best of their knowledge. We call this reasonably common variety of irony, "true-seeming" or "verisimilar". There were at least 15 instances in the briefings laughter files (circa 14% of episodes of implicit irony), for example:

(17) Q: […] I wonder if you could comment on that difference in his position.
MR. MCCURRY: His constitutional thinking has undergone *quite an evolution* in the time. (Laughter.) (WHB)

(18) Mike, why do you think the President is not watching this very closely? Isn't he very interested in what comes out –
MR. MCCURRY: He's *not very intellectually stimulated* by the debate on the Republican side. (Laughter.) (WHB)

In the first, the Democratic podium is sincerely critical of perceived Republican inconsistency, whilst in the second he truly means to say the Republican debate is unengaging. How does the reversal of evaluation theory as expounded here explain such forms?

First of all, these two episodes are clearly examples of understatement. In (17) the dictum "undergone quite an evolution" implies "has performed a complete u-turn, he's contradicting himself", whilst in (18) "is not very intellectually stimulated" implies "is totally uninterested in".

How, then, can understatement be ironic? We have already seen how irony involves a reversal of evaluation – good to bad, or vice versa – on the part of some adjudicator, either the speaker themselves or some participant in the narratives. In understatement or *litotic* irony, the evaluator evaluates an entity as *little* to imply, the opposite, that it is in reality *a lot*, that is, it simply states:

N1 (dictum): Someone understates a value; evaluates something as a little.
N2 (implicatum): Someone emphasizes a value; evaluates something as a lot.

In other words, in litotic irony the speaker performs a reversal of *importance*, closely analogous to reversal of evaluation, especially since whatever is depicted as "highly significant" in the *implicatum* is normally highly significantly *bad*, and its purpose is thus to criticise.

The comic effect is often heightened by stylistic choices; note *stimulated* in (18). The most effective and elegant use of litotic irony in the corpus is the following (the reply to a question on how the podium feels to learn that his retirement is a big news story):

(19) MR MCCURRY: […] we come and go, but we didn't get elected to be anything. And I will *certainly* enjoy whatever *notoriety* I have, and I will *certainly* use it to the good fortune of my family in the future. (Laughter.) (WHB)

The speaker has slipped into self-parody, using a stilted diplomatic register which employs understatement. By the rule of ironic reversal, then, in underemphasising the dictum narrative, he manages to imply an opposing one in some kind of emphatic colloquial register, that he will sell his fame for all it is financially worth. Note that there is still good to bad reversal; the dictum is much nobler than the implicatum. As often in this material, irony is used to tease, here a self-tease.

In practice, speakers also exploit litotic irony in complex ways to achieve particular interpersonal and strategic rhetorical effects. Consider:

(20) Joe, have you read the reports that Yugoslavian TV and movie theaters are showing reruns of the movie "Wag the Dog"?

MR. LOCKHART: I saw that on television.

Q: Do you believe it?

MR. LOCKHART: Do I believe it? Yes. I mean, I believe what I see on television some days. (Laughter.) (WHB)

This is another example of irony ambiguity through indirectness. The speaker means to say something like: "Yes, I believe it since I have no impelling reason to disbelieve what ought to be a truth-telling medium". But this is an *uninteresting* way to answer and so he employs litotic irony, saying "some days" to imply "most of the time". Contemporaneously, he manages to adopt an in-group persona of cynic much appreciated by this particular audience. Note too that his answer is also sarcastic, mildly face-threatening, given his audience partly consists of TV journalists.

### 4.4.4 Irony in questions

Ironical questions, generally taking the form of rhetorical questions, are also often cited as difficult cases and seen a test for any theory of irony, especially for those theories which define irony in terms of propositional (rather than evaluative) reversal, given that some schools of pragmatics claim that the speaker does not commit themselves to propositions in questions, since they have no truth conditions. But, again, evaluation-reversal theory would seem to account well for such cases. In the case, say, of:

(21) Do you have to make that noise while you are eating? (McDonald 1999: 488)

The speaker creates two narratives of the type:

N1 (dictum): (I ask you whether) you evaluate that noise as necessary (i.e. as good)
N2 (implicatum): I evaluate it as unnecessary and indeed irksome (i.e. as bad).

The laughter files contain no less than 16 instances of ironical questions (circa 15% of episodes of implicit irony), including:

(22) Q: If you were Osama bin Laden would you give a live interview right now on satellite feed – (Laughter) (WHB)

This contrasts the two narratives:

N1 (dictum): (I ask you whether) you evaluate [this imagined behaviour] as good
N2 (implicatum): I evaluate it as self-evidently bad

where the *point* is to suggest that the interlocutor must be stupid or naïve. In briefings such episodes very generally also involve a tease which can range from the hostile, like (22), to the more sympathetic, like (23) (emphasis added):

(23) Q: [...] doesn't the President think that was a good question that ought to be asked of many multi-millionaire owners who lay off but don't take pay cuts, *because the President would surely take a pay cut rather than lay off you and Scott, wouldn't he*? (Laughter.).

MR. FLEISCHER: You're half right. (Laughter.) (WHB).

## 4.5 Conclusions on explicit and implicit irony

So far in this chapter, we have examined the use of irony in communicative contexts in the hope of discovering how it works, how it is comprehended and the functions it serves.

The analyses here have shown how the ironic speaker constructs a pair of narratives, both of which are more or less present in the text in explicit irony, whereas in the implicit type only one is apparent and the other is implied. At first sight it might seem that explicit irony merely points out the irony pre-existing in a particular situation but this is far from the case and, as we have seen, both sorts are used strategically and creatively, normally to perform censure, and to align the audience with one's stance (i.e. for persuasion). The criticism is not necessarily hostile (Clift 1999).

Indeed, irony can be affiliative in at least three ways. It can bind speaker and hearer when a third party is the object of criticism (Examples 17 and 18). It can be used in friendly teasing (23), and it can be used in self-deprecatory humour, in self-teasing (19), or a combination of other- and self-teasing as in (16) or:

(24) Q: You can fool some of the people all the time – concentrate on this.
MR. FLEISCHER: That's why I'm here [...] (Laughter) (WHB)

These analyses also lend support to the view that irony is driven by *evaluation*, in particular, the hypothesis corroborated by our observations of this particular data is that the principal mechanism of contrast between the two narratives is reversal of evaluation, the switch, generally, from approval in the dictum to disapproval, criticism, in the implicatum.

What, then, are the main discourse functions of irony? Why do speakers employ it and with such regularity – why do they not simply limit themselves to direct criticism ("Why not say it directly?" ask Dews et al. 1995)? Sperber & Wilson make the following requirement:

> it would then have to be explained how the practice of saying one thing and meaning the opposite could have arisen spontaneously in culture after culture; how children acquire it; [...] why it lends itself to blame-by-praise more easily than praise-by-blame. (1998:290)

The observations we have made in this chapter suggest a number of responses. Given the pervasiveness of evaluation, playing with evaluation for rhetorical effect does not seem at all strange or unforeseeable. More in particular, speakers use irony to be interesting, incisive, dramatic and memorable. This may simply be performed for the purposes of self-display but Brown and Levinson also include "making a good story" among the strategies of positive politeness. A speaker, they say, can "communicate to H[earer] that he shares some of his wants" by intensifying "the interest of his own contributions to the conversation" (1987:106). Allied to this is the intricate face-work it allows speakers to indulge in. Irony and sarcasm, as we have seen on many occasions here, permit speakers to perform face moves indirectly. Indirectness is fundamental to politeness theory which therefore actively predicts that irony should arise in culture after culture. Indirectness has a whole range of interpersonal functions, and it should therefore come as no surprise that such an obvious form of indirectness as irony – evaluation reversal – should appear across human cultures and be acquired as a skill by children (see Chapter 9 for more on face-work and irony).

## Phrasal irony

### 4.6 Case study 3: The form, function and exploitation of phrasal irony

The final case study is of the as yet little-studied phenomenon of phrasal irony, defined as the reversal of customary collocational patterns of use of certain lexical items. The first research question is how phrasal irony is structured. A second, very closely related, question is how, why and where writers use it, and a third question is how it is related to other more familiar types of irony.

During the course of these investigations it was observed that, occasionally, the ironic use of a particular phrase or phrase template is found to be repeated frequently and productively and can therefore be said to have become a recognised usage in its own right. However, it was also noted that by no means all reversal of normal collocational patterning is performed with an ironic intent, and so yet a further research question is how the circumstances when phrasal irony is at play might differ from those of simple counter-instances to the statistically normal collocational patterns of use. The SiBol 93 and SiBol 05 corpora were used in this study since UK newspaper texts are rich in episodes of language play.

#### 4.6.1 Evaluative clash with the phrase

In a seminal article Louw (1993) investigates a particular phenomenon of what we might call language system-internal irony (to distinguish it from the narrative-based kind of utterance irony described thus far), a type occurring within – and by means of – the phrase itself. He examines how speakers or writers sometimes, deliberately or otherwise, upset the normal co-occurrence patterns of lexical items. He notes, in other words, how they sometimes place together two lexical items which do not normally keep company or, rather, which normally in fact *shun* each other's company, as illustrated in the following:

> The modern conference resembles the pilgrimage of medieval Christendom in that it allows the participants to indulge themselves in all the pleasures and diversions of travel while apparently *bent on self-improvement.*
>
> (David Lodge *Small World*, in Louw 1993: 164)

Citing data from the *Cobuild* corpus, Louw shows that *bent on* very generally collocates with unfavourable items: *destroying, harrying, mayhem* and so on. He claims that, by choosing *bent on* to partner the evidently favourable *self-improvement*, rather than more obviously positive or neutral terms such as, say, *seeking, hoping for*, Lodge is searching for an ironic effect. The item *bent on* displays a negative *evaluative prosody* (Chapter 3) and in this particular excerpt, Lodge is exploiting this unfavourable prosody to subvert the normally positive evaluation associated with *self-improvement*.

It should thus be apparent why this kind of effect can be considered a form of irony as defined in the previous section, that is, as reversal of evaluation. The kind of bisociative clash or incongruency that speakers strive to create when they indulge in phrasal irony is an effect created by using an item in combination with an item of the opposite, reversed evaluative polarity to that with which it normally co-occurs.

As we saw above, irony is very generally used to criticise and the butts of David Lodge's criticism are, of course, participants in academic conferences. P.G. Wodehouse (Chapter 6) too realised the comic potential of this technique: "concealed my astonishment that anyone … could *deliberately love* this girl",[1] where the choice of *deliberately*, which co-occurs with negative items,[2] reverses the normal positive associations of love and notifies us that the speaker is not himself enamoured of the young lady in question. One presumes that the butts of the irony are both the girl *and* her admirer.

However, as Hunston (2007) underlines, speakers /writers do not always coselect evaluatively/attitudinally "incompatible" lexical items in order to perform irony; sometimes the effect sought is purely dramatic, whilst on other occasions again there would seem to be very little unusual effect at all. In Section 4.6.8 we will examine how the circumstances when phrasal irony is at play might differ from those of simple counter-instances to the statistically normal collocational patterns of use.

A final point. In examining the *form* of phrasal irony, that is, its internal structure consisting of the juxtaposition of elements of opposing evaluative polarity, we found ourselves unavoidably simultaneously describing its *function*, that of the speaker/writer intending to defeat the listener's/reader's normal collocational expectations (for a variety of local effects, generally including humour and criticism). All this would appear to be a very lucid illustration of how form and function in language are two sides of the same coin.

### 4.6.2 Evaluative oxymoron

One form of phrasal irony is that which we might term the *evaluative oxymoron*. Oxymorons (or *oxymora*) "are traditionally defined as figures of speech that

1. From *The Code of the Woosters* (1991: 53).

2. The SiBol 05 corpus includes: *deliberately infecting women with HIV/killing unarmed civilians/mislead people/scaremongering* and many similarly negative uses.

combine two seemingly contradictory elements" (Gibbs 1993: 268). What is of interest here is a type of oxymoron where the two constituent elements are of opposing evaluative polarity. Examples include *bittersweet, sweet sorrow, tough love*. In each case one of the elements would generally be seen (in context-free terms) as negative, the other positive. The *overall* evaluation may often appear to be neither good nor bad but in practice speakers may shift the balance, as in the corpus examples of *bittersweet*: *rather more bittersweet than hey nonny-no sweet* (SiBol 05: *Times*),[3] *but it was bittersweet applause and Rusedski knew it* (SiBol 05: *Guardian*), both of which are clearly negative in evaluation (In both cases the less than complete sweetness is compared negatively to complete sweetness). Instances of evaluative oxymoron from politics include *champagne socialism*, *the most recent lessons of <u>Chinese democracy</u> were handed out in Tianenmen Square* (*Daily Telegraph*, 1993), *[b]ut, one hundred years later, the Negro [...] finds himself <u>an exile in his own land</u>* (M. Luther King) and *the <u>wisest fool</u> in Christendom*, said of James I of England (VI of Scotland).

Even though evaluative oxymorons contain one favourable and one unfavourable element, the overall evaluation of such constructs in political language tends to be highly unfavourable as well as critical in intent, just as other forms of irony. Plausibly, if an entity or situation is described as less than entirely positive, listeners are psychologically and philosophically inclined to view this as problematic. The most straightforward of these is the last: the description of James is a derisive comment on the difference between how he sees himself (wise: positive) and how others (his enemies at least) see him [fool: negative]. In the third, the "Negro" (Dr. King's own term) being *in his own land*, usually a good thing, actually compounds the negative condition of being *an exile*, though, of course, the exile himself is not the object of criticism here, but those who have consigned him to this piteous circumstance.

In the first two above, in contrast to a presumed positive evaluation of themselves by the two groups, the champagne socialists and the Chinese regime, the overall evaluation is again scornful. The items *champagne* and *Chinese* are not, of course, in themselves negative, but become so when presented in the company of *socialism* and *democracy*. They both of course rely heavily on the audience sharing the same type of knowledge-of-the-world as the speaker.

Even the word itself – oxymoron – can be used to make an argument because of its potential to perform negative evaluation:

3. *Hey nonny no* is the title of an anonymous 16thC *carpe diem* (let us eat, drink and be merry, for tomorrow we die) drinking song.

(25) Mr Adams confirmed in my presence as recently as last week that he did not, and would never, recognise British justice, which he described as an oxymoron.
(Baroness Park of Monmouth, House of Lords debate, 2003)

(26) There may be people – there may even be people in this House – who are so cynical as to suggest that business ethics is an oxymoron
(Lord Borrie, House of Lords debate, 2003)

In (25) Mr Adams is evaluating the British judicial system as [negative: unfair]. In (26) the speaker is suggesting that some people – cynics as he calls them – evaluate all business as unethical.

### 4.6.3 Substitution by evaluative opposite in well-known phrases

Another form of phrasal irony, common in advertising and newspaper headlines, is devised when some part of a well-known phrase is substituted by its evaluative opposite, as in the following literary example:

> That night in Southern Australia brought its first snuffle of *tidings of great horror*.
> (Anthony Burgess: *The End of the World News*)

which is a highly negative reworking of the evaluatively positive *tidings of comfort and joy*, from the well-known Christmas carol *God Rest Ye Merry Gentlemen*.

Other examples of this sort of evaluative substitution in the literature include *Catholic distaste* (from *catholic taste*), which introduces a review of a Dario Fo play in which the author expresses his own "distaste" for the Church, *an all-American villain* (rather than *hero*), referring to Colombus's unpopularity among some native Americans, and *Oxford quick to lose the initiative* (rather than *gain*), which describes an unimpressive performance on the part of the University cricket team (all Partington 1998). Martin discusses *Christmas and New Year tribulations* (*tribulations* instead of *celebrations*, being frequently found in the expression *trials and tribulations*) (1992: 82). Very occasionally, and most germane to the current paper, the reworked phrase becomes a new use and can even then develop into a well-worn canonical one. In SiBol 05 there are 34 occurrences of [*snatch*] *defeat from the jaws of victory* compared to only 19 occurrences of the original version [*snatch*] *victory from the jaws of defeat* (Morley: personal communication).

Such instances are somewhat different from those analysed in the previous sections. There is no inherent internal incongruency as in *sweet sorrow* or *bent on self-improvement*. There is, however, an implicit opposition between the version actually produced and that previously mentally acquired by the reader. As mentioned in the first part of this chapter, there are two types of utterance irony, explicit irony where both the opposing elements are present in the text, and implicit irony, where the opposition is between a *dictum*, that which is actually spoken (or written) and an *implicatum*, that which is unspoken but implied. Evaluative oxymoron, such as *sweet sorrow* or *bent on self-improvement* is thus analogous to explicit irony in that both elements are present, whilst substitution-by-opposite-evaluation as illustrated in this section is a form of implicit irony, in that one narrative is given, but its effect depends upon another quite different unspoken one.

### 4.6.4 The "popularisation" of the ironic usage of a phrase

What is of further interest is that, in the corpus data here, certain phrases or phrase templates where ironic evaluative clash is exploited are found several times, in several reworkings. The ironic use of a template is employed productively and has perhaps come to be recognised as a new version. In other words, writers adopt and reproduce the formulation in its ironic sense and we can presume that writers (and possibly readers) have been primed to recognise this usage thanks to previous encounters.

These fall into two types:

1. reversals where an expected negative element of the template is replaced by something positive;
2. reversals where an expected positive element of the template is replaced by something negative.

### 4.6.5 Replacing an expected negative element of the template with something positive

One example of this kind of reversal-replacement is:

- *an/the outbreak of* NP

The NP, that is, the noun phrase following *an outbreak of* very generally has a negative meaning or connotation. The ironic reversal-replacement upsets the primed expectation of something unfavourable and provides an evaluatively positive NP in the position in the template instead.

The corpus evidence shows that the NP in the template is usually negative. SiBol 05 contained, amongst others, *hysteria* (4 occurrences), *despair* (2), *depression*, *exploding toads* and a large number of diseases, including 27 occurrences of *avian/bird flu*, the media health scare of the moment (in 2005). When *outbreak of* is preceded by *the*, 336 occurrences of *war* were found.

Something which has *broken out* is generally something violent or virulent and is no longer under our control. In Chapter 3 we saw how whatever is "not under one's control" is generally viewed very negatively and this largely explains the negative prosody of *an outbreak of* (see 3.3.7).

However, in several examples the NP is overtly a good thing. There are so many in fact that the clash between the expected unfavourable prosody of the phrase and its reversal in positive seems to have become normalised, an alternative though ironic usage. Examples from SiBol 93 and SiBol 05 include:

> *an outbreak of: candour, clear-sightedness, civility, commonsense* (4 occurrences), *democracy, divine intervention, nutricious nosh, faith* (seen as a good thing by the writer),[4] *peace* (5), *politeness, Anglo-French solidarity.*

There can also be various local meanings to the irony. One of these is the suspicion that whatever has *broken out* may not be sincere:

(27) Those suspicious of the recent outbreak of love between Blair and Brown. (SiBol 05: *Guardian*, letter)

Or that it might be short-lived:

(28) Not for the first time there has been an outbreak of candour at the Home Office shortly after an election. (SiBol 05: *Times* letter)

Or that it was long overdue:

(29) Brussels prefers to keep reality away from the EU project, but this week there was an outbreak of sanity. (SiBol 05: *Times*)

All five references to an *outbreak of peace* were to a hypothetical peace, not yet existing and perhaps difficult to achieve, for instance:

(30) Senior American officials have been playing down the hope that the vote will lead to an outbreak of peace. (SiBol 05: *Sunday Times*)

(31) Despite indications to the contrary, an outbreak of peace between Euro Tunnel and Transmanche Link appears as far away as ever. (SiBol 93: *Times*)

In fact this unreal or hypothetical use of *an outbreak of*, when ironic, is the dominant one. Of the ten occurrences in SiBol 93, seven were unreal, for instance:

(32) So, what hope is there for an outbreak of honesty among Italian journalists? (SiBol 93: *Guardian*)

(33) Is this an outbreak of genius in the land? Sadly, no. (SiBol 93: *Times*)

4. "Outbreak of faith: Wherever disaster has struck this year, compassion has quickly followed" (SiBol 05: *Guardian*, headline).

There are a number of other non-straightforward occurrences of *an outbreak of* which are comic though not dependent on bad-good reversal, in other words, where the NP is neutral rather than good:

> *an outbreak of Scottishness, sudoku, artiness, Egyptomania, Alhambresque architecture, BBC politics*

The effect here is achieved by attaching the expression *an outbreak of*, usually associated with matters of importance and gravity, to mundane or more trivial pursuits; it is in fact a form of *bathos*. In 4.4.3 above we investigated understatement or litotes irony, that is, a sub-type of irony which depends on *large/small* or *important/unimportant* reversal.

– *in a fit of*

Somewhat similar to *an outbreak of* is the expression *in a fit of*, which also suggests a process, especially an emotional one, which has passed out of someone's control, accompanied by a strong implication of temporariness. It normally co-occurs with the semantic set of negative emotions and in SiBol 05 we find *pique* (26 occurrences), *rage* (12), *jealousy/jealous rage* (6) and *despair* (3); in lexical grammar terminology, we would say it displays a semantic preference for items expressing negative emotion. However we also find it followed by *enthusiasm* (2), *benevolence* and *self-improvement* among others, where the negativity is clearly reversed. The rhetorical intention is generally to, firstly, imply that the worthy behaviour is uncharacteristic and also often to poke mild sarcasm, sometimes self-deprecating and rueful, at whoever suffers the *fit*:

(34) In a fit of enthusiasm, I upgraded my iBook […] without checking if my DSL modem would work with it. It doesn't. (SiBol 05: *Guardian*)

(35) […] in a fit of conscience, redistributing her fee […] (SiBol 05: *Sunday Times*)

However, just occasionally, the overall tone is approving:

(36) But this time, in a fit of democracy which could usefully be copied by those companies looking for new directors, there is a proper election. (SiBol 93: *Guardian*)

– *an/the onslaught of*

Bednarek (2008: 127) notes the potential for ironic reversal of the template *an/the onslaught of* (from Monica Ali, *Brick Lane*):

> "Can't stay", she said, "Can't stay", ready to fend off any onslaught of hospitality.

The *OED* defines *onslaught* as "a vigorous or destructive attack or assault" and the earliest quotations are almost all military. There are, however, very few instances in the SiBol corpora of the co-occurrence of this particular template with the semantic set of "war/killing", with only eight occurrences out of 159 in SiBol 05 (including incidentally four references to *suicide bombing*).

The vast majority of uses are metaphorical and semi-metaphorical, *an/the onslaught of tourists/the world's media/the midday sun/age*, and the like, including the following where metaphor is married to bathroom bathos:

(37) […] a wooden seat perched above a wheelie bin filled with sawdust, but was convinced that it would withstand the onslaught of up to 10,000 bottoms over the next seven days. (SiBol 05)

The mechanism at work in the cases considered in this section (*an outbreak of, in a fit of, an onslaught of*) is as follows (where NP = the following noun phrase):

1. in the majority of cases the NP is something *bad*;
2. whenever the NP is something *neutral*, the "badness" priming of *an outbreak* of, *onslaught of*, and so on, rubs off,
3. whenever the NP is something *good* and desirable, the effect can be ironic, comic, dramatic or can create ambivalence (especially in the case of *an outbreak of*). There is a range of individual local effects, for example, that the goodness of the NP is actually being brought into question, that the sincerity of someone is in doubt, and so on.

### 4.6.6 Replacing an expected positive element of the template with something negative

In this section we will examine a number of templates where the irony depends on the opposite reversal-replacement to those seen above, namely of a positive with a negative element.

– [*much/a lot/a great deal*] *to be said for* NP

The phrase template [*much/a lot/a great deal*] *to be said for* usually precedes an entity or situation that would be considered pleasant or beneficial or which the writer is presenting as such. SiBol 05 has, among others, *a stay in a villa, cutting taxes, controllable gas-fired barbecuing,* whilst SiBol 93 has *academic honours, a healthy scepticism* and *being more adventurous*.

However, in SiBol 05, we also come across the following ironic uses in which what is presented as being a good thing would normally be seen as very bad:

(38) Beckett thinks there is *a great deal to be said for* death. (SiBol 05: *Guardian*)

(39) [...] there is *much to be said for* envy if it prompts a sculptor to start chewing his whiskers over the genius of his predecessor Michelangelo, and then to attempt to outdo the master. (SiBol 05: *Telegraph*)

(40) Yet, as Max Beerbohm observed. "*There is much to be said for* failure. It is more interesting than success". (SiBol 05: *Times*)

Again, there is play with evaluation reversal to produce irony. The two corpora also supplied the following endings to the template:

*... to be said for: acrimony, extreme weather, litter, laddish behaviour.*

As can be seen from the examples, this reworked template is a way of introducing a classic hyperbolic style conceit; an outrageously contrarian statement is produced that requires an ingenious explanation, which the writer proceeds to supply or which has already been given in the preceding text.

– MAKE (occasionally DO) *a good job of* NP

The NP here is of a particular kind. It is generally a nominalised verb phrase governed by the preposition *of* and consisting of a gerund and noun phrase.

This template contains the clearest lexical signal possible – *good* – that something positive, desirable, deserving approval is to be expected. However the corpus provides several examples of negative-for-positive reversal-replacement, as in the following:

(41) It may seem a waste of good ink to take apart Robin Cook's arguments when he *has made such a good job of* discrediting himself. (*Times*, 8 April 2003)[5]

(42) The Zimbabwean government spends millions of pounds promoting tourism while the national parks staff seems to *be making a good job of* destroying it. (SiBol 05: *Telegraph*)

There is often a further twist to the ironic use of *a good job of*. Consider:

(43) [...] the British government actively discouraged attempts to assassinate Adolf Hitler on the ground that he *was making such a good job of losing the war*. (SiBol 05: *Times*)

(44) Paul Bremer, for example, the leader of Iraq's Coalition Provisional Authority, emerges as a far darker force than Muqtada al Sadr, the Shia

5. From the CorDis corpus, compiled to examine how the conflict in Iraq was reported (Morley & Bayley, Eds: 2009).

> rabble-rouser whose militias *did such a good job of slaughtering Iraqi policemen* in Najaf last summer. Why? Because he's a free-marketeer and there can be no greater crime than that. (SiBol 05: *Telegraph*)

Although there is a clear evaluative clash between *good job* and *losing the war/slaughtering Iraqi policemen*, there is nevertheless an entity in the co-text for which the action/event in question is projected as a good thing, the British government and the al Sadr militias respectively. Note too how, in Example (44), the italicised phrase is part of a cohesive network of irony which also includes the phrases *darker force* and *there can be no greater crime*, examples of comic hyperbole. There is also a butt to the irony. This example is an extract from a book review, and the irony is at the expense of the leftist author Naomi Klein, not a natural favourite of the conservative *Telegraph*.

– (*enough to/the kind of*) NP1 *that/which* GIVE NP2 *a bad name*

The last set of ironic reversals considered here is one that exploits the phrase template: NP *that/which* GIVE NP *a bad name*, where the first NP is projected as something bad and the second NP is normally – logically – projected as something either neutral or good, but which is being tainted by its association with the first NP, for instance:

(45) [...] an example of the relativism that gives sociology a bad name. (SiBol 05: *Guardian*)

(46) This is precisely the kind of middle class hand-wringing which gives the Guardian a bad name. (SiBol 05: *Guardian*)

The expression is quite common – SiBol 05 contains around 80 examples. Writers in an ironic mood, however, can reverse the evaluative polarity of this second NP turning it, that is, into something that would normally be seen as already bad in itself, another example of positive to negative reversal-replacement. Here are some examples from the corpora:

(47) They are kind of things that gives philistinism a bad name. (SiBol 93: *Telegraph*)

(48) [Mr Monbiot] gives pomposity a bad name. (SiBol 05: *Sunday Telegraph*)

(49) The man gives turf warfare a bad name. (SiBol 05: *Times*)

(50) [...] gives ambulance-chasers a bad name. (SiBol 05: *Times*)

and from the Web:

(51) *National Post* gives stupidity a bad name (headline)

(52) It's Enough to Give Evildoers a Bad Name (headline)

(53) The kind of behaviour that gives hysteria a bad name.

This phrase template is, as can be seen, a format used by writers/speakers to be critical of – or to belittle or poke fun at – the entity or person in question. Given its ingenuity, it constitutes an unmistakable case of writers reproducing a rhetorical format they previously encountered and enjoyed.

The mechanism at work in the cases considered in this section differs slightly from that of the previous section (apart from the obvious inversion of the polarity reversal). The expectation that the entity to be indicated by the NP will be something positive is stronger given the presence in the template of some explicit positive lexical element, for example, *good job* and *give a bad name* (implying it once had a *good* name). The defeating of the expectation is therefore also all the more dramatic. The mechanism might be summarised:

1. in the majority of cases of the template the NP is something *good*;
2. when the NP is something *bad* and undesirable, the effect is dramatically ironic and often comic. As with other reversals there can be a range of individual local effects, and considerations of point of view – that is, good or bad for whom – which can render these effects quite subtle.

### 4.6.7 How such ironic uses become popular

The process of popularisation of the ironic use of a phrase might plausibly have the following psychological mechanism:

1. someone coins a phrase whose effect relies on semantic/evaluative prosody clash
2. other speakers/writers like it so much it gets repeated
3. the semantic/evaluative prosody clash eventually becomes an alternative recognised usage of the phrase.

Alternatively, the ironic use may not have a single author but certain phrases may lend themselves to ironic use to "ironically-minded" speakers/writers, independently of each other. Irony in fact is highly prized in the UK quality press, from which the corpora employed here derive. Nevertheless, it is still reasonable to suppose that there would be a phase (2) in which the ironic use is broadcast, adopted by other writers and speakers and becomes more widely popular.

### 4.6.8 A final twist: When is evaluative reversal ironic clash and when simply a counter-instance?

However, by no means every occurrence of collocational evaluation reversal in the phrase betrays an ironic intent. Very often the effect is simple emphasis or dramatic stress. But, on other occasions, despite the unusuality in statistical terms of the reversal, there is no special effect being sought at all. The reversal is simply a counter-instance to a general trend. We can begin to investigate the difference in the conditions under which special rhetorical effects and simple counter-instances occur by looking at one particular template.

– BORDER *on* NP (occasionally Adjective)

According to the SiBol concordances, various forms of *border* on* are primed to occur as part of a negatively evaluated situation (see also Schmitt & Carter 2004). In a concordance of the first hundred occurrences of these forms, only three referred to real physical locations, for example, "… *bordering on* Tibet", though we do also find "metaphorically physical" locations in "[t]his is O'Driscoll land. It is a place that at first sight appears to be bordering on Larkin country" (SiBol 05; *Guardian*, both named persons being poets). Of the remaining, 69 were unequivocally negative, such as "bordering on the dysfunctional", "on xenophobic", "on malign parody", whilst six were purely descriptive or technical uses, for example, "at times [his music] bordered on swing", "[…]uncompromising themes with comedy that borders on farce" (all from SiBol 05). Many of the remaining occurrences are too ambiguous, at least on first appearance, to assign to one evaluative camp or the other, for instance, "a voice […] he used with great specificity, bordering on deliberation", "a look of panic bordering on mirth".

What interests us here, however, is the expression *border* on* when used in apparently positive environments, of which there were six in this preliminary concordance. Since the typical prosody is negative, does this negativity carry over to the positive uses, as in the cases we saw in Section 4.6.5 above? In other words, are we likely to find it employed in phrasal irony?

To research this question, the full concordance of *border* on* in SiBol 05 was analysed and we find occurrences such as:

(54) […] whose instinctive talent for the work bordered on genius. (SiBol 05: *Guardian*)

(55) "Conviction" is gripping, bordering on brilliant. (SiBol 05: *Guardian*)

(56) […] made a recovery bordering on a "medical miracle". (SiBol 05: *Times*)

(57) […] the Bulls performance last night at times bordered on perfection. (SiBol 05: *Times*)

There is no sense of irony in these instances, in other words, the genius, brilliance and the miracle are not being ironically undermined by an association with *border* on*; the overall positive evaluation endures. Yet, we come across cases where the approval, the positive evaluation is not entirely straightforward or genuine:

(58) Mystifyingly opaque though the Archbishop's utterances may be (and he does have a gift bordering on genius for calling a spade a uni-handled, longitudinal horticultural instrument) […] (SiBol 05: *Times*)

Obviously a strange form of "genius".

It will be recalled that the research question raised at the beginning of this section was: under what circumstances is a statistically unusual combination, a reversal of the usual evaluation, meant to convey an ironical attitude and when is it simply an innocuous counter-instance? We can now begin to examine this issue specifically.

The most typical use of all forms of *border* on* is to talk of an NP1 *bordering on* or which *borders on* an NP2 and most frequently the NP2 term is an implied pejoration of NP1. A simple case would be:

(59) […] monetary incompetence that now borders on sabotage. (SiBol 05: *Times*)

where NP1 is *monetary incompetence* and NP2 is *sabotage*. What is particularly striking, however, is that the linking expression *border on* is itself a signal to the reader/listener on how to view the relationship between the two terms. It is a means of overtly redirecting the reader's evaluation, instructing them to re-read NP1 as (almost) the equivalent of NP2. For instance, in (59) the reader is instructed to view the monetary incompetence in the case in hand as almost equivalent to sabotage. Without this instruction it would by no means clear that *incompetence* and *sabotage* have any natural similarities.

It is very often the case that the NP1 term is not self-evidently inherently negative but *border* on* followed by a genuinely negative NP2 notifies us to read the situation with disapproval:

(60) […] showed a polite interest which bordered on boredom. (SiBol 05: *Observer*)

(61) […] with a smoothness that borders on bland. (SiBol 05: *Guardian*)

(62) […] is so uninhibited that it borders on porn. (SiBol 05: *Telegraph*)

(63) […] allowed to behave with a freedom that borders on impunity. (SiBol 05: *Telegraph*)

Given the reversal of evaluation between NP1 to NP2 at play in such cases, a hint of critical ironic intent is perceptible. On several occasions, *border* on* is used by the writer to forge links between NP1 and NP2 in order to make a particular argument:

(64) […] the "traditional family" rhetoric [of some Conservative politicians] bordered on homophobia. (SiBol 05: *Guardian*)

(65) […] the conservatism of British doctors borders on Luddism. (SiBol 05: *Times*).

In both cases a criticism is clearly being made of the arguments or stance of the group in question. As in these cases, the judgemental function of *border* on* is best seen in cases where there is a shift of point of view from NP1 to NP2, in other words, when the evaluator of NP1 is different from that of NP2. The evaluation of NP1 in such occasions is often projected on some actor, some protagonist in the narrative, whilst the evaluator of NP2 is the observer (the writer), who is being critical of the earlier evaluator. In two more instances:

(66) [UEFA] made a statement that bordered on a harangue. (SiBol 05: *Guardian*)

(67) Sharapova, whose will to win borders on frightening […] (SiBol 05: *Guardian*)

one doubts whether UEFA considered its own statement a harangue, or that Ms Sharapova is frightened by her own will to win. We again sense traces of irony. The positive (self-)evaluation of conservative politicians' family values rhetoric (64), UEFA's "statement" (66), Ms Sharapova's sporting determination (67) are undermined in each case by the addition of what they *border* on*.

There are, as we saw in Example (58), instances where the ironic intent is much more marked, in particular, those instances where the *dictum* is positive in evaluation but where an underlying *implicatum* is more negative and critical. These can be of different sorts:

(68) To allow Vaughan three lives bordered on the sort of charity that warrants tax benefits.

depends upon our rereading the *charity* of the *dictum*, that is the "generosity" of allowing an opposing (cricket) player extra "lives", as "incompetence" in the *implicatum*. The touch of hyperbole, allied to a fantasy script or narrative ("that warrants tax benefits": see Partington 2006a: 69–73 on fantasy narratives in humour) is common to irony and can also be seen in:

(69) As *leaps of faith* go, the International Cricket Association's decision [...] bordered on *the biblical*. (SiBol 05: *Guardian*)

Returning to the earlier example:

(58) Mystifyingly opaque though the Archbishop's utterances may be (and he does have a gift bordering on genius for calling a spade a uni-handled, longitudinal horticultural instrument) [...]. (SiBol 05: *Times*)

the ironic effect depends instead on a parody of mystifyingly pretentious language style whose mastery is termed *genius* in the *dictum*, but the *implicatum* is rather less flattering.

### 4.6.9 Ratio, inherent hyperbole, critical intent

We can now perhaps attempt to answer the question raised in the previous section of why, when the normal critical function of the expression *border* on* is reversed and it is employed to express positive evaluations, it is sometimes obviously intended as ironic, but by no means always so. This distinguishes it from the expressions discussed in Sections 4.6.5 and 4.6.6, where the evaluation reversal was very generally indicative of phrasal irony.

More than one factor is involved in the explanation. The first is how weighted our expectations are. Both the present research and that conducted by Schmitt & Carter found ratios of unfavourable to neutral-or-favourable uses of *border* on* of roughly 7:3. It is likely that such a ratio is simply not sufficiently weighted to one side to set up expectations firm enough to be reliably exploited for irony (in the absence of the cotextual help seen in Examples 58, 68 and 69). The ratio beyond which it is not normally possible to go against the evaluative-prosodic grain of an expression without creating an ironic effect is still another issue which has received little rigorous study.

Another factor is that, as was stated earlier, *border* on* can be used with a purely descriptive function ("his music bordered on swing"), which was rare in the use of the items in Section 4.11. This means that, if there is no contextual help in how to read the author's intentions, statistically unusual favourable instances can be interpreted as semi-descriptive, or at least as non-judgemental and non-ironic, although there can be a degree of tension and uncertainty as to their ironic value, as for instance in:

(70) That matters little to the City who greeted the results with an enthusiasm that bordered on rapture. (SiBol 05: *Guardian*)

A third factor is that the inherent non-hyperbolic sense, that is, the hedging function of *border* on* – if something *borders on love* or *genius*, it still is not quite *love* or *genius* – frequently militates against its use as irony. Phrasal irony is expressed most plainly with the aid of more dramatic expressions such as *bent on*, *in a fit of* or *the onslaught of* which lend themselves more easily to an evaluative contrast with something in their vicinity (we already noted the link between irony and hyperbole in 4.3.1)

Finally the context and cotext play a vital part in priming the reader/listener for ironic intent. There may be hyperbolic or other comic stylistic elements in the cotext hinting that the evaluation being expressed is not straightforwardly or unambiguously positive, as we saw in Examples (58), (68) and (69).

### 4.6.10 Conclusions on phrasal irony

A good number of research questions have been addressed in this final case study. We have examined, firstly, how phrasal irony is structured, namely, by the combination of elements within the phrase of opposing evaluative polarity. This examination simultaneously addressed the question of why it is used: to upset readers/listeners' normal expectations that the evaluation of a particular entity will be straightforward and consistent at any particular point in a text. Form and function were thus seen to be simply two perspectives on the same issue.

We also briefly indicated how phrasal irony relates to the forms of irony investigated in the earlier case studies, in particular in that they are all driven by the mechanism of abrupt reversal of evaluation, either explicitly (the reversal being signalled in the text) or implicitly (the instruction to reverse the apparent evaluation being implied). Additionally, in common with other forms, phrasal irony is conventionally used to express criticism and censure in an indirect fashion.

We then conducted a detailed analysis of different ways in which writers perform phrasal irony, and why they do so. We first looked at how, in many instances of oxymoron, the particular effect being sought involved the forced juxtaposition of two elements of opposing evaluative polarity. We then discussed various examples of the phenomenon of evaluation reversal in texts, both from the expected good to actual bad and vice versa, and in particular we looked in detail at certain templates which are used repeatedly and productively so that the new ironic use of the phrase seems to have become an accepted, recognised version.

Finally, it was stressed that not all evaluation reversal is performed for ironic effect, sometimes it appears to be simply a statistically unusual event, with no particular effect sought or achieved. A number of interlocking explanations were proposed to illucidate the circumstances when collocational irony is intended and instead when simple collocational counter-instance occurs. The issue is highly complex and could well shed some light on why language learners often find irony difficult to detect and to master.

## Suggestions for further research

### Explicit irony

1. Prepare a concordance with c.400 characters of cotext of the items *irony*, *ironic*, and *ironically*. Examine each instance to discover what particular evaluation is being overturned, who or what is being criticised and if there are any other particular rhetorical effects being sought by the writer/utterer.
2. Prepare a concordance with c.400 characters of cotext of *ironic/irony/ironically* followed in a span of 5 words by a contrastive conjunction *while/whilst/whereas*. What exactly is being contrasted and why?

### Implicit irony

1. Prepare a sentence concordance of the phrase *pearls of wisdom*. Are there any examples where the intent is *not* mockingly ironic? What other meanings are being conveyed? Can you think of other phrases whose use is overwhelmingly ironic?
2. Prepare concordances from a spoken corpus with c.400 characters of co-text of the expressions used in mock politeness discussed in Chapter 8. How many instances of irony or sarcasm are there and what other effects are being sought. How do the targets of the irony respond?

### Phrasal irony

1. Further research needs to be conducted to discover which kinds of words and expressions are used by speakers/writers to exploit collocational effects for irony. Given their natural evaluatively hyperbolic function, intensifiers are a promising area; we have already encountered "could *deliberately love*" and other instances are not difficult to find:

   > Tom Watson [...] is the latest card to join the deck of *excruciatingly loyal* Blairites. (SiBol 05: *Guardian*)

Make a sentence concordance of intensifying adverbs with a clear positive or negative evaluative polarity, for example, *excruciatingly*, *wonderfully*, *infuriatingly*, and so on. Are they ever found to premodify an item of opposite polarity such as "wonderfully gruesome", "infuriatingly fabulous" (both Sibol 05) and, if so, what particular effects are being sought?

CHAPTER 5

# Investigating rhetoric in discourse 2

## Metaphor

This chapter follows on from Chapter 4 by investigating another aspect of rhetoric, namely metaphor, and closely links to Chapter 2 by focussing on the use of metaphor as an evaluative device in which selected favourable or unfavourable elements of the source are projected onto the target.

Locke (quoted in Goatly 1997: 1), in arguing against the use of figurative language, stated that:

> all the artificial and figurative application of words eloquence hath invented, are for nothing else but to insinuate wrong ideas, move the passions, and thereby mislead the judgement, and so indeed are perfect cheat.
>
> (Locke 1690, Book 3, ch. 10, p. 105)

As discourse analysts, we might well want to change that ending to: *and so indeed are perfect for investigation*. Metaphor is of great interest precisely because of its evaluative potential, whereby selected favourable or unfavourable elements of the source are projected onto the target (see Chapters 2 and 3).

In this chapter, we look at how a corpus-assisted approach can allow us to examine the two different functions of metaphor: in the first, metaphor is used to make the abstract and unfamiliar more tangible and comprehensible, and in the second, metaphor is employed to make the mundane and familiar appear novel, interesting and entertaining.

### 5.1 Corpus linguistics and metaphor: Methodologies

A corpus-assisted approach to metaphor, as noted in Partington (2006b: 267–268), can be productive both by revealing recurrent patterns of metaphorical usage and by simply making large amounts of authentic data available. The potential contribution of corpus linguistics to metaphor study has received increasing amounts of attention over recent years (for example, see Stefanowitsch & Gries 2006 and Deignan 2005 for volume length studies) and a range of methodologies have been developed. Stefanowitsch (2006:2–6) identifies and elaborates on the following strategies for extracting conceptual mappings:

1. Manual searching
2. Searching for source-domain vocabulary
3. Searching for target-domain vocabulary
4. Searching for sentences containing lexical items from both the source domain and the target domain
5. Searching for metaphors based on 'markers of metaphor'
6. Extraction from a corpus annotated for semantic fields/domains
7. Extraction from a corpus annotated for conceptual mappings.

Corpus-assisted research may draw on several of these strategies within a single study, as illustrated in the two case-studies below.

Charteris-Black's (2004) method of employing corpora in critical metaphor analysis also offers a structured procedure, essentially consisting of stages (1) and (2) above. He advocates starting with the identification of a metaphor, then expanding outwards to manually examine the occurrences in a small number of texts in order to identify *metaphor keywords*, that is, those words which tend to be used with a metaphorical sense. The researcher then expands further outwards to examine these items in a corpus and investigate whether the metaphor keywords are indeed used as metaphors, focussing in particular on the use of conventional metaphor.

## 5.2 Corpus linguistics and metaphor: Challenges and potential pitfalls

Semino et al. (2004) offer a thorough discussion of the methodological problems they encountered in identifying and analysing metaphors in a corpus of conversations about cancer which are relevant for many other case-studies. In particular, they noted challenges in:

i. [identifying] the boundary between the literal and the metaphorical in the identification of linguistic metaphors;
ii. the precise identification of tenor and vehicle in relation to each linguistic metaphor;
iii. the extrapolation of conceptual metaphors from linguistic metaphors; and
iv. the extrapolation of conventional metaphors from patterns in the data.

In terms of potential pitfalls into which we might fall, one of the central issues to recall is that a corpus-assisted study can only tell you about the language in the corpus one is employing and therefore the composition of the corpus will necessarily affect the conclusions that you reach. Let us take a purely hypothetical example. If a researcher were to compile a corpus of newspaper texts using the search term *Road Map For Peace*, s/he would not then be able to use that corpus to comment on which conceptual metaphors were most frequent in the press for the obvious reason that the corpus is highly skewed by having chosen a metaphor as the search-term. If we wanted to identify which conceptual metaphors were most frequent, we would need to compile a corpus using more neutral search terms, such as the names of the countries involved.

Second, as Partington (1998) notes, we can only say that a particular metaphor or group of metaphors is characteristic of a particular discourse type if we have also checked to see its frequency in other types of discourse. The same should also apply to investigations of discourse in the sense of "ways of talking about the world", so before concluding that a particular group is frequently described in terms of water metaphors, e.g. *floods of,* and that this is salient in the representation of that group, we might want to check what else is represented with the same metaphor. In other words, we need to check the relationship in both directions.

## 5.3 Case study 1: Metaphors of *anti-Americanism*

As noted above, in this first case-study we examine how metaphor is used as an explanatory, reconceptualising device. More specifically, a cross-cultural and cross-linguistic corpus-assisted approach is employed to analyse the role of metaphor in the construal of *anti-Americanism* in newspaper discourse from three different countries: the United States, the United Kingdom and Italy, over the period 1999–2007. Within the corpus, four dominant conceptual metaphors of anti-Americanism – as DISEASE, FLAMMABLE, SEA and CRIME – are identified. These metaphors are described and compared with reference to their lexical and grammatical realizations in the 12 sub-corpora. Other targets of these metaphors, within the same discourse contexts, are also sampled and analysed in order to explore the evaluative function that the metaphors serve in illustrating the newspapers' framing of anti-Americanism.

### 5.3.1 Why analyse metaphor in this context?

Newspaper discourse is characterised by the fact that the texts are both forming, and conforming to, the opinions of the reader. The implied reader is, in Goffman's terms, the *principal*, that is to say the "party to whose position, stand and belief the words attest" (1981: 226), and the newspaper's success is dependent on the ability of its journalists to adequately reflect those positions, stands and beliefs. Therefore by analysing the use of metaphor in the press, we can try and access how events and entities are conceptualised by particular groups. For similar reasons metaphors in the press are also investigated in Chapter 8 as part of an attempt to understand how particular groups are represented.

### 5.3.2 Corpora and methodology

For this case-study, we focus specifically on the term *anti-Americanism*, rather than looking at expressions of anti-American opinion, in order to delimit the area of study. The main corpus used here was compiled as part of an interdisciplinary research project regarding the phenomenon of anti-Americanism and contains every article in which the *anti-Americanism* was mentioned over the period 1999–2007 in a set of US, UK and Italian newspapers (shown in Table 5.1).

**Table 5.1.** Newspapers included in the corpus

| US newspapers | UK newspapers | Italian newspapers |
|---|---|---|
| *New York Times* | *Telegraph* | *Corriere della Sera* |
| *Washington Post* | *Guardian* | *La Stampa* |
| *USA Today* | *Independent* | *Il Sole 24* |
| *New York Daily News* | *Daily Mail* | |
| | *Financial Times* | |

The 9.6 million word corpus can be partitioned by date, country of origin, language and individual newspaper. The newspapers were selected opportunistically: whether or not they were available for download, and in terms of coverage: they are all effectively national newspapers, and cover a range of political orientations.[1] The composition of the corpus is summarised in Figure 5.1: as can be seen there was a great deal of variation in the number of occurrences of *anti(-) America** between papers and therefore in the size of the sub-corpora. Overall, as might be expected, the US newspapers were most concerned with discussing the concept of *anti-Americanism*, followed by the UK papers, with the frequencies

1. Average net circulation according to the *Audit Bureau of Circulations* December 2007 release: *New York Times* (1,037,828), *Washington Post* (894,428), *New York Daily News, USA Today* (2,293,137), *Guardian* (310,796), *Independent* (185,029), *Telegraph* (836,750), *Daily Mail* (2,166,312), *Financial Times* (137,315). See http://www.accessabc.com/ www.abc.org.uk

being the lowest in the Italian press. Also as could have been anticipated, the discussion peaked post September 11 2001.[2]

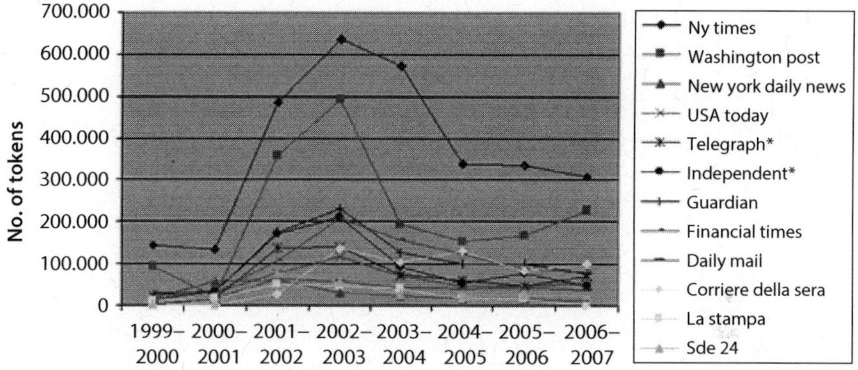


**Figure 5.1.** Size of the sub-corpora

In this case-study, a two-stage approach was taken, incorporating three of the strategies from Stefanowitsch (2006) (listed above).

a. In the first stage, the target, *anti-Americanism*, was isolated and the concordance lines were manually searched for metaphorical use.
b. In the second stage, the linguistic realizations of the metaphors identified in stage one were used to move from source to target. The corpora for this second stage were created ad hoc, by downloading instances of the metaphorical expression in question from the archives of the specific newspaper. This second stage was considered to be important as not only do metaphors trigger associations with the source, but also, within a specific discourse type, the metaphors are primed (see Hoey 2005) by their previous/other collocates and therefore build up evaluative potentialities over time.

### 5.3.3 Results

From the manual analysis of the concordance lines of *anti-Americanism,* four dominant conceptual metaphors emerged; *anti-Americanism* is SEA (158 occurrences), DISEASE (113 occurrences), FIRE (110 occurrences) and CRIME (38 occurrences).

---

2. It is of interest to note that in opinion surveys conducted over the same period, the feelings of *anti-Americanism* were at their lowest post September 11 2001, and rose from there onwards, an almost mirror reversal of the tendency to discuss the phenomenon (for example, Isernia 2005).

Figure 5.2 illustrates the relative frequency and distribution of the four metaphors in the sub-corpora:

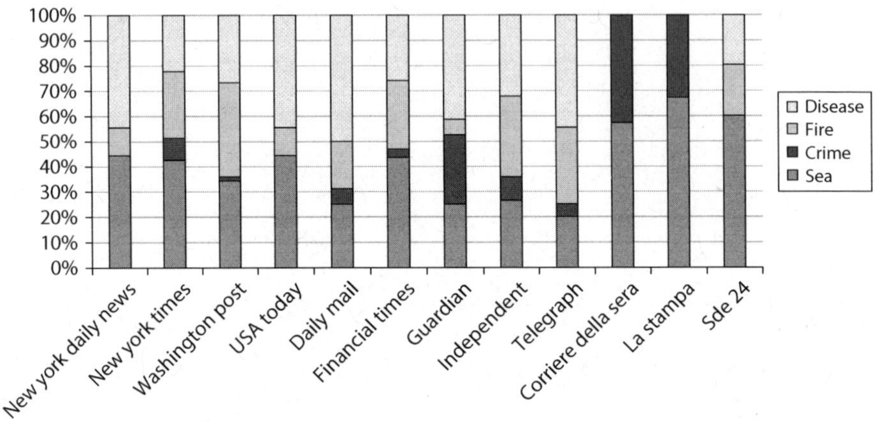


**Figure 5.2.** Relative frequency of the four main metaphors across the individual sub-corpora

*Anti-Americanism is a* S*EA*

Although *anti-Americanism* is a SEA was the most frequent metaphor, it was also one of the most conventionalised, as seen in Figure 5.3, in fact only six per cent of the metaphorical expressions were unique.

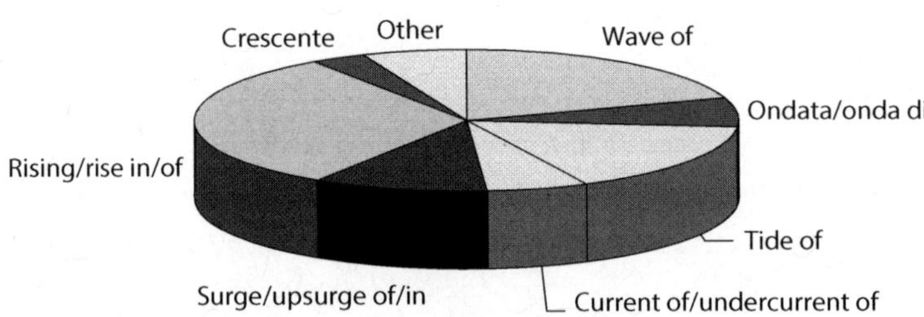


**Figure 5.3.** Linguistic realizations of *anti-Americanism* is SEA

The following concordance lines illustrate the principal linguistic realizations, as well as two illustrative examples from the "other" category:[3]

| | |
|---|---|
| T02 | Chiracs and the Schroders are **riding a wave of** *anti-Americanism* that they have done |
| DM05 | drift away from the Atlantic alliance on **a tide of** *anti-Americanism*, which Schroeder has |

3. Back translations of the Italian language metaphors are supplied in square brackets, although sometimes single words are presented, the translations were chosen after looking at the full context.

NYT01 s is not to deny the existence of **a deep current** of *anti-Americanism* in this Muslim country
WP99 ow call liberalism, with its **deep undercurrent of** *anti-Americanism*, its attachment to quotas,
US02 not a big customer, but Akel is part of **a surge of** *anti-Americanism* that threatens to **erode**
I01 Denying **rising** *anti-Americanism* would not serve any
C01 E preoccupato dal **crescente** *anti-americanismo* di chi, anche in
[is worried by the rising anti-americanism of those, even in]
NYT03 new American order has generated **a tsunami of** *anti-Americanism*, with the United States
C02 vittime civili potrebbero contenere il **dilagante** *anti-americanismo*. <<Non sono un
[civilian deaths could contain the spreading (with reference to water) anti-americanism 'I am no]

As can be seen in Figure 5.3, the group *rising/rise in/of* was the most frequent in the English data, yet, in the absence of the other realizations it is arguable whether it would even have been identified as representing the SEA metaphor. Partington (1998) considers ways of differentiating along the "cline in the originality of metaphorical use, from the unusual, through the well-trodden, to what is usually called the dead metaphor" (1998: 117–118). He asserts that metaphors which are dead for a given discourse community may be identified by their collocates. For example, mixed metaphors, or conventionality of collocation could indicate that the metaphor is dead, whereas if the metaphor is extended across the collocation it is likely to indicate a higher degree of 'liveness' or 'unusuality'. In the case of *rising/rise in/of* there was little other lexis surrounding the collocation suggesting a continuation or extension of the metaphor. Moreover, this was also generally true for the conceptual metaphor *anti-Americanism* is SEA in this corpus.

In the Italian data, the conceptual metaphor *anti-Americanism* is SEA was almost exclusively realised by the metaphorical expression *ondata di* [wave of] as seen in the concordance lines below:

C02 Nell'**ondata** di *anti-americanismo* affiora l'odio contro Israele, si
[In the wave of anti-Americanism, hatred for Israel surfaces,]
C02 anti-Usa Per scongiurare un'**ondata** di *anti-americanismo* e per evitare contestazioni
[anti-US. To avert a wave of anti-Americanism and to avoid protests]
C06 l'<incidente > Calipari, quale **ondata** di *anti-americanismo* si sarebbe sprigionata dalla
[the Calipari incident, what kind of wave of anti-Americanism would have burst out from]
LS00 La distinguiamo nella **crescente ondata** di *anti-americanismo* in Europa e Asia.
[We can recognise it in the rising wave of anti-Americanism in Europe and Asia.]
LS04 giuri sul nascere il rischio di **un'ondata** di *anti-americanismo* nel nostro paese.
[the risk of a wave of anti-Americanism in our country.]
LS04 non possiamo aprire la strada a **un'ondata** di *anti-americanismo*. Nessuno,
[we cannot leave the way open for a wave of anti-Americanism. No-one, ]
LS04 tocca con mano una **crescente ondata** di *anti-americanismo*. E' una questione particolarmente
[touches with a hand a wave of anti-Americanism. It is a particularly]
LS05 nda rischia di provocare un'altra **ondata** di *anti-americanismo*. Tant'e' che Francesco Cossiga ha
[risks triggering another wave of anti-Americanism. So much so that Francesco Cossiga]
S02 oreane ha suscitato nel paese **un'ondata** di *anti-americanismo*. Soprattutto tra i giovani che
[has stirred up a wave of anti-Americanism in the country. Particularly amongst young people w]

| | | |
|---|---|---|
| S02 | Cio' ha sollevato un'improvvisa **ondata** di | *anti-americanismo*: molta gente reclama maggiore |
| | [That has whipped up a sudden wave of anti-Americanism: many people are asking for more] | |
| C04 | poco monumentale: invertire l'**onda** di | *anti-americanismo* che **dilaga** nel mondo a |
| | [least monumental: invert the wave of anti-Americanism that is spreading around the world] | |

It is also noticeable that all except one of these examples come from after September 11 2001, whereas the expression *wave of anti-Americanism* was already in use prior to that date in the UK and US sub-corpora. Furthermore, that one exception in the Italian data was an article from the *Wall Street Journal* which had been translated into Italian for publication in *La Stampa*. This does, therefore, open the possibility of an interesting question regarding the influence of the English language metaphorical representations on the Italian.

As an illustration of the two-step structure of the analysis, we now focus on one linguistic realization of the macro SEA metaphor, *wave of* and the Italian equivalent *ondata di* [wave of] in the *Financial Times*, *La Stampa* and *Corriere della Sera* because the metaphor appeared to be characteristic of these newspapers.[4] The R1 collocates are reported in Table 5.2.

All three newspapers showed a tendency for the node to collocate with items relating to the economy, such as *buying, selling,* and *rincari* [price rises].

For the *Financial Times* (see Table 5.1) there did not appear to be an absolute pattern of *wave of* + unfavourably evaluated entity, for instance, alongside unfavourable collocates like *attacks* and *violence* (marked in bold in the Table) there were also more favourable items such as *optimism, interest, profit,* and (seemingly) neutral words such as *consolidation*. Further investigating the phrase *wave of* + *anti* in all articles from the *Financial Times* over the time period 1999–2007, suggested that *anti-Americanism* was being slotted into an existing frame of *wave of anti* + NATIONALITY:

| | |
|---|---|
| Mr Roh, who was elected on a | *wave* of **anti-American** sentiment |
| ance with Washington, following a | *wave* of **anti-American** sentiment |
| tary vehicle sparked a nationwide | *wave* of **anti-Americanism**, the sc |
| al bank. No such luck. Owing to a | *wave* of **anti-foreign** feeling under |
| s China's efforts to respond to the | *wave* of **anti-Chinese** sentiment in |
| a's efforts to respond to the rising | *wave* of **anti-Chinese** sentiment in |
| half during the past year. And the | *wave* of **anti-foreigner** sentiment i |
| ycle in the midst of a horrendous | *wave* of **anti-Semitism** (initiated fro |
| by a UN commission, provoked a | *wave* of **anti-Syrian** demonstration |
| ion. The assassination provoked a | *wave* of **anti-Syrian** protests and |

Selected concordance lines from the *Financial Times* 1999–2007[5]

4. Metaphors were considered characteristic of a given sub-corpus if the relative frequency for that newspaper was more than one standard deviation above the mean of all the sub-corpora.

5. Every second concordance removed.

**Table 5.2.** Immediate right collocates of *wave* of in the *Financial Times* and *ondata di* [wave of] in *La Stampa* 1999–2007, and *Corriere della Sera* 2002–2007

| **Financial Times** | | **La Stampa** | | **Corriere della Sera** | |
|---|---|---|---|---|---|
| CONSOLIDATION | 169 | MALTEMPO [bad weather] | 181 | MALTEMPO [bad weather] | 61 |
| CORPORATE | 72 | **ATTENTATI [attacks]** | 46 | CALDO [heat] | 55 |
| NEW | 70 | CALDO [heat] | 45 | **ATTENTATI [attacks]** | 23 |
| SELLING | 61 | **ATTACCHI [attacks]** | 42 | CALORE [heat] | 23 |
| MERGERS | 43 | FREDDO [cold] | 38 | FREDDO [cold] | 22 |
| ATTACKS | 32 | **VIOLENZA [violence]** | 35 | SBARCHI [landings] | 17 |
| INVESTMENT | 30 | VENDITE [sales] | 34 | **VIOLENZA [violence]** | 17 |
| VIOLENCE | 26 | SCIOPERI [strikes] | 28 | VENDITE [sales] | 16 |
| OPTIMISM | 20 | ARRESTI [arrests] | 23 | **ATTACCHI [attacks]** | 15 |
| **ANTI** | 17 | **VIOLENZE [violence]** | 20 | GELO [cold/ice] | 15 |
| BUYING | 17 | RINCARI [price-rises] | 18 | ARRESTI [arrests] | 14 |
| INTEREST | 16 | PIENA [peak flood levels] | 16 | SCIOPERI [strikes] | 14 |
| FOREIGN | 15 | ACQUISTI [buying] | 15 | FUSIONI [mergers] | 9 |
| PROFIT | 15 | GELO [cold] | 14 | PROTESTE [protests] | 9 |
| PUBLIC | 15 | **TERRORISMO [terrorism]** | 14 | RINCARI [price rises] | 8 |
| US | 15 | CALORE [heat] | 13 | **VIOLENZE [violence]** | 8 |
| ACCOUNTING | 14 | PROTESTE [protests] | 13 | CLANDESTINI [illegal immigrants] | 7 |
| DEALS | 14 | IMMIGRATI [immigrants] | 12 | IMMIGRATI [immigrants] | 7 |
| EUROPEAN | 14 | POLEMICHE [controversy] | 12 | CRITICHE [criticism] | 6 |
| FINANCIAL | 14 | AUMENTI [increases] | 10 | FOLLIA [madness] | 6 |

Although the items appear to be largely unfavourably evaluated, they are clearly less emotive and more varied than the only other *ondata di anti-* [*wave of anti-*] collocation in *La Stampa* over the same time period, which is *antisemitismo* (antisemitism), as seen in the concordance lines below:

| | |
|---|---|
| . ""Che in Francia ci fosse una nuova | *ondata di anti***semitismo** lo avevo letto |
| e' nel mondo sta montando una nuova | *ondata di anti***semitismo** che vorrebbe |
| alisi dell'Unione europea, della grande | *ondata di anti***semitismo**, del suo car |
| resa e non hanno denunciato la nuova | *ondata di anti***semitismo**. Nessuno si |

Selected concordance lines from *La Stampa*1999–2007[6]

Returning to Table 5.2, the collocates of *ondata di* [wave of] from *La Stampa* and *Corriere della Sera* show a more obviously negatively-evaluated set of events such as: *attentati* [attack], *attachi* [attack], *violenza* [violence], *terrorismo* [terrorism]. It also appears that *ondata di* frequently refers to immigration: *immigrati* [immigrants], *sbarchi* [landings], *clandestini* [illegal immigrants], which may cast further light on how *anti-Americanism* is being negatively framed in these sources.

However, Table 5.2 also shows that another semantic field in the Italian data is weather: *maltempo* [bad weather], *caldo* [heat], *freddo* [cold], *gelo* [cold, literally ice], *calore* [heat]. This semantic field of (unfavourable, excessive) weather also illustrates, despite the similarities, a lack of comprehensive collocational equivalence between the metaphorical expressions *wave of* and *ondata di* in English and Italian (although there is, course, one similar metaphorical realisation in English with the term *heat(-)wave*).

It was also noticeable from Figure 5.3 that in both English and Italian the *anti-Americanism* is SEA metaphor was consistently realised by pre-modifiers, either consisting of adjectives or a noun+*of* pattern. The cases of *wave/tide/current/undercurrent + of* and *onda/ondata +di* are interesting as it is actually difficult to think of non-metaphorical expressions in which they could be employed. This initial intuition was confirmed both by the collocates in Table 5.1, and by looking in another corpus containing US, and UK newspaper data.[7]

*Anti-Americanism is* DISEASE

Similarly to the previous metaphor, *anti-Americanism* is DISEASE was predominately realised by pre-modifiers, as shown in Figure 5.4 and the sample concordance lines below.

6. Every second concordance removed.

7. The *CorDis Corpus*, see Morley and Bayley (2009).

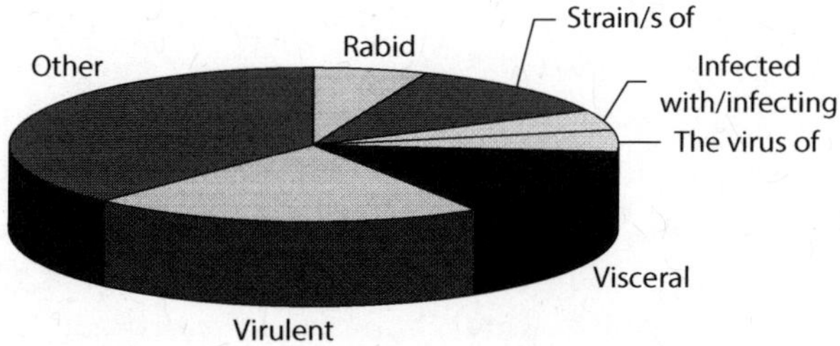


**Figure 5.4.** Linguistic realizations of *anti-Americanism* is DISEASE

Selected concordance lines illustrating the principal linguistic realizations of the metaphor:

| | | |
|---|---|---|
| T04 | But the idea that the most recent wave of **rabid** | *anti-Americanism* stems from mistakes in |
| T03 | timely **antidote** to the more thoughtless **strains of** | *anti-Americanism* **prevalent** today |
| I02 | too many teachers are probably **infected with** the | *anti-Americanism* that they ought to be |
| WP03 | 's a shame, but not surprising, that **the virus of** | *anti-Americanism* has **infected** the |
| DM01 | But then, Miss Short is not alone. The **visceral** | *anti-Americanism* of some in the Labour |
| NYT01 | Whatever the solution to the current, **virulent** | *anti-Americanism*, it certainly cannot be to |

Like the SEA metaphor, the metaphorical expressions are largely realised by pre-modifiers, and there appears to be some correspondence between the grammatical form of the metaphorical expression and the extent to which it has become conventionalised, with the adjectives being more likely to represent 'well-trodden' metaphorical expressions.

Overall, the conceptual metaphor *anti-Americanism* is DISEASE was most frequent per thousand words in the *Telegraph*, and so the analysis was extended to the realization *strain/s of* in the *Telegraph* over the time period 2001–2007.

**Table 5.3.** Right collocates of *strain of* and *strains of* in the *Telegraph* in 2001–2007

| *strain of* + | | *strains of* + | |
|---|---|---|---|
| FLU | 20 | MRSA | 8 |
| VIRUS | 19 | ANTHRAX | 5 |
| BIRD | 13 | DRUG | 5 |
| DISEASE | 10 | FLU | 5 |
| INFLUENZA | 8 | DISEASE | 4 |
| MRSA | 8 | MUSIC | 4 |
| FOOT | 7 | CANNABIS | 3 |
| MOUTH | 7 | RESISTANT | 3 |
| GROWING | 6 | | |
| KILLED | 6 | | |

The collocates in Table 5.3 show that this metaphorical expression is far from being dead in the discourse of the *Telegraph*, and unlike most of the realizations seen so far is predominately used with its literal meaning.

As can also be seen from Figure 5.4, the DISEASE metaphor proved to be one of the most creative and least conventionalised metaphors, with 35 per cent of the realizations being classified as "other" given that they only existed with, at most, one other similar phraseology. The range of realizations is illustrated in the concordance lines below (one line per newspaper):

| | | |
|---|---|---|
| DM04 | lgent, or more stupid, than **the cancer of** | *anti-Americanism* **taking root** in many Western |
| S02 | tinente sia attraversato da **un'epidemia** di | *anti-americanismo*: condizionati dall'11 |
| | [an epidemic of anti-Americanism: ] | |
| I02 | has always been **an unhealthy streak of** | *anti-Americanism* in the Labour Party, a sentiment |
| T01 | and succumbed to the **global pandemic of** | *anti-Americanism*. Britain has stood firm. Britain |
| G99 | ple are working themselves into **a fever of** | *anti-Americanism*. This sort of thing has never |
| US02 | orea and are preparing for **venomous** | *anti-Americanism*. Most large companies have a |
| NYD04 | countries, where they **risk exposure to** | *anti-Americanism*. A goal of the school is to |
| FT01 | n last month has whipped up fresh **bouts of** | *anti-Americanism*. But on the modern cam pu |
| NYT02 | government for addressing **symptoms of** | *anti-Americanism* without addressing an underlyi |
| WP02 | administration. Therefore, his **diagnosis of** | *anti-Americanism* seems not justified. Tho |

This creativity in expression would then seem to suggest that despite the highly conventionalised adjectives seen in Figure 5.4, the metaphor is not considered to be dead by the discourse community, in particular in the UK newspapers.

*Anti-Americanism is* FLAMMABLE

This was the metaphor which was least frequently employed in the Italian sub-corpora, and in contrast to the previous two metaphors it is predominately realised by processes, as can be seen in Figure 5.5 and the selected concordances:

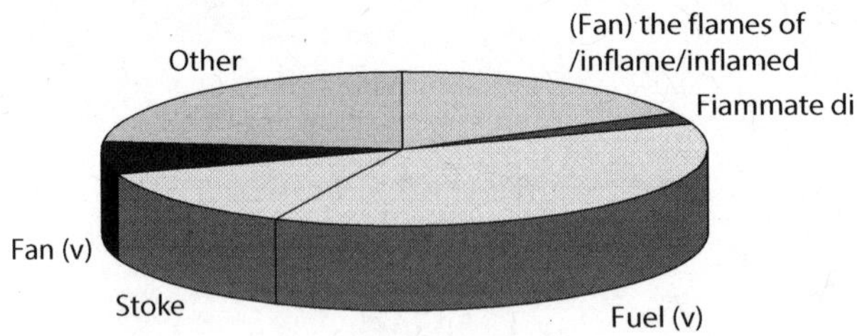


**Figure 5.5.** Linguistic realizations of *anti-Americanism* is FLAMMABLE

Selected concordance lines illustrating the linguistic realizations:

| | | |
|---|---|---|
| DM06 | ed that executing Saddam could **inflame** | *anti-Americanism*, inspire terrorists and further |
| S02 | **Fiammate** di | *anti-americanismo* in Europa non sono nuove |
| | [Flare-ups of anti-Americanism in Europe are nothing new:] | |

| | | | |
|---|---|---|---|
| I02 | state, will one of the main factors **fuelling** | *anti-Americanism* and Islamic extremism across th |
| FT02 | will **stoke the fires of** fundamentalism and | *anti-Americanism*. It may be necessary to strike |
| US04 | e, along with the Iraq invasion, has **fanned** | *anti-Americanism* and filled terrorist camps with a |
| WP00 | twists in the story, **stirring the embers of** | *anti-Americanism*. Almost every major paper |

The *Washington Post*, *USA Today* and the *Financial Times* were the newspapers that employed this conceptual metaphor most frequently per 1000 words. Taking one of the realizations shown in Figure 5.5, the lemma STOKE, the analysis was therefore extended to the whole of the *Financial Times*, *USA Today* and *Washington Post* over the sampled time periods 1991–1992, 1999–2000, 2006–2007:

**Table 5.4.** Right collocates of STOKE in the *Financial Times, USA Today* and *Washington Post* 1991–1992, 1999–2000 and 2006–2007

| Financial Times | | USA Today | | Washington Post | |
|---|---|---|---|---|---|
| INFLATION | 21 | FIRES | 9 | AMERICAN | 23 |
| FEARS | 19 | FIRE | 8 | FIRE | 16 |
| PRESSURES | 17 | LOATHING | 8 | FIRES | 11 |
| DEBATE | 16 | DEBATE | 6 | DEBATE | 9 |
| DEMAND | 11 | ECONOMY | 6 | INTEREST | 7 |
| PRESSURE | 11 | FEARS | 5 | TENSIONS | 6 |
| US | 11 | | | VIOLENCE | 6 |
| PRICES | 10 | | | FEARS | 5 |
| RATE | 10 | | | OUTRAGE | 5 |
| FIRES | 9 | | | INFLATION | 5 |
| INTEREST | 9 | | | BALLISTIC | 5 |
| SPECULATION | 9 | | | BETWEEN | 5 |
| BOOM | 8 | | | CASTRO | 5 |
| END | 8 | | | CATHOLIC | 5 |
| MORE | 8 | | | DEGREE | 5 |
| NEW | 8 | | | CONTROVERSY | 4 |
| WAR | 8 | | | FLAMES | 4 |
| | | | | RAGE | 3 |
| | | | | CONGRESS | 3 |
| | | | | BAD | 1 |

Table 5.4 shows that the only common collocates among the three newspapers are *fires*, *fears* (which is possibly playing on the phonological similarity to fires),

and *debate*. The metaphorical expression in the *USA Today* and *Washington Post* is more extended than in the *Financial Times*, as attested by the collocates of *fire*, *fires* and *flames*. While it may appear that these refer to literal meanings, a closer look at the concordance lines showed that these are also metaphorical, as illustrated in the concordance lines below:

| | | |
|---|---|---|
| US91 | committed monogamy: Keep the home **fire** | *stoked* BYLINE: Marilyn Elias |
| US99 | Racing also gives Gibbs the chance to | *stoke* the competitive **fires** that still **burn** |
| US06 | eks, Senate Democrats have been gleefully | *stoking* the **fires** of this politically fortuitous |

*Anti-Americanism is* CRIME

While the previous three metaphors all refer to natural entities – or possibly in Charteris-Black's (2006) terms, natural disasters: water, fire and disease – the fourth is distinct in that it refers to human activity. It was the least common of the four metaphors and was most frequent (in relative terms) in the *Guardian*, *Corriere della Sera* and *La Stampa* which suggests that is associated with a more liberal political orientation.

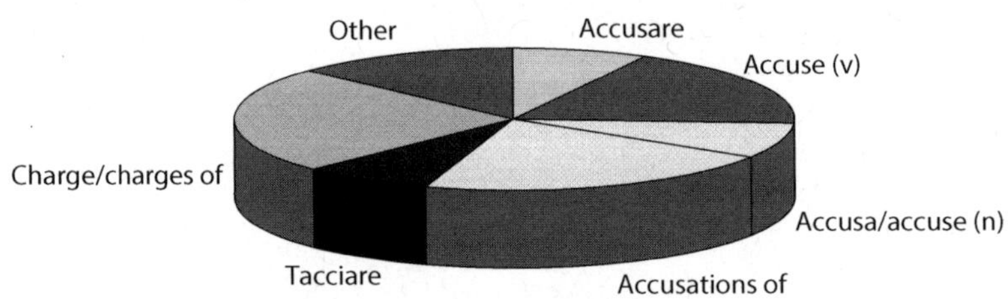


**Figure 5.6.** Linguistic realizations of *anti-Americanism* is CRIME

Selected concordance lines illustrating the principal linguistic realizations:

| | | |
|---|---|---|
| C02 | avvertono: guai a chi osa **accusarci** di | *anti-americanismo.* |
| | [they warn: don't dare to accuse us of anti-Americanism] | |
| G02 | theses, but he has also been bizarrely **accused of** | *anti-Americanism.* |
| LS02 | L'altra scemenza e' **l'accusa** di | *anti-americanismo.* |
| | [the other idiocy is the accusation of anti-Americanism] | |
| I05 | have incited reproachful **accusations of** pinko | *anti-Americanism* |
| C04 | Ovviamente, **tacciare** Fassino di | *anti-americanismo* non sarebbe ne giusto |
| | [Obviously, to charge Fassino of anti-Americanism would be neither right]] | |
| NYT06 | Perhaps partly to disarm **the charge of** | *anti-Americanism*, Mr. Newman also sang' |
| G01 | If in the dock once again for **the thought-crime of** | "*anti-Americanism*". |
| LS02 | anche da persone tutt'altro che **sospettabili di** | ""*anti-americanismo*""". |
| | [even from those who are far from likely to be suspected of anti-Americanism] | |

As the sample concordance lines show, the evaluation appears less straightforward in these instances. While it might seem that equating *anti-Americanism* with crime, like the previous metaphors, offers a clearly unfavourable evaluation, the nesting of the evaluation shows that it is actually most frequently the *accusation* which is being evaluated – unfavourably. To take this into account a more accurate description of the metaphor could be *anti-Americanism* is (TREATED AS) A CRIME (BY OTHER PEOPLE). For this reason it was expected that the extension from source to other targets would prove less fruitful in this case and so this phase was omitted from the case study.

*Other metaphors of anti-Americanism*

In addition to the main four conceptual metaphors discussed above, there were several less frequent macro-metaphors. These included: *Anti-Americanism* is a LIVING ENTITY (29): *alimenta* [feeds], *feed, breed, nurtured, spawning, nourishes*, which was found predominately in the *New York Times*, but also in the *Financial Times, Washington Post, Independent, USA Today, Corriere della Sera, Il Sole 24 Ore.*

*Anti-Americanism* is a TREND (22): *fashionable, old-fashioned, traditional, popular, modish, de riguer, trendy* found in *Daily Mail, Independent, Telegraph, Guardian, Financial Times, Il Sole 24 Ore, New York Times* and *Washington Post*. In these cases *anti-Americanism,* is not only unfavourably evaluated, but also down-graded and dismissed as unserious, transitory and so on.

*Anti-Americanism* is an ENEMY (11): *defeat, fight, curb, combat, fight*, predominately found in *New York Times* and *Washington Post*, but also in the *Guardian* and the *Financial Times, La Stampa*. This is in sharp contrast to the previous set, as anti-Americanism is 'up-graded' and presented as a serious threat.

*Anti-Americanism* is a RELIGION (6): *preach, preach the gospel of, a temple of, the altar of*, found in *Washington Post, New York Times, Independent, Telegraph* and *Financial Times*, possibly also supported by two instances of *fervent* as a pre-modifier.

*Anti-Americanism* (5) is a WIND, found in the *New York Times* and *Il Sole 24 Ore.*

### 5.3.4 Conclusions to case study 1

The dominant areas of metaphor: SEA, DISEASE, and FIRE are all linked by the expression of *anti-Americanism* as an uncontrollable phenomenon (see Chapter 3). This conceptualization also suggests that, in these newspapers, *anti-Americanism* is not a logical, rational entity, indeed one of the most common right collocates of *anti-American* is *sentiment*. A difference should be noted between the first three metaphors and the metaphor of CRIME, as the evaluative pattern in this concept was nested and therefore more complex, and indicative of a different evaluative stance and focus.

There was considerable variation between the four metaphors studied here in the extent to which they were conventionalised or "well-trodden", with the most frequent, SEA, also being the most conventionalised, while DISEASE proved to be one of the most creative. Variations were also noted in the grammatical form which the metaphors preferred, where SEA and DISEASE tended towards pre-modifiers, such as *a wave of* or *a strain of*, CRIME and FLAMMABLE showed a greater variation including realizations in processes, for instance in references to stoking anti-Americanism or accusing (somebody) of anti-Americanism.

The metaphors and metaphorical expressions seemed to be largely conventionalised across cultures in the geographical sense, there were no frequent country-specific metaphors, and a more powerful variable appeared to be political culture. Although in all of the newspapers *anti-Americanism* is evaluated unfavourably, there are differences in the focus of evaluation and the concepts it is paralleled with. The distinction between the metaphors of *anti-Americanism* as SEA, DISEASE and FIRE contrasted with *anti-Americanism* as CRIME seems a useful indicator of the newspapers' positioning.

Although the Italian sub-corpora were much smaller than their US and UK counterparts, the lack of underlying metaphors which were unique to the Italian data was still surprising. The lack of variation across the two languages raises questions for further study, such as whether this may be understood as a reflection of the universality of metaphor in similar cultures, or whether, together with the term *anti-Americanism* itself, there has also been a transfer of framing and metaphor from English to Italian. This may have come about as a result of the translation choices made when reporting English language political speeches and/or English-language news agency feeds. The extent to which metaphors are transferred across languages offers a particularly interesting area for further research and it would be well-suited to a CADS approach.

## 5.4 Case study 2: Metaphor and humour in review articles

### 5.4.1 Metaphors and meaning potential

As we saw from the first case study, metaphors used to describe *anti-Americanism* could be assigned to areas of meaning (sea, fire, disease) which can be defined as natural entities or, for Charteris Black (2004) as natural disasters. Their underlying notion is that of *anti-Americanism* being potentially out of control (see Chapter 3), that is, the fear of a natural force which may not respond to our attempts to control it. Terms such as *virulent, tsunami, inflamed* are indeed related to disease, sea and fire but particularly to the negative aspects of these entities, for instance there are no references to calm beauty of the sea, nothing about healthful air, nothing about wonderful colours. Nor are the warming and useful aspects of fire being called up in these metaphors. It is clear that the pragmatic uses of the metaphor require that only certain features are foregrounded by the metaphor chosen and this is where the generalizations of conceptual metaphor rather miss a point. As Bublitz says "in pragmatic expressions the normal semantic values of a word are not necessarily relevant" (1996: 88).

Metaphors, as many have pointed out, are not explicit about the grounds of comparison. Charteris Black points out that in metaphor:

> statements are made as if they were connected and the reader is forced to consider their relations for himself. The reason why these statements should have been selected is left for him to invest; he will invent a variety of reasons and order them in his own mind. I suggest that engaging in the act of stretching the resources of language involved in metaphor is a way of forging a stronger interpersonal bond between speaker and hearer that extends beyond simply poetry. This is because – like many other features of language – such as a shared regional accent, shared access to a genre or other involvement in a discourse community – metaphor bonds people in a joint act of meaning creation.
>
> Creativity is necessary *both* for those who employ metaphor in everyday language use *and* for those who interpret it. (Charteris Black 2004: 12)

The variable possibilities of interpretation of metaphor are a function of meaning in general. Hanks uses a simile likening meanings to events, claiming that words in isolation have an abstract *meaning potential* rather than clearly defined meaning, and that the precise contribution that a word makes to the interpretation of a complex linguistic expression is generated in context with each event:

> Each content word in a language, like a great international airport, represents a place where things come together, meet, and go off in different directions – a huge set of interchange points with various sorts of connections: internal connections to beliefs in the mind of the speaker, interpersonal connections to the beliefs of other users of the same language, intra-lingual connections to other words in the same language, and putative connections to objects in the world [...] meanings are events – events that are for the most part only momentary, transitory, evanescent. (Hanks 2010: 1)

One anecdotal example of how different meanings of a metaphor can be salient for different people was made clear when, in order to see if there was a stable perception of evaluation, one of the authors once asked a family group what they understood the grounds of comparison to be in the expression *raft of legislation,* in a set of examples found in British broadsheets with the general overall meaning of a noun of multitude. All the family members gave different answers: one said it was a bundle of parliamentary measures around the same topic, linked in the same way as parts of a raft are linked by being tied together; another said it was a set of measures aimed at saving a situation like a life raft; yet another said it was intended to solve a number of problematic situations with a hastily put together vehicle like a raft is put together with minimal ingredients. It is clear that all were focusing on individual but different elements of the meanings of *raft* in order to explain the metaphor. They took different features of the meaning potential, each highlighting a different aspect to make sense of a conventional metaphor. Their interpretations represented a willingness to make approximate sense of a metaphor without troubling too much about exact meanings and it would seem that the metaphor does not carry a stable evaluation. Given that metaphors are not explicit about the grounds of comparison, we can in fact interpret them often in slightly different ways according to the feature which we select as salient for us. This is not because language is a matter of individual meanings. We would not be able to understand each other if that were so. The repetitiveness of social life and interaction provides enough common ground for a shared language which allows us to understand each other, but there are at the same time personal factors because each individual's experience varies and different parts of lexical meanings can be prominent for different people at different times.[8] In much the same way that at a social event such as a party a dentist might be more aware of other peoples' teeth; a hairdresser of their hair colour, a linguist of their accent or idiolect, a person on the lookout for a new partner might focus on a totally different set of features, yet all experience the same event. Similarly, metaphors will activate meaning potential for us, and sometimes there will not always be agreements about exact meanings. This can become apparent from different definitions, even in corpus based dictionaries as we shall see from the following example.

Metaphorical extensions of word meaning enter into the language with considerable frequency, as seen in our corpus of humorous opinion pieces. For example, the set of items, *trouser*, *neck* and *scarf* are the result of such metaphorical extensions departing from their normal use as concrete nouns.[9] It is clear

8. See Chapter 1: the idiom or phraseological principle of language is the dominant, default mode both of *producing* and *interpreting* discourse. We make use of prefabs or schema templates because we rarely recount experiences which are entirely novel and, even if we did, we would talk of them in ways that related them to previously acquired knowledge. Listeners also rely on them heavily in *interpreting* discourse, because phraseological recall requires less time and effort than constant rule-driven synthesis because it helps them to relate what is being said to what they already know and, simply, because it is the way the hearer expects the discourse to be organised.

9. The theory of *norms* and *exploitations*. Hanks (2004) applies the insights of prototype theory and Sinclairian text analysis to the empirical evidence of large corpora. "By studying words in context, we can identify the normal patterns of usage that are associated with each word. A meaning, or meaning potential, can then be associated with each pattern. Thereby, lexical entropy is reduced. A central question in this approach to language analysis concerns metaphors and idioms. Conventional metaphors and idioms are classified as 'norms' (i.e. conventional uses), while dynamic, ad-hoc metaphors are classified as 'exploitations' of norms.

from their colligation patterns and inflected forms (*trousered, necked, scarfed*) that these can act more like verbs than nouns; their pragmatic and textual associations also emerge from reading the concordance lines of their occurrence; the first were mostly from business or sports contexts but in general they were a feature of opinion pieces, often with an ironic or humorous tone. Reading the concordance lines provides encounters with this variation or extension of meaning and enables us to assign some kind of referential meaning from the context, but most of all a clear evaluative prosody of ironic distancing or disapproval. Macmillan *Online Dictionary* definition for *trouser* (vb) ('to get or take money for yourself by stealing') was found to be at odds with the corpus data in terms of referential meaning, as we can see from Examples (1)–(3), which do not fit the definition of stealing.

(1) Top of the charts with a developing nation's debt-busting pounds 250m. But then, everyone (most of all blue-chip sponsors) loves winners. And seven-times champ Michael Schumacher **trousers** nearly pounds 600k a week. (*Guardian 2005*)

(2) So I share Scholey's pain at the sudden loss of a 12-month salary he might have been hoping to **trouser**, in return for a few games in the seconds and a bit of slap and tickle in the Twenty20. I believe the time has now come for players to be prepared for when they strike a run of poor form, like Schofield's last year, or mine from 1983, or Hicky's Test career. (*Guardian 2005*)

(3) The verb "**trouser**" is much loved by the writers of the Guardian's business Notebook. Scarcely a day goes by without them accusing a company executive of **trousering** an inflated bonus or of having **trousered** an inappropriate pension. Rarely can so much indignation have been communicated so succinctly. Like Crystal Palace manager Iain Dowie's "bouncebackability", room must surely be made in the Oxford dictionary for this new addition to our lexicon. Scrutiny of the nation's business leaders by the heavyweight press has increasingly taken on tabloid overtones in recent years. (*Guardian 2005*)

The third example gives us more pragmatic information: *much loved by the writers of the Guardian's business Notebook; tabloid overtones* and clear evidence of the negative evaluative prosody with co-text items *accusing, inflated bonus, indignation*. Clearly the Macmillan corpus did not have many instantiations of this kind and the "stealing" element of the meaning needs revision. The *Cobuild Dictionary for Advanced Learners* is more satisfactory: "if you say that someone **trousers** a

---

However, conventional metaphors can still be distinguished from literal meanings. At least in some cases, conventional metaphors differ from literal senses by their particular syntagmatic patterns." (2004: 274).

sum of money you mean that they receive it usually when they do not deserve it or should not take it". Although there is a difference in the referential meanings given, in both dictionary definitions the evaluation is central to the meaning. We are not just taking a noun and converting it into a verb form when we use the metaphorical extension, we are adding an evaluation.

Further examples are to be found with *necked* and *scarfed* where the negative evaluation seems to suggest carelessness about consequences as well as something about the nature of the product, the amount consumed and the speed with which it is done; (*Macmillan's Online Dictionary* gives: *neck* to drink something very quickly and *scarf,* which they claim colligates with *down*, to eat a lot of something very quickly); though we see from the following examples from the SiBol 05 corpus (as described in 0.4.1), that *necking* is not necessarily drinking a liquid, as we can see in Example (6), and *scarfing* is not always colligated with *down,* as in Example (8).

(4) How this affects the performance is really a question for our sober friend, as it is likely that the rest of the audience will be insensible to such nuances, having **necked** a bottle of house fizz during the all-too- short interval.

(5) As teenagers my friends and I were convinced that there was a correlation between the amount drunk and the likelihood of becoming a supermodel, so we **necked** gallons of the stuff and happily contributed to the phenomenal growth of the bottled-water industry.

(6) Harvey was sacked from the boyband following some unguarded remarks about the drug ecstasy along the lines of: he'd **necked** 12 pills in one night and driven home, plus ecstasy can make you a better person.

(7) Yes, the library. Oh, didn't I say? Adjoining the main dining room was a small library. With books on shelves and lamps and armchairs and all that. And four tables set up. At one point, three Chinese ladies came in and ate there. **Scarfed** big steaming bowls of noodle soup in a library. Weird, man. Like, furry teacup weird. But don't worry, on inquiry we discovered that the bookcases cannot be opened. The books are just for show.

(8) Wiser Democratic heads think that Kerry just was not the right candidate to take on Bush. A fully paid up member of the windsurfing, claret-**scarfing**, bien pensant (he can even pronounce it correctly) East Coast elite, he lacked what it takes to appeal to a majority of the American electorate.

Such extensions are, if we are to judge from these examples, informal and possibly generational. They are neologistic forms as we might judge from the definitions given by online dictionaries and belong to informal spoken or computer-mediated discourse, but are played with in other discourse types, as here.[10] When learning how these metaphorical extensions are used it is the attitudinal flavour that is picked up, while the elements of the actual referential meaning – very fast or just large amounts? liquid or solid? transgressive item or junk food? – are often less easy to pin down. As always, we need to be aware that we cannot always identify which of the semantic features was prominent for the speaker at the time – we have only the co-text to help us. We can again refer back to Hanks (2000):

> The meaning potential of each word is made up of a number of components, which may be activated cognitively by other words in the context in which it is used. These cognitive components are linked in a network which provides the whole semantic base of the language, with enormous dynamic potential for saying new things and relating the unknown to the known. (Hanks 2000: 214)

This is how we make sense of metaphors and how we understand the grounds of comparison which are implicit in their use. The function of relating the unknown to the known and explaining the abstract by means of a concrete concept is part of the pragmatic function of metaphor. As the first case study in this chapter has shown there are a number of conventional conceptual metaphors which evaluate

---

10. *Scarf*: data from online dictionaries:

Online dictionary.com. *scarf*: verb (used with object), verb (used without object) Slang. to eat, esp. voraciously (often fol. by down or up): to *scarf down* junk food. …

Urbandictionary. *scarf*: eat devour inhale consume gorge neck head sweater chow down munch … To pig out or "down" food really fast and hastily. I *scarfed down* the burger. … and used especially when time is of the essence. www.answers.com/topic/

Free online dictionary. *scarf*: To eat or drink voraciously; devour: "Americans *scarf down* 50 million hot dogs on an average summer day" (George F. Will). … *www.thefreedictionary.co.* You *scarfed down* a Big Mac. You inhaled the large fries. You slurped down that double milkshake. But now you have to explain your less than … *digg.com/…/Ten_Excuses_For_Eating_at_McDonald_s* -

Data from websites
21 Feb 2010 … Breakfast sales had grown at a ravenous pace during the boom years as busy workers *scarfed down* sausage biscuits on the way to the office, …*www.huffingtonpost.com/…/unemployment-pushes-fastf_*

26 Oct 2009… making the statement that, "Hey, beating the Raiders is so easy that I can do it while *scarfing down* some delicious wieners. …*sports.yahoo.com/…/shut***down***…/Oakland-hot-dogs-get-a-big-time-endorsement-from?…* – *Stati Uniti* -

I just *scarfed down* a large Pizza Hut pizza General Discussion discussion. *www.physicsforums.com/showthread.php?t=151886* -

10 Apr 2008 … Scarf/*scarfed down* has always been the form we use (in my neck of the woods) when we're talking about eating something very enthusiastically … *forum.wordreference.com/showthread.php?t=908730*

by using one particular aspect of natural phenomena to describe a political stance. We will now look at less conventional metaphors and their use in evaluation but which have the added pragmatic aim of being humorous. The examples of humorous opinion pieces provide many examples of a particular repertoire of metaphor use, involving amplifying and intensifying resources, including hyperbole, irony and the metonymic use of socio-cultural references. Like all metaphors and similes these are comparisons or analogies of a kind but, unlike the use of figurative language to explain or to make clear, they involve metaphorical or metonymic comparisons which would be opaque and bewildering for any reader who is unfamiliar with the wide range of cultural tokens they employ.

### 5.4.2 Humour and metaphor resources

Certain instances of the hedging device *a sort of*, which is essentially a classification or taxonomical metaphor though often used for the purpose of intentional lack of precision, can be applied to many areas of human activity. The examples found in the SiBol corpus frequently involved one salient pattern; they seemed to involve reference to "known" information for evaluative purposes, nearly always involving proper names, place names and brand names or other specifics. The following examples are taken from SiBol 93 and SiBol 05:

(9) **a sort of** cross between Edna Everage and Margaret Thatcher

(10) combines the joys of Julie Andrews with the punch of Arnold Schwarznegger **a sort of** Goldilocks on crack

(11) the Super Soaker **a sort of** Kalashnikov of water pistols

(12) **a sort of** Norman St John Stevas without jokes

(13) **a sort of** Out of Africa twinned with Who's Afraid of Virginia Woolf

(14) Peter Brooke is **a sort of** toffs' John Prescott

(15) Sir John Falstaff **a sort of** upmarket Gazza

(16) Sylvania Waters **a sort of** maritime Chigwell

All these stand out as being non-descriptive and assume the reader's recognition of the names involved and the sharing of certain values in terms of the evaluation that might be applied to the name. A good proportion of the examples came from certain high-profile writers of humorous opinion pieces, in reviews. The reviews were regular features of their papers at the time, many from the Sunday supplements, and evaluation plays a key role. The evaluative style foregrounded is a very culturally constrained one but represents a frequent feature of the British broadsheet press, a style mixing informality with force of opinions and a marked use of irony and figurative language.

In these opinion pieces, ostensibly reviews, an experience (reading a book, watching a programme, driving a car, eating at a particular restaurant), has been delegated to the writer who has the responsibility for evaluating that experience for the readers, thus having to convey both hard facts (for example, price, location, scientific data) and subjective sense impressions (sight, sound, motion, taste, hearing) in order to enable them to make decisions about purchases or a choice of leisure activities, (places to go, productions to watch, cars to buy, food to eat). Conveying experiences through language often involves comparisons and thus metaphor is a useful tool.

However on reading the opinion pieces one becomes aware that the aim is not just that of evaluation since the semantic feature which is being highlighted in the comparison is not always clear, for instance, in Example (14), what has Peter Brooke got in common with John Prescott and why is he considered to be an upper class example of these characteristics? They have another purpose alongside that of simple description, namely, to amuse. The genre uses humour to gain the readers' alignment and humour is the main purpose of the text; idioms, irony and non-literal meanings are part of the repertoire and if not understood or read compliantly as humour the text purpose is lost. The schemata, scripts and narrative shifts called up by the humorous examples given in metaphor form derive from a cultural context shared between writer and readers and often involve parody and pastiche. The corpus under examination might be said to be prototypical but the template is widely used in broadsheets and tabloids.

With the intention of comparing evaluative styles, then, we compiled a small corpus of a series of opinion pieces by columnists of British broadsheets, mostly review articles of a variety of artefacts and events. This corpus contains 256,353 tokens and over 200 texts from 2004 and 2005; this will be referred to as the Humorous Opinion pieces Corpus or the HO Corpus.

As noted in our introduction, we hold that corpus work is essentially comparative, no claims can be made about patterns unless one can say with what the results are being compared, and so another corpus was built to be used as a background corpus. This consists of opinion pieces in the form of reviews published by the *Times Literary Supplement* (also from 2004 and 2005) and will be referred to as the TLS Corpus (216,65 tokens). The reviews in the TLS Corpus, commissioned by the journal from their pool of contributors, are signed and cover the evaluation of new books, films, journals and live performances in much the same way as the HO Corpus does, although the authors are more varied, appear less regularly and do not rely on an established relationship with the reader. The domain is close to the academic though it does not coincide with it as it is intended for a general public rather than a specialist one. It has a serious tone overall; though individual reviewers may use humour and irony it is essentially a restrained publication. This discourse type was chosen because it consists of evaluative discourse of a similar kind, namely, the review, but with considerable differences in the way the evaluation is realised. The purpose of the exercise, then, consisted in looking at how the two sets of writers achieve evaluation through language and how they differ. Is it possible to identify the patterns or repeated regularities of forms in the ways in which the humorous review texts present their evaluations of experiences through language?

The question might also be seen in terms of whether it is possible to identify the tricks in the tool kit of humorous writers by starting with quantitative methods and then examining them more closely via a qualitative analysis of the key resources. Many of the resources of metaphor belong to the open class part of the lexicon and the list of items to be sifted through is varied; it is in the qualitative analysis that we see much of the evaluation. We chose to examine the HO Corpus from the above mentioned 'loud' journalists, comparing it with the reference TLS Corpus of evaluative texts from the more sober or 'quieter' *Times Literary Supplement* to see what the key items might be which differentiate the two evaluative styles. Identifying the sets of key items involved the use of *WordSmith Tools* (Scott 1999) software, in particular *Wordlist* and *Keywords*. Other corpus analysis resources used were *Concgram* (Greaves 2009) and the *Wmatrix* facilities (Rayson 2009) which provided the semantic and POS tagging. Here we will be looking specifically at the use of figurative, metaphorical devices.

### 5.4.3 Figurative language as part of the humorous style

One aspect of the evaluative style lies in how writers seek to negotiate and engage readers, as part of rhetoric or the power of persuasion. One of the functions of evaluation is to construct and maintain relations between reader and writer and it can be used to direct and control behaviour (Chapter 2); in this case it is directed as much to the buying of newspapers as to eating in restaurants, choosing of cars or voting for a political party, since the features are read by many people who have no particular interest or intention of taking up the recommendation. Many people, however, buy the papers in order to read the contributions of these high-profile writers. Such evaluative discourse can reflect and impose a value system beyond that of the individual entity being evaluated. One particular kind of evaluative resource, the use of figurative language and recurrent patterns of metaphorical usage, is of interest to the discourse analyst since it is often used in subtle and even insidious ways in persuasive argument.

We can identify a number of signals which aid computer searches for instances where items are compared through the use of simile with the aim of describing the unfamiliar in familiar terms (we often describe a new experience in terms of a familiar one, using the closest experience we can identify) or to give a concrete parallel for an abstract concept. What Cameron and Deignan have called "tuning devices to negotiate the interpersonal aspects of situationally distinctive uses of language" (2003: pp. 149–160) are often used, almost as if to warn that figurative use of language is about to come into play. Such devices are found in similes and with hedging locutions, for example, *a sort of, kind of, like, a cross between*, which act as overt signals of figurative or fuzzy use of language. Such items are of course identifiable in the wordlist and in comparison with the TLS reference corpus, *sort, like* and *kind* all appear as key words. The search for this type of item falls into the fifth of Stefanowitsch's (2006) categories outlined in the introduction to this chapter.

On examination of the concordances of the abovementioned items the *TLS* examples turned out to involve more imprecise hedging than metaphorical usage while the HO Corpus shows mainly figurative use. Partington points out that there are variations in metaphorical use across discourse types

> The concordances of a *sort of* and *kind of* in newspaper corpora have a completely different story to tell. They were found proportionally far more frequently in metaphorical statements than they were in the [White House] briefings texts. This result, however, tells us more about the nature of the two types of discourse than about the hedges themselves. Newspapers texts are written and have relatively more relaxed time constraints in their production than spontaneous speech. In addition, some types of newspaper writing (notably the so-called comment and magazine-types) display considerable novelty and variety of expression. As a result they exhibit what we might call a much higher general *figurative density* than the briefings. The higher proportion of figurative uses of our hedges is most probably a simple reflection of this overall density. (2006b: 284)

The examples above with *sort of* showed how such figurative uses could juxtapose entities for variety and novelty of expression in ways which are deliberately incongruous. Incongruity is indeed a key feature of humorous uses of metaphor. Writers on humour, from Aristotle to Koestler, agree that incongruity is one of the necessary, though not sufficient, key features of humour.

### 5.4.4 Incongruous comparison

The HO Corpus data contains many cultural metaphors with proper names, brand names and place names being used metonymically or in similes for rhetorical purposes. Unlike much use of metaphor where something abstract is being made clear by relating it to a more concrete entity familiar from the physical world and our common experience (as was the case of the *anti-Americanism* metaphors examined above), here the semantic features which form the grounds of comparison are opaque to the outsider. The reference to shared experience tends to construct the relationship between writer and a particular set of supposedly "in-readers" by referencing pre-supposedly shared experience and thus shared values. To take a similar case from literature, when Hamlet compares his father to his uncle saying it is like comparing Hyperion to a satyr (*Hamlet* I.ii.141–145) he presupposes that the attributes of both are known and the evaluation of such attributes is shared, that all understand the evaluation of Hyperion is positive and that of the satyr is negative, with all that this entails.[11] The writer, in using metaphor, metonymy or simile, links two terms (target and source) according to features they are deemed to have in common, in order to make a comparison, claim similarity or a relationship between the two. If the two have very few features in common, coming from not just different semantic fields but incongruous ones, then the reader has to work hard to identify the features, to understand the comparison, and is thus being encouraged to engage with the text as with a verbal puzzle. If this is achieved after some effort of identification or an imaginative leap the reader is both impressed by the ingenuity of the writer and at the same time congratulates her/himself at having solved the problem (the "smugness effect" which helps create a sense of collusion between newspaper and its readers, Partington 1998: 140).

Although all metaphor and similes might be said to be incongruous, we find instances of particularly incongruous combinations in comparison. Concordance evidence shows how the item *between* links two entities in several different ways. Normally the two entities are meant to be similar in some way, to belong to the same category at least (*between me and you*) and, indeed, in the expression *between a rock and a hard place* they are synonyms. The expression *a cross between* also contains some idea of compatibility, in the sense that, as a metaphor from biology, essentially a breeding metaphor, species can only interbreed, creating a crossbreed, if similar enough. For example:

> […] and what I imagine to be a bison, but turns out to be zubron – a cross between a bison and a cow. (SiBol 05)

When, however, *between* appears in expressions such as *swing between* or *oscillate between* or *the difference between*, they can be antonyms, for example *the difference between extinction and survival, interplay between presence and absence*.[12]

11. Many think Hyperion was a beautiful young man. In fact in Greek mythology he was a god, more precisely, a Titan, with the characteristics of wisdom and watchfulness as the continuation of the quotation indicates. The satyr half-goat, half-man is characterised by drunkenness and lustfulness.

12. Examples from SiBol 05.

If we look at some examples of the use of *between* from the *TLS* corpus:

(17) **Between 1897 and 1903**, Sir William Laird Clowes produced in

(18) had provided for a compulsory exchange of populations **between Greece and Turkey**, but those Greeks,

(19) Edwardian England, a disquisition on the tensions **between law and justice**

(20) an institutional difference **between the USA and much of Europe** to which Lieven

(21) extreme tension; and a witch-hunting consensus **between rulers and ruled**

(22) highlight the disparity **between American wealth and Haitian immigrant poverty**

We see that *between* on its own is also used as a vehicle for comparison of entities from similar categories. In these examples *between* is used to link entities which are clearly from the same or related categories.

In the HO Corpus, on the other hand, in very many cases, the entities which are brought together are deliberately incongruous, the features they have in common are marginal to their definitions rather than prototypical, or are not immediately identifiable. The terms are juxtaposed for humorous effect:

(23) Tory candidates in Liverpool have banded together for mutual support like **a cross between** Al-Qaeda and the Famous Five

(24) ravishingly excellent -an unexpected, juicy **cross between** meaty liquorice and Noggin the Nog's bum.

Example (23) juxtaposes a terrorist group with a fictional children's group while Example (24) uses a cartoon Norse character's anatomy as part of an unexpectedly favourable comparison in a food review. Such comparisons compose a humour of the absurd. In many cases, *between* is used to create images of hyperbolic contradiction of similarity:

(25) the voters, forced to choose **between Mr Davis and being lowered into a vat of boiling pig's urine**

(26) when it comes to politeness, I think the British slot neatly **between the Israelis and the leopard seal**, a blubbery and vicious bastard that kills penguins for fun

(27) most customers would struggle to tell the difference **between a 1945 Chateau Pétrus and a glass of Ribena.**

In this type of figure the contrast lies in the different kinds of relation between [Item 1] and [Item 2]. Item 1 can be something everyday and normal whilst Item 2 is absurd, hyperbolic. Or in terms of evaluation Item 1 can be neutral or positive in evaluation while Item 2 is often exaggeratedly negative. On other occasions we can find instances of register play, Item 1 is middle to high register, Item 2 is often exaggeratedly low register which is a classic structure for performing *bathos*.

There are other signals of comparison to be found in the keywords for the HO Corpus suggesting these participate in salient patterns, in particular *like* and *if* (Table 5.5). These are markers of metaphor which can alert us to the presence of similes (strategy 5 in the list above from Stefanowitsch 2006).

**Table 5.5.** *like* and *if* frequencies in *HO* and TLS

| Word | %HO | %TLS | Keyness |
|---|---|---|---|
| *Like* | 0.41 | 0.17 | 273.8 |
| *If* | 0.34 | 0.18 | 143.9 |

On examination of the concordance lines these turn out to be core items in similes. They mostly rely on script and schemata recall linked to sensory perceptions, so we find terms such as *look like*, *sounds like*, *resembles*. However they all rely on the reader being able to make an imaginative leap and understand an allusion to something which is not always obvious. There is the same challenge to search for similarity in our experience without the comparison either being transparent or involving easily retrievable sensory perceptions. Nor are they immediately obvious in terms of evaluation because the target and source are from deliberately incongruous contexts, moving from formal, public to intimate or domestic,[13] or from banal to high-flown, or recalling incongruous cultural tokens. One of the ways such scenarios are called up is with the phrase *as if*:

(28) Then there are a lot of things that come wrapped up, **as if** they'd been surreptitiously spat into pastry

(29) an alarming way of clearing his throat at the end of a sentence, **as if** about to gob on you.

(30) I am amazed at how many people can pick up a menu and sigh **as if** it were a tax form

(31) It all tastes **as if** it's come in a tanker marked 'Tepid, brown, vaguely oriental'

13. We should perhaps note here that anatomy and physiology are key semantic tags in comparison with the BNC spoken corpus and that one aspect of threats to a speaker's positive face concerns the loss of physical control over the body and emotion leakage, non-control of laughter or tears.

(32) Ask it to power slide and it looks at you **as if** you've invited it for a threesome with the vicar

(33) Mr Paisley made his slow progress towards his seat **as if** to lay eggs on the sand

These examples all call up scenarios whose effect depends on claiming a similarity of sight, sound, or taste between what is being evaluated and some other incongruous entity and rely on the reader to recognise the sense memory called up and appreciate the resemblance.

In other cases, we simply have to use our imagination to visualise some graphic scene:

(34) Countdown is a programme that oozes despair **like** a badly applied tourniquet.

(35) The House was **like** a carp pond after someone had tossed in an electric fire.

(36) The Stuart drove **like** a Buddhist butler.

(37) And so the Multipla was born, the first car to **resemble** an Amazonian tree frog.

(38) It made the Black Hole of Calcutta **resemble** a deserted ballroom

### 5.4.5 Intensification and hyperbole

Another feature of the figurative language in the corpus is an upscaling of the evaluations, by means of lexical build up, repetition and intensification, and the maximisation of lexis. Other effects are created through reversals of force and evaluation. The corpus contains many examples where there is a mixture of force resources, using a maximiser such as *all* or *every,* followed by a bathetic oxymoronic comparison. Table 5.6 shows the relative frequency of these two items in our corpora and as can be seen, both are more characteristic of the HO corpora.

**Table 5.6.** *all* and *every* frequencies in HO and *TLS*

| Word | %HO | %TLS | Keyness |
|---|---|---|---|
| *all* | 0.48 | 0.24 | 145.7 |
| *every* | 0.09 | 0.04 | 147.7 |

(39) the denouement has **all** the anticipatory excitement of a blocked lavatory.

(40) has **all** the aesthetic appeal of a pensioner's diseased gum

(41) the seats have **all** the body-hugging grip of a kitchen chair

(42) with **all** the elegant body language of a beanbag.

The phrase creates the expectation of something with very positive evaluation (*excitement, appeal*) using a pre-modified noun with quite specific positive features (*elegant, aesthetic*) and the expectation is let down by the description of something which is the antithesis of such positive features (*blocked lavatory*). Similar examples are found with just an adjective expressing a positive evaluation followed by an incongruous noun phrase comparison:

(43) truffle oil, which is about **as** Swedish **as** a limerick.

(44) **as** comfortable **as** steamrollers.

(45) **as** attractive **as** a sponsored town centre roundabout

(46) about **as** emotional **as** a tin opener.

(47) about **as** fashionable **as** vicarages.

(48) **As** dynamic **as** someone who's dead.

Many examples of simple hyperbole, exaggerations which suggest a disillusioned expecting-the-worst gloom on the part of the reviewer, are accompanied by fanciful metaphors:

(49) **Every** mouthful of food eaten outdoors in Britain will contain a wasp, and **every** slurp of drink a fly the size of Jeff Goldblum.

(50) lines and actors not given enough time to breathe. Almost **every** utterance had to move great marble slabs of plot.

(51) if you have overhead spots and oversized plates, then **every** wipe mark on the rim shines like tubercular snot.

The item *every* also appears as a keyword in the *HO* corpus. Most exaggerations are examples of extreme case formulations. The writer does not expect to be called to account for the exactitude of the statement but expects the reader to understand that the formulation represents the writer's attitude.

We can also see how the hedge *a bit* combines with the simile signalling device *like* to introduce an incongruous or unlikely comparison, generally expressing a very negative evaluation of the entity being reviewed:

(52) with another Rover 75 to review a car like the Maserati is **a bit like** asking a refugee from Chad to review the Ivy.

(53) said to be the best fish-and-chip shop in London, which is **a bit like** being called the best Relate counsellor in Lagos.

(54) the wallpaper of gaudy flowers that looks **a bit like** they've skinned a dead BA aeroplane tail and glued it on to the wall

Another set involving metonymic reference to people or places involve the presumption of common knowledge both of a person or place and the attendant evaluation:

(55) bandwagon of cosmopolitan holiday orientalism. It's **a bit** Nobu, **a bit** Roka and **a touch** Hakkasan.

(56) It was **all** terribly Tate Modern and jolly pleasing on the eye,

(57) It would have **all** been too Women's Institute

(58) sniffing out tax loopholes **as** fervently **as** a cash-in-hand plasterer

(59) In terms of food, it's **all a bit**, well, a bit Notting Hill.

(60) Ferraris are **just a little bit** disgusting, with a dash of Beckham and a touch of Rio Ferdinand

(61) to be **a bit** more Tracy and Hepburn and **a bit** less Ken Loach does The West Wing

Register echoes depend on familiarity with other genres. In the following example an advertising register is summoned up and the qualities of materials are used metaphorically in the description of the difference between two politicians:

(62) Some people go for the Bakelite retro Aspel, where others prefer the drip-dry, stain-resistant Titchmarsh.

Irony in this discourse type plays with a mismatch or reversal, not so much of the ideational meaning, but of the loudness or weight, and of the evaluation. The kind of word play we have been looking at functions by combining shifts between the open choice and the phraseological principle (see Chapter 1), with disconfirmation of expectations created by idiom signals. The echoing of cliché and register triggers a priming in much the same way as we expect the next track to begin on a familiar CD as soon as the last one ends, and the unexpected shifting of fixed or frozen wording of idioms creates a collocational shock (for example *drunk as a sock, a rabble soothing speech*) just as the incongruous juxtaposition of register creates a shift in narrative with disconfirmation of script recall. Readers are primed by the relationship created by their familiarity with the genre and by the register signals to apply the irony frame in processing meaning. Readers who have not been so primed may well miss the point.

Many of these comparisons, as we saw, involve sense-based scenarios, calling up body-memories. Often intimate and personal scenarios are juxtaposed with institutional figures or entities, a kind of oxymoron. At times we find ironic reversal of evaluation and at others an increase of force of the evaluation with hyperbole and maximum amplification. Hyperbolic signals in the shape of adverbial intensifiers *(deeply, particularly, especially, indeed, certainly, doubly, genuinely, bitterly, supremely)* are prevalent given that hyperbole is the principal key to the comic effects being sought.

The comic effects analysed in this second case study, in particular the use of hyperbole, bathos and register effects, have a good deal in common with some of those found in the humorous writings of PG Wodehouse (see the next chapter), although the repertoire is more limited.

## 5.5 Conclusions

In these two case-studies, we have looked at a number of the techniques outlined by Stefanowitsch (2006), namely, searching for source-domain vocabulary, searching for target-domain vocabulary and searching for markers of metaphor.

As Partington and Taylor (2010) emphasise, metaphors are almost always evaluative in normal (that is, not de-evaluated, Chapter 2.4) discourse, in fact, to evaluate is often their major function ("Juliet is the sun"). One issue that arises in both case studies here, is the need to look at the occurrences in context in order to identify evaluative meanings. In the first case study we saw how the evaluation of the metaphor *anti-Americanism* is A CRIME was actually nested and a more accurate description was a *anti-Americanism* (is treated as) A CRIME (by *other people*). In the second case study, we note how metaphors do not only call up a particular concept, but refer to particular favourable or unfavourable aspects of these concepts. As we have seen in previous chapters this checking of occurrences with the context by going into the text is a constant factor in CADS methodology.

Until recently it was thought that the contribution of corpus linguistics and lexical grammar in the study of metaphor was bound to remain marginal, given that there is no such thing as special metaphorical lexis (see Stefanowitsch 2006: 1–16). In recent times a fair number of imaginative, ingenious studies using corpora have appeared (for example Stefanowitsch & Gries eds 2006).

Nevertheless it remains true that, compared to some other areas of CADS the role of corpus techniques is limited. They have been employed mainly in the collection and organisation of examples, to look for texts which are statistically likely to have a high figurative density, in the comparison of frequency for common metaphors. The lion's share of the more delicate analysis of figurative language remains a task for the human analyst.

## Suggestions for further reading

Introduction (free) to Charteris-Black J. 2006 *Corpus Approaches to Critical Metaphor Analysis*:
⟨http://www.palgrave.com/PDFs/1403932921.Pdf⟩
On metaphor and language teaching:
Sznajder, H.S. 2010. A corpus-based evaluation of metaphors in a business English textbook. *English for Specific Purposes* 29: 30–42.
On cross-cultural/cross-linguistic discourse studies of metaphor
Deignan, A. & Potter, L. 2004. A corpus study of metaphors and metonyms in English and Italian. *Journal of Pragmatics* 36: 1231–1252.
On teaching about the use of metaphor, especially its evaluative function:
Partington A. & Taylor, C. 2010. *Persuasion in Politics,* 2nd edn. LED: Milano, Unit 5 "Metaphors and company: The subtle persuaders" 85–112.

## Suggestions for further research

1. If you have access to any heterogeneric corpus (for example the BNC or bank of English) or a newspaper corpus (in any language), make concordances of parts of the body – head, hand, leg and so on, making sure to make separate concordances for singular and plural forms, for instance, *eye* and *eyes*. What do you observe?
2. Using the same corpus, make concordances of colour terms, *white, black, green, red, gold, golden,* and so on. What do you observe?
3. Compile a corpus of literary texts from *Project Gutenberg* and concordance lexical items relating to weather. Does weather tend to be used as source or target?
4. Compile a corpus of romantic fictional texts from ⟨http://www.millsandboon.co.uk/onlineReads.asp⟩ (see the appendix for instructions on how to do this using *BootCaT*) and look at the collocates of male and female pronouns. Can you identify any patterns of metaphor use?
5. Select a recent political speech, e.g. from ⟨http://www.totalpolitics.com/speeches/⟩ or ⟨http://www.americanrhetoric.com/⟩, and perform a close reading, identifying any possible metaphorical candidates. Then, use the *Corpus of Contemporary American English (CoCA)* to explore how these metaphors are used in other domains.

CHAPTER 6

# Corpus-assisted stylistics

## Investigating author style

Stylistics is usually associated with the study of the language of literature and has been defined as "[t]he science of literary style; the study of literary features" (*OED*), "the study of the language of literature" (Wynne 2006: 223) and "a way of bringing the study of language and literature closer together" (Mahlberg 2007: 219) and certainly the lion's share of work in the area – and the case study in this chapter is no exception – has been carried out on what most people would have no problem in classifying as literature and very commonly on the work of a single, known writer. Among stylistics work which incorporates corpus use we find studies on Dickens (Mahlberg 2007, 2009), Austen (Fischer-Starke 2010) and Wordsworth (Morley 2007). Culpeper (2002) analyses the speech patterns of various characters in Shakespeare's *Romeo and Juliet*, Stubbs (2005) is the study of a single work by Conrad, namely, *Heart of Darkness*, whilst Louw (1993) uses concordancing to shed light on meanings in a poem by Larkin. Beyond the boundary of traditional "literary" texts, McIntyre (2010, 2012) investigates dialogue in Reservoir Dogs and other films.

As Carter insists, there is no clear-cut distinction between literary and non-literary language and "literariness" is best considered both as a complex subjective judgment and also as a cline "with some uses of language being marked as more literary than others in certain domains and for certain judges within that domain" (2004: 69). Indeed we have seen in the previous chapters in this book how stylistic features often associated with literature, such as irony, metaphor and word-play can be frequent in discourse types not normally considered to be literature, such as those to be found in newspapers. Semino & Short (2003) in their book entitled *Corpus Stylistics* recount an impressive and painstaking attempt to devise a system for categorising and annotating the reporting (or, as they term it, the presenting) of language or thought events, that is, direct speech, indirect speech, free indirect thought, and so on, in a large tripartite corpus only one of whose sections is classically literary, the others consisting of news reports and biographical narratives respectively. A further non-literary development of stylistics is forensic linguistics which analyses written documents or transcripts in the attempt to provide evidence in legal cases of disputed authorship (Coulthard 2007). This follows upon earlier work using corpus-derived statistical data for disputed literary authorship identification (see Hockey 1980 for an overview).

What all the various branches of stylistics *do* have in common is the purpose of identifying and describing the distinctive characteristics of a particular authorial style. In most cases the author is known, but in disputed authorship and forensic linguistics study, the identification of the distinguishing style of an author is the point of the exercise, whilst in the case of Semino & Short's news report corpus, we can talk of a "collective" authorial style, characteristic of that particular discourse type. Stylistic studies are by their nature comparative, the particular characteristics of one author or set of authors are only evident and available for evaluation when their work is compared to that of others. On occasion too a researcher may be interested in comparing the characteristics of one of an author's works with another or with the rest of their output. The choice of comparative texts is clearly an important one; comparing texts from entirely different fields of discourse could well result in a surfeit of information, too much noise. With this in mind, Morley (2007) in order to evaluate the features of Wordsworth's poetry, downloaded from the Project Gutenberg site both a corpus of 30,600 words of Wordsworth's works, and a comparative corpus of nearly three million words containing poetry, novels, essays, private letters and magazines from the period roughly contemporaneous with Wordsworth's output, that is, 1780 to 1820. Stubbs constructs two corpora with which to contrast the language features of *Heart of Darkness*, the first, entitled FICTION containing 710,000 words of the "imaginative prose" sections of the Brown, LOB, Frown and FLOB corpora, the second WRITTEN consisting of the one-million word written component of the BNC. Fischer-Starcke (2010) contrasts a corpus containing Jane Austen's novels with another of the novels of her contemporary writers, whilst both Hori (2004) and Mahlberg (2007) do the same for Dickens. The case study reported below avails itself of similar contrastive corpora.

It is not difficult to discern that there is a large area of overlap between corpus-assisted discourse studies and corpus stylistics. In this volume we have stressed repeatedly the methodological importance of comparison among discourse types in CADS work, and stylistics is similarly contrastive. Moreover, as we have seen, the stricture that the subject material of stylistics be literary is not hard and fast and some stylistics work has been performed on entire discourse types like news reports or biographies. In addition, CADS and stylistics share the common aim of uncovering distinctive language features and meanings not easily accessible through other traditional forms of analysis alone. As Stubbs puts it, such studies "must provide results which would be impossible" – we might add *or much harder* – "to obtain without a computer" (2005: 5). Finally, the most influential of corpus stylistics studies have combined corpus techniques with other forms of analyses, in close analogy to the mixed methodology advocated in CADS. Stubbs for instance integrates his statistical analyses, including his concordancing of key items and his computer-assisted searches for common word frames, with extensive background reading of critics of Conrad's work and also with observations from his own close reading of the text, for instance, that it is punctuated with long strings of adjectives and nouns such as "the air was warm, thick, heavy, sluggish" and "their glance was guileless, profound, confident, and trustful" (2005: 15). In light of this we will follow his lead and for the rest of the chapter use the designation "corpus-*assisted* stylistics". Indeed it is our contention that corpus stylistics which refused to avail itself of traditional non-computerised modes of analysis would be rather perverse (unless, of course, the very object of the exercise was to discover the different results obtained with statistical analyses and conventional close reading).

One potential distinction between CADS and corpus-assisted stylistics may reside in the question of *appreciation*, of the expression of value judgement of the linguistic features uncovered and analysed in the course of a study. It is far more customary for the stylistician than for the corpus linguist, even of the CADS variety, to combine the roles of analyst and critic: "In literary stylistics we assume that the artistic effect of a text is something that is noticeable. Literary appreciation and linguistic analyses are not independent" (Mahlberg 2007: 223).

This brings us to the thorny question of whether and how much linguistic theory is able to interpret texts qualitatively, to distinguish between "high" literature and other discourse types. As Stubbs reminds us, Sinclair (1975) argued that "there is a serious gap in linguistic theories if they cannot explain the language of those texts which have the highest literary and cultural prestige" (Stubbs 2005: 6). However it remains doubtful whether formal microlinguistic theories such as lexical grammar, which are concerned with formulating generalisations about language use which are independent of social and cultural norms and personal value judgements, are able to contribute very much to explaining textual appreciation. Take, for example Ahl's assertion that "Europeans [...] are trained to admire irony but to disapprove of puns" (1988: 21). Appreciation training would be more properly a topic of cultural studies rather than lexical grammar. Similarly, an author such as George Orwell is appreciated by many readers for his political acumen and passionate advocacy of tolerance as much as for his prose style and no amount of microlinguistic analysis could explain this admiration.

Other aspects of the limits of microlinguistic theory in evaluating texts qualitatively include the following. Hoey (2005, 2007), Hori (2004) and Partington (1995, 1998), among others, have studied unusuality of collocation as evidence of literary creativeness and collocational phenomena have, of course, been much studied in Firthian linguistics. However, unusual collocations abound in both poetry and newspaper headlines and it is by no means certain that linguistic analysis alone can detect any qualitative difference between their use in the two discourse types.

Morley (2007) is able to detect favoured vocabulary items of Wordsworth, Blake and Keats as well as certain colligational and grammatical information on position in the phrase but these are linguistic facts and they do not tell us who is the "better" poet nor why all three are so rightly revered.

Johnson (2010) employs statistical techniques to compare various English translations of the works of the Nobel-prize winning Italian author Grazia Deledda. She discovers distinct differences in the way points of view are related in the translation, some of which she sees as closer to the original Italian. But we then still come up against the hoary issue of the degree to which faithfulness of translation is excellence of translation, again a question outside the remit of formal microlinguistics.

Partington devises theories of both irony (and see Chapter 4) and word-play (2009b) using concepts derived from evaluation studies and lexical grammar but these theories remain largely descriptions of mechanisms, whilst the efficacy and appeal of episodes of irony and of word-play depend largely on their relation to the context of production, the relationship between participants, and so on.

The one linguistic concept of most use in the course of the case study reported below is that of register, but register is only partly a microlinguistic notion, being also a sociolinguistic and psycholinguistic construct (see below).

But all this is not cause for pessimism. Having raised these caveats, what statistical corpus methods can contribute to corpus-assisted stylistics is to indicate, in analogy with other forms of CADS, particular distinctive tendencies within an author's – or group of authors' – style which may warrant further scrutiny. Such scrutiny will involve a combination of linguistic analysis and critical appraisal. Conversely, on noting the use of a particular language feature during qualitative close reading the analyst can turn to the concordancer to collect and examine other instances. Stylistics is a pluri-disciplinary field and the stylistician is constantly switching linguistic and literary-critical hats, or as Mahlberg puts it, "literary appreciation and linguistic analysis are not independent. In fact they can be described as in cyclic motion" (2007: 223; also Leech & Short 1981: 13).

## 6.1 The comic prose of P.G. Wodehouse

Pelham Grenville Wodehouse is widely recognised as perhaps the greatest humorous novelist in the English language and frequently, also, simply as a great creative genius. According to Gerald Gould, book critic for *The Observer* newspaper: "In the most serious sense of the word [Wodehouse] is a great artist. He has founded a school, a tradition. He has made a language [...] He has explained a generation." Other comic writers are prominent among his admirers. Hilaire Belloc called Wodehouse "the best living writer of English", whilst Douglas Adams tells us, "I have devoured his work repeatedly [...] not merely because he is a great comic writer, but because I think he is arguably the greatest musician of the English language I have ever encountered." However, as Golab notes, "little evidence has been shown to justify this claim", there is almost no literature "attempting to specify the reasons for Wodehouse's success as a humorous writer" (2004: 35). There have been very few linguistic-stylistic studies of Wodehouse's works and certainly none which incorporate corpus analysis.

## 6.2 The corpora

The first step, then, in studying the particularities of Wodehouse's language play was to construct a corpus of his work by downloading the available texts from the Gutenberg site. Due to copyright these are confined to the early works from the 1910s and 1920s. The resulting corpus contains circa 1.1 million words of text. For purposes of comparison, two other corpora were also compiled from Gutenberg, one of ordinary fiction written during the same period consisting of circa 1.5 million words, and another of comic writing, mostly from the same time but, given the relative paucity of material, also from a slightly earlier period, comprising circa one million words. These corpora were named PGW,[1] Novels and Humour, respectively. Their precise contents are listed in the Appendix to this chapter.

Both single-word and word-cluster (from two- to seven-word clusters, technically, 2- to 7-grams) frequency lists were then compiled by means of the *WordSmith WordList* tool for all three corpora, as well as another for Novels and Humour combined. These lists were then automatically compared by the *WordSmith Keywords* program, which thus produced a list of items that are relatively more frequent in the target corpus (PGW) compared to the comparison or background corpora (Novels, Humour and Novels plus Humour).[2] These are known as keyword and key-cluster lists, collectively key-item lists (more technically, key n-gram lists), and the higher in the list an item resides, the more particular (the

1. "PGW" being the initials.

2. The p-value was set at 0.000001.

more key or salient) it is to the set of texts from which it derives (in our case, to PGW). These make it possible to have a roughly objective picture of some of the specialities of Wodehouse's vocabulary and phraseology, at least as compared to other prose of his time.

However, frequency statistics can only begin to give an indication of a writer's style and strategies, and so the list analyses were accompanied by a close reading of the novel *The Code of the Woosters* (1938, henceforth *CW*), of fourteen excerpts from the novel *Much Obliged, Jeeeves* (1971, *MOJ*), reported in Golab (2004), and the short story *The Reverent Wooing of Archibald* (1929, *RWA*) from the collection *Mr Mulliner Speaking*. We also include a number of entries from the *Oxford Book of Modern Quotations* (*OMQ*).

## 6.3 Formality – informality

First of all, the keyword and key-cluster lists were found to contain a good number of words and expressions relating to reporting, perceiving and mental processes. The reporting items include:

> *say, said, uttered, speak, speech, words, remarks, mention, confide, what I mean, I'm bound to say, I mean to* say.

The perceiving items include:

> *perceived, eyed, gaze, become conscious/aware of, the spectacle of, became aware that, get* or *under the impression that.*

The mental processes items include:

> *suppose, idea, thinking, meditations, brooded, occurred to* (as in *it occurred to him that*), *to ascertain, the recollection of, to my mind, it seemed to me/to him.*

All these are ample evidence of how much of Wodehouse's prose, even when as here compared to other fiction, is composed of dialogue. Moreover, even when the writing does consist of narrative it is framed as talk. The Wooster stories are narrated in first person as a kind of internal dialogue, with the occasional reference to a potential "public" ("but one must be honest with one's public", "if I were to take it for granted that my public knows all about Gussie Fink-Nottle…"), whereas the *Mr Mulliner Speaking* tales are explicitly framed as stories being told by Mr Mulliner to the fellow members of the *Angler's Rest.*

The single most striking aspect of the key-items lists then is the number of words and expressions they contain which reflect imitation of everyday speech. First of all, we find a number of pronouns high in the keyword lists, that is, among the first 200 keywords: *you, I, me, he, him, your* and *my*. Just as striking is the number of contractions among the top 200 keywords: *it's, I'm, don't, you're, I've, didn't* and *wasn't*. These two groups of items are both of course further indication of the interactive-dialogic nature of Wodehouse's prose (dialogue at times with the reader and at times between characters).

The key-item lists also include several kinds of non-grammatical speech-indicating lexis, including upper-class slang like *blighter, dash it, by jove, rummy*, conversational constructions, including *you know, I mean, I suppose, awfully sorry, it's all right* and colloquial items, such as *chump, bloke, baffled*.

However, the lists also contain, conversely, a considerable number of strikingly formal items of various kinds. These include simple words like *injudicious, ascertain, enabled* but also more complex constructions such as, among others, *endeavouring to, proceeded to, the latter, as regards, at this juncture, the recollection of, had been compelled to, to the exclusion of all else/other things* etc., *the work of a moment, would be paltering with the truth*.

Concordancing some of these items revealed how Wodehouse employs them as part of various interesting comic techniques. First of all, he frequently mixes formalisms and informalisms very closely in the same segment of text, as was evident in the concordance of *as regards*, a relatively formal item often followed by slang or colloquialisms (our italics):

(1) **As regards** the fusing of her soul and mine, therefore, *nothing doing*.

(2) **As regards** his *getting blotto* …

(3) … **as regards** the foodstuffs *and what not* …

and, equally, of *endeavouring to*:

(4) He darted rapidly away, and the cabman, **endeavouring to** detain him, *snatched* at his overcoat.

(5) … and had *sat in a corner* behind a potted palm perspiring shyly and **endeavouring** to make conversation to a formidable nymph in pink.

(6) … where Bill, the fox-terrier, had encountered an acquaintance, and, to the accompaniment of a loud, gargling noise, was **endeavouring to** *bite his head off*.

The concordance of *the work of a moment* reveals how Wodehouse also combines the mixing of formal and informal language with deliberately over-intricate grammatical complexity, to comic effect:

(7) The makings were neatly laid out on a side-table, and to pour into a glass an inch or so of the raw spirit and shoosh some soda-water on top of it was with me **the work of a moment**.

(8) In short, he was one of Nature's rubbernecks, and to dash to the rail and shove a fat man in a tweed cap to one side was with him **the work of a moment**.

(9) It was nicely perched up on the grass, and to have plunked it on to the green with an iron should have been for any reasonable golfer **the work of a moment**.

Another aspect of Wodehouse's comic style was evident in the concordance of both *as regards* and *endeavouring to*, namely the recounting of banal, mundane events in high-flown language. This is most apparent when the character Jeeves is speaking:

(10) 'Mr. Fink-Nottle appears to have realized at this point that his position **as regards** the cabman had become equivocal. The figures on the clock had already reached a substantial sum, and he was not in a position to meet his obligations.'
'He could have explained.'
'You cannot explain to cabmen, sir. On **endeavouring to** do so, he found the fellow sceptical of his bona fides.'

A more qualititative analysis, that is, a close reading, of the excerpts contained in Golab (2004), highlights how Jeeves's linguistic role in the Wooster stories consists largely in formulating an account of events and, especially, in reformulating other characters' accounts, in a formal, even grandiloquent register (all *MOJ*, our emphasis in bold):

(11) 'I'd hate to be a fox, wouldn't you, Jeeves?'
**'Certainly I can imagine more agreeable existences**, sir.'

(12) 'Was this you, Jeeves?'
'Sir?'
'Did you put Ginger up to doing it?'
**'It is conceivable that Mr Winship may have been influenced by something I said**, sir.'

The following contains three reformulations hard upon each other's heels:

(13) '... Then I succeeded in diverting his attention for a moment, and while his scrutiny was elsewhere **I was able to insert a chemical substance in his beverage which had the effect of rendering him temporarily insensible**. [...]
'You mean you slipped him a Mickey Finn?'
'I believe that is what they are termed in the argot, madam.'
'Do you always carry them about with you?'

> **'I am seldom without a small supply, madam.'**
> 'Never know when they won't come in handy, eh?'
> 'Precisely, madam. **Opportunities for their use are constantly arising.'**

And Jeeves's frequent literary quotations also tend to be hyper-elegant reformulations of another speaker's previous sentiment:

(14) 'How quiet everything seems now.'
'Yes, sir. **Silence like a poultice comes to heal the blows of sound.'**

One of the principal underlying and recurrent comic techniques employed by Wodehouse, then, is *humour of register*. Hasan and Halliday (1989) see a register as a cluster of associated [linguistic] features having a greater than random tendency to co-occur in a given situation. More informally we might define it as a way of speaking or writing regularly associated by a set of participants with a certain set of contextual circumstances. Register is thus a linguistic but also a social and a psychological phenomenon. It is linguistic in being characterised by a particular vocabulary and phraseology, a particular syntax, a particular discourse organisation and, if spoken, very possibly by special intonation patterns and voice quality. It is social in that there is a consensus in a given discourse community about which features normally belong to or are appropriate in a given context, that is, whether the register matches the situation. And it is psychological in that any individual member of the community can recognise whether a piece of discourse which has been produced is appropriate in the current situation.

Attardo defines register humour as "humor caused by an incongruity originating in the clash between two registers" (1994: 230). This definition would certainly relate to the reformulation examples reported above, as well simpler, but rapid-fire juxtapositions of different registers such as (both *MOJ*, formal in bold, informal in italics):

(15) I had given him the Spinoza at Christmas and he was constantly immersed in it [...] he tells me it is ***good ripe stuff***, well worth **perusal**.

(16) **I could appreciate** that this ***put him in quite a spot***, **the feudal spirit** making him wish to ***do the square thing*** by the young master, while a **natural disinclination** to ***get bunged out of*** a well-loved club **urged him** to let the young master ***boil his head***.

These are all instances from the character Wooster's narration of which, in fact, the constant movement between the elevated and the mundane is characteristic.

By far the most common sort of humour register clash is bathos, that is, the sudden bathetic shift from something elevated to something low and mundane, often both of language and of topic.[3] There is no shortage of examples in Wodehouse's prose, as in the following (both *RWA*):

(17) Algy moved on, and Archibald, **his soul bubbling within him like a Welsh rarebit at the height of its fever**, sank into a chair **and stared sightlessly at the ceiling. Then, rising, he went off to the Burlington Arcade to buy socks.**

But Wodehouse's work also includes innumerable instances of a less common form of humour, that is, the reverse, a shift from the low, colloquial and mundane to the elevated in language and topic; in the following two examples, elevation to the philosophical and the poetic respectively (both *RWA*):

(18) The process of buying socks eased for awhile the turmoil that ran riot in Archibald's veins. **But even socks with lavender clocks can only alleviate: they do not cure.**

(19) 'Suppose that aunt of yours wants to come and visit us … what, dearest would be your reaction to the scheme of **socking her on the base of the skull with a stuffed eelskin**?'
'**I should like it**', said Aurelia warmly, '**above all things.**'

We can use the term *upgrading* to describe this less-studied form of register humour (Partington 2006a: 75–76, 78–80).

Register humour does not necessarily involve an explicit clash and it can also occur when "a mismatch is perceived between speech events which have actually been produced and those that might be expected in the current situation" (Partington 2006a: 74). In practice, this kind of register humour occurs when the speech events produced are normally felt to be characteristic of a different situation from the one actually pertaining, in other words, that a speaker/writer has fallen into a register different form the one expected. This definition relates to instances

3. It is very common in canned jokes:

> A mountain climber slips over a precipice and clings to a rope over a thousand-foot drop. In fear and despair, he looks to the heaven and cries: 'Is there anyone up there who can help me?' A voice from above booms: 'You will be saved if you show your faith by letting go of the rope.' The man looks down, then up, and shouts, 'Is there anyone *else* up there who can help me?'

and that the humorous writings of Woody Allen is almost entirely bathetic:

> Authentic Being, reasoned Needleman, could only be achieved at weekends and even then it required the borrowing of a car (1997: 301)

such as Jeeves's account of an altercation with a cabman (Example 10) and the many instances in Wodehouse where mundane entities or events are recounted with high-flown (pseudo-)elegance:

(20) 'These eggs, Jeeves,' I said. 'Very good. Very tasty.'
'Yes, sir?'
'Laid, no doubt, by contented hens. And the coffee, perfect. **Nor must I omit to give a word of praise** to the bacon' (*MOJ*)

These can, of course, also be counted as instances of upgrading.

## 6.4 Hyperbole and litotes

In the previous section we looked at one type of register shift, that between formal and informal language. The PGW corpus keyword lists, however, bear traces of another kind of register play. They contain a considerable number of intensifying items, that is, expressions of hyperbole. Some of these are in informal 1920s upper-class register such as *deuced, topping, infernal, frightful/frightfully* but many more are items which can be found across a wide range of discourse items, such as *extremely, thoroughly, perfectly, extraordinarily, undoubtedly, absolutely, undeniably* (all found in the first 1000 keywords).

However, at the same time, the lists contain a number of expressions of litotes, that is, understatement, such as *a bit of, sort of.*

Turning to a closer reading, we find, in fact that both hyperbole and understatement are, indeed, very important stylistic strategies. The first, exaggeration, is an almost constant feature of Wodehouse's prose:

(21) 'I can remember the days,' said the Gin-and-Ginger-Ale, 'when **every other girl you met stood about six feet two in her dancing-shoes**, and **had as many curves as a Scenic Railway**. Now **they are all five foot nothing and you can't see them sideways**. Why is this?'
The Draught Stout shook his head.
'Nobody can say. It's the same with dogs. One moment the world is **full of pugs as far as the eye can reach**; the next, **not a pug in sight, only Pekes and Alsatians**. Odd!' (*RWA*)

Another relatively common hyperbolic technique is pluralisation, thus one girl becomes "…all these girls in your bedroom", a certain Pauline Stoker becomes several "Chuffnell Hall … should have been entirely free of Stokers", and in "Jeeves had no right to say that fellows went down to the village […] when they didn't", "fellows" refers to the narrator, Wooster.

Turning to understatement, sometimes known as *litotes*, we find, for instance:

(22) 'Shakespeare said **some rather good things**.'
'I understand that he **has given uniform satisfaction**, sir.' (*MOJ*)

A particularly effective and characteristic technique is the recounting of sudden or hurried or violent activity in sedate language:

(23) How simple it would have been, had he not been a Mulliner and a gentleman, to remove the weapon [a battle-axe] from its hook, spit on his hands, and haul off and dot this doddering old ruin one just above the imitation pearl necklace (*RWA*)

Grammatically, the single leisurely sentence is slowed down by a complex clausal structure, elegant syntactic inversions ("How simple it would have been", "had he not been") and lexically we find a number of deliberately undramatic items: *simple*, *remove*, *dot* [her] *one*.

The sudden shift from the hyperbolic to the trivial in topic may also be seen as another form of bathos:

(24) The great thing in life, Jeeves, if we wish to be happy and prosperous, is to miss as many political debates as possible. (*MOJ*)

## 6.5 Playing with degrees of precision

The keyword and key-cluster lists also contain a number of items generally used to express a degree of vagueness in conversation. Vagueness of language can, of course, be a very useful tactic when a speaker is unable or unwilling to give more information than s/he is currently doing (Channell 1994; Carter & McCarthy 1997; Cheng & Warren 1999). But it can also be used for surprise comic effect. Items found in the key-item lists include *stuff* (*about*), *and generally, something about* and (some/any/no-thing) *in the nature of, and all that, what not, all that sort of thing/rot, in a* [adjective] *sort of way*. Concordancing these revealed some interesting pays on precision, for example:

(25) He mentioned **something about** scooping out your insides (PGW)

(26) Of **anything in the nature of** a girl in heliotrope pyjamas there was absolutely no trace (*CW*)

The effect is partly achieved by a contrast in register, *stuff* (*about*) and *something about* being conversational and can be used with higher register vocabulary:

(27) You know, I rather agree with those poet philosopher Johnnies who insist that a fellow ought to be devilish pleased if he has a bit of trouble. All that **stuff about** being refined by suffering (PGW)

Conversely, *in the nature of* is rather academic and can be used with lower register vocabulary. But what these locutions have in common is a vagueness of reference and when used to refer to something very precise – *scooping out your insides* (25) or *a girl in heliotrope pyjamas* (26) (note, not simply any pyjamas) – the effect can be arresting.

Another technique of playing with precision-vagueness is what we might call metonymic reference, that is, the circumlocutive description of some quality or behaviour associated with an entity by means of which the reader is challenged (usually a mild challenge) to recognise the entity in question. A couple of simple and recognisable examples are "the old eight hours", meaning a night's sleep and "the man behind the prayer book" referring to the vicar. Others need more contextual explanation, for example, "the Five-Year Planner" is the "socialist" butler, exacting his personal revenge on the English upper classes in the form of Wooster (all *CW*). Metonymic references are obviously much less communicatively precise than simple reference but can be seen as an inventive form of stylistic variation.

## 6.6 Colourful imagery

Golab expresses the opinion that "the hallmark of Wodehouse's fiction is his imagery" (2004: 40). For Hall too, his similes and metaphors are striking and colourful due to:

> the wide range from which he draws his comparisons, using them in every instance to emphasise resemblances which at first glance seem highly incongruous (and hence provoke the reader's laughter), but which at the same time are highly appropriate to the particular person or situation described.
>
> (Hall 1974: 106–107)

However, since incongruity is not necessarily in itself humorous (Ritchie 2004: 63; Partington 2006a: 43–49), this raises first of all the question of what kinds of incongruity Wodehouse employs, and what makes some kinds of incongruity humorous. Furthermore, since metaphor is common to many prose styles, in fact to practically all language, the second proper question is, what is singular, if anything, about Wodehouse metaphors. Finally, what is especially striking about Wodehouse's imagery is his characteristic employment of *simile*.

Starting with the last, the question of the precise relationship between metaphor and simile is beyond the scope of the current paper. Miller sees similes as relating very closely indeed to metaphor and containing all the same mysteries:

> [S]imiles can pose all the apperceptive problems that metaphors can [...] when Eliot writes, for example, "the evening is spread out against the sky like a patient etherized upon a table," it challenges us to search for the similarity in our experience of evenings and etherized patients – and may well affect the way we see an evening sky thereafter.[4] (Miller 1993: 375)

Here, we will follow Miller in considering simile a category of metaphor, but a category perhaps used in special ways.

Similes, of course, by definition, contain an overt lexical sign linking the two items to be compared. Miller lists a number of these simile signals: *like, is like, acts like, looks like, as, is as* Adj *as, resembles, reminds me of, is the same as, is similar to* and *the same way* (1993: 371). All of these items can, of course, be concordanced.

The first particularity to be noted about Wodehouse's similes is the remarkable array of linguistic means of introducing the comparison statement, which goes far beyond Miller's list. For instance, *a sort of* was found in the key-item lists of PGW (and see also 5.4.2) and when it was concordanced the following were forthcoming:

(28) She regarded Eustace as **a sort of** medicine. A second dose might not be necessary, but it was as well to have the mixture handy (thus the simile is: Eustace IS LIKE a medicine)

(29) The Wanted column of the morning paper is **a sort of** dredger, which churns up strange creatures from the mud of London's underworld (the Wanted column IS LIKE a dredger)

(30) [...] he was inclined to think of his luck as **a sort of** special train which would convey him without effort to paradise (his luck IS LIKE a train)

Close reading unearthed many much more exotic and striking linking expressions, such as the following, all from *CW*:

(31) Her attitude to a recalcitrant nephew **would closely resemble that of** ...

(32) ... the odd **suggestion he conveyed of** having bought the place

(33) it's **not unlike** the Scottish express going through a tunnel ...

---

4. Apperception is a term borrowed from Herbart (1898) and indicates the mental processes required when new things are learned by being related to things already known.

(34) his expression was **almost identical with** that of … the face of a fish I once …

(35) … something [in Gussie's *timbre*] … **reminding the hearer** partly of an escape of gas …

(36) I couldn't have made a better shot, **if I had been** one of those detectives who see a chap walking along the street and deduce that he is a retired manufacturer of poppet valves names Robinson, with rheumatism in one arm, living at Clapham

alongside the following from *RWA*:

(37) …which gave him **something of the look of** an earnest sheep

(38) …and all I can do is **stand there feeling like** a piece of Gorgonzola that has been condemned by the local sanitary inspector

As for the special effects Wodehouse creates with his metaphor and simile (see also 5.4.4 on incongruous comparison for humorous effect), we might consider:

(39) We are the parfait gentle knights, and we feel that it ill beseems us to make a beeline for a girl **like** a man charging into a railway restaurant for a bowl of soup. (*Thank You, Jeeves* as quoted in Hall 1974: 107)

Such constructions clearly display the kind of bathos described in 6.3, that is, their effect depends upon a sudden dramatic fall from high to low register and, possibly also, topic. Wodehouse compounds a number of highly literary items in the first part – *parfait gentle knights* (the allusion is to Chaucer's *The Knight's Tale*), *we feel, ill beseems us* – to be followed by a comic fantasy narrative of the hungry and hurried railway traveller, complete with colloquial language *charging, make a beeline*. We have already encountered a similar instance in Example (17) (*his soul bubbling within him like a Welsh rarebit*).

In other episodes of simile, for instance:

(40) […] whose demeanour was now rather **like** that of one who, picking daisies on the railway, has just caught the down express in the small of the back. (*The Inimitable Jeeves* in *ODQ*)

the effect is similar to that described in 1.3, that is, the sudden intrusion of an extremely hyperbolic fantasy narrative – being struck by an express train – into an otherwise tranquil scenario – the picking of flowers.

Finally in the following type:

(41) As a rule … I'm not lugged into Family Rows. On the occasions when Aunt is calling to Aunt **like** mastodons bellowing across primeval swamps … the clan has a tendency to ignore me. (*The Inimitable Jeeves* in *ODQ*)

we find language hyperbole (*mastodons, bellowing*) combined with a highly fanciful fantasy narrative script revolving around prehistoric beasts. Notice too how the preciseness of the details used in the fantasy narrative adds to the comic effect: it is not just an express, it is the *down* express, she is picking not simply flowers but daisies, she is caught in the *small* of the back and the animals are specifically *mastodons*.

And the sheer imagination, indeed far-fetchedness verging on the absurd, of the juxtaposed fantasy narrative script – together with, as Hall implied, its perfect aptness (appropriate in its very inappropriateness) – is another characteristic of Wodehouse's imagery:

(42) But the change in him, I soon perceived, was purely superficial. The manner in which he now tripped over a rug and cannoned into an occasional table, upsetting it with all the old thoroughness, showed me that at heart he still remained the same galumphing man with two left feet, who had always been constitutionally incapable of walking through the great Gobi desert without knocking something over. (*CW*)

and see Example (21) ("every other girl ... had as many curves as a Scenic Railway").

## 6.7 Playing with co-occurrence

In the last Example (42), "upsetting [the table] with all the old thoroughness" is quite striking. There appears to be an evaluative opposition given the normally positive sense of *thoroughness* and the fact that upsetting the furniture is generally frowned upon. Moreover, concordancing *all the old* in PGW produced three instances:

(43) At the moment, no doubt, she might be wishing that she could hit him with a bottle, but deep down in her I was prepared to bet that there still lingered **all the old** affection and tenderness.

(44) Tuppy, I could see, despite that painful scene in the larder, still loved Angela with **all the old** fervour.

(45) But underneath it **all the old** love still remains. Am I correct?

all of which are evaluatively positive and so we might presume that Wodehouse indeed meant *all the old thoroughness* to be taken as a good thing in this case, very probably with undertones of affection (in the notation introduced in Chapter 2, good: endearing).

One more singularly striking technique used frequently by Wodehouse, then, is what we might term "creative collocational inappropriateness" or "clash" (an important aspect of what Partington 1998 terms "unusuality" in which primed expectations are upset, see also Chapter 4 on phrasal irony), that is, the juxtaposition in the text of items *of a type* rarely found in each other's company, which, in fact, would normally be primed to avoid each other. The following is a similar example:

(46) [...] concealed my astonishment that anyone...could **deliberately love** this girl (*CW*)

Very generally, *deliberately* either co-occurs with items which are evaluatively bad or, when they are neutral, it tends to lend a negativity to the overall meaning of the phrase (see also 4.6.1). Of the former case, PGW contains, among others: "you have deliberately deceived me" and "there seemed to be something deliberately fat-headed ...". Of the latter case it includes: "why does a man deliberately choose a job like writing plays?" (and, in this instance, the text goes on to argue how play-writing is so arduous [negative] that it requires the patience of a Job). The negative evaluative weight of *deliberately* is enough in Example (46) to reverse the normal positive associations of love and notifies us that the speaker (Wooster) is not himself enamoured of the young lady in question.

Because such combinations as *deliberately love* are nonce juxtapositions, there is no chance at all that any sign of them will appear in key-item lists and such instances are normally discovered during close reading. However, once one has been stumbled across it may be possible to unearth similar examples using the concordancer, and indeed a search through PGW for *deliberately* produced the following:

(47) Genevieve was tall and blonde, a destroyer of masculine piece of mind [...] Yet here was this one **deliberately selecting** her, Katie. It was almost a miracle.

(48) You **deliberately assert** that you loved that weird Gawd-help-us (Madeleine Bassett)?

In these cases, although the R1 items – *selecting* and *assert* – are seemingly evaluatively neutral, there are other very positive items – *a miracle* and *loved* – to which *deliberately* is semantically connected. In (47) the *miracle* retains its positive evaluation since it describes the event from Katie's viewpoint, whereas (48) is akin to (46) in that *deliberately* counteracts the positive evaluative polarity.

Not all instances of creative collocational inappropriateness rely on a contrast in evaluation, for instance:

(49) …unshackle the eggs and bacon (*CW*)

The verb *unshackle* is very rarely found in a non-metaphorical sense (in either the SiBol corpora or the BNC Sampler) but when it is it does not normally co-occur with items outside a very restricted set (*irons*, *chains*), which certainly does not include foodstuffs.[5] A similar instance is a reformulation of a renowned literary quotation (another common Wodehouse technique):

(50) …if you have butter, prepare to shed it now

(the original being "if you have tears prepare to shed them now" Mark Antony, *Julius Caesar*, III: II). The verb *shed*, when used in a rare literal sense is also normally primed to cooccur with a limited set of items (SiBol 05 includes: *tears, light, weight, blood*), again not including food. Given the mundane nature of food, these too can be considered examples of comic bathos.

Other discourse types where this form of collocational play is likely to be found include advertising, UK newspaper headlines and, of course, poetry. It is also clear that many of the techniques found here are also employed in the humorous opinion pieces in Chapter 5. It may well be that the columnists picked up some of their comic skills by reading Wodehouse.

## 6.8 Conclusion

The aspects of corpus methodology involved in the current research have included the compilation of the various corpora, the comparison of the corpora using the Keywords program and the concordancing of keywords and key-clusters which caught the analyst's attention to examine their use in context, normally a limited context (although it is certainly possible to go from the concordance line to reading the text from which it derives).

A good deal of time, effort and care was required in designing and building the target and comparison corpora. The question needs to be asked whether that time and attention could have been better spent simply studying a wider selection of Wodehouse texts than were eventually subjected to close reading. In other

5. Even the rare instances where *unshackl** cooccurs with apparently literal 'restraining irons', the sense can still be metaphorical:

> The afternoon session certainly belonged to Hampshire (County Cricket team) as Terry, then Morris, unshackled their chains. (SiBol 93)

words, what was the added value, if any, of introducing corpus techniques? We might begin to answer this somewhat perversely by posing the inverse question, namely: what can close reading uncover that corpus analysis cannot?

There were, indeed, a number of kinds of observations arising from close reading in the current study which it is hard to imagine would have been available to mechanical inspection. Instances of pluralisation ("all these girls in your bedroom"), unusual co-occurrence ("deliberately love"), as well as metaphor and metonymic reference are all far more likely to be happened upon while reading than through statistical analysis.

Secondly, there are observations arising from the key-item analyses which would not surprise even the most distracted Wodehouse reader, the prevalence of upper-class slang in the dialogues would surely lie in this category. There are others perhaps which an attentive reader might well have strongly intuited. However, in such cases, one must also be careful to distinguish between active and passive realisations (also known as the "hindsight effect"), when an observation reached by starting from the statistical data appears self-evident to the reader, but only after it has been pointed out to them. The frequent shift between different kinds of register might fall into this category, including Jeeves's role as elegant reformulator of previous utterances.

In many such cases, however, corpus methods can provide statistical evidence to support reader's impressions and suspicions and give a more objective measure of the strength of the phenomenon, in particular how frequent and how prominent the lexis associated with the language feature in question is in the key-item lists, as well as providing much more detail. For instance, it may well be obvious to all that Wodehouse is peppered with comic upper-class hyperbolic expressions, such as *deuced, topping, infernal, frightful/frightfully*, and so on, but much less evident to the naked eye, though not to the keyword tool, that many other more widely used intensifiers as *extremely, thoroughly, perfectly, extraordinarily* and so on, are just as much a feature of his prose. Similarly, the sheer number and variety of reporting, perception and mental expressions used by Wodehouse was something of a surprise to us initially but on reflection (hindsight) we might have anticipated them.

Alternatively, statistical evidence may in fact *fail* to support the reader's hypothesis. This may not mean the hypothesis is unfounded, it may instead mean that the phenomenon is not salient enough to show up on the statistics, that is, it may lie above the threshold of statistical significance being employed or, perhaps, that a different set of reference texts would be required to make the suspected language feature stand out.

If we turn to what was indeed rendered more accessible by the statistical analyses, it becomes difficult to make objective pronouncements. To say that a certain language phenomenon was new to us when analysing the key-item lists is not to claim that other readers may not have had their own intuitions about it. Caveats made, there were a number of indications of peculiarities for further research that previous reading had not made so visible, and these include: the number of formalisms, the range of non-slang intensifiers, the litotic expressions and the range of vague-language expressions.

Secondly, the concordance tool enabled many more examples to be collected in a very short time of many of the sets of words so far mentioned, including some unusual co-occurrences (specifically, involving *deliberately*, see 6.6), and having an abundance of examples often led to particular insights. For instance, a study of Wodehouse's formalisms demonstrated how frequent is Wodehouse's shift not only from high-to-low register (bathos), but also from low-to-high register (upgrading). This is just as true of course for phenomena first observed during first reading, for instance, on noting the use of a particular simile marker the analyst can turn to the concordancer to collect more instances. Moving from one occurrence of a linguistic phenomenon to many gives, not just a bigger and better picture, but, by potentially revealing *patterns* of use, can mean the difference between having or not having a picture at all. Illustrations of this are, firstly, the discovery, by looking at a number of literary similes in context, that they were often to be found in text-initial position with a forward-looking (cataphoric) function. They frequently introduce a kind of conceit for which an elucidation is produced in the following text (see Examples 28 and 29). Secondly, that *practically* (the second highest **ly* adverb keyword, after *absolutely*), when concordanced in PGW, proved very frequently to perform the function of introducing a hyperbolic metaphor ("we're practically castaways on a desert island", among many more). By comparison in the reference corpus Humour there were no such metaphorical uses of *practically* and in the Novels corpus, only one. Finally, that *might have been*, when concordanced, was often found to be a sophisticated *grammatical* means of constructing a simile ("but so thickly did it bristle with obstacles that it might have been a mile of No Man's Land", is equivalent to "it was as full of obstacles as a mile of No Man's Land") (Partington 2006b). Sinclair's pronouncement that "[t]he language looks rather different when you look at a lot of it at once" (1991: 100) is one of the standard dicta of corpus linguistics, and part of what is meant is that any linguistic feature can be seen to behave in unsuspected ways when you look at several instances of use in context.

It would seem then that a case can be made for the inclusion, in some circumstances at least, of corpus methods in author-stylistic research. The kinds of utility can be broken down as follows:

- some language features may be apparent to corpus analysis alone (at both the key-item phase and the concordance example-collection phases)
- corpus analysis can lead to hypotheses which need to be tested by close reading of the data
- corpus analysis may corroborate (or fail to corroborate) pre-statistical impressions

And finally:

– corpus analyses can lead to serendipitous discoveries.

As an illustration of this last, the item *rummy*, with 101 instances, was high in the PGW keyword list. Curious about its precise meaning (it turned out to signify "strange", "funny"), we concordanced it and read the extended text for some of the lines. We came across the following example of metonymic reference (incidentally the only one we have found of apposition, that is, where the reference of the metonym is found immediately adjacent to it, that is, *husbands* and *lads of the for-better-or-for-worse brigade*):

(51) Yes, the dear girl had been **rummy** at breakfast. She had not exactly said anything or done anything out of the ordinary; but – well, you know how it is. We **husbands, we lads of the for-better-or-for-worse brigade**, we learn to pierce the mask. There had been in Lucille's manner that curious, strained sweetness which comes to women whose husbands have failed to match the piece of silk or forgotten to post an important letter.

This fortuitous instance of serendipitous discovery alerted us to the copious and rich use of metonymic reference in Wodehouse's prose (6.4).

Having said all this, the most striking impression left at the end of this research is that there is little point to corpus author-stylistics *tout court*. If we had taken an author unknown to us and subjected his or her texts only to comparative computer analyses, our findings, we feel, would have been poor indeed. Intuitions, impressions and suspicions arising from our knowledge of this author's work informed and enriched our analyses at every level, and reading of at least some of the corpus (in the original literary sense) of an author's work in concomitance with the machine analyses is highly productive. The two can corroborate each other's findings and even when they do not this can act as a spur for further investigation to discover why this is. Corpus stylistics, then, would be a limited enterprise but corpus-*assisted* stylistics can be a worthwhile pursuit.

## Appendix: The contents of the three literary corpora

### PGW

*The Adventures of Sally*; *The Clicking of Cuthbert*; *A Damsel in Distress*; *Death at the Excelsior*; *A Gentleman of Leisure*; *The Girl on a Boat*; *The Indiscretions of Archie*; *Jill the Reckless*; *The Little Nugget*; *The Man with Two Left Feet*; *A Man of Means*; *The Man Upstairs*; *My Man Jeeves*; *Piccadilly Jim*; *Right Ho, Jeeves*; *Something New*; *Uneasy Money*; *A Wodehouse Miscellany*.

Novels

*The Valley of Fear*, by Sir Arthur Conan Doyle; *Women in Love*, by D.H.Lawrence; *Three Soldiers*, by John Dos Passos; *The Age of Innocence*, by Edith Wharton; *The Path of the King*, by John Buchan; *Short Stories, 1909 to 1922*, by Lucy Maud Montgomery; *The Land That Time Forgot*, by Edgar Rice Burroughs; *She and Allan*, by H. Rider Haggard; *Scaramouche*, by Rafael Sabatini; *The Beautiful and Damned*, by F. Scott Fitzgerald; *Tales of the Jazz Age*, by F. Scott Fitzgerald; *Main Street*, by Sinclair Lewis; *Twelve Men*, by Theodore Dreiser; *Crome Yellow*, by Aldous Huxley; *The Mysterious Affair at Styles*, by Agatha Christie.

Humour

*A Humorous Romance of Outdoor Life*, by Frederick Upham Adams; *Journeys to Bagdad*, by Charles S. Brooks; *The Innocence of Father Brown*, by G. K. Chesterton; *The Wisdom of Father Brown*, by G. K. Chesterton; *The Story of Doctor Dolittle*, by Hugh Lofting; *The Diary of a Nobody*, by George Gossmith; *On Nothing & Kindred Subjects*, by Hilaire Belloc; *On Something*, by Hilaire Belloc; *Three Men in a Boat*, by Jerome K. Jerome; *Three Men on the Bummel*, by Jerome K. Jerome; *The Unbearable Bassington*, by Saki; *Beasts and Super-Beasts*, by Saki; *Humorous Masterpieces from American Literature*, by Various; *The Best American Humorous Short Stories*, by Various; *Little Masterpieces of American Wit and Humor*, by Various; *Little Masterpieces of American Wit and Humor 2*, by Various; *Nonsenseorship*, by G. G. Putnam.

CHAPTER 7

# Cross-linguistic discourse analysis

## Investigating the representation of migrants in the UK and Italian press

In this chapter we present a cross-linguistic case study in which the methods of CADS are used to analyse the representation of migrants in the Italian and UK press. In addition to the cross-linguistic analysis, another aspect of CADS (corpus-*assisted*) methodology illustrated in this chapter is the integration of extra-corpus statistical information in the research process. We start by surveying some of the previous work in this area and then move on to the case study, which is divided into three main phases. In the first phase, Section 7.4, terms referring to racism and xenophobia were concordanced to investigate how the newspapers presented and used these terms. In the second phase, Section 7.5, drawing on research carried out by a team of researchers from Lancaster University (see, for example, Gabrielatos & Baker 2008), we focus on the terms *refugees*, *asylum seekers*, *immigrants*, *migrants* (and Italian equivalents, taken from Taylor 2009b) and the various nationalities associated with these terms were identified. This information is then compared to "real-world" statistical data in order to identify any mis-match between the estimated numbers of migrants from a given country and the amount of attention that they receive in the media. This simple comparison of estimated populations and media visibility aids in identifying groups which are foregrounded and which could then be subsequently analysed.

### 7.1 Cross-cultural/cross-linguistic CADS

#### 7.1.1 Previous research

In this chapter we refer to cross-linguistic corpus-assisted discourse studies, but this will include consideration of work which identifies itself as bilingual CADS (e.g. Freake et al. 2011) and there is some overlap with comparative corpus-based discourse studies.

One of the early applications of CADS to multi-lingual corpora as part of a large-scale venture was the *IntUne* project which ran from 2005–2009 and investigated the theme of citizenship in Europe (see Bayley & Williams 2012).[1] For the project, a 150 million word corpus of news reporting from France, Italy, Poland and the UK was collected and analysed. Resulting research employing the CADS methodology included studies of the representation of broadcast news, such as Thornborrow et al.'s (2012) study of discourses of European identity in British, Italian, and French TV news, and studies of the print media, such as Dugales and Tucker's (2012) analysis of European institutions in the French and British Press.

The scarcity of previous research in this area is emphasised by Moschonas and Spitzmuller (2010: 18), who argue that "there is an urgent need to devise methodologies for the processing of large corpora, and particularly for the use of comparative corpus-based – or even corpus-*driven* – discourse analysis" within language ideology research. In their study they compare language ideologies through the analysis of a relatively small corpus of 160 articles which contained references to *media language* in Greek and German newspapers. Murphy (2005) also focussed on a cross-linguistic dimension of newspaper discourse in her study of lexico-grammatical markers of attribution or reporting in two comparable corpora of English and Italian opinion articles. In both these examples, a cross-linguistic CADS approach is employed with a mainly comparative drive. In the second example, Murphy (2005), the focus is very much on the language itself in the comparison of genre conventions. This is a kind of comparative study with very practical implications, for instance, for translation work. However, in the former, the focus is on cultural differences in language ideologies and the fact that the two subcorpora are in different languages is almost secondary, what is of interest is how the issue of language ideology is represented in the press. Similarly, in the case study discussed below, we were interested in investigating representations in UK and Italian media because these two cultures have a different history of migration. In contrast, Taylor (2012) analyses the meta-references to mock politeness and the linguistic realisations of mock politeness in English and Italian, and therefore the focus is very clearly on comparing the two languages.

More recently, Freake et al. (2011) compare the discursive construction of nationhood and belonging in Quebec through the analysis of a corpus of public consultation briefs submitted to the Bouchard Taylor Commission (2.7 million tokens, 95% in French, 5% in English). They created "comparator" corpora for each sub-corpus and then used the keywords for each language as a starting point for the analysis. This is an interesting example, as the use of two languages is not

1. ⟨www.intune.it⟩

driven by a comparative focus, as in the cases above, rather the cross-linguistic focus is an attempt to ensure minority voices are not excluded. This means that the subcorpora were not balanced in terms of size but they function as a means of aiming for a "completeness". The documents which were compiled into corpora were originally submitted in two languages, and therefore to exclude one of those languages would mean excluding a set of voices. Similarly, in the *IntUne* project, in trying to describe how European identity is constructed, if the researchers had limited their research to one language then it would also have been limited to one (dominant) culture and would not have allowed them to approach the issue of *European* identity.

### 7.1.2 What methodological challenges might the researcher face?

Cross-linguistic CADS brings a range of additional challenges, some of which are outlined in the following section.

First, if we are going to compile our corpora using search terms, or choose comparable search terms for collocation analysis, the primary consideration is how to identify comparable items in the different languages. As Tognini-Bonelli & Manca state:

> to translate means (1) to identify a specific function together with its formal realisations in L1, (2) to compare it with another set (function + formal realisation), or other sets, in L2 and finally, in the light of the previous stage, (3) to attempt to encode the given function into a chosen formal realisation in the target language. (2004: 371)

Identifying functional equivalence for search terms therefore involves looking at meanings in context. In Taylor (2009b) one of the authors of this book carried out a para-replication of work into the representation of refugees, asylum seekers, immigrants and migrants (see, for instance, Baker & McEnery 2005; Baker et al. 2008; Gabrielatos & Baker 2008; Baker 2007). In the first stage, three bilingual dictionaries were used to identify possible translations for *refugees, asylum seekers, immigrants* and *migrants*. However, this in itself raised some serious doubts about the validity of the available translations, for example two of the three dictionaries did not include *immigrato* [*immigrant*] as a translation for *immigrant*. Furthermore, as a proficient speaker of Italian and reader of Italian newspapers, the author had sufficient background knowledge to see that a range of additional translations were missing from the bilingual dictionaries, such as *clandestini*, which is described in the *Oxford Paravia Concise* (henceforth *OPC*) as "(*immigrato*) illegal alien; (*passeggero*) stowaway". Thus, this phase highlighted the fact that there was a lack of cohesion between the English to Italian definitions and the Italian to English definitions: for instance, looking for Italian translations of *immigrant* we did not find *extracomunitari* [literally *non-EU*], but in the English translation of *extracomunitari* the word *immigrant* is present. In the second phase, to check the actual usage of the terms which had been identified through reference to the bilingual dictionaries and to the author's background knowledge, the frequencies of the English and Italian terms were compared in two large corpora. This showed that the most literal translation of *asylum seeker* (*richiedente asilo*) was in fact not a functional equivalent as it was used significantly less frequently in the Italian corpus. This stage also highlighted that the apparent translation of *refugees* (*rifugiati*) was rarely used to refer to migrants in Italy and nearly always referred to marginalised others elsewhere. We would therefore caution that considerable care needs to be taken in this initial phase of identifying comparable search terms, as the subsequent construction of the corpus will, naturally, determine the research findings. Another, very important consideration in identifying functional equivalence is the general evaluative meaning of the terms in each language. Two or more items cannot be considered translation equivalents if they are usually embued with different evaluative sense in different language communities, and evaluative differences in apparently cognate items across languages have been documented in a range of studies; see, for instance Xiao & McEnery (2006) on English and Chinese, Partington (1998), Tognini-Bonelli (2001) and Stewart (2010) on Italian and English, Lewandowska-Tomaszczyk (1996) on English and Polish, Berber-Sardinha (2000) on Portuguese and English, Munday (2011) on English and Spanish.

Second, another translation-related challenge, which we have already had to address in writing this chapter, is the choice of how to report the findings. In this case, we have briefly discussed some issues involved in cross-linguistic research using English and Italian, but we are writing in English and assuming no knowledge of Italian. This is naturally not a new question, particularly for researchers who carry out their research on English or a similarly widespread/powerful language but it is a question that we always have to consider in cross-linguistic research. When providing translations, should we try and provide a literal back-translation or a functional translation or something in-between? For instance, in Chapter 5 of this book we refer to the metaphorical phrase "dilagante anti-Americanism" in which the conceptual metaphor is one of water as *dilagante* comes from *dilagare* which is used in a similar way to the verb *flood*. However, "flooding anti-Americanism" holds very limited meaning for the English-speaking reader and translations of *dilagante* from bi-lingual dictionaries would identify *widespread* or *rampant* as equivalents. These alternatives would then convey the functional meaning more effectively but then the original metaphor is lost, and clearly this is problematic when reporting on a linguistic analysis of metaphor. Finally, in terms of the presentation of findings, another key limitation to using translated data is the use of KWIC style concordance lines which are highly appropriate in reporting language patterns but will not necessarily function in highlighting patterns around a translation equivalent.

Third, in addition to a need for awareness of translation-related theory and good practice in dealing with cross-linguistic study, there are also issues relating to the cross-cultural variation. For instance, in this case study we are looking at newspaper discourse, but newspapers in Italy and the UK are different in many respects. One way in which they differ is that the major division in UK newspapers between "broadsheet" (also referred to as "quality") versus "tabloid" (or "popular") newspapers is not really relevant to Italy, where a more salient distinction is between nationally circulated and local/regional newspapers.

Fourth, when interpreting our data, as Freake (2011) emphasises, we need to be wary of attributing differences between corpora to the language variable when they could have been affected by a number of other variables, not least the extent of comparability between the different language corpora. Similarly, she notes that we should be careful not to assume that each language corpus is a homogenous entity.

Fifth, Freake et al. (2011) and Freake (2011) also note some methodological difficulties relating to the use of keyword analysis. First of all, the keywords cannot be compared directly if they are in different languages. Second, they note that "when a word has a different keyness from its translation in another language, it is difficult to assess whether this is due to significant differences between the focus corpora or differences between the reference corpora" (Freake et al. 2011: 30) and therefore, by way of solution, they suggest that rather than comparing keyness values, a more useful and valid indicator is the comparison of relative rank orders of keywords.

## 7.2 Representation of migrants in the Italian and UK press

In any kind of cross-cultural research the different contexts of production need to be taken into account, and Italy and the UK have different recent histories regarding immigration and emigration. Both countries have seen considerable external emigration and internal movement but within Italy *immigrazione* [immigration] generally meant internal migration, particularly in the post-war period and the items *immigrazione* [immigration] and *immigrati* [immigrants], when used to refer to *immigration* and *immigrants* in the (British) English sense, are still often post-modified by *stranier** [foreign]. However, in recent years this situation has changed somewhat and, as the data in Table 7.1 shows, Italy actually has a lower a rate of emigration than the UK, and the number of "foreigners" ("stranieri", calculated by citizenship) resident in Italy is now quite similar to that in the UK. Table 7.1 also includes 1999 data to allow for some comparison of how the situation has developed in the two countries as this variable is likely to affect newsworthiness.

**Table 7.1.** Demographic data for the UK and Italy in 1999 and 2009 (data from Eurostat unless marked with * which is from the UNHCR)

| | 1999 | | 2009 | |
|---|---|---|---|---|
| | UK | Italy | UK | Italy |
| Population | 58,785,246 | 56,923,524 | 61,595,091 | 60,045,068 |
| Foreign-born persons usually resident | n.a. | n.a. | 6,769,300 | 4,375,240 |
| Foreigners usually resident (based on citizenship) | 2,297,947 | 1,116,394 | 4,184,011 | 3,891,295 |
| Long-term immigrants entering | 354,077 | 185,052 | 566,514 | 442,940 |
| Long-term emigrants leaving | 245,340 | 64,873 | 368,176 | 80,597 |
| Asylum applications | 71,160 | 18,450 | 50,025* | 17,525* |
| Refugees | n.a. | n.a. | 269,363* | 54,965* |

## 7.3 Corpora

Two sets of corpora were created for this investigation: the first containing articles from Italian newspapers and the second from British newspapers. The papers were downloaded from *Nexis UK* and were chosen according to their availability on the database. Although practical, this is naturally an imperfect selection process, as unfortunately it means that some Italian newspapers with a high circulation, such as *La Repubblica*, were omitted because they were unavailable on *Nexis UK*. The newspapers were divided into four categories (newspapers in each category are listed in order of circulation, see Appendix A to this chapter for more information):

UK broadsheets: *Telegraph, Times, Guardian, Independent*
UK tabloids: *Sun, Mirror, Daily Star, Express, Daily Mail*
Italian national newspapers: *Corriere della Sera, La Stampa*
Italian regional/local newspapers: *Il Resto del Carlino, La Nazione, Il Giorno*[2]

The first group of subcorpora contained all articles from 2009 which contained the search term *racis**, which retrieved *racism*, *racist* etc. and the Italian

2. The three regional newspapers overlap considerably as they belong to the same editorial group and carry many of the same articles.

equivalent *razzis**. The second set of subcorpora contained all articles which contained *xenophob** or *xenofob**. For the third group, the English language corpora were built using the search terms *refugee**, *asylum seeker**, *immigrant** and *migrant** (RASIM), where the wildcard allows for singular and plural forms to be retrieved, and the Italian corpora were built using the search terms *immigrat** [*immigrant*], *clandestin** [*illegal immigrant*, but also *clandestine* which creates some "noise"], *extracomunitar** [*non-EU*] and *stranier** [*foreign, foreigner*] (for which we adopt the acronym ICES), in this case the wildcard *allows for a range of endings (gender and singular/plural). These search terms were chosen based on Taylor's (2009b) analysis of functional equivalents as outlined above. The sizes of the subcorpora are reported in Table 7.2. As can be seen, each of the three groups is larger than would be comfortable to analyse manually without using sampling or a similar technique. It is therefore clear that a corpus-assisted approach can also be of use here in simply providing a way of handling the data.

**Table 7.2.** Summary of corpus size

| | racis*/razzis* | xenophob*/xenofob* | RASIM/ICES |
|---|---|---|---|
| Italian national newspapers | 848,448 | 193,458 | 4,459,334 |
| Italian regional newspapers | 839,430 | 185,066 | 10,880,021 |
| UK broadsheet newspapers | 3,979,302 | 3,979,302 | 3,979,302 |
| UK tabloid newspapers | 992,560 | 25,012 | 1,406,462 |
| Total | 6,659,740 | 4,382,838 | 20,725,119 |

The differences in size also give us an initial indication of the interests of the different newspapers. However, the size of the corpora alone may be misleading given that broadsheet newspaper articles tend to be longer than tabloids, and, as noted above, there is some noise or irrelevant data in the Italian corpora due to the polysemous lexical items. Therefore, we will discuss the number of articles and number of occurrences rather than corpus size in the following section.

The various corpora were analysed using *Wordsmith Tools 5* (Scott 2008) and *SketchEngine*. For the purposes of this paper, the main advantage to *SketchEngine* is that the corpora are POS-tagged as they are uploaded. However, because *SketchEngine* requires the user to upload their corpora (rather than downloading the software, as is the case with *Wordsmith Tools*) it can be time-consuming and there are financial limitations on the size of corpora that can be processed because the user pays per million word allowance.

## 7.4 *Racism* and *xenophobia*

In this section, we aim to look briefly at how racism and xenophobia are presented in the press. As an initial measure of newspaper interest, we looked at how many articles there were in each newspaper containing the search terms.

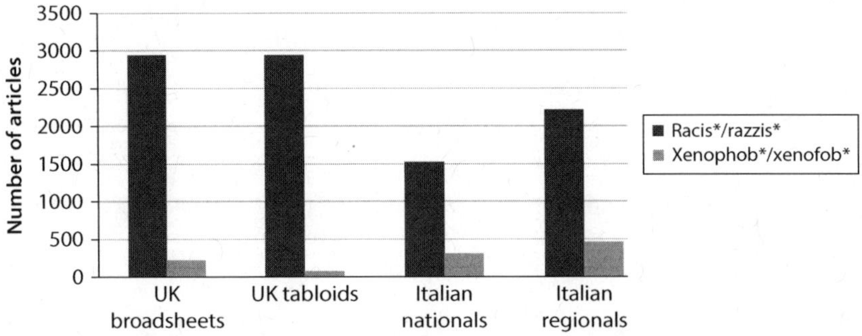


**Figure 7.1.** Number of articles containing references to *racism* and *xenophobia*

Counting the number of articles was considered a more reliable indicator of newspaper interest than simply looking at the size of the corpus retrieved from *Nexis UK* because of the differences in standard article length. It was also considered to be more useful than counting the number of occurrences because this can be skewed by single articles with a very high frequency of usage. From Table 7.3 we see that the UK tabloids and broadsheets were very similar in terms of the number of articles referring to racism. In contrast, *razzis** occurred almost half as frequently in the Italian national newspapers than *racis** did in the UK broadsheets.

### 7.4.1 Racism

We started the analysis of the references to racism by analysing the collocates and n-grams (also referred to as clusters). The analysis of the 3-grams revealed a number of expressions indicating denial of racism (as discussed in van Dijk 1992), with the following phraseologies featuring in the 15 most frequent clusters: *not a racist* (both UK broadsheets and tabloids), *il razzismo non* [*racism + not*] (Italian broadsheets), *non siamo razzisti* [*we are not racist*] (Italian regionals). As might be expected, in the UK broadsheets, these were predominantly attributed to some other voice than the newspaper's, as illustrated in (1), rather than averred in its own (attribution and averral are discussed in Chapter 2.5), as shown in Example (2), (only three out of 42 occurrences):

(1) She sighed when asked about immigration. "I am absolutely *not a racist*," she said. "I have friends of other colours. I have travelled the world, I was born in Malaysia myself." (*Guardian*)

(2) But this is *not a racist* country, even if it has people with racist opinions. With the exception of BNP voters, most people think that non-white Britons born in the UK are just as British as white citizens. (*Telegraph*)

The instances in the tabloids were also predominantly attribution through reported speech (67 out of 76), but there were also three examples from letters to the newspapers, one instance from a columnist and five instances from news and features sections, as in Example (3), which suggest a slightly higher tolerance for the denial of racism rhetorical strategy (van Dijk 1992):

(3) PRINCE HARRY is an idiot but *not a racist.* (*Sun*)

Of the instances of *il razzismo non* [*racism + not*] in the Italian national newspapers, the most common construction (eleven instances) was *il razzismo non c'entra* [*it's nothing to do with racism*] and once again they were all instances of attribution. Similarly, all the instances of *non siamo razzisti* [*we are not racist*] in the regional newspapers were reported speech, but they were not contested by the newspapers, even when the speaker was someone who had set up two Facebook groups called "No alla moschea di Sesto" [No to the mosque in Sesto] and "Via i rom da Sesto San Giovanni" [Move the roma from Sesto San Giovanni].

Therefore, we can see that the newspapers vary in terms of which voices they choose to include, which is significant in terms of the overall ideological position that they present, but all are quite careful to avoid using the denial formulae themselves in averred statements.

The next question then, is who or what is evaluated as racist in the various newspapers? From an initial overview of the collocates, shown in Table 7.3, some interesting patterns emerge.

All four newspapers refer to the situation of racism within football, though this gathers more attention in the Italian press. The UK broadsheets appear more interested in institutional racism than their tabloid counterparts and although they also refer to racism with regard to the British National Party (*BNP*, a right-wing political party), the identification of racism with the BNP in the tabloids seems more marked (the items *BNP, party, Griffin* – the *BNP*'s leader – all being relatively more frequent). This may indicate a simplification or narrowing of what constitutes racism as compared to the broadsheets, an impression which could be explored and tested in further research.

All four sets of newspapers have *accused/accusations* in the most frequent collocates, but another strong collocate of *racis** in the UK tabloids is *branded* which seems to suggest some ambiguity – the act of "branding" generally having a very negative evaluation, the corpus-based *Macmillan Online Dictionary* defines *brand* as "to describe someone or something as a bad person or thing, especially when they do not deserve this". A closer analysis of the concordance

**Table 7.3.** Most frequent collocates of *racis*/razzis** divided into thematic groups (approximately three miscellaneous items, such as *yesterday*, have been omitted from each paper category)

| | Broadsheets | Tabloids | Nationals | Regionals |
|---|---|---|---|---|
| Racist what? | *abuse*, 129; *attacks*, 67; *behaviour*, 66; *language*, 77; words, 67; *comments*, 65 | *abuse*, 235; *attacks*, 76; *language*, 116; *comments*, 104; *remarks*, 74; | *confronti*, 34; *violenza* [violence], 26; *cori* [chants], 164; *insulti* [insults], 48 | *violenza* [violence], 60; *episodi*, 65; *confronti*, 80; *cori* [chants], 246; *insulti* [insults], 86; *scritte* [writing], 52; *frasi*, 59 |
| | *football*, 59 | *football*, 73 | *Balotelli*, 80 | *calcio* [football], 63; *Balotelli*, 101; *presidente* [president], 52 |
| | *BNP*, 96; *party*, 85 | *BNP*, 163; *Griffin*, 73; *party*, 100 | | |
| Who/where? | *institutional*, 83; *police*, 130 | *police*, 111 | *paese* [country], 34; *Italiano* [Italian], 30; *l'italia* [Italy], 23 | *italiani* [Italian/Italians], 59; *paese* [country], 26; *societa'* [society/ football club], 48 |
| Labelled as | *accused*, 114; *called*, 61 | *accused*, 132; *branded*, 109; *alleged*, 80 | *accusa* [accusation], 25; *accuse*, [accusations], 28 | *accuse* [accusations], 47 |
| Associated with | *sexist*, 59; *homophobic*, 65 | – | *xenophobia* [xenophobia], 48 | *xenophobia* [xenophobia], 74 |
| | *black*, 111; white, 111 | *black*, 99; *white*, 99 | – | *colore* [colour], 48 |
| Events | | *hate*, 73 | *conferenza* [conference], 111; *Ginevra*, 33; *ONU*, 34; *Durban*, 39 | *conferenza* [conference], 44 |

lines from the UK tabloid corpus showed that references to *racis** and *branded* very frequently co-occurred with a semantic set of fear as illustrated in the concordance lines in below.

EX eaking English they are **afraid** of being *branded* a *racist* or being accused of belonging
EX ity groups to integrate for **fear** of being *branded racist*. Britain is in a rotten state. But i
EX ite working class without **fear** of being *branded* as *racist*." City banker Mr Miraj, 35,
EX t with as people were **frightened** to be *branded racist*. "There is no one less *racist* than

| | | |
|---|---|---|
| EX | e to express them without **fear** of being | *branded* a *racist*." But former Labour Minister F |
| EX | eel unable to complain for **fear** of being | *branded racist*. The stark report warned there w |
| EX | blicly on such matters for **fear** of being | *branded* as *racist*. To ignore or trivialise the |
| EX | ith as people were **frightened** of being | *branded racist*. "There is no one less *racist* than |
| MAIL | SIAN PUPILS FOR **FEAR** OF BEING | *BRANDED RACIST* HE GAVE HIS name as He |
| MAIL | o tolerance' approach for **fear** of being | *branded racist* themselves. They worry that by |
| MAIL | ice their worries 'without **fear** of being | *branded racist*'. In the furore that followed, Fran |
| MAIL | king English they are **afraid** of being | *branded* a *racist*.' Mr Kumarasiri grew up in a vi |
| MAIL | ottingham says neither a **fear** of being | *branded racist*, nor intimidation from his landlo |
| MAIL | ass immigration 'without **fear** of being | *branded* a *racist* when all they really want are |
| MAIL | out their worries 'without **fear** of being | *branded* a *racist*'. The findings, produced by M |
| MAIL | lay blame because we **fear** we will be | *branded racist*. I travelled to Ethiopia at the |
| STAR | **fear** that if they complain they will be | *branded* "*racists*" in politically correct Britain |
| STAR | ut, " he said. "They are **afraid** of being | *branded* a *racist*. "I don't expect immigrants to |
| STAR | pproach in this country. **We fear** being | *branded* a *racist* if we speak out. "He's come he |
| SUN | Government that lives in **fear** of being | *branded racist* if it criticises such non-integratio |
| SUN | with the local council **fearful** of being | *branded racist* by persecuting a "minority". Ho |
| SUN | d to speak up. They are **afraid** of being | *branded racist*. "Perhaps it's a view better comin |

Concordance lines showing the co-occurrence of *racis**, *branded* and fear (EX = *Daily Express*).

In this discourse, then, being branded a racist is therefore something that people are afraid of, and those who were portrayed as being in danger of this were included: *A BOY of nine playing soldiers with a Polish pal*, *a six-year old girl*, *an elderly couple* and *a brilliant head* [teacher]. These were the four most common stories in the newspapers and in these cases exhibit a favourable stance taken towards the potential "brandees". Alignment with those who might be or have been "branded" is also frequently expressed by presenting the reason for potential "branding" as actually inoffensive and also by the use of inclusive pronouns, as seen in (4) below, where the reason for being "branded" is opposing a supposedly "lunatic" policy, whilst the victims of the branding are an "us" group:

(4) But, like all opponents of Labour's **lunatic** open-door policy, **we** were branded "racist" and ignored. (*Sun*)

In Example (5) we see one of the clearest expressions of what does and does not count as racism in the *Daily Mail*, with the distancing of anti-immigration stances from racism.

(5) **Dominic, his youngest son, was adopted from Croatia, so Mr Magill can hardly be described as someone with a hatred of foreigners.** But he is under no illusions about why people from his area were involved in the violence. [...] 'You get branded a racist if you speak out about the issue of immigration. But I think I'm being a realist, not a racist, when I say that this is something we must address. (*Daily Mail*)

Once again, this view is presented through reported speech, but the voice is legitimised through the careful specification of why, according to the article, the speaker cannot be considered racist (in bold).

It is also interesting to note that while the UK broadsheets associate racism with other forms of discrimination (collocates shown in Table 7.3 included *sexist* and *homophobia*), there are no similar items in the most frequent collocates for the UK tabloids.

The Italian newspapers appeared much more concerned than the UK papers with the relationship between the whole country and racism, as can be seen from the collocates in Table 7.3. Once again, it should be noted that the majority of these were in reported speech or in the letters sections. From reading the concordance lines, it became clear that the references to *paese* [*country*] most frequently did refer to Italy itself (16/24 in the nationals, 22/26 in the regionals), and the same was true for *società* [*society*, although *società* also means *football club* in some instances here]. One difference between the two types of Italian newspapers was the extent of dis/agreement with the proposition that Italy is a racist country; in the Italian nationals only two instances, both reported speech, disagree with this. In contrast, in the regionals, almost half expressed disagreement, once again, through the use of attribution, as in (6) which was from the letters section and (7) which contains direct reported speech.

(6) E non parliamo di razzismo ad ogni frase un po' sciocca. E' razzista un Paese dove si assegnano più case popolari agli immigrati che agli italiani? [Let's not talk of racism after every silly comment. Can a country be racist if it assigns more council housing to immigrants than Italians?]. (*Il Resto del Carlino*)

(7) la posizione di Marcello Lippi, ct azzurro, è condivisa da Galliani: "Non siamo un paese razzista, è vero che nei nostri stadi c'è molta maleducazione e che bisogna fare attenzione a non sottovalutare il problema, ma credo che certi cori siano opera più di imbecilli che di razzisti" [Marcello Lippi's interpretation is shared by Galliani: "We are not a racist country, it's true that in the football stadiums there is a lot of uncivil behaviour and we have to make sure we don't underestimate the problem, but I think many of these chants are the work of idiots rather than racists"]. (*Il Giorno*)

### 7.4.2 Xenophobia

As noted above, in the Italian press, references to racism and xenophobia collocated strongly, 76% of the occurrences of xenophobia co-occurred with *razzis** in the Italian regional newspapers. Generally, they were linked with a coordinating conjunction or as part of a list (approximately 95% of uses), but at times they were contrasted as illustrated in (8).

(8) Per questo un numero crescente di italiani guarda con sospetto gli immigrati. **Non è razzismo: è xenofobia**. Non è una gran consolazione, sono d'accordo. [This is why an increasing number of Italians are suspicious of immigrants. It's not racism: it's xenophobia. It's not much consolation, I agree.] (*Il Giorno*, Letters section)

In the UK tabloid press, as was seen in Figure 7.1, there were fewer references to *xenophob**. Of these reference 39% referred to a single story in which Peter Mandelson, then Business Secretary, commented on a strike at UK factory saying "We should keep our sights set firmly not on the politics of xenophobia but on the economics of this recession". Therefore, in these cases, the occurrences of *xenophob** are generally instances of "mention" rather than "use" (Quine 1940), that is, no particular individual or group is being accused of xenophobia. In another 30% the references co-occurred with *racis**, in a similar way to the Italian data. In the remaining instances, it was seen to co-occur with *out of touch* and *insular*. There were also some similarities with the use of *racis**, for example, there were instances in which xenophobia is clearly distinguished from an acceptable patriotism, (Examples 9 and 10), and the use of the label is on occasion portrayed as a means of (unfairly) attacking and controlling an "us" group (Example 11):

(9) NO ONE wants a blind or bigoted **patriotism** that manifests itself as *xenophobia* and ignorant rejection of all that is foreign. It is good to be open to others but self-hatred is neither attractive nor constructive. (*Express*, editorial)

(10) To be **patriotic** is to appreciate and be grateful for all that is valuable in the country you live in. It does not require you to be a *xenophobe* or a blinkered nationalist. (*Sun*, editorial)

(11) Similarly, as politicians of all parties ganged up to agree that there was no alternative to Britain being a member of the EU, anyone who queried this was **denounced** as a *xenophobe* and **vilified** as a **swivel-eyed lunatic**. (*Mail*, columnist)

In the British broadsheet newspapers, 38% of instances co-occurred in coordination with *racis**, showing how the two terms are equated. Just 37% referred to xenophobia in the UK while 53% referred to xenophobia elsewhere, mainly in Europe. Of those referring to the UK, the majority were affirming the existence or potential for xenophobia (Example 12), rather than denying or challenging the label, as seen in the tabloids, although there were a few instances, as shown in Example (13).

(12) And Labour, as a pro-Europe governing party, deserves much of the blame. Not only has it failed abjectly to champion the European cause over its 12 years in power, but it has done far too little to nip the *xenophobic* tendency in the bud. (*Independent*, editorial)

(13) For a decade we trusted what we didn't understand. Global capitalism was intricate beyond all reckoning. Polite Indian voices answered when we rang our banks, Spanish firms owned our airports, the Germans bought our water, Dubai controlled our ports. Our homes were flooded with imported clothes and toys and electronics so cheap that you daren't think too hard about who made them or how. **To question any of this was to be *xenophobic*, a Little Englander – or worse.** (*Times*)

From this, necessarily, brief investigation of how racism and xenophobia are constructed in and by the newspaper's themselves, we can see that discussion of racism in UK and Italian press is frequently presented through the use of attribution. The UK tabloids seems to envisage a narrower scope of the term *racis** than do the broadsheets, restricting it more frequently to discourses around the *BNP*. Moreover, they often take up a stance of sympathy towards those who are labelled or risk being labelled as racist. In the Italian press there was greater discussion of whether Italy is a racist country and there was more disagreement with this notion in the regional newspapers where potential racism may be downplayed/downgraded as ignorance or stupidity.

In the next section, we compare data on the estimated number of migrants in each country with the visibility that nationalities have in the press.

## 7.5 RASIM and ICES geographical identities: Frequencies

In the next phase we calculated which geographical identities collocated most frequently with the terms *refugee**, *asylum seeker**, *immigrant** and *migrant* in the UK broadsheet and tabloid newspapers. In order to do this, we initially looked at all collocates of RASIM words within a span of 10 items to the left and right, and identified those which referred to countries or nationalities, therefore, where we have listed Poland, for instance, this refers to all co-occurrences of RASIM with *Poland, Polish, Pole* and *Poles*. Subsequently, we used the concordance tool to check the co-occurrence of each identity with RASIM. We have chosen the rather vague term "geographical identities" because we found that the newspapers often group and amalgamate nationalities, for instance referring to "Africans" rather than referring to a country. In Table 7.4 we present the geographical identities which collocate most frequently with RASIM in the UK newspapers alongside the statistics reporting the estimated population in the UK by foreign nationality. We have also included information about the percentage change in the number of foreign nationals from 2008 – 2009 because any sudden change within the year of study would be likely to affect the newsworthiness. The intention here, and in Table 7.5 which reports the same data for Italy, is to identify those nationalities which seem to receive a disproportionate amount of media attention in relation to their numbers. Naturally, not all of the references to nationalities in association with RASIM/ICES, refer to the presence of those nationalities in the UK or Italy. In the UK broadsheets in particular there is considerable interest in reporting on RASIM elsewhere and this will be taken into consideration in the discussion below. However, this rather rough measure does give us a systematic and replicable starting point for selecting nationalities/identities for analysis.

### 7.5.1 UK data

**Table 7.4.** Comparison of ranking of nationalities present in the UK and (geographical) identities with a high visibility in the press in 2009

| Estimated population resident in the UK, July 2009 to June 2010 | | % change from 2008 | Geographical identities which co-occurred with RASIM: Broadsheets | | Geographical identities which co-occurred with RASIM: Tabloids | |
|---|---|---|---|---|---|---|
| Poland | 541000 | +10 | France | 272 | Ireland | 267 |
| Republic of Ireland | 342000 | −1 | **Palestine** | **217** | France | 230 |
| India | 322000 | +12 | **Afghanistan** | **165** | **Africa** | 114 |
| Pakistan | 165000 | −10 | **Africa** | 163 | Poland | 111 |
| USA | 150000 | +15 | USA | 160 | **Eastern Europe** | 109 |
| France | 122000 | −1 | Italy | 156 | **Afghanistan** | 89 |
| Germany | 116000 | +23 | **Iraq** | **151** | China | 78 |
| China | 104000 | +18 | China | 136 | **Iraq** | 75 |
| Italy | 104000 | +3 | Pakistan | 130 | Italy | 65 |
| *South Africa* | 101000 | 0 | Poland | 122 | USA | 64 |
| *Nigeria* | 97000 | +10 | **Eastern Europe** | 109 | Germany | 58 |
| *Portugal* | 95000 | +7 | Germany | 108 | **Romania** | 49 |
| *Lithuania* | 88000 | +52 | **Tamil** | **107** | Nigeria | 47 |
| Australia | 77000 | −9 | Ireland* | 92 | Pakistan | 45 |
| *Bangladesh* | 75000 | +12 | India* | 86 | Australia | 44 |

In Table 7.4, the countries and/or identities which are marked in bold are those which receive more attention than might be expected based on a presumed correlation between the number of people from a given country and their visibility in the media. Those marked in italics received less attention than might have been expected.

From the list of nationalities, we note that South Africa, Portugal, Lithuania, and Bangladesh are somewhat under-represented in both the broadsheets and the tabloids. Lithuania ranked 17th on the tabloid scale and therefore is not exceptional, but the others ranked much lower, in particular Portugal. Australia just fell outside the cut off for the broadsheets, as did India in the tabloids and therefore is not considered exceptional either, but Nigeria ranked very low in the broadsheets. It is also interesting to note that although people from India are one of the most populous national groups in the UK, the ranking is relatively low. There is of course an old and continuous history of migration between India and the UK and this may go some way to explaining the relatively low amount of attention paid, alongside a preference for other, more vague, markers of geographical identity such as *Asian**.

Moving on to those nationalities which seem to gather more attention than might be expected, we start with the broadsheet data. The references to Palestine, most frequently in the form *Palestinian refugees* (89 occurrences) in the broadsheets refer to the situation outside the UK, and this explains the mismatch in the number of references and the number of people in the UK. The same applies to Tamil, which again most frequently occurred with the term *refugees*. This would also suggest that *refugee** may not actually be a productive search term when looking for references to migrants within the UK. Regarding the presence of Afghanistan in the broadsheets, only 25% clearly referred to people in the UK, although an additional 30% of instances reported on the situation in France which is presented as having an impact on the UK because the migrants are described as waiting to enter the UK. This is perhaps evidence that this group is portrayed by some source at least as posing a potential threat to UK social equilibrium. The same applies to Iraq, African and East European and so these terms would be included in any subsequent analysis. Of the references to Africa, we may break them down in to references to the whole continent, South Africa (19%), north Africa (6%) and west Africa (2%). Only 19% referred to people within, or migrating to, the UK and so the frequency reflects the broadsheet tendency to report international news rather than a local preoccupation.

With reference to the tabloid data, as can be seen from Table 7.4, the identities which seem to have a greater visibility than might be expected are; Africa, Eastern Europe, Afghanistan and Romania. The only addition to the broadsheet data is the presence of Romania. Therefore, these would all be potentially interesting for further study.

### 7.5.2 Italian data

In order to calculate the collocates in the Italian data, *SketchEngine* was used because when the corpora are uploaded they are automatically POS-tagged. This meant that in the search for collocates it was possible to specify that the terms *immigrat** [*immigrant**], and so on, should all be nouns. This allowed us to remove "noise" deriving from the fact that terms like *clandestin** are also used in an adjectival form, for instance in *scommesse clandestine* [*illegal/unauthorised betting*]. In addition, we had to address the fact that several articles are shared across the regional newspapers and therefore the figures given below only refer to unique occurrences. So, for instance, if the same article appeared in all three regional newspapers, it was only counted once. Duplicates were eliminated manually from the concordance lines.

**Table 7.5.** Comparison of ranking of nationalities present in Italy and (geographical) identities with a high visibility in the press in 2009

| **Estimated population resident in Italy, 2009** | | **% change from 2008** | **Geographical identities which co-occurred with ICES: Italian national newspapers** | | **Geographical identities which co-occurred with ICES: Italian regional newspapers** | |
|---|---|---|---|---|---|---|
| Romania | 796477 | +27 | **UK/GB/England** | 62 | Morocco | 410 |
| Albania | 441396 | +10 | Romania | 58 | China | 382 |
| Morocco | 403592 | +10 | **Africa/North Africa** | 54 | Albania | 238 |
| China | 170265 | +9 | **Eastern Europe** | 48 | Tunisia | 238 |
| *Ukraine* | 153998 | +16 | **France** | 46 | **Eastern Europe** | 212 |
| *Philippines* | 113686 | +8 | Morocco | 40 | Romania | 189 |
| Tunisia | 100112 | +7 | China | 35 | **Africa/North Africa** | 174 |
| *Poland* | 99389 | +10 | Egypt | 34 | Senegal | 161 |
| India | 91855 | +19 | Tunisia | 28 | Egypt | 131 |
| *Moldova* | 89424 | +30 | **Libya** | 26 | **UK/GB/England** | 96 |
| *Macedonia* | 89066 | +14 | India | 23 | **Germany** | 90 |
| *Ecuador* | 80070 | +9 | **Rom** | 21 | **Nigeria** | 79 |
| *Peru* | 77629 | +10 | **Somalia** | 21 | **Pakistan** | 76 |
| Egypt | 74599 | +7 | **Eritrea** | 20 | **Rom** | 68 |
| *Sri Lanka* | 68738 | n.a. | Albania | 19 | **France** | 61 |
| *Senegal* | 67510 | +8 | **Spain** | 19 | India | 51 |

Table 7.5. shows the relative rankings of the most populous foreign nationalities in Italy and the visibility of various nationalities or identities in the Italian press; as previously, the items marked in bold are those which appear to be over/under-represented in the newspapers in this corpus. From the list of nationalities, we can see that people from the Ukraine, Philippines, Poland, Moldova, Macedonia, Ecuador, Peru, Sri Lanka and Senegal are discussed less frequently in

the Italian press than might be expected. In looking for an explanation for under-representation, we need to look outside the corpus and in this regard it is interesting to note that in a report issued by the social research foundation Censis, entitled *Dare Casa alla Sicurezza* [*Giving safety a place in the home*] the nationalities which are most frequently involved in domestic work are: Romanian, (19,4% of the total domestic workforce in 2009–2010), Ukrainian (10,4%), Philippines (9%) Polish (7,7%) and Moldavian (6,2%). The same report noted that the majority of those working in domestic fields are women (more than 80%). Thus, we may hypothesise a relationship between the domestic, controlled sphere in which these nationalities tend to work and the lack of newsworthiness in the press (one possible exception is Romanian, to which we will return below). Another factor may be the frequent use of the more general reference to East European.

In contrast, if we look at the data which reports on the nationalities with the largest number of business owners, according to Censis (Rapporto Sopemi 2010), the nationalities are, in order: Moroccan, Romanian, Chinese, Albanian, Swiss, Senegalese, German, Tunisian, Bangladeshi, Egpytian, Serbian and Montenegrin, French, Nigerian and Pakistani. If we refer back to Table 7.5, it is clear that this second list matches very closely the list of newsworthy identities in the Italian regional newspapers.

Moving on, therefore, to the nationalities which appear to attract more attention than might be anticipated from numbers of residents alone, we note the high frequency of discussion of the UK (grouped together with Great Britain and England because in reality in the press analysed here they are frequently conflated), France and Spain in both newspaper types but since these frequently occurred in discussion of the policies towards migrants in those countries they are not included in the analysis below.

In a similar way to the UK newspapers discussed above, the Italian press tends to group non-Western European nationalities and favour vaguer terms, therefore we have items like *africa** [*africa**] and *nordafrica** [*North Africa**] and a range of terms referring to Eastern Europe in place of references to individual countries. These assimilative terms appeared in the frequent geographical identities for all four newspaper subcorpora.

Another key item in both the national and regional newspapers is *rom*, which is related to the English *Roma*. However, the term was not present in the three bilingual dictionaries mentioned earlier, nor in several monolingual Italian dictionaries (e.g. *Zingarelli Minore*). In the *Corriere* monolingual dictionary (Dizionario Italiano di Sabatini Colletti), *rom* is defined as:

> **agg.** Del popolo nomade degli zingari: [adj. of the nomadic peoples of gypsies]; **s.m. e f.** Nel sign. dell'agg.: *una comunità di rom* [noun, masc. and fem. In the meaning of the adjective: *a community of rom*]

Given the high frequency of usage in associations with *ICES*, this would be included in subsequent study, but that is not to suggest that we consider *rom* to be a nationality.

In the Italian national newspapers, references to people from Somalia and Eritrea also seemed to be marked. When examined, they were found to be occurring in very similar contexts (although several references to Eritreans were driven by a single event regarding five Eritreans who were the sole survivors of a shipwreck) and in both cases, the majority of references were to groups of Somalis or Eritreans coming towards Italy. The majority of occurrences seemed to take a sympathetic stance, as in Example (14).

(14) E' il dramma di un'altra carretta del mare, respinta dai nostri vicini: un barcone con duecento clandestini (molte le donne e i bambini, probabilmente sono eritrei) che da due giorni sta navigando in acque di competenza maltese e ha rischiato di essere riportato in Libia. [It is the tragic story of another unsound boat, sent back by our neighbours: a boat with 200 illegal immigrants aboard (many women and children, probably Eritrean) which for two days had been sailing in Maltese waters and risked being taken back to Libya]. (*La Stampa*)

Similarly, the references to Libya and Libyans also tended not to refer to people within Italy. The most frequent lexical collocate of Libya/Libyans in the context of ICES was *respinti* [*sent back*], and the majority of occurrences referred to the migration route from Libya to Italy, and to the agreement between the Italian and Libyan governments which had been effected the previous year, under which Italy agreed to paid $5 billion in damages for its pre-WWII occupation of Libya, and Libya agreed to take back refugees who had tried to reach Italy from the Libyan coast. When the concordance lines were examined, the migrants were rarely actors in the clauses, they were acted upon in terms of being sent back, handed over, repatriated and so on.

To summarise, the nationalities which seemed to be foregrounded and which referred to migrants within Italy are (North) Africa, (East) Europe, and "rom" for both sets of Italian newspapers, in addition to Romania for the Italian national newspapers, and Nigeria for the regionals. Other candidates for examination in the regional newspapers, given their ranking in Table 7.5, would include: Pakistan, Senegal and Egypt.

This section has described an initial entry point into the data, a replicable way of identifying which groups to focus on, and the next stage would be a linguistic analysis using CADS techniques. The aim of such an analysis might be, for instance, to attempt to find out more about why certain groups were given relatively high visibility, how positive or negative it was, and if negative, whether there was evidence of prejudice against them.

## 7.6 Conclusions

In this chapter we have raised some of the issues surrounding cross-linguistic corpus-assisted discourse studies. In particular we have emphasised the need for the researcher to have an awareness of translation issues and practices. This is precisely the kind of area where we can learn a great deal from a neighbouring discipline. We have also focussed on another methodological issue, namely the utility of looking at other sources of information outside our corpus. In discourse analysis, we are analysing language in context and therefore to treat the corpus as an isolated black box is often methodologically unsound and unfruitful. In this chapter we looked at external data both to try and interpret and explain our data and also as a means of identifying areas for analysis from a more objective and replicable starting point.

In analysing the way in which the terms *racism* and *xenophobia* are used, we have seen some evidence that certain sections of the press may exploit attribution and the inclusion of other voices through letters sections in order to express alignment or sympathy with prejudiced viewpoints. The analysis has also highlighted some similarities between the British broadsheets and the Italian national newspapers, and the British tabloids and the Italian regional newspapers, reflecting the similar readerships.

Through examining any mismatch between expected and actual levels of prominence in the press we identified geographical nationalities which were foregrounded and in a longer study this information would then form the starting point for the analysis of representation. This type of study could be very usefully enhanced through the use of programs such as the *UAM CorpusTool* (O'Donnell), a free piece of annotation (and interrogation) software which is designed for this type of qualitative analysis.

In conclusion, from a methodological viewpoint, we feel that cross-linguistic CADS is an exciting area as there has been relatively little work done to date, with even less conducted on more than two languages and this offers new researchers the opportunity to influence the development of the field. We have outlined various possible areas for extension activities below, but these are simply some starting points which are thematically tied to the topic of this chapter.

### Suggestions for further research

1. Find out which terms would be the equivalent to RASIM in at least one other language that you know. You could then identify the nationalities which co-occur most frequently with RASIM and/or the equivalents that you have identified and investigate how they are represented.

2. You could repeat the basic comparison of frequency and newsworthiness in the press for two different countries whose language you know and then continue the process by investigating the representation of those nationalities in a para-replication study.
3. In a simplified para-replication of Moschonas and Spitzmuller (2010), concordance “language” in (at least) two press corpora in languages that you know. What evidence do you find of linguistic prescriptivism?
4. A good number of language issues are treated in this volume. You might like to investigate whether the observations we make about them are also valid in other languages, ideally by examining them in similar types of corpus to those we employ. For instance is the concept of irony perceived and described in similar or different ways to that seen in Chapter 4, and are explicit irony markers, equivalents that is of *it is ironic that*, *ironically*, *the irony was*, and so on, used in similar or different ways?
5. In Chapter 5 we identified a number of recurring metaphors which were used in relation to immigration. What metaphors are used to depict immigration in other languages? What metaphors are used in different languages to portray other social issues such as crime/criminals, unemployment, prostitution, emigration, and so on?
6. If it possible to access or compile corpora in another language which are similar to those used in Chapter 9, it would be most interesting to investigate what kinds of politeness and impoliteness strategies are adopted by speakers and compare them to those outlined in this book.

CHAPTER 8

# Interactive spoken discourse 1

## Managing the message

### 8.1 Introduction and review

In this chapter and the following one we turn our attention specifically to spoken discourse. This chapter begins with an overview of studies performed using corpora of spoken language and then presents a couple of related case studies into what we have called *forced priming*, that is, the strategic flooding of messages favourable to speakers or their clients into an ongoing discourse and also into competition amongst speakers to have their messages accepted. We concentrate on two forms of institutional interactions, namely press briefings and judicial inquiry. Chapter 9 follows on the theme of conflict talk but examines it through the prism of face and facework and, as the chapter's title implies "CADS and (im)politeness", we will pay as much attention to aggressive facework as to more traditional themes of speaker face enhancement or mitigation of face threat to others.

Spoken interaction has historically been the poor relation in linguistics for both ideological and practical reasons. Writing was very often considered to be the nobler form of the language, especially in societies where only a small elite could read or write. As Biber et al. note:

> The Greek origin of the word *grammar* itself (from *gramma* 'a letter', 'a piece of writing') reminds us that the Western grammatical tradition is founded almost exclusively on the study of the written language, a bias which still exists today. However, conversation is not a 'special' or 'unusual' register. In fact, conversation is the most commonplace, everyday variety of language, from which, if anything, the written variety, acquired through painstaking and largely institutional processes of education, is to be regarded as a departure. (1999: 1038)

In more recent times, Chomskian linguistics for one has tended to marginalise speech, seen as more prone to "performance error", and therefore a more debased version of language, furthest away from competence, the true object of linguistic attention. But the very practical difficulties of obtaining a record of speech events also militated against their study. The Latin proverb *verba volant, script manent* ("speech is transient [literally "flies"], writing is permanent") encapsulates both the ideological prejudice and the practical predicament in studying the spoken word.

The diffusion of the tape recorder, which allowed transcripts to be produced, was the first great technological leap forward, leading to the birth of conversation analysis and also the first section of spoken language in a corpus of English, Quirk's Survey of English Usage, begun in 1959.[1] The second breakthrough was, of course the arrival of the Internet, which meant that a wide variety of spoken texts, already transcribed by a third-party and available in machine-readable form, became accessible for linguistic analysis, including the datasets investigated in this chapter (interestingly in the light of the material employed here, as Nelson Francis [1982: 15] points out, the transcripts of the Nixon White House tapes, published as a result of the Watergate investigation, was perhaps the first set of transcripts which became "accidentally" available to linguists in this way).

The effort and expense of transcribing and, even after the advent of the Web, that of annotating for prosodic information, has thus resulted in a disproportionate amount of attention being given to written language. The BNC corpus, for instance has a ratio of 90% written to 10% spoken. More recently though, most of the large heterogeneric general corpora compiled for lexicographic purposes include spoken language and some have provided valuable data for language description (the Cobuild, CANCODE and Longman corpora have been used to produce grammars of the English language and all pay attention to the spoken language as a distinct variety, see 8.2 below). Such large heterogeneric spoken corpora have been sampled for sociolinguistic variables such as social class, sex, and age, and this information is available to the user (see Kennedy 1998 for a description of various widely used corpora and Edwards 1992 on the problems of transcription). However, the cost and complexity of collecting spoken data involving recording and transcription and the provision of metadata does not solve the difficulty in obtaining contextual information from very large corpora. Intonation and paralinguistic features such as gesture, facial expressions, and so on, are rarely fully included in transcription (as Baker points out, even the opening of a door can be seen as part of interaction in a discourse, 2005: 34). To meet this need, some researchers are experimenting with so-called aligned corpora, where it is possible to move from a transcript to the recording from which it derives (for example discussed in Adophs & Knight 2010).

Given this background of difficulties in obtaining a record of spoken discourse, many studies have employed pre-existing general corpora (rather than

1. ⟨http://www.ucl.ac.uk/english-usage/index.htm⟩

a specially compiled bespoke monogeneric corpus (see next paragraph). The spoken sub-corpora of these have been interrogated for specific word forms or phrases with a particular function, especially where these form a limited set and are therefore good candidates for word-string searches, for instance, Stenstrom (1994) on hedging devices and Fung & Carter (2007) on discourse markers. Schauer & Adolphs (2006) looked specifically at expressions of gratitude. Other language aspects studied include the study of a wider set of conversational routines, where more or less fixed expressions are used for apologizing, thanking, requesting, offering etc. (for example the use of *Why don't you X?* for offering advice) and Aijmer's (1996) study used speech acts as an organising principle to investigate data from a number of spoken corpora in the London–Lund corpus, whilst Adolphs (2008) investigated pragmatic functions in spoken discourse in a book length study looking at language patterns linked to conversational routines using the CANCODE corpus. Channell's work on vague language included data from spoken corpora (1994). Cameron & Deignan (2006) studied metaphorical language in spoken discourse from a number of settings to explore the words and expressions that regularly appear in the cotext of both conventional and innovative metaphors. The 1.5-million-word sample from the CANCODE spoken English corpus has been used by Carter & McCarthy (2006) to study how certain forms are used in interaction and the corpus evidence used to evaluate the terms upon which a grammar of English might be developed for the understanding of interpersonal features. McEnery's (2006) analysis of swearing in English uses the spoken section of the BNC as a part of his study.

For many features of interactive spoken discourse, however, researchers have found it more fruitful to compile specialised corpora for their own particular purposes where the context of the interaction, the relationships and communicative purpose may be more finely delimited, carefully chosen and clearer than in the case of generic corpora.

There are a number of specialised corpora of spoken language which have been compiled and sometimes annotated for the analysis of particular discourse types. For example, the CORD historical corpus of English Dialogues containing "authentic dialogue", that is, written records of real speech events (trial proceedings and witness depositions), and "constructed dialogue", that is to say, texts which contain non-actual, imaginary, authored dialogue such as drama, instructional treatises in dialogue form or other didactic works (Culpepper & Kytö 2010). Cheng, Greaves & Warren (2008) have conducted cross-cultural studies on differences in conversational discourse practices between native and non-native speakers of English using the Hong Kong Corpus of Conversational English (HKCCE), compiled at the Hong Kong Polytechnic University, which contains around 50 hours (around half a million words) of transcribed natural conversations involving 340 participants, with eleven different occupations, 48% of the conversations being produced by native speakers and 52% by non-native speakers. The transcriptions were marked up with prosodic information based on the discourse intonation system devised by Brazil (1997). Much of their work focused on differences and similarities between the two speaker groups in intonation patterning, for example, the intonation of declarative-mood questions, of yes-no and *wh*-questions, of disagreement, of extended phrases and of vague language, and in differences in speakers tone choices (rise and rise-fall tones) to exert dominance and control.

Others have concentrated on gathering one domain type, often a context involving some kind of institutional discourse where there are constraints on the kind of discourse allowed in the situation. Recurrent language patterns can thus be studied in relation to the constraints. The insights gathered from such analyses can often be used for teaching purposes. Examples are the MICASE corpus of spoken academic English begun in 1997 at the University of Michigan (Simpson et al. 2002) and, the BASE corpus compiled in the UK, to provide a British point of comparison (see Appendix for websites).

Other studies on institutional talk include forensic investigations such as the seminal Coulthard (1993) paper comparing witness statements with police statements using transcripts of spoken interviews or statements (see Coulthard 2007 for an overview on forensic linguistics and Cotterill 2003 for an example of the analysis of courtroom discourse). A similar discourse type is found in the language of official inquiries with fact-finding and cross-examining phases which can be useful in the investigation of pragmatic features (see Duguid 2007 on the Blair government testimony, Taylor 2007, 2008, 2009a, 2011 on politeness, mock politeness and impoliteness on the Hutton Inquiry and Bondi 2007 on the Saville Inquiry, named after its chairman but also known as the "Bloody Sunday Inquiry"). Other studies range from discourse types as diverse as Farr's (2010) monograph on the language of teaching practice feedback and Friginal (2009) on the language used in out-sourced call centres.

Other researchers have concentrated on media discourse. Haarman & Lombardo (eds 2009) describe a corpus-based approach to the study of TV news broadcasts, of which contains the description of an ad hoc markup coding system for the interaction types found in TV news (Cirillo et al. 2009). O'Keeffe (2006) explores spoken interactions in the media, drawing on contemporary sources from the English speaking world including chat shows, radio phone-ins and political interviews. These discourse types have varying degrees of scriptedness but provide ready recorded material and some even provide transcripts.

All the institutional business of politics is, of course, conducted through language and there are several corpus-assisted data sets of various types of recorded and transcribed spoken institutional discourse (see Adel 2010 and Partington 2012 for overviews). The CSPA is a Corpus of Spoken Professional American English which contains two separate discourse types, the first consists of interchanges between academics, and the second of press conference transcripts from the White House and policy statements by White House officials. So far, most studies using this material have been concerned with linguistic rather than sociopolitical observations, such as Liu (2003) on the use of idioms and Iyeiri et al. (2005) on gender and style.

There have been a good number of studies of political speeches (for example Fairclough 2000 on the discourse of New Labour), and the interactive nature of political spoken discourse has received considerable attention, but this attention rarely includes exploiting of the kind of quantitative data which corpora can help provide. *Discourse and Society* contains 188 references to political press conferences but without a reference to corpus linguistics and 181 references to corpus linguistics but these do not deal with interactive spoken data. For example, Bhatia (2006, 2011) examines hedging and evasion in press conferences, with a corpus of 20 press conferences in the first case, but uses a critical discourse approach and not a corpus linguistics approach. There have been corpus-based studies of the parliamentary discourse of the House of Representatives and the UK House of Commons (e.g. Bayley (ed.) 2004; Baker 2006; Miller & Johnson 2009; Bayley & Bevitori 2009). The interface between politicians and the press has also provided a source (Partington 2003, 2006a; Riccio 2009 on White House press briefings). A good number of these studies employ corpora consisting of pre-transcribed texts in machine-readable form accessed from the Web, as mentioned earlier, and were thus carried out at minimal expense, often by single individuals. In many cases they would not have been feasible previously.

Fictional writing has also been employed as a source of data for spoken interaction, in particular, film and television scripts, given their ease of access as sources of contextualized data; for example Biber & Burges (2001) looked at dialogues from Star Trek for diachronic purposes; Baker (2005) employed CADS techniques to analyse 107 scripts of the American TV sitcom Will and Grace in his investigation of public discourses of gay men; Bednarek has produced a monograph (2011) on the language of fictional television in a case study of a series The Gilmore Girls.

## 8.2 The grammar of spoken discourse: Is it distinct from most forms of writing?

One of most intriguing and informative studies in the field of corpus-assisted spoken discourse studies is Biber et al.'s Chapter 14 on "The grammar of conversation" (1999: 1037–1125), which draws on spoken data in the Longman Spoken and Written English Corpus (LGSWE). The authors attempt to answer the fundamental question of whether there is a distinctive grammar of spoken language, of which conversation is generally taken to be the "bedrock" form from which all other types of speech derive (Scannell 1991: 12), in other words, whether speech operates by laws different from those of the written language. Their initial opinion, expressed in the introduction to the chapter, is that by and large the grammar of conversation can be described using the same parameters as those employed to describe writing:

> [...] the main answer to this question provided by this book is already clear: the evidence of the analyses presented in earlier chapters is that the same 'grammar of English' can be applied to both the spoken and the written language. (1999: 1038)

They can both be described using a shared set of main categories: adjective, noun phrase, relative clause, linking adverbials, and so on.

However, as they discuss in more detail the grammar of conversation, it becomes steadily more apparent that very many features of speech have no equivalent in writing, or are quite rare in forms of writing which are not imitations of speech (as found in, say, novels).

Such features include (but this is by no means an exhaustive list): politeness forms, greetings, farewells, prefaces and tags as in:

> north and south London (*preface*, often non-clausal)
> they're different worlds (*body*, usually clausal)
> aren't they, in a way? (*tags*) (1999: 1072)

utterance launchers (including "overtures" such as *the trouble is, I'll tell you what*), backchannels (*mhm, uh-huh*), expletives and other interjections, vocatives (*guys, Dad, Mike*), repetition and echo, the set of inserts which include: discourse markers (*well, right, I mean*), attention signals (*hey*), response forms (*yeah, dunno*), response elicitors (*right?, eh?*), in fact, the whole system of interrogatives which is much richer than in writing. Indeed conversation is characterised by a large set of items which enable real-time interaction to occur, most of which are all but absent from writing.

There are also a number of items whose use is strikingly more or less frequent in speech than in writing, for example pronouns and other deictics, contractions (*it's, we'll, wasn't, they've*) and negation/contradiction (predominantly expressed by *but* and *no*) are all much more common in most forms of speech.

On the basis of this evidence, the authors begin to have a change of mind on the symmetry of the grammar of speech and writing:

> In some cases of grammatical divergence, written registers and spoken conversation may have simply developed along different paths. (1999: 1051)

They move on to considering the very different way conversation is *constructed* which also makes it entirely distinct from writing. The limitations of on-line planning means spoken discourse proceeds *incrementally* (Brazil 1995), with one add-on following another, generally in the form of short clauses (the average length of clauses in the LSWE corpus is just seven words) interspersed with grammatical fragments or non-clausal units (average length 2 words) which include the inserts listed above and a prevalence of unembedded clauses, such as *when you're ready, if you don't mind,* and there is little of the complex subordination or embedding of clauses possible in many forms of writing. Conversation is also much richer in prefabricated and semi-prefabricated expressions (Biber et al. talk of "lexical bundles") than most forms of writing. Moreover, conversation exhibits a strikingly lower lexical density, defined as the proportion of lexical word tokens (nouns, verbs, adjectives, adverbs) to grammatical word tokens, than almost all written discourse types. It also exhibits a much lower type-token ratio, partly because of the frequency of prefabs and various constraints on vocabulary choice, for instance, of time, memory and generic habit. The grammar of speech, conclude Biber et al. is "dynamic" in the sense that it is constructed and interpreted under real-time pressure. In contrast, they say, "the grammar of writing is more architectural". The written sentence has a "static existence" and its various elements can be placed in more hierarchically ordered relations to each other.

On the basis of this accumulation of evidence, the authors end up with a radically different focus concerning the relation of speech to writing from the one they started out with:

> Focusing now on how the grammar of conversational English is constructed, it may be useful to see the grammar of conversation as to some extent a different system with different rules from the grammar of written English. (1999: 1066)

These conclusions have considerable implications both for linguistic analysis and for language pedagogy. With very few exceptions, notably question tags, the particular features of conversation are rarely included in language descriptions designed for the teaching/learning of English. Even today, these grammars of "English" rely almost exclusively on the concept of a grammar common to writing and speech but historically, as remarked in (8.1), the description of the "common" English grammar was in fact designed to account almost exclusively for the written form of the language. Two recent learning-oriented publications which do include information on speech are Biber et al. (2002), which was developed from Biber et al. (1999), and Carter and McCarthy (2006), which draws on data from the Cambridge and Nottingham Corpus of Discourse in English (CANCODE).

## 8.3 Studying institutional adversarial talk

Returning to the theme of our case studies, in our view, some of the most interesting types of interactive discourse are those in which adversarial situations arise where the participants have conflicting aims, are under pressure and, above all, are accountable to authority. It is in such situations that the strategic use of language can best be studied. In these accountable and adversarial high profile situations, what is said will be seen by a wider audience beyond those physically present and participating in the interaction, a record will remain after the event and one or more beneficiaries of the event (the *beneficiaries* are "the reason why the discourse is enacted" [Partington 2003: 57], that is, the party for whom the discourse is ultimately designed [Partington 2006a: 168]) have professional or even judicial power to judge and punish. Therefore, it is vital for participants to present their view of events carefully and to make sure that it is the view which prevails, while respecting the ratified routines, including politeness norms. Such discourse types, which include press conferences, courtroom discourse and accountability interviews (usually media interviews of public figures) allow the study of bias, neutrality, adversarialness and holding to account (Montgomery 2007). These discourse types have received a great deal of attention from traditional discourse analysts and media studies (Harris 1991; Clayman & Heritage 2002; Hutchby 2005) but a corpus-assisted approach can reveal some of the non-obvious patterns of interaction as well as uncover the core items of routines, turns and speech acts. For this reason we have chosen to illustrate the CADS approach to spoken interaction with a case study of adversarial discourse types, focusing on press briefings and a high profile judicial inquiry.

Two key concepts will be examined. Firstly, *forced priming*, the repetition of certain lexical items and constructions to encourage particular interpretations which are favourable to the user and, secondly, *priming competition*, that is, competition among parties to have their particular messages accepted by the other party and by the particular beneficiaries of the discourse event.

## 8.4 White House press briefings

White House press briefings are press conferences held on a regular basis, in normal times, daily. They are a particular type of *institutional talk* (Drew & Heritage eds 1992), which is defined as talk between professionals and lay people, but the definition can be stretched, as here, to include talk between two groups of professionals with an audience of lay persons (the TV and Internet audience). Briefings are a particularly fascinating genre of institutional talk in that they combine features of informal talk, given that the participants meet so often and know each other well, and confrontational or "strategic" talk. The two parties involved – the spokesperson or podium (officially known as the White House Press Secretary) and the press – have very different interests and aims, which are in conflict on several levels. The podium wishes to project his or her political ideas and particular view of the world, the press to test that view, often suggesting more critical alternatives. The press hopes to uncover ever more information, including any evidence of weakness, malpractice, internal dissension and so on, the podium ideally wants to give as little away as possible outside the official line of his employers (Partington 2003).

Two corpora of briefings are employed in this study, WH-Bush containing briefings from the first George W. Bush administration (c. 3,400,000 words, compiled by Riccio 2009), and WH-Obama, containing all the briefings of the Obama administration in the year from December 2010 to the end of November 2011 (c. 1,300,000 words, compiled by Franconi 2011).

## 8.5 The Hutton Inquiry

The Hutton Inquiry, lasting from August to October 2003 was described as "one of Britain's most powerful judicial hearings" (Rogers 2004: ix). Lord Hutton's terms of reference were "urgently to conduct an investigation into the circumstances surrounding the death of Dr Kelly". David Kelly was a leading scientific advisor on weapons of mass destruction in Iraq who committed suicide after becoming caught up in conflicts between the government and the *BBC* regarding the government dossier *Iraq's Weapons of Mass Destruction: The Assessment of the British Government* published in September 2002. The row between the government and the *BBC* centred on *BBC* journalist Andrew Gilligan's claim that the dossier had been "sexed up". As the dossier formed part of the government's case for using military force against Iraq, many expected the inquiry to cover issues of use of intelligence and the reasons for going to war.

The Hutton Inquiry heard from seventy-four witnesses over approximately one hundred hours of examination, including testimony from members of the government, the Ministry of Defence, and the *BBC*. It was divided into two phases: the first stage of the inquiry was intended to be "devoted to obtaining in a neutral way, by counsel to the inquiry, an account of the events which took place" (Lord Hutton, opening statement, 1 August 2003). In the second stage some witnesses were re-examined by the various counsels. We can, therefore, distinguish between four distinct examination types in the Hutton Inquiry which move along a cline of "hostility":

- cross-examination by the witness's own counsel, henceforth referred to as "friendly examination";
- direct examination by counsel to the inquiry;

- cross-examination by counsel to the inquiry;
- cross-examination by counsel representing persons or bodies who have an opposing view, henceforth referred to as "hostile examination".

The effects of these different examination types on the witness discourse are clearly discernible in terms of the amount of talk contributed, as Table 8.1 illustrates.

**Table 8.1.** Average witness turn length in different examination types

| Examination type | Average no. of words per witness turn |
|---|---|
| Friendly | 25.50 |
| Direct | 17.00 |
| Cross | 15.49 |
| Hostile | 13.80 |

The results are strong evidence that the lawyers successfully control the quantity of the witnesses' discourse and therefore exert institutional power despite the fact that the witnesses were powerful figures outside the specific context of the inquiry (Taylor 2009a).

## 8.6 Similarities and differences between the two discourse types

White House briefings and a judicial inquiry such as the Hutton Inquiry have a good deal in common. First and most obviously, like almost all institutional talk, they follow a question – response (Q–R) format in which questioners seek to extract information, clarification, and so on. They are collaborative in that respondents are institutionally expected to provide at least some kind of meaningful response to the questions and also in that some questioning is supportive of the respondent as in, for example, the abovementioned "friendly examination". But they are also very frequently adversarial, even confrontational, in that the very different interests and aims of (categories of) participants lead them to verbal conflict.

They both consist very largely of talk about language. In the case of Hutton, about government reports and dossiers and about the discussions which led to their creation, and in both cases many questions are requests for clarification of, or challenges to, statements made by either the respondent or one of their governmental clients. In the case of briefings, about administration announcements, its reaction to news reports, what the President has said, and what the podium had previously said.

And they both generate still more language. They are important news-generating events themselves. Language is, of course, the topic of as well as the expression of media messages. In politics and in the reporting of politics, language is constantly being reworked and adapted from other speech events: reports, opinions, announcements, reactions, discussions, and what have been called news performatives and performative documents (Bell 1991; Fishman 1980). Such documents have been created not just as part of the political process but also as part of the communication of that process to the public. As Fishman noted, "[j]ournalists love performative documents because they are the hardest facts they can get their hands on" (1980: 99). Bell too remarks, "[j]ournalists love the performatives of politics where something happens through someone saying it. The fusion of word and act is ideal for news-reporting. No other facts have to be verified" (1991: 207). The only fact is that somebody said something, although what precisely was said and *meant* provides ample food for debate.

Finally, in both cases the stakes are very high. What transpires in briefings can be extremely important and highly delicate from a political perspective:

> Anything McCurry [press secretary during the Clinton administration] uttered from the podium magically attained the status of official White House policy, and if he deviated later on the administration would be accused of the dreaded sin of flip-flopping. (Reaves White)[2]

Not only are the podium's words often treated by the press as White House policy, but they risk interpretation by non-American bodies as official US policy. Since they are broadcast both on television and on the Internet, "any misstep can be beamed instantaneously around the world" (*CNN-allpolitics*).

As for the Hutton Inquiry, the amount of attention which it drew meant that each day's proceedings and the performances of both witnesses and lawyers were also analysed and discussed in the public domain. The witnesses were not only representing themselves in the inquiry but also their respective employers and therefore there were also issues of shared face; individuals were scrutinised and judged on many fronts. Many of the witnesses possessed a high absolute status outside the specific courtroom context, and were both familiar with and adept at interacting within the constraints of a question-response discourse type, and may therefore be closer to the expert witnesses described in Stygall (2001). Furthermore, the witnesses, either individually or collectively, risked being presented/perceived as responsible for the death of David Kelly, which is undoubtedly a very different and more formidable type of risk from the face threats generally envisaged in most work on spoken discourse analysis.

2. From a review prepared for the Amazon US website.

The differences between the two, instead, are largely due to dissimilarities in the powers and resources of the participants, which in both cases are asymmetrical but in different ways. By asymmetry in this context is meant "differential access to such common speech acts as questions, directives, accusations, assertions" (Harris 1995: 122) and so on. Harris, in fact, uses the example of questions in court, which are the prerogative of representatives of the institution and which "appear to be used […] as a mode of control, making it difficult for non-institutional participants (i.e. defendants, witnesses) to put forward propositions of their own" (Harris 1995: 122). This, she suggests, makes it difficult for them to challenge the questioner's view of the world. As mentioned above, the Hutton interchanges however, are rather different from normal courtroom talk in that both sides, questioners and respondents, are representatives of institutions and in most cases experts in communications.

Differential access to discursive resources clearly plays a major part in the briefings too, but the cards are, once again, not stacked against the podium as respondent in the same way as in most institutional questioning. He or she has a large say in setting the agenda, in deciding which topics can legitimately be discussed and for how long, since he or she has greater rights than most respondents to withhold information and has the ability to control turn-taking by the power to nominate next speaker as well as, importantly, to interrupt current questioners. Like many of the chief politicians interviewed in Hutton, the podium also has a staff of wordsmiths to help him or her prepare for being grilled.

The *beneficiaries* of the discourse are largely the same for both discourse types, including other journalists and ultimately, the general public. But in Hutton there is also an immediate beneficiary present in the room, the presiding Lord Hutton, who will be writing the final Report. This authoritative judicial presence can be used as an extra resource by the questioner to constrain a respondent to reply in a compliant fashion, as in the following:

(1) Q Gompertz: This was the draft which became the material which was approved for use; yes?
R Hatfield: If you tell me it is.
Q Gompertz: That is the *evidence*. I would like you to *tell his Lordship*, please, (18 September 2003)

## 8.7 Asserting the administration's message, imposing primings in briefings

From the point of view of the White House, the whole raison d'être of briefings, the reason they were instituted in the first place, was to affirm the administration's favoured view of events to the press and through them to the public. To this end, the podium's discourse is replete with repeated phrases, often with minor variation. A concordance of *realise* in the WH-Bush corpus yields 25 occurrences of *help* the Iraqi people realise a better future/a better and brighter future/a free and peaceful future*. A concordance of *job* in the same corpus reveals how the podium uses it to praise some party, typically some member of the government or service personnel abroad. Of the 250 occurrences, 23 are of the form, *do* an* [intensifier] *job* (for instance, the President/Secretary Rice/our troops are *doing an outstanding/superb/terrific job*). Others are of the form *we greatly appreciate the job they are doing* or we will *make sure our troops have all the tools /resources they need to get the job done/do their job*. This use of *job* in expressing messages of praise is entirely absent from the press's language; indeed commendation of any kind is much rarer in journalists' turns.

In the first six months of the WH-Obama corpus, on the other hand, in times of economic crisis, *job* collocates 101 times in the podium's speech with *grow* and *growth* in constructions like [our aim is to] *drive/increase job creation and economic growth* and, in fact, *grow the economy and increase job creation* is the most common long cluster in the corpus.

It is true that, as Biber et al. remark, spoken discourse is particularly characterised by an abundance of (semi) prefabricated phrases (see Chapter 1):

> Time pressure makes it more difficult for speakers [compared to writers] to exploit the full innovative power of grammar and the lexicon: instead they rely heavily on well-worn, prefabricated word sequences, readily accessible from memory.
> (Biber et al. 1999: 1049)

but the kind of repeated sequences we see here are far longer and syntactically more complex than Biber et al.'s examples of prefabs (or "lexical bundles") from conversation, such as, *Can I have a …?, Do you know what …?*

In the same six months, the podium uses *we* + WORK a total of 198 times, often accompanied by an intensifier: *we are working avidly, we have worked assiduously/diligently/aggressively/very hard/every day*. In a keyword list comparing WH-Obama with the one-million word spoken section of the BNC Sampler (a collection of diverse discourse types) the following items all appeared among the top 200 keywords: *continue* (as in *continue our efforts, continue to work on …*), *forward* (*move the economy forward, as we go forward to create an America that …*), *action, progress, effort/efforts, measures, steps, commitment, decision/decisions*. The attempt is made to portray the White House and their political affiliates generally as active to the point of workaholism. However, the impression is not shared by at least one person in the room:

(2) Q Why does the Congress and the President and Washington generally act like a college kid and wait until the last minute to get everything done? (20/12/2010)

The items *message* and *messages* themselves are used in complex ways to try to impose the government's message. In the podium's speech in WH-Bush, Riccio (2009) found that the White House was repeatedly represented as the addressee of *messages*, as in *we/the President gets the message*, painting a picture of an attentive, listening administration.

More common however was the White House as sender or principal ("the party to whose position the words attest" Levinson 1988: 226) of the message. Three of the top five verb collocates of *message* in WH-Bush, namely *send, think, sending, get* and *sent*, are forms of SEND. The main recipient countries of the White House's messages in WH-Bush are both friend and foe: *North Korea* (30), *Iraq* (17), *Israel* (15), *Syria* (12), whilst the main personal recipients of messages are *Saddam Hussein* and *Bin Laden*. In WHB-Obama this honour falls upon *Qaddafi*. Riccio argues that, in the case of foes, *message* acts as a palatable synonym for "warning" or even "threat", as in the following:

(3) Mr. Fleischer: All of these actions by the United States and our allies – and we have worked every step of the way with our allies – have, I believe, **sent an unmistakable message** to regimes that are seeking or that possess weapons of mass destruction: these weapons do not bring the benefits of security, as the President stated; they bring isolation and unwelcome consequences. (19/12/2003)

(4) Mr. Fleischer: I think Saddam Hussein needs to get the very clear understanding and **message** from the United States and from the world that he needs to disarm, that this is indeed serious. (17/01/2003)

The top qualifier of *message* in both briefings corpora is *clear*, followed by *strong* and *important*. All podiums, unsurprisingly, attempt to project an image of their President as strong and decisive.

The briefings journalists also use the item *message* with considerable frequency but in a different way. As often as not it is a way of testing, of questioning the administration's clarity, resolve or wisdom, of asking the podium in other words whether he feels the administration is sending the wrong message, a dangerous message or a garbled message:

(5) Can we just put this kind of in a broader context in terms of campaign finance reform? What kind of **message** does it **send** if he goes and presides over this dinner, where most of the money being raised is soft money donations? (12/12/2002)

(6) Q: ... troops that are going to be in the Northern territories. Is that not **sending a message** to the Chinese? (11/11/2011)

(7) Q And second, just a **clarification**. When you talk about the President's long-term vision for the economy and industries that in the future will create jobs, I mean, what kind of **message** does that take to the kids getting out of college today that can't find any jobs anywhere? I mean, do they wait – are they supposed to be patient and wait for this? (09/06/2011)

Occasionally, *the message* becomes the object of explicit attention. In the following episode, the podium is asked specifically about the Obama administration's communication strategy, its pervasive occupation of every available space to *get its message out*, and whether in fact this might amount to opportunism:

(8) Q Jay, the White House has made great use of Facebook in terms of its **messaging** strategy. Could the appearance today at Facebook headquarters be construed as an effort to also promote Facebook, to thank Facebook?

MR. CARNEY: Absolutely not. I mean, Facebook has half a billion users, I think something like that – more people than you can possibly imagine. The President – **we get our message out** in a variety of ways and the President appears in a variety of private enterprises to have events. And this is not about endorsing a specific company; it's about accepting an invitation for a forum to speak to the American people. (20/04/2011)

And it is sometimes possible, with the benefit of corpus techniques, to observe how the White House message evolves, how the exact nature of the primings being flooding into the discourse changes, which provides the clearest evidence possible of deliberate attempted linguistic engineering. In January 2011, *Libya* or *Libyan* is not mentioned in the briefings room. In February, both the podium and press are comfortable in discussing the Libyan *government*, which is mentioned 32 times, but in March only nine times, and after that never at all (except a couple of times in the context of freezing Libyan government assets). In the same February, there are six mentions of the Libyan *regime* and six of the *Qaddafi regime*. By March, however, *regime* is used a total of 58 times, 37 co-occurring with *Qaddafi* and 21 with *Libyan*. In the final six months of the year, we find only *Qaddafi* with *regime* and never *Libyan*. The *Libyan government* has rapidly been replaced in briefings discourse with the *Qaddafi regime* in a very clear priming shift to create diplomatic distance between the White House and the Libyan administration. Perhaps the most interesting aspect is that *Libyan government* disappears from the journalists' speech almost as quickly as from the podium's. They clearly acquiesce to the White House's message on this issue or, if we prefer, the administration's priming flooding has been entirely successful.

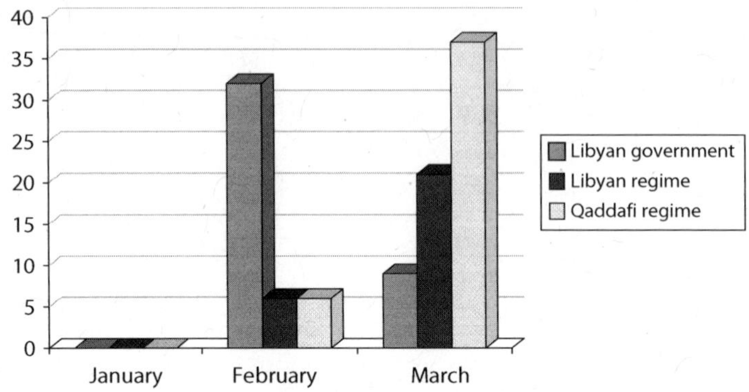


**Figure 8.1.** How the briefings participants refer to the Libyan administration in the first three months of 2011

There is a similar process of diplomatic distancing regarding Syria in WH-Obama, but the process is far slower and not complete. In the first six months of 2011, we find 48 occurrences of *Syrian government* and only 3 of *Syrian regime*. In the second six months, there are 34 references to *Syrian regime* but it is still called *government* 18 times, all by the podium. The podium's language towards the Syrian leader is also gentler than that used about Qaddafi. Throughout the year he continues to be called "*President* Assad", whilst Qaddafi moves from "*Colonel*" or "*Muammar* Qaddafi" to predominantly just "Qaddafi". When the White House in August 2011 finally deems the Syrian leader to have "lost his legitimacy", he is asked to "step aside" (previously simply to "change course" or "cease the violence") and there is no talk of "remove"/"removal" from power, as for Qaddafi.

There is also an evolution in the administration's message regarding Egypt, but once again a very different one. The administration in general and the podium in particular are clearly wrongfooted and embarrassed by events. Although occasionally simply "Mubarak" for the press, the podium refers throughout the year to "*President* Mubarak". He is initially praised as "a close and important partner with our country" (27/01/2011) and the President even praises the Egyptian army just before news breaks of its failure to protect protestors (02/02/2011). The podium cannot bring himself to condemn the President:

(9) Q And as you stand today, you still back President Mubarak?
MR. GIBBS Again Egypt is a strong ally. (26/01/2011)

As the violence grows, much of it reportedly committed by supporters of the President, the podium is asked the straight question:

(10) Q Do you think Mubarak is a dictator?

Realising this phrasing might afford the Podium some room for footing evasion (perhaps "it's not important what I think"), the journalist switches the target or *recipientship* (Partington 2003: 51) of the question to the President:

(11) Q More importantly does the President think Mubarak is a dictator?

But they are still not obliged with a straight answer:

(12) The administration believes that President Mubarak has a chance to show the world exactly who he is by beginning this transition which is so desperately needed in his country and for his people now. (02/02/2011)

Instead the podium's repeated message is that of urging (maximum) "restraint"/"nonviolence", sometimes "on all sides". One journalist at least becomes frustrated at this priming flooding:

(13) Q "Deeply concerned", "urging restraint" – to this point, from my knowledge, no US official has come out and condemned the violence. Is it time to condemn the violence?

This seems indeed to shame the podium into slightly stronger language:

(14) MR GIBBS: Let's be clear Mike. Urging restraint and then seeing violence is obviously very counter to what we believe should be had. And we would strongly condemn the use of violence on either side during this situation, absolutely. (28/01/2011)

But note "on either side". And "condemn the violence" (and also the still more distancing "the *use of* violence"), is not the same as directly condemning the perpetrators of the violence. This can be compared to the following statement at about the same time on the Libyan government:

(15) MR CARNEY: Well, let me just say that the President strongly condemns [...] the bloodshed perpetrated by the Libyan government in Libya. (23/02/2011)

No mention is forthcoming, regarding Libya, about the violence committed by opponents of the regime, nor reference to condemning violence "on both/all/either side(s)", as was the case with Egypt.

By the beginning of February, alongside "restraint" in Egypt, the White House also begins to flood the discourse with calls for "(orderly) transition" (67 occurrences in the month) which at times must "begin now", and for "progress", "change" and "free and fair elections" (this last phrase is used by the podium 39 times, beginning on the 28th January to the end of February):

(16) MR GIBBS [...] I think this underscores precisely what the President was speaking about last night, and that is the time for a **transition** has come and that time is **now**. The Egyptian people need to see **change**. We know that that **meaningful transition** must include opposition voices and parties being involved in this process as we move toward **free and fair elections**. But that process must **begin now**. (02/02/2011)

Analysis of keywords and key clusters lists reveals other repeated Middle East foreign policy messages. The podium affirms that in Libya, Syria and Egypt "people" have "legitimate aspirations" (19) "legitimate grievances" (16) (but "Bahrain is a very different case", 21/03/2011). Because a "humanitarian crisis" is unfolding in Libya, the US provides "humanitarian assistance/relief", which includes, rather bizarrely, "non-lethal" humanitarian relief:

(17) MR DONILON: [...] And again, it would have to be worked out with the opposition group that control various aspects in the east, but they could also be air provisions of non-lethal humanitarian relief. (10/03/2011)

which would make air provisions of *lethal* humanitarian relief an intriguing euphemism indeed. To stress that the US is not acting alone, in the keyword lists we find *partners, allies, together with, international, coalition* and *multilateral*, but to avoid any accusation of lack of initiative or of weakness, also *US leadership*. Finally, *each/every country* co-occurs forty times with *different*, for example:

(18) MR. CARNEY: Well Dan, as we've said, **each country** that has been affected by this unrest is **different. Each country** in the region is **different. Each country** has **different** traditions, political systems and relationships with the United States and other countries around the world. (24/02/2011)

which illustrates the podium's stock response to questions on why the administration's reaction to the various regional uprisings was so different, from bombing in Libya, to diplomatic pressure in Egypt, to kid gloves over Syria and Bahrain (see also Franconi 2011).

Our knowledge, use, and expectations of language are, of course, determined by our exposure to language in context but, as we see in briefings, not all exposure is the result of random personal experience. The above episodes constitute what we have called *forced priming*. Frequently repeated phraseologies – *getting the job done, each country is different*, and so on – result in messages being deliberately flooded into the discourse for a particular purpose. Institutions and enterprises spend considerable investment in encouraging priming through planned repetition, a process Fairclough has called the "technologization" of discourse (1996: 71–83), and for this reason it can be illuminating to employ concordancing and key-item comparison to examine frequency data in institutional discourse. In an age of mass communication and near instant reproduction of multimedia material, there is an increased care and attention paid by institutions to how their desired messages are conveyed. Those who have the information gatekeeping role, including the podiums in the White House, as well as the special advisers employed by the Labour government who were called to appear before the Hutton inquiry, are professional discourse technicians.

## 8.8 Repeated messages and forced primings in Hutton respondents' discourse

If we turn to the language of respondents in the Hutton Inquiry, in particular those representing the British government, in stark contrast to the projection of the speaker's and clients' *clarity*, *strength* and *control* we found in the briefings, their language is characterised by the forced priming of a sense of passivity, lack of personal control and therefore lack of personal responsibility for the events surrounding the death of Dr Kelly. Duguid (2007) compiled a specific corpus of the contributions of three government representatives, namely, Tony Blair and his media advisers Alistair Campbell and Jonathan Powell, entitled Men at Work (MaW) and she found that this sub-corpus was characterised by various strategies of vague language use, many of which were revealed in a keyword and key cluster comparison with All Hutton, the main corpus, comprising the whole Inquiry. The first inkling of this projection of passivity in the key items is the prevalence of the modal HAVE TO giving the impression of being under obligation and not acting from choice, personal desire or conviction. Its relative frequency as a percentage of the total word count of the All Hutton corpus is 0.07%: whereas the Men at Work corpus has a frequency of the lexeme (that is to say including the different forms of *have+to*) as 0.20% of the total word count of that subcorpus. Sometimes it is a discourse marker (*I have to say*) but usually it expresses some constraint, constriction or pressure: e.g.

(19) You then reach the point when you really **have to** take a decision

(20) It was unfair for any of us to **have to** appear at any these select committees

(21) It is going to **have to** happen and therefore let us work out all the steps that then **have to** be taken

(22) Here we were saying: this is a big problem, we **have to** deal with it

(23) I think on that night certainly it was something I was **having to** deal with

### 8.8.1 Impersonal constructions

When compared to All Hutton, the key cluster data shows a significantly greater use of impersonal constructions:

**Table 8.2.** Existential constructions found in the clusters, as percentage of total word count in the respective corpora

| Cluster | All Hutton | Men at work |
|---|---|---|
| *this was* | 0.07% | 0.19 % |
| *that was* | 0.15 % | 0.27 % |
| *it was* | 0.07 % | 0.63 % |
| *there were* | 0.15 % | 0.27 % |
| *there is* | 0.09 % | 0.21 % |
| Total: | 0.53 % | 1.57 % |

Such impersonal constructions have several effects. One is that of depersonalisation; no one gets singled out or named and so no responsibility is assigned, for instance:

(24) **there was** a renewed sense of urgency on the question of rogue states

(25) **there was** a sense that Iraq as it were fitted a special category

(26) **there was** a feeling in Downing St that the Government was not being properly represented by the BBC

(27) **there was** really a sense of frenzy in the media

The audience is none the wiser regarding who precisely has the *sense* or *feeling* mentioned, and no-one can be summoned by the Inquiry to confirm whether or not they had had it.

The use of constructions with *it*, *this* and *that* (also among the keywords) acting as impersonal protagonists is also frequent (the use of *it* is found in several evaluative patterns highlighted by Sinclair & Hunston 2000: 84–101 in their construction of a local grammar of evaluation). Many of the expressions carry negative evaluation (*it was grim, it was hugely complicated, it was getting worse, it was giving rise to concern, it was becoming impossible, it was an extremely difficult and unusual set of circumstances*). The working reality constructed by these forms builds up into a picture of impotence in the face of difficult, uncontrollable and unpleasant circumstances that the three government respondents are less frequently the originators of any actions and more often the perceivers of an existing situation. This finding is corroborated when we look at the content nouns in the Men at Work keywords list.

### 8.8.2 Key nouns: Vagueness in reference

Impersonal constructions do not involve any identifiable person as protagonist which, as we have seen, is an important factor in the construction of a working identity in terms of who does what. In fact, all the nouns in the list of keywords would need further context to be properly interpretable. They are general nouns (Halliday & Hasan 1976), which can be used with the vaguest of reference.

**Table 8.3.** Key nouns found as subjects

| Noun | All Hutton | Men at work | Keyness |
|---|---|---|---|
| *thing* | 0.03% | 0.15% | 90.1 |
| *sense* | 0.03% | 0.12% | 66.3 |
| *issue* | 0.06% | 0.19% | 63.9 |
| *people* | 0.08% | 0.21% | 58.6 |
| *point* | 0.14% | 0.29% | 45.4 |
| *story* | 0.07% | 0.19% | 52.9 |
| *discussion* | 0.05% | 0.12% | 28.0 |

*Thing*

The noun with the highest keyness value (in proportion Men at Work has five times as many occurrences as All Hutton) is one of the vaguest nouns of all: *thing*. It is often hedged (*sort of thing, kind of thing*) which suggests lack of engagement or even a distancing from the precise detail of such aspects of work.

(28) this **thing** was already washing around the media

(29) it was the sort of **thing** that would be good to put into the dossier

(30) it is not untypical of the kind of **thing** that they would publish

Francis (1994) calls these general nouns "text labels" and discusses the difference between their use as retrospective or prospective labels, commenting that they are often used with "fuzzy reference", remarking "it could even be argued that referential indistinctness of this kind could be used strategically […] to creative or persuasive effect, perhaps providing scope for different interpretations or blurring the lines of specious or spurious argument" (Francis 1994: 88). Whether used strategically or not we find repeated patterns in the use of *thing* where one element is foregrounded for strategic persuasive effect, either by the use of a ranking qualifier, for example, *the first thing, the only thing, the one thing, not the major thing, the whole thing, one salient thing, the key thing, the important thing* or by the use of evaluative terms such as *the right thing, the best thing, a good thing, a very clear thing, a deeply unpleasant thing, not a sensible thing*. Most uses of this label express a justification of decisions made with a limited number of options to choose from, that we were trying to do our best in difficult, constraining circumstances.

*Issue*

The item *issue* is another key general noun of very vague reference which seems to have a threatening presence in the world of our government representatives

(31) During August this **issue** had really built up quite significantly and seriously

(32) we were months away from deciding our strategy on this **issue**

We find that the strategy for confronting an *issue* often involves further vague lexis including agentless passives:

(33) a select committee is **looking at an issue** that is such a huge and hot political issue

(34) **this issue had to be returned to** by the international community

(35) it was an important **issue to be discussed**

Yet again, the listener is often left with little information over the precise nature of the *issue* being discussed. A further advantage to this term is that, unlike *problem*, it is non-evaluative and therefore does not even commit the speaker to a value judgement on the various events surrounding Dr Kelly's demise.

*People*

The collective general noun *people* appears in similar patterns to *thing*; and is often preceded by a ranking or evaluative qualifier, as in *the best people, the only people, the right people, the senior people*. Quite who the *people* are involved in each case is not clear, and so no-one can be summoned and asked whether what is said about them is true.

(36) […] someone was being interviewed and re-interviewed and presumably **people** were talking about it within the system

(37) […] it was done as far as possible by consensus in a way that **people** were content with…

(38) Contrary to what some **people** might say I appoint the people but after consultation with the opposition

(39) 'Why now?' – **People** ask. I agree I cannot say "this month, or next, or even this year"

*Point*

Some of the uses of *point* are in fixed phrases such as *at that point, to the point where, point of view* (which indicates the dialogistic positioning of various interlocutors, for instance, *the BBC's point of view*), but others are evaluative as *no point in, little point in* and others rank and evaluate, such as *a key point, a salient point, an important point, a perfectly fair point, a hindsight point* and a set of occurrences take part in emphatic or foregrounding constructions which attempt to angle the interlocutor's attention to one aspect of an argument (Biber et al. 959–962), often with a contrastive or corrective disclaim function:

(40) I think that is a separate **point**. That was the **point** who should sign the foreword. John Scarlett's **point** about ownership was he had to own the whole document.

(41) The **point** was he was not involved in the intelligence part of the dossier; he could not know whether or not the 45 minutes had been added by No. 10 Downing Street.

(42) The whole **point** of it is to meet in private so it can consider intelligence material. He was therefore strongly opposed to it.

(43) When I talk about making "more of the **point** about current concealment plans", I am simply making the **point**, given that we knew he had an infrastructure for concealing his WMD programme, that should be brought out more in the dossier.

(44) I am not making a **point** here about Dr Kelly, but it is important to remember that was part of a report that almost half of the Committee did not sign up to,

(45) The fact is that the entire original allegation was an attack on our integrity. I want to make this **point** because it is important. I do not mean that in a sense I was being unduly sensitive about this.

(46) The **point** we had been trying to make, as I said earlier, Tom Kelly, in particular, was to find a way that the BBC could find a ladder on which to climb down gracefully and admit they got it wrong.

The item *point* can be very vague indeed, its significance can vary from, "idea", "issue", "argument", "purpose", "reason" and "deeper meaning", and it is often difficult for the listener to know which is meant. But it is not always as vacuous in its use as some of the previous general nouns we examined. It is often used simply as a kind of discourse place-holder, which precedes and announces the advent of further, more detailed information. This is part of its function in most of the examples above.

The forced priming of a particular message – that we government representatives were at the mercy of events over the death of Dr Kelly – is much less blatant than those we witnessed in briefings discourse. It is characterised not by the deliberate flooding into the discourse of fixed and semi-fixed phrases, hammering home a specific view of events, but by the steady crafting of the message by framing it in certain lexical-grammatical constructions which are much less obvious to the naked ear. It is essentially a multi-pronged strategy, directing the focus elsewhere, claiming mitigating circumstances, emphasising how important their job is and pleading no culpability. The assistance of corpus-analytical techniques were particularly valuable in uncovering this particular non-obvious meanings (Introduction 0.3).

This representation of themselves as disempowered is both very rare in political discourse (indeed, as we have seen in this volume and especially in Chapter 3, claiming lack of control – and it being a good thing for the claimant – is unusual in any discourse) but at the same time highly strategically effective given the situation and dangers they faced. In many quarters of the press and public, Mr Blair, Mr Campbell and Mr Powell were perceived as expert and aggressive media managers, able and eager to exert excessive control in driving their messages out into the arena of public debate. It was vital for them, therefore, to counter this impression of expert control in the particular case of the events leading to the death of Dr Kelly, that far from being in command of this particular situation, they were powerless in the face of the slings and arrows of misfortune. It could well be that they were not being in any way insincere and have truly felt this was the case. However this may be, it still required considerable communication skills to impose this very novel version of their situation and powers on the discourse beneficiaries, and the fact that the message was broadcast subliminally, in the lexical grammar rather than by simple outright protestations of innocence and impotence, made it all the more effective.

## Suggestions for further research

1. One good introduction to studying the nature of spoken discourse is to compare the spoken sections of the BNC to the written sections. Keyword lists of spoken versus written and written versus spoken can be consulted at http://ucrel.lancs.ac.uk/bncfreq/. The Longman Grammar of Spoken and Written English has a brief account of some of the differences between

conversation and written news reports (Biber et al. 1999: 9–12) and you might like to follow up some of these (for example, in conversation there is a predominance of verbs of thinking and feeling but in news reports of verbs of saying. Make a list of the verbs you find in each variety of discourse). The same work also contains an excellent introduction to the special grammar of conversation (Biber et al. 1999: 1037–1125), which includes a selection of topics, some of which can be investigated using concordances. Questions to research might include: in which types of discourse is swearing most and least common? What are the most common verbs and in what form are they (past, present, *-ing* form)? Which discourse type has the widest and which the narrowest range of *-ly* adverbs? Some *numbers* are significantly more frequent in the BNC spoken than in the written sections. What is the reason for this?

2. Look at the behaviour of the word *absolutely* in spoken and written corpora. Do the same for *like* and *so*. What differences do you observe?
3. The spoken section of the BNC is composed of several different discourse types, from "spoken demographic" to "spoken context-governed" ("business", "education", "institutional" and "leisure"). These sections can be compared using keyword lists. What are the particular characteristics of the more conversational "demographic" speech and the more formal and scripted "context-governed" speech, and vice versa?
4. Look at the Number 10 website of the British Prime Minister's office. There are transcripts of speeches and interviews which could be used for corpus work on political discourse ⟨http://www.number10.gov.uk/news-type/speeches-and-transcripts/⟩
5. One rich topic might be reformulation in adversarial interaction. In normal circumstances briefings questioning would be classified as neither hostile nor friendly. The journalists' professional competence face is enhanced by projecting an image of scepticism towards the White House's accounts of events but without preconceptual bias. However the questioning does share with hostile interrogation the intent to test the respondents' versions and, where appropriate, to suggest much less agreeable alternative versions. The way this reformulation of versions is performed by questioners can be analysed in the concordances of the lexical signals of reporting in questioner discourse. These include, again, reporting verbs especially *saying*, as in *is what you're saying …? are you saying that …? you're not disputing that …?* Other lexical signals of reformulation for concordancing include *in other words, is that correct, is it fair to say, just to be precise*, especially when these are preceded in the question by *so*. A number of lexical markers such as the intensifiers *seriously* and *really* may indicate sites of adversarial questioning of another

speaker's version, as in *are you seriously suggesting…?*, *are you saying…?* The item *but* is very frequently the first word in the questioner's turn, indicating they are nor entirely satisfied by the previous response. These '*but* questions' can be concordanced and analysed to judge the degree of dissatisfaction and how the questioner seeks further enlightenment.

White House press briefings are available online ⟨whitehouse.gov⟩. Download all those available for the previous month or so to analyse some of the items and expressions mentioned here.

6. You might then like to look at reformulation of questions by the respondent. Clayman (1993) analyses the use of reformulation of the question by respondents as a method for evasion or for shifting the questioner's agenda in their favour. He then looks at the ways in which these attempts are in turn resisted by questioners. In the terms we adopt here, he is studying competition between participants' attempts at enforcing dominant primings. He also lists a number of the prevailing features of other-reformulation. In general, he notes, "the reformulation occurs within a discrete unit of talk which is syntactically disjoined from the ensuing response". In other words, the respondent usually takes time off to rephrase the question in a sort of preface to the response. Moreover, "subsequent talk initially builds upon the reformulation rather than the original question" (1993: 164), hence its potential for avoidance. However, those that are most "dangerous", in Clayman's terms, those most likely to pass unnoticed, are "embedded" reformulations where there is no separate passage containing the reworked version. For example, and perhaps most commonly, assertions of agreement to a part of the question may actually serve to ignore other parts. Summarising the question may also be a way of glossing over the threatening parts and altering the emphasis. In the context of the case studies presented in this chapter, we can see such activity as competition among speakers to have their primings accepted. These tactics may be studied by concordancing lexical signals of respondent reformulation which include, most obviously, *no* and *not*, lexis of disagreement *question*, *dispute*, *disagree* and, once again, reporting verbs in expressions such as *what I'm saying is*, *what I'm trying to tell you is* and also the expression [not] *a question/matter of*, in the following preceded by an adversative introductory expression, namely, *Look* (used 712 times by the podium in WH-Obama):

> Q: Jay, just to follow up on Pakistan, Senator Lindsey Graham today said, "You cannot trust them and you cannot abandon them." Do you agree with that assessment?
>
> MR. CARNEY: Look, I **don't** think it's **a question of** trust. I think it's a question of the interests that we share and the cooperation that we've forged. It's a complicated relationship. There's no question. And we do have our differences […] (03/05/2011)

7. When investigating features of an interactive spoken corpus it is usually very useful to be able to access the turns of different categories of speakers individually (for example, in briefings, to separate out the podium's turns and the questioners' turns). This, of course, can be laborious: it can be achieved either by mark-up or manually (cut and paste). Differences in the speech patterns of each category can then be analysed, perhaps beginning with keyword and key cluster comparisons. This can afford intriguing insights into discourse strategies adopted by different interlocutors.
8. Adversarial questioning in institutional Q–R discourse is another potential topic. A number of judicial inquiries, including Hutton are available on-line. In friendly examination the lawyer and witness share a common, although differently motivated, goal or set of wants, and therefore the type of facework enacted is cooperative. The lawyer's competence face, in this context, is dependent on enhancing the face of the witness. In contrast, in hostile examination the two participants in the interaction have opposing and incompatible goals, which means that the facework is aggressive. The lawyer's aim is to threaten the witness's face, to portray him/her as untrustworthy and so on in order to discredit his/her narrative and therefore privilege the lawyer's own narrative. There are a number of lexical indications of aggressive questioning which can be concordanced for analysis. Taylor found that question tags such as *isn't it? didn't you?* "which restrict the response turn and therefore the witness's 'freedom of action' to tell his/her own story" (2009a: 217), for example "When you told parliament that the intelligence was 'extensive, detailed and authoritative', that wasn't true, *was it*?" (Paxman to Blair, BBC interview). She also found that negative interrogatives such as *is it not, was it not, did you not* and *do you not* question tags featured very prominently as key clusters in a comparison of hostile and friendly examination, for instance, "*Do you not* agree that Dr. Kelly was treated shabbily in relation to this episode?"

   Other features of adversarial questioning include quoting the respondents words back to them, "but you said last week that", "but it was you who told the select committee …". Reporting verbs such as SAY, TELL, ASK and so on can be concordanced, especially with context words such as *you* and *but* and also *what* given that cleft construction are often used for emphasis in aggressive questions, for example, *what I'm asking you is* … Be careful to also analyse the tactics respondents adopt in responding to aggressive questioning, and what this might imply about the contextual powers they are able to exercise. For example, questions in *respondent* discourse are potential markers of conflict talk.
9. Another topic of study might be other kinds of aggressive questioning include repetition of the question, which may be detectable by looking for clusters.

10. Radio interviews of politicians and other public figures are an interesting source of interactive data. Collect a week's recordings of the BBC Radio 4 *Today* programme, for example, and try to identify questioning and answer strategies and their formal instantiations.

    As a start, read the following transcript and look at ways in which aggressive questioning and reformulation is being carried out:

BBC Today programme 08.10.11, on the government's plans to effect changes in investment in the National Health Service (NHS).

Q: Don't you have an obligation to admit to people that although the government says there is a real-terms increase on paper year on year in the NHS in England, it means in day to day for a lot of local health providers that cuts are having to be made?
A: Well, I certainly accept that these are challenging times for the NHS um simply because the sheer scale of the economic mess that the last Labour Government …

Q: Yeah but do you accept that there are cuts when you are saying that there is an increase?
A: Well what.. No what I am... saying is that the way in which NHS funding has always been determined has been through the GDP deflator and the erm measure the Government uses for inflation which was 2.4% at the time of the er spending decisions, now 3, –2.9% and what we have made is a 3% cash increase in funding for the NHS.

Q: Do you accept that despite that figure…
A: Yeah

Q: Many local health providers are having to impose quite severe cuts? Do you accept that?
A: What I accept is that…

Q: No look sorry it's a terribly simple question. You've avoided it twice, please don't avoid it again
A: No I…

Q: Are they having to make deep cuts?
A: If you let me finish…. What I accept is that there are challenges and what the NHS has got to do and is doing is look for improving um the efficiency and effectiveness of delivering care which will save money that can then be ploughed back into front line services and you can see it across the NHS the audit commission has said last year there was £4.3 billion pounds worth of efficiency savings which will then be ploughed back into the NHS but yes, it is a challenging <u>time</u> for them and they are having to cope with the problems that we inherited.

Q: It's a challenging time, look sorry fourth time do you accept that people are having to make deep cuts despite the fact that the Government is saying that there is real-terms increase in funding in England?
A: No what I think and believe is …

Q: You don't accept that
A: No what I believe should happen … is happening is that they are looking at greater erm efficiency and effective ways of delivering services

Q: D'you mean cuts?
A: They are cutting back on um levels of management that is um erm top-heavy and that is […]

Q: You don't think any patient services are being cut?
A: No because there are great pressures

Q: You see managers have been telling us, and some of them don't want to be named cos they might get into trouble, and these are not politicians these are people and you well know in your own area and in others who are trying to deliver the best services they can and they say it is a deceit on the public in practice to say on the one hand there is a real-terms increase but in fact because of the savings they are being asked to make and the money they are being asked to hold back they in fact are having to cut services and leaving the public completely confused because they're told on the one hand by the Government "We're putting more money into the NHS" and their local hospitals are saying " Sorry. We're taking money out. "Don't you understand that the public is confused by that.
A: Well, I understand that if it is put like that it will cause confusion but I don't accept that that is the way it should be put. The way it should be put is to explain to people there are great challenges on the finances, for more effect this has got to be…

Q: You sound like the sort of PR people have been coming in here and saying "I'm cutting this service but I don't call it a cut I call it a great challenge".
A: Well, it is challenging and what we've got to make sure what we have got to ensure…

Q: Can a challenge ever be a cut? Cutting? It can
A: yes it can be a cut but the way

Q: Why not call it what it is?
A: because what we are looking for is for different ways of providing a service more effectively … if I could give you some

Q: It sounds like a …
A: could give you some…

Q: Yeah ok ….

Do you feel this is an effective method of conducting interviews?

CHAPTER 9

# Interactive spoken discourse 2

## CADS and (im)politeness

### 9.1 Overview of corpus linguistics and (im)politeness

(Im)politeness studies are generally concerned with trying to understand the role of face and facework in communication, and how different types of facework are expressed. The term (im)politeness is used here to make it clear that we are as interested in aggressive facework as we are in mitigation of face threat, or face enhancement.

Research combining corpus linguistics and (im)politeness may be broadly divided into two categories; in the first and less frequently used method, the corpus is used to build up an understanding of first order (im)politeness (impoliteness1), that is the lay-person's notion of (im)politeness; while in the second, the corpus is used to investigate second order (im)politeness (impoliteness2), that is, the scientific/academic notion of (im)politeness. The distinction between first and second order politeness was introduced by Watts, Ide and Elich who stated that:

> We take first-order politeness to correspond to the various ways in which polite behaviour is perceived and talked about by members of sociocultural groups. It encompasses, in other words, commonsense notions of politeness. Second-order politeness, on the other hand, is a theoretical construct, a term within a theory of social behaviour and language usage. (1992: 3)

Although the distinction is at times a fuzzy one, many would argue that in order to analyse the theoretical notion we need to start with the lay notion, that is, the idea that the participants in any interaction have about what is polite, appropriate, and so on, and this is where corpus linguistics can make a truly significant contribution, by allowing us to examine large quantities of naturally occurring data.

To date the interaction between (im)politeness and corpus linguistics has been somewhat one directional, there are no articles which have been published in the last four editions of the *International Journal of Corpus Linguistics* with (im)politeness or facework in the title or abstract, while there are at least four articles from the last two years in the *Journal of Politeness* which mention corpora. The adoption of any particular methodology raises interesting questions about the relationship and the sequential order between theory and methodology: such as whether the resulting analysis is primarily data-driven or hypothesis testing. If we look at previous studies in this field, it becomes clear that the theoretical framework of (im)politeness has been used in combination with corpus linguistics for a range of purposes and at a variety of stages in the research process:

1. The theory may be applied to the data to account for the findings of a study, for instance, in the discussion and interpretation of keywords obtained from comparing two different corpora or sections from corpora. For example, Archer and Culpeper (2009) compare the language used in different social interactions in a corpus of historical English. This type of inherently comparative approach is particularly useful in cross-cultural pragmatics though see also Taylor (2006) on comparing different phases of courtroom discourse.
2. Alternatively, the corpus may be marked up with the specific aim of testing a hypothesis, as in McEnery et al. (2002), who annotated their data for pragmatic information about the sense and force of utterances in order to investigate directness and indirectness. In this kind of analysis the annotation may be very time-consuming, but it also forms an integral part of the interpretation of the data. The *UAM Corpus Tool* facilitates this type of detailed annotation without requiring advanced computer skills (see Appendix).
3. More recently, Culpeper (2008) has used corpus linguistics to investigate the evaluative force of the expressions *over-polite* and *too polite*, and thus highlights the potential of a corpus semantic approach to metalinguistic labels of (im)politeness. This approach is also evident in Hardaker's (2010) analysis of first order (im)politeness notions of "trolling" in computer-mediated communication.[1] She examines over 2000 references to *troll** in her chosen discourse type in order to see how this community perceives troll behaviour and to form a working, user-based definition of trolling for future research.
4. Most frequently, the corpus is used as a resource for examples of a given (im) politeness feature, and research using this combination ranges from Kohnen's (2008) study of Anglo-Saxon address terms to Beeching's (2006) study of *quoi* in contemporary French.

This categorisation aims to show the range of possible intersections available between corpus work and (im)politeness, starting from the most data-driven.

1. Trolling is generally understood as the deliberate creation of social discord in online communities, though see Hardaker's article for a full definition.

In reality, of course, there is likely to be some overlap between the groupings and the extent to which the full scope and potential of corpus linguistic methodologies are applied varies greatly.

In terms of what additional value a corpus approach to (im)politeness might offer, it can provide a new means of deciding what to analyse as (im)politeness; a way of addressing both first and second order notions and therefore responding to criticisms about the lack of interaction between the two within (im)politeness studies; it enables the researcher to provide information about how frequent a phenomenon is; and also permits research into the process of conventionalisation of im/politeness formulae and pragmatic meaning shift.

However, there are also, naturally, some limitations and potential pitfalls with this type of analysis. First, there is a risk that the importance of context may be neglected. This is less likely to be a problem in CADS where corpora are often created by the analyst his/herself who is aware of the context of interaction of the texts s/he includes, but where so-called general, heterogeneric corpora are used, it is essential to note where each set of data comes from. Secondly, politeness and impoliteness studies would ideally avail themselves of spoken and/or multimedia corpora which include information on intonation and other paralinguistic features, but even today few such corpora are readily available and they still require a good deal of time, effort and expense to build. Third, the use of a corpus does not in itself guarantee reliability or validity – a cherry-picked example from a corpus is still a cherry- picked example. Fourth, and connected to this last point, as with all corpus research, there is a danger of referring to corpora as though it will automatically confer scientific value; this obviously depends on the corpus, the questions asked, the amount of interpretation and number of generalisations drawn, and so on.

## 9.2 A case study: When "politeness" is not being polite

In the following section we employ a case study to investigate what, in practice, a corpus approach to (im)politeness may involve. The aim of this piece of research was to analyse the use of conventional markers of respect such as *with respect* or *sir* and challenge the blunt assumption that a polite form will necessarily be doing politeness work. Using corpus evidence, we aim to demonstrate that the use of such forms can perform a number of different functions in discourse other than respecting an interlocutor's face. Indeed, they are sometimes used as a deliberate ploy to attack it.

In the first stage of the case study, we illustrate how corpora may be employed to identify sites of potential impoliteness in a systematic, replicable way and in the second stage, we use the corpora to examine occurrences of the markers of conventional negative politeness and identify patterns of usage within different discourse types.

### 9.2.1 Introduction

> Humphries: Minister, with the greatest possible respect –
> Hacker: Oh, are you going to insult me again?
>
> (*Yes, Minister*)[2]

This case study examines the variety of functions which negative politeness forms fulfil in institutional discourse. The potentially confusing term, *negative politeness*, does not of course refer to impoliteness, but to politeness which is directed at an individual's negative face, that is to say the right of the recipient to maintain their distance (Goffman 1967: 72). This is counterbalanced by positive politeness through which a speaker may show his/her appreciation for another participant and, as Goffman notes, the two are frequently in opposition:

> To ask after an individual's health, his family's well-being or the state of his affairs, is to present him with a sign of sympathetic concern; but in a certain way to make this presentation is to invade the individual's personal reserve. (1976: 73)

Here we focus on the use of negative politeness in institutional discourse in order to add to the increasing literature which demonstrates that negative politeness features are clearly not limited to mitigation of the effect of an

2. A BBC political sit-com from the 1980s. From the episode "The Greasy Pole", available at ⟨http://www.youtube.com/watch?v=NoQY3BGbteY&NR=1⟩ (5 January 2011).

unavoidable face-threatening act (FTA) on the addressee (e.g. Harris 2001, Blas-Arroyo 2003). Rather, as the quote above from *Yes, Minister* illustrates, in certain contexts some "polite" phraseologies have become so conventionalised that, like Hacker, most competent English speakers would be primed to treat them as discourse markers indicating that a (possibly avoidable) face threat is about to follow.

Within the institutional discourse types studied here, polite phraseologies, while superficially expressing distance and deference, are seen to perform a variety of overlapping functions such as showing awareness of the discourse norms, allowing the participant to be "consciously aggressive in an acceptable way" (Locher 2004: 90), demonstrating that the participant can "handle it" (Mullany 2002), marking sections of the interaction for attention, and, finally, functioning as an integral part of an impolite move in the case of mock politeness, where mock politeness is used to refer to instances where "the FTA is performed with the use of politeness strategies that are obviously insincere, and thus remain surface realisations" Culpeper (1996: 356).

### 9.2.2 Negative politeness

Negative politeness is a fundamental concept in much politeness research. Brown & Levinson define it as follows:

> redressive action addressed to the addressee's negative face: his want to have his freedom of action unhindered and his attention unimpeded. It is the heart of respect behaviour, just as positive politeness is the kernel of 'familiar' and 'joking' behaviour [...] it performs the function of minimizing the particular imposition that the FTA unavoidably effects. (1987: 129)

Combining this with work by Lakoff (1975), and O'Barr and Atkins (1980) on women's speech and courtroom discourse respectively, it has been posited that negative politeness features are characteristic of powerless speech, that is to say, they are a set of forms most commonly resorted to by the less powerful participants in interactions. However, a growing body of literature on institutional discourse has cautioned against equating institutional and interactional power (e.g. Johnson 2002; Mills 2002; Thornborrow 2002), and subsequent quantitative research has shown that, while the presence of negative politeness strategies may correlate to a lack of institutional power, it does not necessarily correspond to a similar lack of interactional power (for instance Taylor 2006). The implication of this non-equivalence between interactional power and the use of superficially deferential strategies is that the negative politeness strategies must be performing additional functions, and this is the focus of this study.

Harris (2001) can be credited with drawing attention to the potential of institutional discourse for impoliteness studies: she highlights the way in which "systematic impoliteness is not only sanctioned in Prime Minister's Question Time but is rewarded in accordance with the expectations of the Members of the House (and the overhearing audience)" (2001: 466). Secondly, she notes the regular co-occurrence of intentional face threats and negative politeness features in this discourse type. Perez de Ayala also analysed the adversarial nature of Prime Minister's Question Time and similarly concluded that, within this context:

> the function of politeness changes: politeness strategies are not the linguistic means necessary to avoid conflict. Question time *is* conflict. Politeness strategies become the means at the Chamber's disposal to be able to work and progress, even in the middle of conflict. (2001: 164–165)

Politeness markers then become a way of "getting away with it". In these cases, it is not so much a case that politeness "makes possible communication between potentially aggressive partners" (Brown & Levinson 1987: 1) but makes communication between *explicitly* (and *necessarily*) aggressive partners possible. This view is repeated in Ilie (2004) where she notes that in both her UK and Swedish parliamentary data mitigation strategies are used alongside deliberately offensive rhetorical acts in order to avoid being institutionally sanctioned (2004: 81–82).

Christie's (2002) study of UK parliamentary discourse focuses on apology behaviour, and challenges the default categorisation of apologies as politeness strategies. She notes the range of functions which apologies fulfil in this context, and, of particular interest to this chapter, she describes the way in which apologies are used to enhance the speaker's own standing. For instance apologies may be used to (favourably) differentiate the speaker's behaviour from that of other participants, and, where they occur for putative offences, the apology allows the speaker to display their integrity and respect for norms. The importance given to this explicitly egotistical motivation recalls Goffman's statement that "[i]n aggressive interchanges the winner not only succeeds in introducing information favorable to himself and unfavorable to others, but also demonstrates that as interactant he can handle himself better than his adversaries" (1967: 25).

Among the research on broadcast interviews, a rhetorically similar institutional discourse type, Piirainen-Marsh finds that:

> the [interviewer] combines conventionally polite forms and a neutralistic posture with a challenging use of interrogative syntax. By doing so the [interviewer] seems to build on what is appropriate or within the expected politic behaviour of the interaction and uses it as a resource in constructing an accusatory question agenda. (2005: 208–209)

In addition to conforming to situational norms, other research has noted the importance of the public nature of political interviews on the use of politeness strategies, for example Mullany (2002: online) notes that in her data, an interview between Hilary Armstrong (a government minister at the time) and John Humphrys (a well-known radio presenter), the interviewee uses mitigating language tactically to avoid conversational breakdown which "would be damaging both for HA and the Labour Party she represents if she is perceived to be unable to cope with JH's aggressive style". The importance of the public dimension naturally also applies to parliamentary discourse, and in particular Prime Minister's Questions which usually has a much larger audience than most debates, a fact at least partly due to the entertainment value perceived in the inherent confrontation.

### 9.2.3 The discourse context

Given the importance in any analysis of the situation of production, the discourse context is described, albeit briefly, with particular reference to the potential impact on facework and (im)politeness. The main corpora used in this chapter contain UK data from parliamentary discourse, a public inquiry and political interviews (the corpora are described in more detail in Section 9.4.2). These three discourse types were chosen because they are all instances of public, institutional discourse consisting of a restrictive turn-taking format, in which "sanctioned aggressive facework" (Watts 2003: 260) may form part of the expected behaviour given the lack of common goals. Additionally, the participants in each of the three contexts were similar given that the interactions featured predominantly politicians, in fact some speakers appear in all three corpora.

Although the power structure is asymmetrical, in particular in courtroom discourse and broadcast interviews, it is critical to recall that *both* participants, the questioner and the respondent, have been assigned an institutional role and are constrained to interacting within the limitations of that role and the situational norms more generally. For instance, although the questioner may have greater topic control, in unmarked discourse s/he is still limited to introducing information through a turn-type that may be recognised as a "question".

In terms of contextual norms, the three discourse types differ in the extent to which they are rule-bound, from the explicit regulation of parliamentary discourse, to the presumed knowledge of expected behaviour in a broadcast interview.

Furthermore, and this is perhaps the most important feature of these discourse types, the participants are interacting with the primary aim of displaying information for the *beneficiaries* of the discourse, rather than exchanging information. As noted in Chapter 8, the beneficiaries of the discourse are "the reason why the discourse is enacted" (Partington 2003: 57), and what all three discourse types have in common is that they were public and the beneficiaries included the media and wider (voting) public. On this point, we might recall Brown & Levinson who note that "in general, persons want their goals, possessions, and achievements to be thought desirable not just by anyone but by some particular others especially relevant to the particular goals" (1987: 63), and these *some particular others* may be seen to broadly correspond to the beneficiaries in the discourse types studied here.

Given that the interaction is enacted for (largely) non-participatory beneficiaries, it also follows that facework is predominantly directed at those beneficiaries rather than the interlocutor, which is to say that by conforming to the expectations of the discourse context, the participants seek approval – to gain face – from a third party.

The three discourse types also represent something of a cline in terms of expected aggressive facework. At one extreme, we have hostile cross-examination in the Hutton Inquiry, where the witness is examined by Counsel for another (opposing) party, whose primary goal is discrediting the witness's narrative and attacking his/her face in the eyes of the beneficiaries. At the other end of the continuum, we have two forms of friendly examination, the first where the witness is examined by his/her own lawyer, the second in display questions and interventions put to an MP by a sympathetic member of his own party. The *Breakfast with Frost* interviews are also typically perceived as being towards the "softer" end of the spectrum, as the following quote from the Frost_media corpus (see following section) illustrates:

(1) "[…] It's pointless being confrontational when you don't have the smoking pistol, because all you do is shut people up." This approach of Frost's is less professional than dispositional. One suspects that he regards all confrontation as ungentlemanly; […] Frost's great talent is for schmoozing guests onto his show in the first place and it is based, largely, on his understanding of the workings of male vanity. (*Guardian*, 27/10/2003)

### 9.2.4 The corpora and corpus interrogation tools

Three types of corpora are used in this chapter; the first set contains the institutional interaction which is the focus of the analysis, the second contains meta-comment on those interactions, and the third is a reference corpus.

The first set is composed of three corpora, each consisting of institutional interactions from 2003:

a. HoC contains c. 960,000 tokens from House of Commons debates on the Iraq war,
b. Hutton contains c. 840,000 tokens from the Hutton Inquiry, a public inquiry set up to investigate the circumstances surrounding the death of Dr. David Kelly which heard from seventy-four witnesses including members of the government, the Ministry of defence, and the BBC (see also Chapter 8),

c. Frost contains c. 480,000 tokens of interviews with Labour politicians on the *BBC* television programme *Breakfast with Frost*.

The first two, HoC and Hutton, are part of the CorDis Corpus which was created as part of a larger project into the discourse of the Iraq war (see Cirillo et al. 2009 for details of compilation), while Frost was created for this project. The Hutton corpus is further sub-divided according to the examination types. Reference will be made to *direct examination* when witnesses were examined for the first time by the one of the inquiry's QCs, *cross-examination* when the witness is re-examined by one of the inquiry's QCs, *friendly examination* where the witness is examined by his/her own QC, and *hostile examination* where the witness is examined by another party's QC.

It is important to note that all three corpora are actually small enough to be read and analysed without necessarily viewing them through corpus interrogation software. The ability to access the data in a variety of ways is an important part of CADS methodology. However, it should also be noted that unfortunately there are no corresponding sound files for any of the three corpora since they were not available from the respective sources; the Hutton Inquiry, Hansard and BBC websites. This limits the potential analyses, particularly in the study of mock politeness.

The second set of corpora were created specifically for the research question investigated here, using the *LexisNexis* database and these are:

a. Frost_media (c. 2,888,000 tokens)
b. Hutton_media (c. 23,256,000 tokens)

These ad hoc corpora contain all the UK newspaper articles available through *LexisNexis* from 2003 which referred to *Breakfast with Frost* and *Hutton Inquiry* respectively.

The third corpus-type is that represented by the heterogeneric British National Corpus (BNC), which is employed in order to extend research to a larger corpus, and to look into a variety of discourse types.

Three different types of software were used for the corpus interrogation: *Xaira*,[3] *Wordsmith 5* (Scott 2008), and, to a lesser extent, the freeware *AntConc*.[4] For comparative work across the three main sub-corpora *Wordsmith Tools* was

3. *Xaira* (XML Aware Indexing and Retrieval Architecture) developed at Oxford University is the XML version of *Sara*, the software originally developed for interrogating the British National Corpus. For further information: ⟨http://www.oucs.ox.ac.uk/rts/xaira/⟩ [Accessed 01/09/2008].

4. *AntConc* 3.2.1w (Windows). Developed by Laurence Anthony, Waseda University, Japan.

used because it is more flexible than *Xaira* and can also be used to process plain text files. *Xaira* was preferred for detailed analysis of the concordances and collocates of HoC and Hutton (which are in an annotated, XML format). *AntConc* was used for analysis of distribution as the parallel plot display is very helpful for comparison.

### 9.2.5 Identifying impoliteness

It has been noted that one obvious limitation of corpus study is that the analysis requires the identification of lexical items, for instance Rühlemann states that:

> [t]his requirement means that, in a corpus, only those phenomena can be studied fully whose lexical form(s) and pragmatic function(s) display a straightforward one-to-one relationship […] Where there is a complete form-function mismatch, as in cases of conversational implicature, a quantitative corpus study will be useless. (2010: 290)

However, if there is such a complete form-function mismatch, then it should be possible to locate these phenomena by identifying clashes of context or co-text. Furthermore, in this chapter we propose that corpus analysis may be used to identify potential sites of (im)politeness without recourse to lexical forms. Once such events of significant facework have been identified, they may subsequently be analysed in terms of frequency and distribution/location as well as through appropriate qualitative techniques. The location of (im)politeness events may be found through pragmatic annotation, for instance if a corpus contains information about speech volume or occurrences of laughter (e.g. Reershemius 2012). In the institutional context studied here, some ways in which corpora may be used to identify sites of impoliteness would include looking for:

1. meta-pragmatic comment on the discourse norms (discussed in Section 2:1)
2. reception/judgements of impoliteness from an addressee
3. reception/judgements of impoliteness from third parties i.e. neither the speaker nor the addressee (discussed in Section 2:1)
4. shifts from transactional to interactional mode (discussed in Section 2.2).

Clearly, there is much overlap in these sets, in particular with the first three which all refer to first order notions of impoliteness (impoliteness1), that is to say common sense/usage notions of impoliteness. It should also be noted that the third set, reception/perception of impoliteness by other parties, is quite wide-ranging, for example it could refer to immediate reactions, such as the call to order by the Speaker in parliamentary discourse, or to delayed reactions, as is the case in press reporting. Theoretically, there should also be the fifth possibility of looking for the speaker's own evaluation, but this post-utterance narration is so unlikely in the discourse types studied here that it has been omitted.

It should also be noted that the choice or relevance of any of these approaches will depend on the theory of (im)politeness with which the researcher is working, for example none of these can contribute to a theory of (im)politeness that is centrally dependent on intention. While intuitively intention does seem to be key to the perception of (im)politeness, and this is supported by evidence such as the concordance lines below, it is difficult to see how a definition which was entirely dependent on speaker intentions can be operationalised, given the impossibility of an observer being able to reliably access them.

| | | |
|---|---|---|
| A0F | I don't | *mean* to be rude, but how on earth are you going to |
| CA3 | I'm sorry, dear boy, I don't | *mean* to be rude |
| F9C | He didn't | *mean* to be rude. |
| G0P | I'm sorry, I don't | *mean* to be rude. |
| G0X | He doesn't | *mean* to be rude,' explained Betty. |
| GY7 | You see you see I don't | *mean* to be erm rude or anything but as I'm sure you |
| H8X | said breathlessly, 'I didn't | *mean* to be impolite |

Concordance lines from the *BNC* of MEAN + *rude/impolite* within a span of 5. The code on the left tells the user which section of the corpus the line has been extracted from.

Therefore, for practical purposes, exchanges will be analysed as sites of potential impoliteness in one of two ways. Firstly, if they have been verbally marked as such by participants or by a third party, that is, by observers to the event such as members of the press. Secondly, if the behaviour can be seen to go beyond the discourse norms operating in the specific context of production.

### 9.2.6 Looking for meta-pragmatic comment

In looking for comment either from participants, or from observers, we suggest that three types of search terms may be used:

1. The first set is formed of terms which evaluate and classify events or utterances using meta-pragmatic politeness terms such as: *rude*, (*im*)*polite* etc.
2. The second set, in the search for impoliteness, would include terms which indicate that aggressive facework occurred such as *feisty, confrontational* etc.
3. The third set is made up of terms which refer to the norms, and exceptions to them such as: (*in*)*appropriate*, (*un*)*usually* etc.

The precise choice of which items to include in these sets is of course subjective, but semantic work of the sort suggested by Culpeper could assist in construction, for instance, by analysing the use of *rude* within a relevant corpus it may be possible to reliably identify other salient terms. For this study, because the corpora were relatively small, it was most productive to look at comment from third parties of the type belonging in the second set above and this will be discussed below. However, the data also contained a certain amount of explicit meta-pragmatic comment of the first type, for instance, from HoC we find the following exchange (our italics):

(2) Francois (Con): On a point of order, Mr. Deputy Speaker. I fully appreciate that the Minister can take the decision not to give way, but as someone who served in the regiment that hon. Members have been discussing, I must put it on record that I think that it was extremely *discourteous* that he did not give way to me. Do you not think that he is being *impolite*?

Lord (Deputy-Speaker): That is a matter not for the Chair, but for debate. In any case, the hon. Gentleman has now put his point on record. (HoC)

Interestingly, Francois professes to acknowledge his awareness of the norms, *I fully appreciate*, but nonetheless unfavourably evaluates the action and actor as *discourteous* and *impolite* respectively, and invites the Speaker, the institutional arbiter of the norms, to agree with him. The Speaker, however, rejects the invitation to agree, but draws attention to the supposed aim of the intervention: putting the perceived impoliteness on record, and ensuring that others notice it.

In the following example, also from the House of Commons corpus, the impolite label is similarly used to draw attention to another MP's supposed intentions:

(3) Garnier (Con): I have the *greatest_respect* for the right hon. and learned Member for North-East Fife [Mr. Campbell] for the manner in which he advanced his case this afternoon and for the *clever* way in which he said that this afternoon's debate should not descend into party-political argument. That makes it hugely *impolite* to be *rude* about the Liberal Democrat motion. I shall not be *impolite*, but I will have one or two things to say about it. (HoC)

Garnier starts by apparently positively evaluating Campbell: *greatest respect, clever*, but then inverts expectations and his evaluation in the second sentence, starting from *[t]hat makes it*, using the contrast to highlight what he portrays as an attempt at manipulating the debate.

Analysis of the second set of search terms, those which are likely to indicate aggressive facework, proved more fruitful. For instance the Frost_media corpus contained one particular interview with Tony Blair which was adjudged by press observers to contain a considerable amount of aggressive behaviour, as illustrated in the extracts below:

(4) This is what Mr Blair is certain to do in his speech tomorrow – saying, as he did in his *unusually feisty performance* on Breakfast with Frost yesterday – that what really motivates him is crime, asylum, health, and education. (*Scotsman* 29/09/2003)

(5) Mr Blair used a *combative interview* on BBC1's Breakfast with Frost to *confront* his critics and tell them he was in no mood to back down. (*Telegraph* 29/09/2003)

(6) Mr Blair again showed his resilience yesterday in a *combative performance* on the BBC One show Breakfast with Frost. (*Times* 29/09/2003)

(7) Mr Blair gave a *combative performance* on BBC's Breakfast With Frost programme (*Independent* 29/09/2003)

(8) It wasn't just a *belligerent performance* he gave on Breakfast With Frost, it was *arrogant*. (*Mirror* 29/09/2003)

(9) But nor was the refusal to back down on Iraq, NHS reforms or student top-up fees couched in the *confrontational language* Mr Blair *deployed* in his conference warm-up interview with BBC1's Breakfast with Frost. (*Guardian* 01/10/2003)

Each of these, from five different papers, with different political affiliations, referred to an interview of Blair by Frost which took place on 28/09/2003 and highlighted it as a site of potential impoliteness. If we then move from focussing on the reception corpus, Frost media to the interaction corpus, Frost, a comparison of the wordlist for the response turns of this single interview with the response turns in all the rest of the Frost corpus showed that the keywords included *you* (2.16 compared to 1.31 occurrences per thousand words) an indicator of directness. A large proportion of these consisted of Blair's characteristic interpolation, *you know*, used as an utterance launcher and discourse marker which invites consensus (Duguid 2007). However, in ten out of the 81 occurrences he was directly addressing his interviewer as illustrated in the concordance lines below:

| | |
|---|---|
| they use those weapons, then I just tell | *you* the economic insecurity that will result from that, t |
| ly in relation to this. But let me just tell | *you* and tell the public the other side of the picture |
| things by deals. Okay? And as I said to | *you* earlier, the British people decide who the prime |
| nquiry. But let me just say one thing to | *you*, I also hope people understand that sometimes the |
| ese things. But I just simply say this to | *you*. If we had received this intelligence, with all the hi |
| it is. In saying that, I emphasise this to | *you*, in the end the British people decide who the prime |
| ing public services but all I'm saying to | *you*, it's interesting just in the last couple of weeks, two |
| ssary to spend but again I would say to | *you* that just realise the consequences of having a stable |
| ry often a mystery to me, as they are to | *you* I should suspect. |
| cross to people. I mean I grew up with, | *you* grew up with, the concept of the Second World Wa |

Concordance lines of *you* addressed to Frost in Blair's responses in the 28/08/2003 interview.

Referring to the interview, the *Guardian* leader the following day described Blair as having been "astonishingly direct". While the examples above do not necessarily indicate impoliteness, the reactions to the interview clearly show the effect of a shift from established norms on the audience. Although it is interesting to note that the evaluations differed: for the *Times* the performance was evaluated favourably as showing *resilience*, while for the *Mirror* Blair appeared *arrogant*.

### 9.2.7 Looking for shifts from transactional to interactional mode

An alternative means of identifying sites of potential (im)politeness could be that of looking at the norms of the discourse situation, and subsequently identifying what goes beyond such norms. This draws on Locher & Watts's conceptualisation of (im)politeness, and, as Locher & Watts (2005: 17) note, it entails the researcher knowing *a priori* what is (in)appropriate.

Following Brown and Yule (1983), many researchers adopt their "analytic convenience" of distinguishing between transactional and interactional language. Transactional language is primarily used to convey "factual or propositional information" while interactional language is primarily used to "establish and maintain social relationships" (Brown & Yule 1983: 1–3). Partington (2006a) takes this distinction and proposes describing interactional and transactional as modes rather than functions of language, and notes that they are "also psychological notions, especially with regard to institutional settings: speakers are in transactional mode when they feel they are doing institutional business" (2006: 59). Therefore, although the term transactional is used, this is certainly not to suggest that face concerns and facework are irrelevant in this mode, but to indicate that the participants "felt" they were doing institutional business. Thus, what is meant when talking of a shift into interactional mode, that is, away from "playing the interview game" (Clayman & Heritage 2002: 148), is that the participants are behaving as if they feel that discourse is no being longer enacted and displayed for the original beneficiaries.

As this transactional-interactional shift constitutes a clear move away from the norms and expected behaviour in the institutional discourse contexts discussed here, it is suggested that identifying movement between the two modes offers a way of locating potential (im)politeness, and another way of approaching the identification of (im)politeness from a systematic CADS perspective.

For example, in the Frost and Hutton corpora, where the discourse is largely enacted for non-participatory beneficiaries, the use of the second person pronoun to address the interviewer, as illustrated in the Blair concordance lines above, suggests that Blair feels that his face is under threat and has started to interact personally with Frost, as opposed to following the conventions normally adopted when displaying for an audience. One example of a key phraseology we can employ to explore this is *you are +ing*, given that its employment suggests both a shift to focus on the present time and place and, more importantly, to a repositioning of the beneficiary. Figure 9.1 shows the distribution of *you are +ing* in the *Breakfast with Frost* interviews (the Frost corpus) and the exchanges during the different interaction types of the Hutton Inquiry. Each vertical line indicates an occurrence of *you are +ing.*

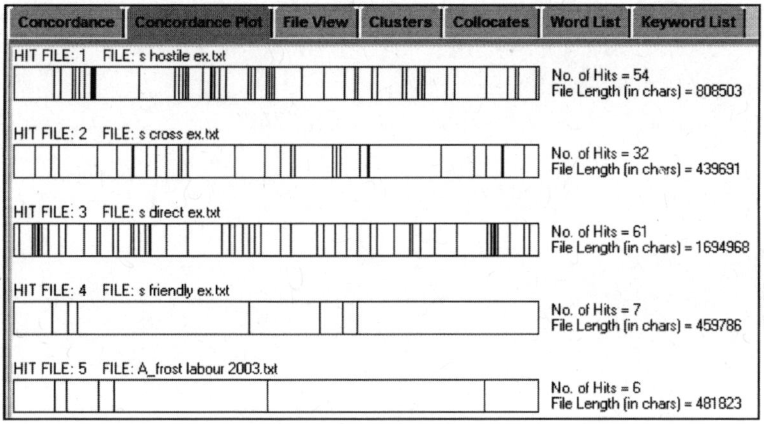


**Figure 9.1.** Distribution of *you are +ing* in *Frost* andthe different phases of *Hutton*

As predicted, the distribution analysis shows a higher frequency of occurrences in hostile examination than in friendly, and what is also noticeable from the visual plot is that the occurrences tend to cluster together. This continuum across the different discourse types does then seem to corroborate the hypothesis that in this type of institutional discourse it is a useful phraseology for identifying shifts from transactional to interactional mode.

A closer reading of the occurrences of the phraseology shows that, in a small number of cases, within the immediate cotext of the directness of *you are + ing* there are also distancing mechanisms, associated with negative politeness (in bold):

(10) R. Tebbit: **I think, if I may say so,** *you are coming* still at that we had a stratagem to reveal the name, we did not.

(11) R. Tebbit: As I have said to you before, the problem here is *you are assuming,* **if I may put it like that**, there was some process to reveal Dr Kelly's name. There was not a process to reveal Dr Kelly's name.

(12) R. Hoon: Well, I **apologise** for repeating the same answer, but *you are putting* the question in another way.

In each case the witness is moving away from the situational norms and is criticising the QC, and attacking his *competence face* (Partington 2006a) by challenging the questioning. However, in order to avoid being sanctioned for this shift away from the expected norms, the FTA is accompanied by negative politeness markers:

*I think, I apologise, if I may*, which do not mitigate the effect of an unavoidable FTA on the addressee, but function as a means of rendering the aggressive utterance acceptable to the beneficiaries.

In the third corpus, HoC, looking for second person pronouns would not be productive given it is not used between members, but we can look at the phraseology *is + *ing* and isolate those examples referring to members of parliament. Of particular relevance here are the instances where the speaker was evaluating and labelling a language behaviour as inappropriate as illustrated in the examples below:

(13) Cormack (Con): The hon Gentleman *is using unparliamentary language* about being duffed up.

(14) Speaker: The right hon Member for Hitchin and Harpenden *is disrupting* the speech.

(15) Deputy speaker: The hon Gentleman's intervention *is going rather wide* of the motion.

(16) Galloway (Lab): The Chief Whip *is heckling* me but this is a free Parliament and I will be heard in it.

### 9.2.8 Two illustrative markers of negative politeness

Having identified sites of potential conflict, certain negative politeness markers which repeatedly occurred within the co-text were then analysed in greater detail and concordanced throughout the corpora. For reasons of space, only two instances are discussed here by way of illustration.

#### 9.2.8.1 *With (*) respect*

If we look at the occurrences of *with (*) respect*, the marker used in the *Yes, Minister* quote which opened this case study, the instances where it is used to address the interlocutor are unequally distributed across the three corpora, with the highest concentration in HoC (39), followed by Hutton (5), while there were no occurrences in the less hostile Frost. In the majority of cases, the phrases prefaced a contradiction, as illustrated in the sample concordance lines below:

*With due respect* to the Foreign Secretary, that is **not** the point at issue
*With great respect*, I was cleared, but I do **not** want to go into that issue because it would
*With great respect* to the hon Gentleman, I do **not** believe that the Basra road is a good
*With great respect* to them, I do **not** believe that they understand the Islamic world.
*With respect* to my hon Friend, I am **not** ignoring that.
*with respect*, I do **not** know of anyone on either side of the House who is pro-Saddam.
*With respect* to my hon Friend, I do **not** accept his use of the terminology a conquering
*With respect* to the Hon and learned Gentleman, he has **not** been here all afternoon, but those

*with respect* to my hon Friend – I do **not** want to get drawn into issues of where we go.
*With the greatest respect,* it is **not** us who have to justify why we are putting down a
*With respect,* Mr Speaker, that was **not** the question

Concordance lines of *with+respect* in HoC.

Within this particular discourse context, we may surmise that the phraseologies have become so conventionalised that they are to be interpreted simply as discourse markers showing that the speaker is superficially conforming to the expected respect behaviour and that an opposition to a preceding statement will follow. It is therefore acting as a means of achieving interactional power in putting forward an alternative narrative.

It is also of interest to note that these markers of respect for negative face predominantly accompany threats to positive face. Even in instances like the last concordance line, where the speaker is addressing a more institutionally powerful figure, we may hypothesise that the effect of the mitigation is once again to show knowledge of the norms and avoid sanction, and is therefore not primarily attempting to protect the addressee's face.

In a smaller number of cases, the face threat appeared to be simultaneously strengthened, as illustrated in the representative examples below:

(17) *With all due respect*, there is **not the slightest** danger of Zimbabwe becoming a forgotten tragedy. (*Mullin*, HoC)

(18) *With all due respect* to the people involved, that is an **extremely** hard case to believe. (*McCabe*, HoC)

(19) *With respect*, the right Hon Gentleman has heard **very clearly** today **from one of his own Hon Friends** why that argument has **no** credibility **whatever** (*Rammell*, HoC)

(20) *With respect*, that **demolishes** the Hon Gentleman's argument. (*Rammell*, HoC)

In each case, the speaker has made a choice to emphasise the FTA, in (17), (18) and (19) by the selection of intensifiers: *not the slightest*, *extremely*, *very*, neg+*whatever*, and in (20) by the use of the hyperbolic *demolishes*. Additionally, in (19) the face-threatening information is attributed to a member of the same political party as the addressee, thus making it much more difficult to dismiss or counter-attack. Given this simultaneous intensification of the FTA, it is difficult to see how it may be argued that *with* (*) *respect* is attempting to mitigate the effect of the FTA on the addressee. Rather, the clash between the deference and attack serve to mark the utterance for attention, particularly where the politeness feature is fronted and thematised as in Examples (17)–(20), thus leading to a sort of garden-path mechanism where the hearer is initially misled into expectations of deference. Furthermore, in these contexts, the greater the respect expressed, the less likely it is to be sincere, as exemplified in (21):

(21) *With the greatest respect*, the Foreign Secretary is doing what the Prime Minister and the Leader of the House have been doing for the last two days: answering different questions from the ones that are being put to him. (*Clarke*, HoC)

In the data from the courtroom discourse there were just five occurrences of *with* (*) *respect*, of which one was plainly deference marking, and mitigating the face threat of correcting Hutton the law lord chairing the inquiry. The deference marking is extended with the use of title and the minimiser *just*:[5]

(22) Q. HUTTON: Did you regard him in his conversation with you on 22nd May as challenging the Government's claims?

R. GILLIGAN: *With respect my Lord* I said charges rather than challenges. I do not think he set out to sort of take on the Government in that sense. I just think [...] (Hutton, *Direct-examination*)

However, there were also instances similar to (17) to (20) where the witness was clearly challenging the QC and intensifying the face threat, as the following example shows:

(23) R. HOON: I think, *with the greatest respect*, that is a **very** bad point. I cannot anticipate what Ms Teare had with her at the time. I gave you the evidence to the best of my knowledge and recollection. *If I may say so*, I thought that you **seriously** misled Pam Teare as to the facts [...] (Hutton, *Hostile-examination*)

Hoon combines the respect formula not just with a contradiction, but with an intensified FTA on the QCs positive face.

The other instances of the *with* (*) *respect* phraseology in the courtroom discourse also consist of management of aggression and conforming to norms but, similarly, not to mitigation of the FTA directed at the addressee. Our knowledge of the context of production tells us that where used by the QC, the questioner, to address a witness *with* (*) *respect* is highly unlikely to be functioning to show deference. In the longer extract in (24) the QC is cross-examining a witness, Teare, about the MoD's procedure for releasing Kelly's name to the press. It was a moment of high tension and the face threat to Teare, both as an individual and as a representative of the MoD, was particularly high:

(24) Q. KNOX: That was one part of the strategy. The other part of the strategy was to give out further details if the right questions were asked. **That is right, is it not?**

5. 'Q is used to mark question turns and 'R' to mark response turns, these represent the institutional roles rather than the function of each utterance.

R. TEARE: No, **you are suggesting** this is a strategy. **What** I am saying **to you** is the production of Q and A material is standard practice to back up a statement; that is one thing.

Q. KNOX: Yes. *With respect, Ms Teare,* **the answer to my question** is **surely**: yes, we would give out further details about Dr Kelly's identity to journalists if they asked the right questions. For instance: is he in Iraq? You would answer: no, though he visited Iraq recently for a week. **That is the position.**

R. TEARE: The Q and A represents a balance. Its contents represent a balance between not identifying Dr Kelly personally but being able to answer factual questions that journalists could legitimately put to us.

Q. KNOX: *Ms Teare,* **the answer to my question** is "yes", **is it not**? You would give out more information to journalists if they asked you the right questions. That was part of the Q and A material.

R. TEARE: Yes, we would answer – (Hutton, *cross-examination*)

In this sequence Knox puts the question to Teare, who objects to the use of *strategy* to describe the procedure, the QC then rejects her response, and proscribes the "correct" answer to his question. This is an outright contradiction of Teare's initial answer, *no*, and moreover represents an additional face threat by suggesting that she is not complying with the essential discourse norms: that the QC will ask questions, and the witness will provide an answer. The QC's unfavourable evaluation is strengthened by the final assertion [*t*]*hat is the position*, infringing negative as well as positive face and therefore markedly contrasting with the turn-initial *with respect, Ms Teare*.

#### 9.2.8.2 *Vocatives*

The extended Example (24) also serves to illustrate the use of vocatives in the cotext of impoliteness. The QC twice uses the vocative *Ms Teare*, both times before forcibly establishing a new narrative of the events under discussion. If we then look at the whole Hutton corpus, which has been annotated for vocatives, we find they are distributed as illustrated in Figure 9.2:

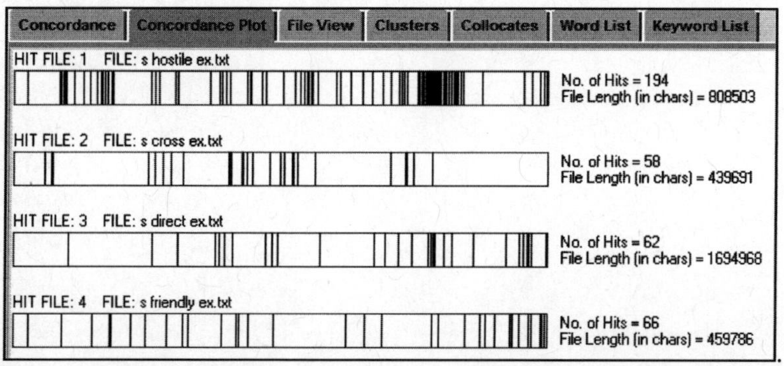


**Figure 9.2.** Distribution of vocatives in the different stages of the Hutton Inquiry

As the distribution plot shows, there was an increased use of vocatives in the most aggressive stage of the inquiry, and, like the occurrences of *you are +ing* (Figure 9.1), they tend to cluster together. Given that both speakers and turns are predetermined by the discourse type, the vocative must be doing additional work beyond simply specifying who the speaker is addressing, such as demonstrating the stance taken towards the addressed participant (Lerner 2003). Brown and Levinson noted that the use of titles and names as address forms outside of greetings, hails and attention getters:

> is only appropriate where the speaker is performing an FTA (face threatening act) [...] such usages are typical in legal proceedings, the title and name accompanying questions that are intended to nail the defendant for instance, rather than small clarifications of fact. (1987:184)

The main cluster of vocatives highlighted in the dispersion plot for hostile examination (Figure 9.1) came from the examination of Mr Gavyn Davies (from the BBC) by Mr Jonathan Sumption (Counsel for the Government). The evidence from Hutton_media indicates that this exchange was perceived in the press as both hostile (25)–(28) and entertaining (27)–(28):

(25) Mr Davies was *fiercely and repeatedly challenged* by the Government 's lawyer, Jonathan Sumption. (*Evening Standard*)

(26) In earlier evidence yesterday, the BBC was *thrown on to the defensive* as the chairman of the corporation's governors came under a *gruelling cross-examination*. (*Scotsman*)

(27) FROM THE moment Gavyn Davies, BBC chairman, *squared up to* Jonathan Sumption QC yesterday, you could almost smell the money. As the million-pound-a-year former whizzo banker took on the million-pound-a- year whizzo lawyer, this was clearly the inquiry's *battle of the big-wads*. (*Independent*)

(28) *It's fantastic entertainment* to watch these giants trying to tear each other to bits. I'm reminded of those old Japanese movies with titles like Godzilla versus Mothra: you might not care who wins, but those special effects make for a terrific 90 minutes. Yesterday saw the fabulously rich Gavyn Davies, the chairman of the BBC, in *deadly combat* with the almost as fabulously rich Jonathan Sumption, [...] The phrase "Mr Sumption" was used lavishly, the impression being given of the local toff speaking to a dense rural constable who nevertheless has the power to make his life difficult. (*Guardian*)

It is interesting to note from (28), that the *Guardian* sketch-writer remarked on the use of the vocative *Mr Sumption*, and described the effect as condescending, given that condescension is noted as a strategy of negative impoliteness in Culpeper's model (1996; Culpeper et al. 2003). Within this one examination sequence, Sumption referred to *Mr Davies* six times, and Davies referred to *Mr Sumption* 26 times. In order to show the pattern of co-occurrence of vocative and unambiguous FTA, a selection of the concordance lines are included below:

| | | |
|---:|---|---|
| I believe it gives a fair account **entirely**, | *Mr Sumption*. | I have conceded that the words "senior |
| DAVIES: | *Mr Sumption*, | the **whole** point of our decision was |
| If we had taken a decision on the night, | *Mr Sumption*, | **you would be standing here** saying I |
| , **we could not** have got the information, | *Mr Sumption*. | There was **no way** of obtaining the |
| tepad. Therefore it is **very** customary, | *Mr Sumption*, | for the journalist's memory to be |
| all the other Governors. **Bear in mind**, | *Mr Sumption*, | that this e-mail came several days |
| sition? It is **absolutely not** the position, | *Mr Sumption*. | I **do not, at any stage** in my life, igno |
| ck on our impartiality and our integrity, | *Mr Sumption*, | that I think it was **perfectly** reasonabl |
| 45 minutes claim"? **What that means**, | *Mr Sumption*, | is **whatever** emerges about the right |
| *I think* I have **just** explained to you, | *Mr Sumption*, | that it was *rather* difficult for the |
| ce Services? Well, **bear in mind here**, | *Mr Sumption*, | that I **myself** did not know who this |
| | *Mr Sumption*, | the word "investigated" is a **strong** |
| have already formed? I agree with that, | *Mr Sumption*; | and **if you knew** my colleagues **you** |

Selected concordance lines showing the co-occurrence of *Mr Sumption*

As can be seen, there is a systematic co-occurrence of the polite address form *Mr Sumption* with: intensifiers such as *entirely, absolutely, perfectly*; cleft constructions which foreground and emphasise the contradiction such as *what that means is*; imperative structures like *bear in mind*; assertions about the addressee *you would be standing here*. We can also see other markers of negative politeness in the context such as the hedges *I think* and *rather*. However, once again it is evident that these markers are being strategically deployed, not to mitigate the effect of the FTA on the addressee but to do additional work such as marking the interaction for the beneficiaries and allowing the speaker to be aggressive while seeming to remain within acceptable boundaries.

### 9.2.9 Mock politeness

The marked use of *Mr Sumption* shown above may also be interpreted as an instance of mock politeness where the excessive use of the politeness marker is used to aggravate the recipient while remaining deniable. Mock politeness is probably the most interesting of the various uses of negative politeness features investigated here because, as noted in the introduction, it involves an absolute inversion of effect; far from functioning to mitigate the FTA, the politeness forms constitute the FTA. Culpeper (1996: 356) defines mock politeness/sarcasm as cases of impoliteness where "the FTA is performed with the use of politeness strategies that are obviously insincere, and thus remain surface realisations", and also notes the close relationship to irony. While I would not equate mock politeness with sarcasm for the reasons set out below, the connection between mock or surface politeness, irony, and sarcasm is particularly interesting. Following our definition of irony as the reversal of good/bad evaluative meaning (rather than necessarily ideational meaning; Chapter 4), the effects of mock politeness may be described as arising from a reversal of face evaluation: from respect for face to attack on face. It appears that, while the recipient superficially gains or is given face in some way, there is also a concurrent and incompatible attack on face, and the resulting face loss may well be greater given how the earlier expectation of face gain is defeated, deluded, and perhaps derided. Intuitively, it seems that the end effect is a greater act of impoliteness than would have been achieved by a direct, unambiguously on record impolite strategy, as also suggested by Culpeper et al. (2003), but this remains an area for later investigation.

Mock politeness in the corpora analysed here seems to be realised in two main ways; in the first, the effect is created through a textually explicit clash of evaluations achieved through the juxtaposition of easily recognised negative politeness features (marked in italics) and the intensification of an FTA (marked in bold), as illustrated in (29) and (30):

(29) Could the Home Secretary *forgive a tinge of* scepticism, as it *appears* that all that **stuff** about weapons of mass destruction was got from a website by **Mr Campbell's young things?** It was not **even** run past the Joint Intelligence Committee, which was **only 50 yards** up the corridor. (*Dalyell*, HoC)

(30) I hope that *my right hon Friend will forgive me* if I tell him that the statement **smacks of desperation – desperation to attack** Iraq. (*Tynan*, HoC)

The two examples of the first type, (29) and (30), also illustrate the way in which the reversal of face evaluation is emphasised by the register shift, from *tinge of scepticism* to *stuff*, and *hope… will forgive me* to *smacks of*. The importance of register shift was also briefly seen in the analysis of *with* (*) *respect*, and investigating and identifying such (re)placement could be another fruitful use of corpus linguistics in the study of impoliteness.

In the second type of realisation, the politeness is intensified beyond credible interpretation, given knowledge of the context of production, as in Example (31), which comes from the same tense exchange as the concordance lines above in Section 3.2.

(31) R. DAVIES: *I think* you *would* have to, *if you do not mind, Mr Sumption*, tell me what aspect of the issue you are talking about. (Hutton, *hostile-examination*)

I would hypothesise that it is the second realisation that is most likely to be equated with sarcasm, while the first type may fulfil a wider range of functions, such as creatively marking the utterance for attention (of the beneficiaries). For this reason I would be cautious of equating mock politeness with sarcasm. The investigation of *sarcas** in the Hutton_media corpus seemed to tentatively confirm the association of sarcasm with the second type of mock politeness – intensification of the politeness beyond credibility given the context – both in the type of instances cited to illustrate sarcasm as in Example (32):

(32) One of the joys of the Hutton Inquiry is that people so accustomed to this status find themselves compelled to answer to someone else. [...] Mr Scarlett twitched. "I never called it a dossier, my Lord. I called it an assessment." "*I am sorry* for the loose use of language," replied counsel to the inquiry James Dingemans QC, whose appetite for *sarcasm* has been growing as the days have passed. (*Scotsman*)

And also in the references to the prosody of the utterance in (33):

(33) Andrew Caldecott, QC, who appeared for the BBC, has been generally voted the star performer in this inquiry. [...] He noted, *sarcastically*, that "in government, note-taking has become a forgotten art." (*Times*)

In each case the surface politeness is marked through the mis-match with the context, in particular the power roles of the participants, and are therefore to be interpreted as mock politeness. Examples (32) and (33) also serve to emphasise the delight that the press took in observing and reporting the impoliteness examined here referring to the *joys of the Hutton inquiry* and *the star performer* framing the judicial inquiry as an act of entertainment, and this of course would form another interesting research question in itself.

## 9.3 Conclusions

In this case study we have attempted to briefly draw attention to the variety of functions fulfilled by negative politeness features, and to explicitly investigate the potential value of corpus linguistics to the study of (im)politeness. By examining three different institutional discourse types it has been possible to look at patterns of usage and illustrate that the multiple functions of negative politeness markers are not limited to one discourse type. Negative politeness markers are seen to fulfil and accomplish a range of functions, from directly conveying the FTA in the case of mock politeness, to focussing the beneficiaries' attention on the interaction in the case of polite address forms, to conventionally marking disagreement in the first set of *with* (*) *respect* concordance lines. While our results undoubtedly challenge the acritical notion that the function of markers of negative politeness is necessarily that of mitigation of an FTA, it should not be interpreted as attempting to deny that form-function relationships exist. Indeed, the analysis has also shown that, even when negative politeness forms are not used principally to be polite, within a given context the other functions we identified were often expressed by particular phraseological patterns.

We have also presented a novel experimental technique in this chapter of combining the use of corpora of primary sources, namely Hutton, House of Commons debates and political interviews, with corpora containing secondary sources, reports, comments, and suchlike, upon those primary sources, namely the Hutton_media and Frost_media corpora. This allowed us both to track the development of opinions on the events in question and also, crucially, gave us insights into what commentators other than ourselves interpreted to be (im)polite behaviour. As noted in the first two case studies on irony reported in Chapter 4, it is sound methodological practice, wherever possible, to have some separation among (i) the definition of the terms used in the research, (ii) the data analysis and (iii) the data interpretation, and taking into consideration interpretations by parties other than the data analysts (that is, us) is a good way to achieve a partial separation.

The corpus analysis represents a methodology which goes beyond treating the corpus as a resource bank and shows how corpus-assisted discourse study may contribute not only to facilitating the identification of patterns of usage in specified contexts, but also to offering a more objective, less researcher-dependent identification of potential (im)politeness events than has usually been the case.

## Suggestions for further research

Below we list some research questions which could form the basis for further projects.

1. Choose a particular discourse community to investigate in terms of first order conceptions of impoliteness (impoliteness1). What kinds of language behaviour are described or classified as impolite? A potentially interesting source would be online forums which are created for expatriate/migrant communities because discussion here often centres on cross-cultural differences in im/polite behaviours. Another fruitful source is the forum entitled "Am I being unreasonable?" on the website www.mumsnet.com because this also frequently involves discussion and interpretation of impolite behaviours. You could use BootCaT (see Appendix at the end of the book) to collect your corpora.

2. Concordance the use of the terms *banter* and *teas** (that is *tease, teasing, teased,* and so on) within a specified discourse context – what type of language events are described? How aggressive and face-threatening are they? Do you notice any difference in terms of who participates in the event? You could use one of the large online corpora such as Brigham Young University's Corpus of Contemporary American for this type of question (see Appendix).
3. Within a particular discourse context, for example the readers' comments on newspaper articles published online, how do the participants perform disagreeing? To what extent is the act of disagreement mitigated? Are there any conventionalised disagreement formulae (Culpeper 2010) and do they differ across discourse types/languages? You might compile a corpus from one of the online discussion forums for this using a tool like *BootCaT* to speed up the process. It could be interesting to compare the style in different forums.
4. Look at a corpus of political radio/television interviews – is there any correlation between who is being interviewed and the frequency of shifts from transactional to interactional mode?

CHAPTER 10

# Modern diachronic corpus-assisted discourse studies (MD-CADS) 1

## Comparisons over time in lexical grammar and discourse practices

Most of the studies in this volume in which the SiBol/Port corpora (see the Introduction 0.4.1) are employed are essentially synchronic, the corpus being used to investigate language patterns at a particular period in time, or alternatively are "time-less", where corpora are used to throw light on the way, say, irony or metaphor or evaluation function in general terms. In this chapter, instead, we illustrate how two or more "sister corpora", that is, corpora constructed to be as similar in content, composition and structure as possible, might enable an analyst to track how language patterns and meanings, as well as the discourse practices these might reveal, can change over comparatively brief periods of modern times, a form of corpus linguistics we have named *modern diachronic corpus-assisted discourse studies*. In the next chapter, we will attempt to illustrate how comparisons among such sister corpora can shed light on the social, political and cultural issues considered worthy of attention in different times and how differently or similarly they are represented.

Using corpora in diachronic studies of language, that is, the study of language change over time (Gr. *dia*, "through", "across" + *chronos*, "time"), itself a specific form of the study of *language variation*, is, of course, by no means a novelty. McEnery goes so far as to say that "[d]iachronic study is perhaps one of the few areas which can only be investigated using corpus data [...] because the intuitions of modern speakers have little to offer regarding the language used hundreds or even tens of years before" (2006: 96). Rissanen, perhaps the most celebrated corpus-assisted diachronic linguist, is less pessimistic about intuitions, but stresses the need to bolster them and to guard against:

> the risk that corpus work and computer-supported quantitative research methods will discourage the student from getting acquainted with original texts, from being on really intimate terms with his material and thus acquiring a profound knowledge of the language form he is studying. (1989: 16)

We might talk about "learned intuitions" acquired through close acquaintance with a discourse type, even if from a different time period. In any case, the process is little different from having to "learn intuitions" about a current discourse type with which a speaker has little original familiarity.

Be this as it may, most previous research into contemporary language change has employed relatively small corpora, for instance, the so-called "LOB family" is a (growing) series of corpora of British English each of a million words (Baker 2009) which have been used in the main to conduct studies of changes in the behaviour of frequent words or constructions; such studies are therefore largely on grammar. Having at our disposal much larger corpora, studies of less frequent structures as well as of *lexical* – as opposed to *grammatical* – words also becomes feasible. As Baker notes:

> My own experiences with corpus research would suggest that a million words is probably acceptable for examining usage of high frequency words (most grammatical words and a couple of hundred lexical words) but only very cautious conclusions can be made about other lexis. (2009: 314)

Entirely new avenues of research in modern diachronic linguistics are opened; we can study meaning change, especially of *sets* of lexical items, in relationship to both internal linguistic factors and also in response to external social influences. Being in a position to study lexical patterns and how they differ in the two corpora we are able to study changes in discourse processes as well. In this chapter for instance, we will touch upon how UK "quality" newspapers appear to be adopting some of the language practices once thought typical of their downmarket counterparts, the tabloid papers.

A final introductory consideration is that, when a corpus is reduced to representational form for the sake of statistical analysis, for instance, to the form of a list of keywords, different patterns inevitably stand out to different researchers. As Taylor observes of the first collection of MD-CADS work (Partington (ed.) 2010):

> each researcher brings his/her own primings in terms of theoretical, methodological and ideological background to the development of the research question. There is indeed "more to seeing than meets the eyeball" (1958: 7), as Hanson put it in his seminal *Patterns of Discovery* and, even though we are all working with a similar methodological approach, each of the contributors to this collection saw something different when looking at the two SiBol corpora and the initial keyword lists. (Taylor 2010: 223)

Different items will obviously attract attention if the focus of interest is on changes in grammar rather than on sociopolitical issues. When items attract attention they can be individually concordanced in the corpus in question. In this way, the analyst can begin to formulate hypotheses as to why particular items are more salient in a given set of texts. The presence in the list of an individual item may simply be a question of chance or a feature of an individual writer's style. It is when sets of similar or related items are uncovered that real evidence of changes in linguistic or discourse practice may be found. In this chapter, we look at some of the differences among our sister corpora, describing first the software-generated "facts" in terms of relative frequencies and keyness scores. The discourse analytical approach subsequently exploits the quantitative analyses and, by examining the linguistic patterns perceived, an attempt is made to find significant generalisations about the corpora by a search for items that could be assigned to semantic sets, glossed according to what they have in common. The appearance of these sets in the keywords for SiBol 2005 seems to point to changes over time in newspaper discourse style when compared with the SiBol 1993 corpus. In some cases we have added data from the Port 2010 corpus.

## 10.1 Comparing the 1993, 2005 and 2010 corpora: Corpus wordlists and keywords

At the start of the project, wordlists were compiled using *WordSmith Tools 5* and two keyword lists formed using the Keywords tool: one consisting of the key items in the 2005 newspapers as compared to the 1993 data, and the other of the key items from the 1993 set of texts as compared to the 2005 items. We confine ourselves to analysing the first 2,500 items in each list, an arbitrary cut-off point adopted entirely for practical reasons.

The most striking feature of the 2005 keyword list from the grammatical perspective is the salience of first- and second-person personal pronouns. We find *you* in fourth place in the list (after three Internet-related items), closely followed by *I*, *your*, *my*, *we*, *me* and *us*. We also come across *yourself* and *myself*.

Perhaps the second most apparent characteristic of the list is the very large number of verb contractions among the first one hundred salient items. These are accompanied by a large variety of negative contractions. The top 500 keywords include *don't*, *didn't*, *doesn't*, *can't*, *wasn't*, *isn't*, *won't*, *couldn't*, *wouldn't*, *aren't*, *haven't*, *hasn't* and *weren't*. We also find that a considerable number of items which can be used either as "empty subjects" or deictically are very prominent in the 2005 list, either alone or as part of contractions, (e.g. *it's*, *that*, *that's*, *there's*, *it*).

The most salient verb is *get*, followed by *can*, *think*, *want*, *got*, *know*, *like*, *see*, *do*, *need*, *make* and *look*, all items commonly found in conversational forms of the language.

Along with verb contractions and negative contractions (see above), Leech and Smith (2006) include the increased use of the progressive among their "changes apparently indicative of colloquialisation". Among the first 1000 items of the 2005 keywords are *going, getting, looking, doing, playing, drinking, thinking, watching, working, having, using, eating* and *wearing*. There are no equivalent *-ing* verb forms among the top 1000 keywords for 1993. Leech and Smith also claim that "questions of all kinds" are indicative of colloquialisation, and the 2005 list indeed includes *where, when, why, how* and *what*. Concordancing confirmed that the increase was due to their use in questions rather than as relative pronouns/ relativisers or complemetisers (Biber et al. 1999: 87–88).

Turning to the 1993 keyword list, we come across a good number of formal terms of address or personal appellation. These include *Mr, Mrs, Lord, Dr, Sir, Lady, Rev, Herr, Signor* and even *President*. The UK press seems to have curtailed in recent times its use of courtesy forms.

Another significant lexico-grammatical change is in the relative frequency of the type of linkers present in the lists. In 1993 we find items such as *therefore, moreover, nevertheless* and *indeed*. The 2005 keywords instead include *and, but, because* and *also*. All these sets are indications of an increase in the personalisation or familiarisation or "de-formalisation" of newspaper register over the twelve years between the two corpora. This finding is perhaps unsurprising: Fairclough (1995) has written on what he terms the *conversationalisation* of media discourse; others talk of *political cross-discourse* (Alvarez-Cáccamo & Prego-Vásquez 2003). As regards newspapers in particular, McNair (2003) describes what he calls the *tabloidisation* of UK so-called quality newspapers, whilst Carter & McCarthy note two particular linguistic features used to attempt this familiarisation with the reader:

> journalists also achieve impact and get on a "conversational" wavelength with their readers by using common spoken discourse markers and purposefully vague language in a projected conversational exchange. (2006: 238)

To check that these sets were not apparent simply due to the growth in the size of papers over the period due largely to the of expansion of magazine-style sections, we made a list of comparative keywords from the one newspaper which had not increased in volume, namely the *Telegraph*, and these sets were still found to be very prominent. Nevertheless, by no means all the items in the lists indicate a progressive stylistic informalisation in all newspaper sections: some must, indeed, be the product of the change in paper format and the relative growth in the magazine, non-hard news sections given the recurrence of certain domains and contexts. As one might expect, the list of keywords from 2005 contains a good number of items relating to the technological advances which have taken place since 1993: *www, internet, online, dvd, email, mobile*, and so on. When we compare Port 2010 to SiBol 05 we see the technological advances which took place as keywords include: *twitter, tweet, youtube, facebook, Ipad* and *Iphone*.

It is equally unsurprising to find changes in a large number of proper names of people and places, reflecting those events which came into the news in 2005, but which were not there in 1993; for instance, *Bush* as opposed to *Clinton* and *Blair* as opposed to *Major*, whilst *Obama, Cameron, Clegg, and coalition* become keywords in 2010. There are items produced by current newsworthy events such as *tsunami* and *Katrina* (and *hurricane*) in 2005 and *Chilean, miners, trapped* in 2010. Unsurprisingly, in 2005 we find several *Iraq*-related items (*Iraq, Iraqi, Shia, Sunni, Sunnis* and *insurgents*), whereas in 1993 we have Balkans-related terms (*Bosnia, Serbs, Sarajevo* and *Croats*). In 2010 high in the keywords list, even when compared with 2005, we find *Afghanistan, Afghan, Helmand, Taleban.*

The 2005 list includes items relating to high finance or venture capitalism, including *FTSE, bid, takeover, executive,* and *hedge* (funds), as well financial institutions such as *Deutsche* and *HSBC* (both banks). In contrast, in 1993 we find a few items from the sphere of high finance but far more relating to the national economy in general: economic *recession, recovery, inflation* and *economy*; to national economic problems, such as *unemployment*; and to industrial matters: *coal, chairman* and *industrial.* When we turn to Port 2010 we find that both financial and economic terms are prominent with the aftermath of the financial crisis of 2008 (*banks, banking* and *bankers, bailout, recession, deficit, debt, inflation, quantitative easing*).

In terms of topic or event focus it was noticed that sport had become a major interest in the broadsheets since 1993; the single most noticeable feature of the 2005 keywords, in terms of content words was the very high proportion of top keywords relating to sport, especially to football. Of the first 100, as many as twenty-one refer to sport or sporting personalities (for instance, *Premiership, Chelsea* and *Beckham*), whereas in 1993, the top 100 keywords contains only two sporting items (namely, *soccer* and *Gooch*, a cricketer). Port 2010 reveals cooking and food have become recurrent topics (for instance, *chop, chopped, cook, baking, butter, onions, soufflé, sauté, purée* and *crème*).

## 10.2 The methodology of set identification: Evaluative lexical keywords

As Scott argues (2006: 25), a wordlist will nearly always contain, firstly, a small number of highly used items, the most frequently used of these being grammatical items, followed by a long list of items which occur very infrequently. In terms of lexical choice, the high frequency lexical items used over a wide variety of texts, such as in a corpus of one entire year of newspaper output, represent well-worn paths as opposed to new ones. In examining the keywords lists we can see how, over time, some previously little-frequented paths have become well-trodden, while, as it were, the grass has grown over others. In analysing the 2005 keyword list, we identified three particular sets of lexical words which were distinctive but which shared the lexicosemantic properties of evaluation (see Duguid 2010a for a fuller description). All three sets also bear traces of informal register; and many of their members are described as being more frequent in spoken language in Biber et al. (1999) and Carter and McCarthy (2006).[1]

As a means of comparison, the definitions given for each one in a corpus-based dictionary (*Macmillans English Dictionary for Advanced Learners*, henceforth MEDAL) were consulted, and terms which were repeated in these definitions were employed to characterise the common features of the set. MEDAL assigns a star rating to words to indicate frequency in their corpus, where three stars are assigned to very frequently occurring words. Some examples are included in the text for illustration purposes.

## 10.3 Language in the press: Patterns in the keywords list

The keyword items seemed to divide fairly neatly into two sets, with a number left over (for a full account with the lists of keywords and their keyness score see Duguid 2010a). The first set contained items involving implicit superlatives (Carter & McCarthy 2006: 443), which have a high intensity element in their meaning; for example, adjectives like *overjoyed* and *exhausted*, as opposed to *happy* and *tired*. They express some kind of extreme degree or exaggeration, and are frequently used for effect rather than description alone. They all express positive (or, indeed, highly positive) evaluation. As Hunston and Francis (2000) have noted, we need to find a convenient descriptive umbrella term for what items in a group have in common. Here "hyperbole" was chosen as a convenient term. The list consisted of evaluative adjectives with intensity in their meaning and adverbs with functions such as intensification, upscaling and maximisation. To corroborate whether intensification was carried in the meaning, we checked their definitions in MEDAL (the terms used in the dictionary definitions were *extremely*, *very*, *completely*, and so on), and we then further subdivided them into subsets, namely, those concerned with size and ranking, amplified evaluation and intensification (Section 10.6.1.2 below).

1. See ⟨http://www.euppublishing.com/doi/abs/10.3366/cor.2010.0102⟩ for full lists with keyness scores.

A second set was identified because the items were classified as all being related to vagueness or lack of precision: their dictionary definitions including terms such as *imprecise* and *undefined*.

There was a third set with some of the same properties, that is, they were for the most part adjectives with subjective evaluative meaning, being terms of praise or blame expressed in various ways. It is more difficult to find a convenient denomination for this set, but "vague and informal evaluation" seems to cover the meanings. The words have in common with the first two sets their informality (informality was in the definitions of most of these items in MEDAL). In reference to our earlier discussion on conversationalisation, some of the items in our sets were from quotations of direct speech, that is to say, they are a written representation of spoken language and are not always directly attributable to a journalist. This represents the journalist's desire to provide another voice in the discourse. However, as much as any real desire to reproduce someone else's direct speech accurately, it often also heralds a wish to be dramatic or to provide "witnessing", where a first-hand account of an issue or event is given in the form of a narrative from personal experience.

In the following section, we will look at some of the items from our sets in more detail to see in which phraseologies they occur and what they have in common. One question to address is why such a group is appearing in the keywords, why *overt* evaluation is so much what 2005 papers are "about", there being considerably fewer *intrinsically* evaluative adjectives in the SiBol 93 keywords.

## 10.4 Informalisation

The first findings indicated an increasing informalisation. A number of linguistic devices were identified which are usually associated with informal registers, a conversational tone, marked by features of informal spoken language previously identified as a feature of the tabloids and of print advertising (Cook 1992; Lombardo 2001; Hundt & Mair 1999; McNair 2003).

As we saw above, second-person pronouns are high in the 2005 keyword list. Hundt and Mair (1999), too, in their tracking of changes in newspaper prose between 1960 and 1990, noted a greater use both of contractions, and first- and second-person pronouns, where these oral features were adopted in an attempt to appeal to a wider reading audience. This trend appears to have accelerated in the 1990s and into the 2000s. The writers expect those they address to respond to the value positions they propose. The projected relationship reflected in the corpus is also signposted by a set of items uniting informality and vagueness or lack of precision (see Channell 1994). Vagueness is a strong indication of assumed shared knowledge, the referents of vague expressions being assumed to be known by the reader (Carter & McCarthy 2006: 202).

## 10.5 Language in the press: Hyperbolic evaluation

The first of our sets was labeled *hyperbolic evaluation* (containing words like *fantastic, gorgeous, amazing, fabulous*). The keyword analyses revealed how a large number of hyperbolic evaluative expressions have become more frequent in broadsheet language. McCarthy and Carter (2004) provide a useful discussion of what they call "purposeful exaggeration" in everyday conversational British English. Using evidence from corpora, they demonstrate how speakers exaggerate narrative, descriptive and argumentative features and make assertions that are overstated, literally impossible, inconceivable or counterfactual in many different types of discourse contexts. Such hyperbolic expressions usually pass without challenge by listeners, who accept them as creative intensifications for evaluative or affective purposes, such as humour and irony (McCarthy & Carter 2004: 184).

At the same time, they remind us that hyperbole in written contexts was a feature of classical rhetoric, associated with persuasive speech and the exercise of power. Such rhetorical exaggeration has been examined in previous studies of broadsheet opinion pieces (see Chapter 5, which looks at the kind of opinion pieces where the use of humorous hyperbole abounds). McCarthy and Carter (2004) illustrate some of the most frequently recurring lexical-grammatical types of hyperbole in everyday contexts, finding that hyperbole (like metaphors) can be both conventional and creative. For them, what is of great interest is the evaluative context of hyperbole/overstatement and how speakers use it to express affective meanings, and how the interpersonal function is paramount in its use. In newspaper use of the rhetoric of the vernacular, the fact that such features imitating spoken language, particularly evaluative adjectives and adverbs, appear to predominate among the 2005 keywords provides more corroboration for the hypothesis that broadsheet newspaper language is becoming conversationalised. Other grammatical features associated with evaluation include intensifiers and quantifiers, comparators (such as comparatives and superlatives), ways of being vague, adverbs indicating affect, certainty and doubt, and hedges and emphatics (Hunston & Thompson 2000). All of these are present in our 2005 keywords list. Grouping them as patterns into sets and subsets enables more powerful statements about changes in these newspapers' language habits to be made.

The use of a simulated orality is also a feature of promotional or advertising language. It has been suggested that press release material is being used more often as a basis for articles, and phrases are frequently taken *verbatim* by the journalists from press releases.[2] A report entitled *Quality and Independence of British Journalism: Tracking the Changes over 20 Years*[3] in 2008 found that 60 percent of press articles come wholly or mainly from "pre-packaged" sources. The findings suggest that public relations often does much more than merely set the agenda: it was found that 19 percent of newspaper stories were verifiably derived mainly or wholly from public relations material, while fewer than half the stories appeared to be entirely independent of traceable PR. This would account for the conventionalisation of certain positively evaluative terms which form part of the communicative function of promotion. However, newspapers are also self-aware and conscious of these changes, some descriptive items become perceived as promotional rather than descriptive, and newspapers, in turn, dedicate a certain amount of comment on their use. Ironic exploitation, as we saw in Chapter 5, with a reversal of evaluation from positive to critical, is perhaps also a result of irritation with PR's reiterated and strategic enthusiasm. Such interest in language and an attempt to confront the question of journalistic spread and devaluation of turn of phrase can be seen reflected in the keywords for 2010 where we find the items *cliché, clichés* and *clichéd* and a range of concordance lines deprecating clichés while in the act of reiterating them. We find reference to *the old cliché, overused, lazy, tired, predictable clichés, widely peddled and overworked clichés* but also many concordance lines with *it may be a cliché but, it's a cliché I know but, it may sound like a cliché but* and *it has become a cliché but.*

## 10.6 The keyword sets

### 10.6.1 Hyperbole and extremes in evaluation in the keywords

One subset of the hyperbolic evaluation set shows a concern with relative size or ranking (e.g. *biggest, huge*) as a parameter of evaluation, though this is often metaphorical and has to do with fame, importance or distinction; in short, this is a combination we denominate as "size and ranking" (see Section 10.6.1.1).

Another set consists of positive keywords which are used to construe objects and events in terms of rank or of exceptional, outstanding aesthetic quality (e.g. *pivotal, iconic, gorgeous*) also functions to amplify positive evaluation. The third subset consists mostly of intensifying adverbs (e.g. *absolutely*). A fourth subset

2. See: ⟨http://www.guardian.co.uk/books/2008/feb/09/pressandpublishing.society⟩

3. This report was prepared by Lewis et al. at the Cardiff School of Journalism, Media and Cultural Studies.

consists of *all* and *every*, and other indefinite pronouns and quantifiers (*everyone* and *everything*) which present extreme case formulations. The MEDAL definitions for these items contain glosses which reflect their inclusive nature (usually using *all* and *every* in the definition) and often add the idea of emphasis, agreement or disagreement. Such emphasising also involves elements of intentional imprecision; the indefinite quantifiers allow language users to make generalizations (e.g. *everyone, everything*).

#### 10.6.1.1 *Size and ranking and relative importance*

Here are some of the items related to "size and ranking". It is clear from the data that there is a considerable overlap of the semantic preferences of these items because of the repetitive nature of newspaper discourse, and so we find business and sport represented frequently in the size and ranking list, but also fame and significance, impact and effect as the papers carry out their task of setting cultural agendas.

> ***huge***: The collocates in R1 position suggest a semantic preference for words dealing with impact and effects, either emotional or in terms of fame or significance (*huge significance, scope, row, surprise, shock, sense, relief, pressure, demand, success, star hit, hits, setback, blow, loss* and *losses*).
>
> ***bestselling***: In SiBol 05, this item indicates the concern with success in commercial terms. It is both hyperbolic and vague. The main right collocates indicate a relatively restricted domain (*author, book, novel, writer, novelist, memoir, series, newspaper, album, single DVD*) and three words which reveal a distortion due to a particular product: *da, vinci* and *code*.
>
> ***top***: The concordance lines reflect a penchant for lists (*top ten, two, four* and *three*) – the search for the best and the importance of striving. The principle domains are those of sport, the performing arts, cooking and restaurants, and travel; all of these areas are covered by supplements or dedicated pages.
>
> ***key***: As an adjective, this item is inherently comparative in meaning, indicating a judgement about importance. It co-occurs with many general nouns: *key thing, man, question, point, element, moment, area, witness, worker, member, ingredient, component* and *difference*.
>
> ***pivotal***: R1 collocates appear to be related to strategic issues concerning people, places or times, often in a sports context (*pivotal role, moment, figure, point, part, position, player, year, figure, character, factor, decision, scene, stage, event, game, day* and *match*). Both *pivotal* and *key* seem to be serving the same function, that of claiming high ground and visibility by declaring importance.

#### 10.6.1.2 *Positive and amplified evaluation*

The following items all contain amplification in their meanings (that is, the definitions all contain a gloss which expresses intensity in one way or another) or they are accompanied by intensifying adverbials.

> ***iconic***: This is a media word which has been the subject of much comment. Its collocates are nearly all linked with fame, fashion and visibility, and most contexts are connected to the arts (*iconic status, image(s), figure, brand, design, fashion, moment(s), event, photograph(s), film, movie, performance, piece* and *work(s)*).
>
> ***perfect***: This item displays a semantic preference for "things to be sought after" (*the perfect risotto* and *the perfect roast chicken*), but it is also a sports metaphor (*a perfect 10*).
>
> ***beautiful***: The frequency of this item suggests the importance of physical appearance and aesthetic reactions in the value system adopted (its R1 collocates include *beautiful game, people, woman, place, things, day, city, house, daughter, places, beaches, country* and *girls*).
>
> ***gorgeous***: In our material this item relates mostly to aesthetic or sense experiences (MEDAL gives it as an alternative to *beautiful*, especially with reference to clothes and hair). We also find the idiom *drop dead gorgeous*, meaning "exceptionally gorgeous".
>
> ***terrific***: This item is nearly always connected with arts and aesthetics (*looks, sounds, performance(s), form, value, appearance, record, animation, film, cast, ensemble, story* and *achievement*).
>
> ***compelling***: The R1 collocates mostly concern the arts or literary artefacts, hence *compelling story, account, drama, narrative, viewing, performance, series, portrait, book, documentary, read, film* and *study*).
>
> ***incredible***: This item's collocates mostly relate to competition and performance. Its R1 collocates include *journey, amount, story, thing, run, success, speed, pressure, range, skill, strength, energy* and *achievement.*

Such open hyperbole can be contrasted with the limited number of evaluative adjectives from SiBol 93 keywords: *considerable, substantial, modest, cautious, satisfactory, inadequate, limited.* The only evaluations in the keywords of SiBol 93 which could be regarded as remotely hyperbolic are *distinguished* and *necessary*. When Port 2010 is compared with SiBol 93 the same words appear in the keywords suggesting that the hyperbolic style persists into 2010.

#### 10.6.1.3 *Intensification and emphasis*

This subset involves a variety of intensifying features, usually adverbial, and a few are analysed here:

> ***so***: This item is also used to emphasise a quality, feeling or amount but not all uses are emphatic. A keyness comparison of n-grams would provide further insights into the changing phraseology of broadsheets since we find the unit *so not*, employed to express a new emphatic negation with a variety of colligations, to be found mostly in first-person accounts or direct speech, for instance:

(1) The dining room was pretty much the communal place where the TV was and where we did our homework. The front room is the sacred zone. **You are so not allowed in the front room** – it was only used when there were visitors. (*Sunday Times* 2005)

***hugely***: This adverb shows similar semantic preferences to *huge* but with a stronger association with emotional impact (*hugely impressive, enjoyable, entertaining, disappointing, respected, satisfying, inhibiting, exciting* and *embarrassing*), or the extent of the impact (*hugely popular, successful, important, influential, significant, ambitious, controversial, powerful, inflated* and *competitive*).

***absolutely***: This item appears to show a semantic preference for denial (*absolutely no, nothing* and *not*) and for justifying (*absolutely right, clear, necessary, sure, certain, essential, vital, crucial, true, central, critical* and *correct*). It also adds emphasis by maximising words which already express strong emotion (*absolutely staggering, hilarious, ludicrous, horrendous*, and *appalling*), especially strong emotion where intensification is already part of the basic meaning (*absolutely delighted, devastated, gutted, terrified, thrilled, knackered, shattered, stunned* and *gobsmacked*) and it is these last two preferences which account for most of the increase in use.

Perhaps not surprisingly, the same intensifiers are found in the Port 2010 vs SiBol 93 keywords list as in the SiBol 05 vs SiBol 93 list. In contrast, only two intensifiers appear among the keywords of SiBol 93 vs SiBol 05, namely *greatly* and *wholly*, which belong to a more formal register. There are also a number of downscaling adverbials (*scarcely, merely, nearly* and *virtually*), which exemplify a choice of focus rather than force. Martin and White define the latter as being values by which speakers graduate (raise or lower) the interpersonal impact, force or volume of their utterances, and the former as being values by which they graduate (blur or sharpen) the focus of their semantic categorizations (2005:37). This fits in with the general finding that more recent UK "quality" newspaper prose uses greater force via hyperbole and less focus through vague language, as we shall see in the next section.

### 10.6.2 Vagueness

In the second set of keywords, we observed how a lack of precision can also be combined with either hyperbole or understatement to achieve vagueness. Hyperbole is, very frequently, vague to some extent, for instance, when it includes all, or most, or worst-case scenarios, it avoids precision by its inclusiveness.

***bit***: This item appears in a number of evaluative patterns: *a bit* + evaluative adjective, *a bit* + of + evaluative noun, and also as a downtoner or hedge – *a bit worried, nervous, disappointed, tired, sad, surprised, mad*, which all indicate a need to avoid certainty in classifying emotions.

***stuff***: This item often functions as a cohesive substitute for a general noun, but it also indicates informality and collocates with items that indicate unusualness (*new, interesting, exciting*), as well as usualness (*usual, same, old, boring, basic, obvious, everyday, dull, familiar, routine*). A number of frequent clusters reflect a concern with emotional impact, both positive (*important, fascinating, gripping, stirring, weird, heady, interesting, impressive, thrilling, terrific, entertaining, wonderful*) and negative (*hard, bad, rough, tough, scary, heavy, dangerous*).

***thing***: All definitions contain glosses of imprecision. Like *stuff*, it is a general noun and is useful in creating lexical cohesion, enabling people to refer vaguely to categories, assuming shared categorisations.[4] However, it is also a way of actually performing categorisation (*a boy thing, a Zen thing, a C4 thing, a Catholic thing, a status thing, a playboy thing*).

***something***: As Hunston and Sinclair (2000) and Bednarek (2006) have pointed out, this item is often part of an evaluative pattern (*there's something* + adjective group), which appears frequently in the dataset considered here. R1 and R2 collocates of *there's/there is something* include a number of clearly evaluative items, like *special, different, similar, wrong, good, sinister*.

Although most of the above are recognisable clusters occurring with a certain frequency we can also see how journalists attempt to ring the changes to provide variety and perhaps some creativity by creating new patterns. We find: *something disappointingly prosaic, something commendably old-fashioned, something queasily imitative, something unsatisfactorily static, something laudably ambitious* and *something utterly beguiling*. In all of these examples, intensifiers co-occur with *something* so that the vagueness of *something* is given focus and/or force by its collocates, and the informal imprecision can be juxtaposed with a choice of lexis which is both precise and formal. The priming expectations that *something* should indicate vagueness and informality are thus overturned and exploited to creative and novel evaluative effect.

### 10.6.3 Vague and informal evaluative lexis

The items in the third set of SiBol 05 keywords, (for example items like *dodgy, quirky, funky, edgy*, see Duguid 2010a for full list and keyness scores) all share the features of informality and an underlexicalised vagueness in their definition, where the attitude of the writer is clear, but the grounds for that attitude are less clear. Many are the short words from the Old English part of the lexicon which are associated with informal language and are one- or (at most) two-syllable words,

4. See also Chapter 8 the second case study on spoken discourse where *thing* is a keyword and used for strategic purposes.

which have been defined as "often of colloquial tone" (Quirk et al., give the examples *meaty*, *comfy*, *gushy* and *runny* [as in nose], 1985: 1553).[5] In SiBol 2005, some items, such as *bling* (Oxford Dictionary's word of the year 2009) or *chav* (Oxford Dictionary's word of the year 2004),[6] are neologisms, often discussed as such in the press. This newspaper interest in language means that such terms become salient both because they did not exist in the previous corpus and also because they occur as objects of reflection – as citation forms in discussions of their use, rather than because they are particularly popular with newsworkers. Of the occurrences of *bling* in SiBol 05, more than 5% are in scare quotes and for *chav*[7] this proportion rises to 9.5% with a large number of mentions or citation forms as opposed to use, for example:

(2) but for me in London town, and with "chav" the insult du jour, I run the risk of being mistaken for a wannabe glamour model. (*Guardian* 2005)

(3) Reactions to this new animated series will depend on whether viewers find the word "chav" to be acceptably jocular or a nasty bit of modern snobbery. (*Sunday Times* 2005)

(4) Speaking of tolerance and snobbery, isn't it odd that the word "chav" is now so freely used, making it into the new edition of the Oxford Dictionary of English yesterday? (*Times* 2005)

A subgroup of this set is notable for the shared morphology of its members, that is, two syllables ending with *y* (phonetically [i]): *sexy*, *easy funny*, *funky*, *tricky*, *dodgy*, *quirky*, *cheesy*, *moody*, *creepy*, *clunky*, *edgy*, *grumpy*, *classy*, *spooky*, *yummy*, *handy*, *shiny*, *sparkly*, *feisty* and *geeky*, which all give an adolescent, even infantile, flavour to the evaluations. The word *edgy* can have a positive sense of avant-garde and unconventional, as opposed to a negative sense of agitated and nervous, which is the meaning it nearly always has in sports reporting. It is used in our corpus as a positive term of appraisal (urban dictionary.com gives the meaning as "involving a tendency to challenge societal norms and reveal the dark side"), as in this example:

(5) Nighty Night is all infantile self-indulgence. Perhaps enthusiasts slap themselves on the back for enjoying such "**edgy**" fare. And, yet, far from being **edgy**, the result is curiously anachronistic, a mammary and member-obsessed world about which Benny Hill might have found himself tumescent. (*Times* 2005)

5. For a discussion of the *-y* suffix, see also Adams (2009).

6. ⟨www.askoxford.com:80/world of words/wordayear⟩

7. The corpus contains a large number of related neologisms (*chavette, chavvy, chavdom, chavellers, chavistocracy, chavtastic*. (see also Renouf 2007).

(6) This is not an exciting series. It isn't **edgy** or groundbreaking and you won't find Davina McCall suddenly popping up in a woolly hat. It's the sort of programme, in fact, that the Prince of Wales would probably enjoy. (*Times* 2005)

As we can see from the examples below, many occurrences are used in distancing quotation marks or are direct quotations where the writer makes sure we know the choice of words is someone else's, as in the following concordance lines for *vibrant* and *edgy*:

(7) And when M&S does try to get its act together, it's excruciating. Every few months you would swear that some bright spark, who probably saw David Brent as a role model, has sent a memo to the shop floor telling the check-out staff to be "friendly" and, Lord help us, "**vibrant**". (*Times* 2005)

(8) From all this delirium Barham brings home a reassuringly positive message. He liberally sprinkles his text with hurrah-words such as "**vibrant**" and "passion", and figures that whatever the kids want to do is OK. (*Guardian* 2005)

As well as the use of distancing scare quotes, Examples (5) to (7) also illustrate how important shared cultural references are in the accumulation of meanings around such items when they are being considered reflexively. The target or implied reader is expected to have a set of evaluations connected with Benny Hill, the Prince of Wales, Davina McCall and David Brent (see also Chapter 5.4).

## 10.7 Evaluative meanings in the keywords and diachronic conclusions

All items in the first set of keywords carry positive evaluation (with the single exception of *desperate*), in apparent contradiction to the renowned claim that news values tend to favour the negative over the positive (Galtung & Ruge 1973: 72) or an indication of the stable frequency of negative terms, but an increase in the positivity may also suggest that newspapers are no longer mainly concerned with news reporting. It may well be, as we remarked earlier, an indication of an increase in the proportion of soft news and magazine material relative to hard news, and that promotional material – which is, of course, largely positive in tone – might be the source of many of the stories.[8] The set of vague items are all MEDAL three-star

8. A closer manual search for other hyperbolic items in the wordlists, for example, *mega* and *uber*, reveals they are words that are on their way to becoming popular, though they are not yet frequent enough to appear among the keywords. *Uber* however does appear in the keywords of Port 2010 vs SiBol 05. The hyperbole set of explicitly evaluative lexical items is used to perform exaggeration, but of a rather unfocussed type.

words which appear in a number of phraseological patterns, and their frequency is a result of this ability to collocate in clusters which are informal and imprecise. As Carter and McCarthy remind us, "being vague is an important feature of interpersonal meaning" (2006: 202).

Many of the other items in the list evaluate in terms of fame, success, sexual attraction, unusualness, newness, excitement, style, quality and emotional impact. These might be said to represent some of the key values expressed in modern UK broadsheet discourse. They convey an attempt to differentiate some product or performance from the rest of what is on offer. If we extend our analysis of the keywords list from 2,500 to 5,000, we find yet more examples of promotional and informal discourse. We come across a group of words related to consumerism, materialism and competition: *elite, exclusive, classy, luxury, aspirational, wealthy, significant, upmarket* and *glamorous*. There is also a group of advertising copy type words: *comfortable, natural, sleek, floral, proud, modern, festive, stylish* and *fairytale*. Another group of words is related to entertainment reviews: *brilliant, hilarious, talented, clever, wonderful* and *legend*.

When we looked at the SiBol 05 keywords, it became apparent that the informal items are not just the modern equivalents of some older evaluative terms, given that there are very few explicitly evaluating items in the keywords of SiBol 93. So, we might ask ourselves whether the new contexts (new supplements and features sections which account for the increase in size) and the new relationships created to attract readers (the emphasis on beauty, fame, size, importance, success, and the informality with which they are expressed) generated the values. These parameters of evaluation do indeed seem to belong to their time and to their genre; there are no formal or high register alternatives in the 1993 data for the values expressed by the 2005 corpus, so there is not, simply, a different choice of register, but also a change of contexts. However, all this does not correspond to a new creativity, the fact that many of the items are three starred words for the MEDAL dictionary also suggests that this "hype" (derived, of course, from "hyperbole"), far from indicating creativity in language usage, denotes, rather, a well-worn and clichéd use of language. What is more, we saw that in Port 2010, among the keywords in comparison with SiBol 05, we find *cliché/clichés/clichéd* with collocates *the, those* (suggesting shared experience), and the concordance lines indicate an awareness of the well worn paths of language use. The question remains, then, of why such emphasis, informality and familiarity have increased. The newspapers under investigation here seem by 2005 to have expanded their role as commenting and reviewing at the expense, proportionally at least, of news reporting, in an attempt to provide something the rolling news programmes cannot provide. Partington (2010) noted that *yesterday* – an item that is famously frequent in the first sentence of hard news stories – was a keyword in SiBol 93 compared with

2005, along with a good variety of verbs in past time reference form that are typical of hard news reporting. This new expanded role of commenting and reviewing is reflected in the increase in size and variety of newspaper supplements.

An example of how newspapers are aware of language change, and sometimes discus it openly, was found in a review item. The hyperbolic nature of advertising-speak and corporate jargon was detected by the *Oxford English Dictionary* monitoring programme, and was discussed in a book on language by Dent (2005) which was reviewed thus in the *Telegraph*:

> (16) As part of the 'bigging-up' or 'supersizing' trend, she identifies the use of 'ova', 'uber' or 'mega' prefixes to beef up words. Miss Dent said: 'Linguistic supersizing is on the increase, and it may show the influence of advertising-speak and corporate jargon on language, in which everything needs to be hyped to get noticed. It means that some of our greatest words are losing their power. Add to this the "hyperinflation" of our language, as just detected by the Oxford English Dictionary. Prefixes such as "ova" and "uber" and "mega" are diluting the power of our words. One of its experts said this week that to be called a hero used to be the highest honour. Now you have to be a superhero to make an impact.' (*Telegraph* 2005)

All three broadsheets included a review and comment on this book, implying at least that it was considered worthy of note. However the fact that they all used the same examples and the same quotation suggests they are not exactly aware of the root of the problem in that, perhaps, the reviews themselves were, ironically, taken from a press release. This multiplied the number of times the words under discussion appeared in our corpus and neatly illustrates the way the forced priming (see Chapter 7) of promotional material works.

What the items considered here have in common is that they are all used to evaluate, many of them hyperbolically, and that they mimic spoken and informal language use. The appearance in the keywords lists of these high intensity items is a strong indication that a particular discourse function has grown considerably over the period. If these words have become salient, then the nature of broadsheet language has changed considerably, that it has adopted the use of less measured language, and has become more imitative of the orality and informal language that used to be a characteristic of the tabloids and of advertising. One aspect which is very frequent in the data is that of ironic usage, tongue-in-cheek evaluations or distancing-quote usage as we saw with *vibrant*. It is very difficult, however, to quantify this kind of knowing reversal of evaluation (Chapter 4.3).

Finally, the frequent use of very common terms of evaluation (the three-star words from our reference dictionary) may suggest that the journalists are writing to ever more strict deadlines, and often resort, as a result, to dead metaphors and set phrases.

CHAPTER 11

# Modern diachronic corpus-assisted discourse studies (MD-CADS) 2

## Comparisons over time of social, political and cultural issues

In the last chapter, we saw how comparing and contrasting the contents of two or more sister corpora could permit the analyst to make evidence-based inferences about developments over recent time in UK newspaper language and discourse practices. In this chapter we present two case studies showing how similar analyses can shed light on developments over recent times in newspaper attitudes to political, social and cultural issues. The first study is on how antisemitism is reported and discussed, the second on the ways the items (and concepts) boy/s and girl/s are represented. The emphasis will be as much on the methods of analysis we employed as on the results we observed. In both studies, the second in particular, attention will be paid not only to how representations of these issues have changed over recent times, but also on what remained the same. Whilst it is true that humans, like all biological entities, tend naturally to be interested in change since changes of state often prove to be especially significant, "sameness" is, as we shall see, more complex than might at first sight appear. As Heraclitus famously put it, "nothing persists except change", we both can and cannot step in the "same" river twice.

### 11.1 Antisemitism: The longest hatred

#### 11.1.1 The statistical consistency of discourses around antisemitism

The initial spur for the current piece of research was an observation made by Duguid (2010b) in an MD-CADS study into the differences and similarities over time in the use of the prefix *anti* in Sibol 1993 and SiBol 2005 that the items *anti-semitism* and *anti-semitic* retained exactly the same place in the rankings, that is, 4th and 8th most frequent respectively. Discourses in these newspapers relating to *antisemitism* had, therefore, remained not only very frequent but statistically very consistently so. However, a closer comparison of the contexts of the two items suggested that there might be important differences in the kinds of discourses around antisemitism and consequently in the way it was being represented. This was obviously partly due to references to particular events which took place in the two years, but she also found discussions of "more long-term concerns about rising numbers of attacks on Jews in Britain and France" (Duguid 2010: 212). We considered this worthy of further investigation.

In this paper we adopt the non-hyphenated spelling of *antisemitism* in this paper following a practice recommended by the Jewish philosopher Emil Fackenheim: "the spelling ought to be antisemitism without the hyphen, dispelling the notion that there is an entity 'Semitism' which 'anti-Semitism' opposes" (1977: 11).

### 11.1.2 A working definition of *antisemitism*

The OED defines *anti-Semitism* (hyphenated) as "[t]heory, action or practice directed against the Jews". The US Holocaust Memorial Museum defines it simply as "prejudice against or hatred of Jews".

Most forms of racism are predicated on the purported inferiority of the target group. Antisemitism historically – and paradoxically – combines this with varied conspiracy plots depicting Jews – as a collective – as extremely powerful and manipulative of international events and processes, always in a clandestine way (Partridge & Geaves 2008) and always with malign ends (see Section 11.1.12 below).

Several voices in the data maintain that antisemitism is often not treated as seriously as other forms of racism (Examples 17 and 20). It may be that this perception in some eyes of Jews as (over)empowered disqualifies them from victim status, even in cases where they are clearly targets of abuse.

This however is somewhat abstract. Much of what concerns the press in their 2005, 2009 and 2010 reporting is actual physical harm or threats of it and damage and defacing of places such as synagogues and graves, taking place within the UK.

The working definition of antisemitism for The European Monitoring Centre on Racism and Xenophobia (EUMC) supplies a number of examples of what it considers to be antisemitic acts which range from outright violence, to "making mendacious, dehumanizing, or stereotypical allegations about Jews".[1] This would be uncontroversial for all three newspapers but another much-debated question

1. ⟨http://fra.europa.eu/fraWebsite/material/pub/AS/AS-WorkingDefinition-draft.pdf⟩

is whether a perceived "singling out" of Israel for supposedly excessive vituperation can sometimes contain elements of antisemitism, as the EUMC definition also specifically claims (and see Foxman 2003):

(1) Are the readers, in the SWP's usually magisterial and definite opinion, right to "feel" that the distinction between anti-Semitism and anti- Zionism is being blurred, or not? (*Times* 2005)

and whether in particular this can lead to an encouragement of anti-Jewish feeling (Sections 11.1.11, 11.1.13). This raises the question of whether some behaviours may not be antisemitic *in intent* but may be antisemitic *in effect*, in parallel with other forms of racism.

### 11.1.3 Averral and attribution

It is often important to ascertain whether what is being claimed is done so in the name of the newspaper or at least one of its writers, that is, whether the opinion, the representation being expressed is asserted – *averred* – by the paper. Alternatively the opinion/representation can be explicitly attributed to some other external primary source, and the newspaper is purporting to act as conduit, as secondary source (see also Chapters 2.5 and 7.4.1 on averral and attribution). The attribution is often in the form of direct quotation, but not always. In researching issues like racism, it is also important to note how much and what kind of evidence is provided by both internal and external sources for the way they represent their view. Instances of averral can be seen in Examples (4) and (5) and elsewhere, instances of attribution can be seen in Examples (8) and (9) and elsewhere. Where relevant, attention will be paid to whether a representation is averred or attributed (Sinclair 1988; Tadros 1993).

The present case study is on analyses the way antisemitism has been reported and discussed in the UK press. What, however, will not be within the scope of the current paper are *instantiations* of antisemitism, that is, episodes where writers are *performing* antisemitism (invented example: "Those Jews – they control the media, the banks, US foreign policy"). Such performed episodes of antisemitism are not flagged by a keyword search for *antisemit**.

### 11.1.4 Methodology

To study the similarities and changes in the way *antisemitism* is talked about in the UK press, four datasets were prepared from SiBol 93, SiBol 05, Port 2010 and also, since the research began in mid 2010, from a collection of all the articles in which *anti-Semit** or *antisemit** apppeared from the same newspapers in 2009, downloaded using Lexis Nexis. In order to extract all and only the episodes in context where antisemitism is mentioned or discussed in the four years, the concordance-keywords procedure was adopted (Taylor 2010), as follows:

1. Using *WordSmith Tools* (Scott 2008), a concordance was prepared of the search terms *anti-semit** and *antisemit** in SiBol 93. A span of 300 characters of co-text was specified, equivalent to approximately four lines of text in a standard word processor.
2. The concordances of *anti-semit*/antisemit** were saved in .txt format to compose a separate new corpus consisting of the concordance lines (called a "concordance-corpus"). Any instances of duplicated text were eliminated, when appropriate.
3. The process was repeated for SiBol 05 for the 2009 dataset and for Port 2010, resulting in three concordance-corpora, henceforward AS93, AS05, AS09, AS10.
4. The *WordSmith Wordlist* tool compiled lists of the words contained in each concordance-corpus in order of frequency.
5. Using the *WordSmith Keyword* tool, keyword lists were prepared for each of the concordance-corpora as compared to each of the other two, producing nine lists in all:

   AS93 vs AS05; AS93 vs AS09; AS93 vs AS10
   AS05 vs AS93; AS05 vs AS09; AS05 vs AS10
   AS09 vs AS93; AS09 vs AS05; AS09 vs AS10

   The first names in each pair is the target corpus, the second the comparison corpus. The p-value, indicating the level of statistical significance which needs to be met, was set at 0.01 (a higher value than sometimes used, but appropriate when comparing relatively small corpora since at lower values very few items will be collected) and the minimum frequency at 5 items (a reasonably high figure, which helps to counterbalance the high p-value and ensure that items are not included by chance).

The analyst thus has at their disposal every single incidence of use in context (300 characters) of the item *anti-semit** and *antisemit** in the three newspapers in each of the four years.

### 11.1.5 Blending stretches containing duplicated text

When intending to compare the contents of the various concordance-corpora of *antisemit** a major problem became apparent, that of how to eliminate duplicated segments of text. It is very often the situation that, within the span of one concordance line, a second (or even more) instances of the search-item can occur. The likelihood of this happening increases, of course, proportionally to the amount of co-text chosen for the concordance and, as we have already mentioned, it is very generally convenient in corpus-assisted discourse studies to stipulate considerable amounts of co-text, from 300 characters upwards. To illustrate, *The Times* 2009 concordance-corpus contained the following two lines:

> 158 or the memory of the six million Jewish victims of the Shoah, and to pray that humanity will never again witness a crime of such magnitude. Sadly, **anti-Semitism** continues to rear its ugly head in many parts of the world. This is totally unacceptable. Every effort must be made to combat **anti-Semitism**.
>
> 381 Sadly, **anti-Semitism** continues to rear its ugly head in many parts of the world. This is totally unacceptable. Every effort must be made to combat **anti-Semitism** wherever it is found. During my stay in Jerusalem, I will have the pleasure of meeting many of this country's distinguished [...]

The stretches of text underlined are clearly duplicates. For the purposes of any kind of frequency counting and in particular for comparing the words and clusters in this concordance-corpus with those in the others, one of the stretches has to be eliminated and the two lines blended. If this is not done then the items in the repeated stretch will be counted twice when a word-frequency list is made, skewing the resulting frequencies, and since there proved to be many instances of such overlaps, the resulting lists would be illegitimate. Moreover, blending is preferable to simply eliminating one of the lines, since this would involve removing one or other segments of co-text. If the first line above was cancelled "or the memory of the six million Jewish victims of the Shoah, and to pray that humanity will never again witness a crime of such magnitude" would get removed, whereas if the second was cancelled "wherever it is found. During my stay in Jerusalem, I will have the pleasure of meeting many of this country's distinguished" would get removed. These segments, instead, should be available for frequency counts.

Before line-blending can be effected, there is the real problem of locating the two or more lines with overlapping text to be run together. Left or right-sorting fails to locate and juxtapose them because the immediate co-texts of the two occurrences of *anti-Semitism* in the overlapping lines above are entirely different; they would be:

> crime of such magnitude. Sadly, **anti-Semitism** continues to rear its ugly head

and

> Every effort must be made to combat **anti-Semitism** wherever it is found

### 11.1.6 When not to remove duplicated text

Matters are further complicated by the fact that it is not possible to simply employ a short program to eliminate all duplicated text of a certain length from our concordance-corpora. Fairly long strings are often found to be repeated, not quite by chance but contingent on the topic of discussion in hand. For instance, the 2009 material included two occurrences in entirely separate articles and therefore with completely different co-texts of the following rather sizable fragments: [Chelsea fans] "made racist and anti-semitic chants before their 2–1 ..." and "the Latvian part in the Conservative's European coalition". These may well be particularly numerous in newspaper texts, given how most news reporting articles are reworkings of press agency reports, so different newspaper writers are often working from the same starting text. Moreover very many articles are reworkings of various other previously published stories on the same topic ("Frankenstein" pieces). There are also numerous smaller chunks, whose status is somewhere between random cluster and set grammatical expression, such as "it should be acknowledged that", "as often happens when", as well as proper names like "the Protocols of the Elders of Zion". Obviously none of these should be removed if occurring more than once.

We also quite frequently find the same quotation repeated in different articles, for instance:

(2) A Royal Court spokesman urged people to see the play before judging it. "**It is possible to criticise the actions of Israel without being anti-Semitic**," he says. (*Guardian*, February 14th 2009)

and

(3) He said "While Seven Jewish Children is undoubtedly critical of the policies of the State of Israel, there is no suggestion that this should be read as a criticism of Jewish people. "**It is possible to criticise the actions of Israel without being anti-Semitic**." (*Guardian*, February 19th 2009)

### 11.1.7 The procedure we adopted

The solution to the problem of removing unwanted duplication whilst ensuring the retention of desired duplications which was eventually adopted here was to use cluster-searching following by manual inspection. Each concordance-corpus for each newspaper for each year (so, nine in all) was fed into *WordSmith*'s *WordList* Tool, with the cluster length setting activated at eight items (8-grams), with a minimum frequency of two. By trial and error we discovered that collecting clusters of smaller length produced too many distracting "normal" stretches of text, and even this setting gave several hundred clusters for each newspaper concordance subcorpus. Very many clusters of course related to the same stretch of replicated text, for instance the duplicated stretch of text: "He claimed he himself had been the victim of the far-right in Poland after being attacked for a statement he made on antisemitism in the European parliament" (*Guardian* 2009) produced, among several others the following 8-grams:

> AFTER BEING ATTACKED FOR A STATEMENT HE MADE
> ATTACKED FOR A STATEMENT HE MADE ON ANTISEMITISM
> BEING ATTACKED FOR A STATEMENT HE MADE ON
> FOR A STATEMENT HE MADE ON ANTISEMITISM IN
> IN POLAND AFTER BEING ATTACKED FOR A STATEMENT

These clusters could then be used to search for duplicated stretches within the concordance subcorpus itself. When the two entries containing the identical stretch were found (using the Word edit *Find* tool), the decision then was necessary on whether they needed to be blended (as in the example above in 11.1.5: "Sadly, anti-semitism continues to rear…") or whether they should be left as they were, as in the cases illustrated in the previous section. Though somewhat laborious, the procedure proved to be a very effective way of clearing out unwanted duplicated text from the various corpora and thus making them legitimate entities for cross-comparison. Fortunately, not all concordance-corpora contain as much duplicated text as those employed here. Taylor (2010), for instance, found very few episodes of duplication in her concordance-corpora of the expression *the science* simply because it seldom appeared twice in close proximity in the same text.

### 11.1.8 Looking for similarities across the datasets

We decided to look firstly for similarities across the datsets, what was constant in discussions of the topic in hand in the three time periods, and to do this a separate keywords comparison was made of each concordance-corpus with the contents of both the two million-word BNC sampler corpus (henceforth BNC(S), a selected portion of the 100 million-word British National Corpus of "general" British English) using the *WordSmith Keywords* tool and of the BNC 10-million word sample using *Sketch Engine*. The four keyword lists have several items in common, many of which were largely to be expected, for example: *Hitler*, *Nazi* – *Nazis*, *racist* – *racism*, *Zionist* and *anti-Zionist*. The item *Holocaust* was high in all the lists, but closer scrutiny revealed that in 1993 it collocated with *memorial* and *survivor(s)*, whilst in the later data only did it also collocate relatively frequently with *denier* and *denial*.

The items *Israel* and *Israeli* were present in all the lists but had become relatively more frequent in the more recent datasets. So too, as a first hint of corroboration of Duguid's discovery of discussions of "more long-term concerns about rising numbers of attacks on Jews in Britain and France" (Duguid 2010: 212), was the word *attacks* and *incidents*. Baker (2011) has coined the term "lockword" to indicate items which retain their keyness or "popularity" of use over time in a particular discourse type (see 11.2.3.5). Some items are clearly more locked in relative popularity position than others.

### 11.1.9 Discourses on *antisemitism* in AS93

We then turned to investigating the differences in discourses on antisemitism over time by examining the various concordance keywords lists, beginning with the three lists showing the key items from the 1993 concordance corpus, namely AS93 vs AS05, AS93 vs AS09 and AS93 vs AS10. Although the concordances were the starting point, whenever appropriate the option of analysing the whole articles in which they occur was always available. Taking AS93 vs AS10, the most salient items of all in the latter were *Russian* (34 occurrences), *Russia* (21), *Polish* (19) with *Poles* (8) not far behind. There were also twelve occurrences of *Soviet* and thirteen of *Communism.*

Many of the first of these arise from various discussions of Russian history, for example:

> (4) **Anti-Semitism** was initially suppressed by Communism, but in the last years of Stalin's rule the campaign against "rootless cosmopolitanism" threatened savage executions and deportations which were averted only by the tyrant's death. Since then **anti-Semitism**, usually under the cloak of anti-Zionism, had a respectable place in the Communist Party. (*Times* 1993)

As we shall see, just how much antisemitism resides under the cloak of anti-Zionism, not in the Soviet Union but in modern Europe including the UK, becomes a lively topic of debate in the more recent newspaper material.

However, the majority of instances of *Russian* are part of an extensive discussion of the rise of Mr *Zhirinovsky* (prominent in all AS93 lists), leader of a Russian nationalist group and widely credited with antisemitic views. The appearance of *Poles* and *Latvia* is equally due to a mix of references to both historical antisemitism and the possibility of current renewed nationalistic antisemitic attitudes, *nationalism* (15 occurrences) and *nationalist* (14) both appearing high in the AS93 lists. The Iron Curtain had of course fallen only three years before 1993, and so a major theme of the UK newspapers is what effect the new independence and the reassertion of nationality on the part of various Eastern European states would have upon their minority populations, given the relatively recent historical precedents of intolerance.

We also find *Christian* (18), *Christians* (8) and *Catholicism* (6). These appear both as part of a general discussion of historical Christian antisemitism:

(5) Given the Jewishness of Christianity, the relations between the two religions have been a historic tragedy of unimaginable proportions. Christian **anti-Semitism** is one of the worst stains on the record of Christianity. (*Times* 1993)

and also because, in 1993, an agreement between Israel and the Catholic Church contained a commitment by the latter to cooperate in combating antisemitism.

Another set of prominent keywords, *Coren*, *Jacobson*, *Judas*, *Nureyev*, *Wells* and *Wagner* are proper names and all turn out, when the concordance-corpus is investigated, to have some literary or artistic reference. The Jewish writer Howard Jacobson produced and acted in a TV documentary drama called *Sorry, Judas* which included discussion of how much antisemitism the Judas story had provoked over the years. H.G. Wells and Nureyev are discussed in terms of various antisemitic remarks they may have made. The item *memoirs* also appears, largely thanks to discussions of literary biographies. The most intense discussion however revolves around the question of whether Wagner's music can still be enjoyed despite his notorious antisemitism.

(6) If the traditional (and bogus) dichotomy between Wagner the vile, egoistic **anti-Semite** and the composer of sublime music were to break down, Wagner could lose his place in the pantheon as an indispensable element of Western culture. (*Times* 1993)

Similar questions can be asked of several major works of English literature from Chaucer's *The Prioress's Tale* to Dickens's *Oliver Twist* (see Julius 2010).

In sum, then, a large proportion of the UK newspaper discourse on antisemitism in 1993 is historical or deals with the biography of past writers and artists. Although a reputed or potential resurgence of antisemitism in modern times is a common theme too, it is presented as a phenomenon potentially occurring in faraway places.

### 11.1.10 Discourses on *antisemitism* in 2005, 2009 and 2010

The 2005 discourses around antisemitism still include numerous historical references, but the overall picture of representations of antisemitism is also radically different. As mentioned earlier, the AS05 vs AS93 keyword include *attacks* but also *incidents, offence* and *levels, rise* and *highest*. They also include *Britain, UK, London* and *Manchester* as well as proper names from British politics.

There are numerous reports, generally attributed by the newspaper to external primary sources (reports, Jewish bodies, politicians, etc) about antisemitism on home soil and much concern that the number of incidents has reached levels never known before:

(7) A total of 532 "anti-semitic incidents" – defined as malicious acts on Jewish people or property – were recorded in 2004, according to the Community Security Trust, a body that monitors levels of **anti-semitism**. The figure was a 42% increase on the 375 anti-semitic incidents recorded in 2003 and considerably more than the previous record of 405 in 2000. (*Guardian* 2005)

(8) John Mann, chairman of the parliamentary committee against **anti-semitism**, said the problem had moved into the mainstream. "Anti-semitism is back in fashion," he said. (*Guardian* 2005)

The situation in France is reported as worse still, with *French* among the 2009 keywords:

(9) [*La Commission nationale consultative des droits de l'homme*] said in its annual study that 1,565 threats and acts of violence against mainly Jewish and Muslim victims were registered in 2004, compared with 833 the previous year. "Manifestations of racism and **anti-semitism** are multiplying dangerously in France and last year reached an exceptional and disturbing peak " the commission said. The report said **anti-semitic** acts represented more than 60% of all the incidents recorded: 970 compared with 601 in 2003, most committed by people of "Arab-Muslim origin". (*Guardian* 2005)

Judging by these statistics, the small numbers of Jewish people as a proportion of the general population of France and the relatively high percentage of racist incidents which they experience means that the chances of any Jewish individual suffering a racist act is much higher than for many other minorities. Moreover, there are no reports in any of the newspaper subcorpora of any incidents in which Jews were the *perpetrators* of a racist incident.

By 2009 the situation is reported as having deteriorated still further:

(10) [Headline] **Anti-Semitism study**
The Metropolitan Police report four times as many anti-Jewish incidents in recent weeks as Islamaphobic events. The respected Community Security Trust, which records anti-Jewish attacks with scrupulous rigour, reports as many attacks on Jews – verbal, vandalism and some violent – in the first weeks of 2009 as in the first six months of last year. (*Guardian* 2009)

(11) On average, there is an **antisemitic** attack of some kind every single day in the UK: graffiti, vandalism, arson and occasionally actual physical assault. Jewish schools have been granted extra protection. (*Guardian* Editorial 2009)

(12) [Headline] **Anti-Semitism is rife, says minister**
BRITAIN has failed to eradicate the "utterly unacceptable cultural ill'" of **anti-Semitism**, a Foreign Office minister has admitted. (*Guardian* 2005)

(13) Last month a 32-year-old IT worker, Michael Booksatz, was beaten up in the streets of north London by two hooded men shouting about Palestinians. Jewish students at the London School of Economics – home to many brilliant Jews who fled Hitler's Germany – are now frightened by anti-Jewish abuse from Islamist students. Graffiti such as "Kill the Jews" or "Jihad 4 Israel" appear close to synagogues in London. (*Times* 2009)

And, as in 2005, in 2009 antisemitism is also represented as being rife in Western Europe:

(14) In Belgium a Molotov cocktail was thrown at a synagogue [...] *Joods Actueel*, a Jewish magazine, has received a dozen death threats including those by an anonymous man who threatened a suicide attack [...] A Jewish home was firebombed at the weekend. (*Telegraph* 2009)

(15) A report this week by the New York-based Anti-Defamation League complained of what it claimed was a rise in **anti-semitism** across Spain [...] "we [have] seen viciously **anti-semitic** cartoons in the mainstream media, and street protests where Israel is accused of genocide and Jews are vilified and compared to Nazis." (*Guardian* 2009)

In some of these passages, for Example (10) and (14), the language used is relatively neutral but in others the negative evaluation of the representations of current antisemitism is reinforced by the use of intensifiers, sometimes averred by the writers themselves ("every single day" Example 11), sometimes attributed to other participants ("utterly unacceptable cultural ill" Example 12, "viciously" Example 15).

### 11.1.11 The perpetrators

Those accused of antisemitic views and/or behaviour include, not surprisingly, far-right groups in all three corpora. When compared to the BNC(S) (rather than to each other), all three keyword lists feature prominently *Nazi* and *Nazis*. The item *nationalists* is a keyword in 1993 tending almost exclusively to refer to Eastern European groups, whereas *BNP*, a home-grown far-right organisation, appears amongst those of AS09 along with the name of its leader Mr Nick *Griffin*. *Fascism* and *fascist* are most prominent in the 1993 keywords data; it falls a little out of favour later.

The company kept by *anti-semit**, that is, the traits and groups it is felt to aggregate with, is, as would be expected, unpalatable:

(16) When the new European Parliament convened this week, its ranks included Hungarian gypsy-haters, French Holocaust deniers, Dutch Islam-baiters, Austrian **antisemites**, Italian racists, and Flemish separatists, (*Guardian* 2009)

We also find *anti-semit** often paired with *misogyny/misogynist* and, especially in the more recent corpora, *homophobic/homophobia* (these appear as follows, AS93, 3 times; AS05, 16; AS09, 32; AS10, 27).

If an association of bigotry – and worse – with the far right is taken for granted in all three concordance-corpora, one major difference between the 1993 data and the three more recent datasets is the considerable debate in the latter surrounding a supposed rise in antisemitism on the left. This is not entirely new (Cohen 1984) and there are references to historical leftist antisemitism in France, in Germany where "The anti-semitism of the terrorist Left was revealed when a radical group bombed a Jewish hall in West Berlin in 1969" (*Times* 2010), in the Soviet Union, and in Poland, as one letter-writer remarks:

(17) Garton Ash links anti-Semitism in Poland with the right [...] In reality it is unfair to limit such criticism to one side of Polish politics; for decades the motor of modern **antisemitism** in Poland was the left. After the second world war the ruling communist party drove Poland's remaining 200,000 Jews from the country in successive waves. (*Guardian* 2009)

But there are also discourses, again very generally attributed by the newspaper to some external primary source, over a purported contribution of the left to current levels of antisemitism in the UK:

(18) She also criticised how prejudice against Jews was seen by some on the left as "second-class racism". (*Times* 2005)

(19) "**Anti-semitism** is back in fashion," he said. "It was once considered solely a problem of the far right, but this is no longer the case." He said the "liberal and progressive left" could not absolve itself. (*Guardian* 2005)

The speakers here are, in (18), a member of the executive committee of the National Union of Students, who resigned, according to the *Times* report "after being abused and spat at by left-wing undergraduates and Muslim activists because she is Jewish" and in (19) John Mann, chairman of the parliamentary commission into antisemitism.

Explanations are also offered, this time generally averred by the newspapers themselves. One *Guardian* writer believes that some on the left have simply forgotten its core values in pursuit of a false and simplistic dualism:

(20) Too often, however, members of today's left have abandoned their task of creating a better, more just world in the name of just such a blind and aimless struggle between an "us" and a "them". And because the powerless sometimes hold the values of homophobia, misogyny, racism, mass murder, and **anti-Semitism**, the left has found itself championing or at least excusing these values in the name of its Manichean struggle. (*Guardian* 2005)

The second argument contends that the left has become so totally preoccupied with the Middle East that it has little interest left in guarding against antisemitism.

Example (21) is from a leading article, thus the authoritative averring voice of the newspaper:

(21) The government has also recognised that [...] "unlike other forms of racism, **antisemitism** is being accepted within parts of society instead of being condemned." The left fought a long and honourable battle for racial equality, but some within its ranks now risk sloppily allowing their horror of Israeli actions to blind them to **antisemitism**. (*Guardian* 2009)

Another *Guardian* columnist, Jonathan Freedland, himself Jewish, warns against the "affinity for Israel" test (*Guardian* 2009) designed to divide British Jews "into good Jews and bad Jews", the former being those who denounce Israel, the latter those who refuse to disaffiliate from it, a form of test (not to mention also false dichotomy) which would undoubtedly, as Mr Freedland implies, be seen as racist if applied to any other minority group.

Prominent among the AS05 vs AS93, AS09 vs AS93 and AS10 vs AS93 keywords, we find *Muslim* and *Muslims*, with *Islam* and *Islamophobia* somewhat lower down. An initial conjecture was that these items might be salient when compared with data from 1993 or the *BNC(S)* (most of whose texts date from the 1980s and 1990s) simply because there are more Muslims in British social, cultural and political life. To test this hypothesis, a keyword comparison was conducted between AS05 and the entire SiBol 05 newspaper corpus, both data sets being therefore from the same moment in time. *Muslim* and *Muslims*, however, still appeared very high on the AS05 keyword lists (ranked 28th and 37th respectively), with *Islamophobic* and *Islamic* also appearing (78th and 144th respectively), evidence that these items were indeed highly salient in AS05.

*Muslims* are discussed in terms of both perpetrators of antisemitic acts and also as fellow victims of prejudice.

As regards the first, all the papers are very careful to make a distinction between ordinary Muslims and violent extremists (usually denominated *Islamists*):

(22) [Conservatives and Labour join] in saying it is time for the Parliaments of the democratic world to take action against **anti-Semitism** – especially Islamist attacks against young Jewish students on university campuses. (*Times* 2009)

In the entire SiBol 05 corpus there are only two instances of *muslim* attack**, both of which are metaphorical (*Muslims attack BBC* and *Muslims attack ban on ...*), compared to thirteen instances of *Islamist attacks*, all of which refer to episodes of physical violence. The depiction in 2010 is more complex. A concordance of *islamist** and *attack** (span 2L, 2R) afforded 30 results in all of which Islamists were the perpetrators of physical attacks. A concordance of *muslim** and *attack** (span 2L, 2R) yielded 28 occurrences. In 14, Muslims were the victims of attacks, in 11 Muslims were the perpetrators, but in all cases but one of the latter, when the attacks took place in the west, the term *Muslim(s)* is qualified by *extremist(s)* or *fundamentalist(s)*. However, in recounting violence in Nigeria, the two sides are referred to simply as *Muslims*, with no qualifiers, and *Christians*.

Returning to alleged Islamist antisemitism, very generally, it is organised political associations rather than individual incidents which excite most discussion:

(23) If taxpayer-funded schools were run by supporters of the BNP, there would be an outcry. Hizb-ut Tahrir is an Islamic version of the BNP: not actually violent, but openly **anti-Semitic**, racist, and an enemy of liberal society. (*Telegraph* 2009)

The *Telegraph* is averring the negative appraisal. And there is mention of widespread institutionalised antisemitism in some Muslim-majority countries, again averred by the newspaper itself, here the *Guardian*:

(24) TV stations across the Muslim world have been running this garbage [Holocaust denial] for ages, along with lurid **anti-semitism**. Jordanian TV's Ramadan special this year was Al-Shatat, a Syrian- produced series that speaks of a "global Jewish government" and depicts the ancient blood libel: the accusation that Jews use the blood of Christian children in preparing food for Passover. (*Guardian* 2005)

As regards the second relationship, there are twenty-eight representations of Jews and Muslims as fellow sufferers of rising xenophobia in AS05, AS09 and AS10, of which the following is a brief sample:

(25) It is hard to believe that, 60 years on, we are witnessing a resurgence of intolerance, incitement, harassment and violence against Arabs, Muslims and Jews in the form of **anti-Semitism**. (*Telegraph* 2005)

(26) They may take new forms, but even in the post- Enlightenment era **anti-semitism** and Islamophobia are alive and well. (*Guardian* 2005)

(27) The BNP are [...] as homophobic, Islamophobic and plain, downright racist as they are **anti-semitic**. (*Telegraph* 2010)

and see Example (16). In the majority of such cases the newspapers are averring the existence of anti-Muslim and anti-Jewish prejudice. The newspapers in question would appear to be more at ease in asserting a rise in more generalised prejudice than in asserting growing antisemitism alone, possibly because the latter comes as news to many readers and therefore needs more substantiation.

### 11.1.12 "The global Jewish conspiracy"

In 11.1.2 we mentioned how anti-Jewish prejudice is often justified by conspiracy theories. Concordances of *conspirac** and *plot** within a nine-word span of *Jew** showed how reports of Jewish-conspiracy accusations have developed over time. In the 1993 data, we find references to far-right beliefs that clandestine Jewish plots brought down Germany and the Nazis and to nostalgic communists accusing the Jews of destroying the Soviet Union and plotting to control the new Russia (or Poland or Hungary).

By 2005, however, the Jewish tentacles have spread. There are more mentions of Jewish conspiracies; 55 compared to 29 in 1993. As one commentator remarks ironically "the Jews are responsible for everything. For 9/11, for Iraq, for the spread of Aids, for all political unrest" (*Times* 2005). There are more references to modern conspiracy theories sited in the West: new plots to ruin Germany, to take over the USA "using African-Americans as their subhuman foot-soldiers" (*Times* 2005), even Ireland is contaminated:

(28) "[...] He was exercised by what he saw as a Jewish plot to take over Irish politics. 'They are infiltrating all the parties.'" (*Times* 2005)

The numerical increase is also partly due to an awareness of another strain. There are 19 mentions of right-wing antisemitic conspiracy theories both contemporary and in the last century, seven of left-wing theories, but 16 mentions of Islamist theories, mostly in Muslim-majority countries but also in Europe, including outbursts by an adviser to the Prime Minister who reportedly "is a Holocaust-denier and thinks the Iraq war was cooked up by a conspiracy of Freemasons and Jews" (*Telegraph* 2005).

Such people could be dismissed as cranks, but their antisemitism is feeding from and into much wider strains. The Islamist version, for instance, according to one commentator, draws from the "conspiracy theory of a Jewish-crusader network to subjugate the Islamic world" (*Times* 2005) and can allegedly find official sanction amongst governments: "senior members of the ruling dynasty [of Saudi Arabia] ... still believe that the downing of the twin towers was a Jewish conspiracy" (*Times* 2009).

There is a clear parallel among the strands. For one group the Jews used their clandestine financial power to destroy the Soviet Union, for another to bring down Nazi Germany, for another they are using it to control America, the West, the World, and for yet another to destroy Islam.

All this conspiracy plotting is of course *attributed* to some party. Is there any conspiracy accusation averred by any of the newspapers? Unsurprisingly there is nothing overt, except for the *Guardian*'s applying the term "the Jewish lobby" to the varied opponents of an academic boycott of Israel (Section 10). After complaints, it specified that the reference was to The Union of Jewish Students and the Board of Deputies of British Jews, a well-respected, elected body, neither of which seems to merit the appellation. The same newspaper says in 2009, "there is no 'Jewish lobby' in the conspiratorial sense the slur implies".

### 11.1.13 Differences in focus of the three newspapers

It is both clear and unsurprising that all the newspapers evaluate antisemitism very negatively. Several of the extracts included here contain instances of explicitly negative lexis, for instance, "Wagner the *vile*, *egoistic* anti-Semite ..." (Example 6), "... openly anti-Semitic, *racist*, and an *enemy* of liberal society" (Example 23). But are there any significant differences in the way the three newspaper report and discuss antisemitism? To answer this question the concordance corpora relative to the three most recent datasets were reorganised by individual newspaper, with 2009 and 2010 combined into one. Keyword comparisons were then made among them using *WordSmith* (p-value maximum 0.01, minimum five occurrences).

The *Telegraph* 2005 keyword list includes *Labour, posters, Fagin, pigs* and *Howard*. Unsurprisingly the right-leaning *Telegraph* was the paper to make the most of a dubious Labour party election poster campaign depicting the Jewish leader of the Conservatives as a flying pig and as Dickens's malevolent Jewish character.

The *Times* is by far the most interested of the three in religious discourses and the relation between Jewry and the Church. The item *Vatican* is first in its lists, which also contain *Pius, Pope, Church, Benedict, beatification, priest* and even *God* and *vicar*.

The top item in the *Guardian* lists is *Israel* with *Israeli* close behind. In 2010, the newspaper uses these two items a combined total of 5,806 times (15 times per million tokens), compared to *The Times* 3,519 times (9 per million tokens) and the *Telegraph* 3,141 times (8 per million tokens). Given the tumultuous events of the following year – 2011 – in the rest of the Middle East, it is interesting to note that, in contrast to its pervasive coverage of Israel, the *Guardian* in 2010 mentions *Libya* and *Libyan* just 480 times, *Syria* and *Syrian* 499 times and *Tunisia* and *Tunisian* a mere 121 times.

The *Guardian* also uses the item *Zionis** and *anti-Zionis** far more than the other papers put together, (in 2010, 186 times, compared to *The Times*'s 49 and the *Telegraph*'s 36). The *Guardian* and *The Times* display a different emphasis. The *Guardian* warns of the need to distinguish between anti-Zionism and antisemitism, which "has become a growth industry for every university department of cultural criticism." (*Guardian* 2009):

(29) There is a thin and permeable line between anti-Zionists and Jew haters; just as there is such a line between those who produce critiques of Islamism and those who are simply racists. (*Guardian* 2005)

*The Times* on the other hand is more ready to aver in its own voice instances where it feels that the two have been conjoined, either openly and deliberately, as by Ahmadinajad who "has used his speech [to the UN] to voice anti-Semitic and anti-Zionist rhetoric" (*Times* 2009), or unwittingly as in the UN Goldstone Report "based largely on interviews with Hamas which panders to anti-Zionist (even anti-Semitic) opinion" (*Times* 2009), or guilefully and viciously:

(30) Criticism of Israel is not anti-Semitic. But all anti-Semites hate the existence of a Jewish state and hiding behind code words such as anti-Zionism increases the density and viciousness of their anti-Jewish utterances. In Italy, the streets of Milan are daubed with slogans urging Italians not to buy goods at Jewish shops – an echo of the Nazi slogan "Kauft Nicht Bei Juden" [...] In anti-Semitic demonstrations in Berlin, placards stating "It was a good idea to use gas" and "I'm anti-Semitic and that's good" were carried. (*Times* 2009)

The *Guardian* lists also contain *NUS*, *student* and *campus*, and we noted above the items *boycott* and *campaign* amongst the 2005 keywords. These derive from a controversy that year concerning a proposal by the Association of University Teachers (AUT) to institute an academic boycott of certain Israeli universities and a counter campaign to lift the ban. The affair was much discussed in the *Guardian* and its sister paper, the *Observer* but practically ignored by the other papers: of the 55 lines of a concordance of *AUT* and *boycott* (occurring within 9 words of each other) 50 were from the *Guardian* and *Observer*, four from *The Times* and just one from the *Telegraph*. It is recounted largely through attribution rather than averral, that is, through the eyes of the protagonists, for example, the following is from one of two letters to the *Guardian* signed by 200 academics:

(31) The **boycott** leaders may not see themselves as antisemitic, but they are guilty of inadvertently feeding into a growing anti-semitism on British campuses and helping to create a feeling of insecurity among Jewish students, who no longer feel safe in what should be one of the most secure and free spaces in public society. (*Guardian* 2005)

When it speaks with its own voice, the *Guardian* is largely unsympathetic to the boycott. The movement which finally overturned the boycott vote is called *grassroots*, a word with a strong positive connotation. But the strongest condemnation comes in a piece attacking the boycotters' declared motivation for singling out Israelis:

(32) [they] argue that Israeli universities should be singled out for sanctions "because Zionist influence [that is, Israeli influence] spreads far beyond its

own immediate area of dominion, and now widely influences many key domestic agendas in the west ... Unlike the Chinese, Russians and other oppressive regimes, the Israelis and their supporters directly influence the policy-makers of our own countries." (*Observer* 2005)

The commentator suspects the same old global Zionist conspiracy theory dressed up in the latest clothes:

(33) In other words, the **boycott** of a small Israeli university where Jews and Arabs study and work side by side represents a courageous blow against some kind of imaginary international monster, whose tentacles reach out into the heart of the western world. I leave it to readers to decide what kind of mindset lurks behind such prose. (*Observer* 2005)

### 11.1.14 Discussion and conclusions on *antisemitism*

(34) **Anti-semitism** today is more often taught as history; the assumption is that it no longer has any real significance. Yet, as MacShane points out [...] there has been a recent reinvention of age-old prejudices. The chairman of a parliamentary commission of inquiry into **anti-semitism**, he has seen the evidence for the renewal of anti-Jewish hatred and his chapter of samples from a year's worth of recent crimes and violence against Jews makes deeply depressing reading. (*Times* 2009, and see MacShane 2008)

In 1993 antisemitism was certainly being discussed in the UK quality press mainly "as history", whilst the main preoccupations concerned whether the newly-achieved independence and emerging nationalism of various Eastern European states would awaken traditional anti-Jewish sentiments.

By 2005, the picture painted by the UK press had changed considerably. Although the previous discourses to some extent remain, they are joined by new, more urgent ones, relating to antisemitism in the British and Western European here-and-now. From official figures showing a distinct upsurge in antisemitic acts (2009 saw the highest number of recorded incidents),[2] ranging from murderous slogans on walls or during demonstrations to actual attacks on individuals, synagogues and Jewish schools, to rumours and allegations of exploiting antisemitic prejudices in sections of the population for electoral advantage, antisemitism in the 2000s in the UK was said to be "rife", "back in fashion".

2. ⟨http://www.thecst.org.uk/docs/Incidents%20Report%202010.pdf⟩

## 11.2 Case study 2: Girls and boys in the UK press

As in the previous study, in this section we will make use of the three Sibol/Port corpora. However, rather than using keywords as our starting point, or entry point to the data, we will explore the range of resources that are available to focus on *similarity*. More specifically, we aim to look at methods which are accessible to language researchers who may not have a strong background in programming and/or statistics.

### 11.2.1 Why search for similarity?

In many ways corpus linguistics is founded on the search for similarity because it involves the search for "usuality" and repeated patterns of behaviour. However, we are generally most used to explicitly focussing on similarity and comparability as key concepts at the stage where we are selecting or creating comparable corpora or reference corpora and this is the aspect that is often emphasised in introductory texts. As discussed in the first case study, there is also the problem of identifying similarity at the level of duplication of texts in corpora and what counts as an unwanted duplicate. In this case study, we examine how the search for similarity can also be profitably expanded beyond the corpus selection/creation stage into the discourse analysis, and that at present this aspect is somewhat neglected. For instance, by way of anecdotal evidence, we concordanced *same/similar/similarity/similarities* in a corpus of 47 corpus linguistics articles (created for Taylor 2008) – there were 555 occurrences (512 of which for *same*), compared to 722 for *different/difference/differences*. This pattern was also found in the British Academic Written Corpus (BAWE), in which there were 7,866 occurrences of *same/similar/similarity/similarities* (of which 5,009 for *same*) compared to 12,808 of *different/difference/differences* showing that this focus on difference is certainly not exclusive to corpus linguistics.

In an early MD-CADS paper, a study of the representation of the European Union (Marchi & Taylor 2009a), it was argued that MD-CADS "allows us both to track *changes* in language usage and to account for extra-linguistic *changes* (social, political, cultural, historical etc.) that language reflects" (2009a: 203, emphasis added). This dual focus on language change and change reflected in language is clearly central to MD-CADS and, indeed, as Partington suggests:

> [h]umans, like all biological entities, tend naturally to be more interested in change than stasis, since changes of state often prove to be especially significant – for good or bad, threatening or rewarding, and so on. Change is also generally intriguing since it tends to demand explanation in a way that stasis often does not. (2010: 105)

However, here we also suggest that there are two principal, interrelated, reasons why we might also want to focus on similarity in corpus approaches to discourse studies. The first is simply that by concentrating on differences alone, we would effectively create a blind spot which means that rather than aiming for a 360 degree perspective of our data, we are actually starting out with the goal of achieving only a 180 degree visualisation. Therefore, the search for similarity can add a new range of starting points into our data and allow us to start with a more ambitious aim regarding the "completeness" of the analysis. In contrast, the potential neglect of patterns of similarities in the data leads to another significant threat to the balance of the analysis, which is that, by setting out to look at difference, that is exactly what the analyst is likely to find and report. Such findings are potentially highly misleading as it may be that in quantitative terms the similarities between two corpora or topics considerably outweigh the differences. As Baker (2010a) explains:

> [N]ot publishing or sharing such findings can result in what has been called 'bottom drawer syndrome'. For example, imagine that ten sets of researchers, working independently from each other, all build a corpus of Singapore English and compare it to a similar British corpus, looking at the same linguistic feature. In nine cases the researchers find that there are no significant differences, decide that the study is therefore uninteresting and assign the research to the bottom drawer of their filing cabinet rather than publishing it. However, the tenth researcher does find a difference and publishes the research, resulting in an inaccurate picture of what the general trend is when such a comparison is undertaken. (Baker 2010a: 83)

This then leads on to the second major motivation for highlighting the role of similarity, which is that the deliberate and systematic "looking in both directions" may offer some kind of counter-balance to the issues of cognitive bias. As Scott and Tribble (2006) have argued, we are pattern perceivers, indeed "it seems to be a characteristic of the *homo sapiens* mind that it is often unable to see things 'as they are' but imposes on them a tendency, a trend, a pattern" (2006: 6). As they say, this insight and imagination can have positive implications when manifested in our ability to identify patterns and is essential for discourse work, but there is also the risk of perceiving tendencies where there are none, or where they are the result of ignoring much of the data, as mentioned under the first point. In an article titled "Did aliens help to line up Woolworths stores?", the science journalist Ben Goldacre (2010) entertainingly and effectively criticises a piece of work reporting the systematic and mathematically complex distribution of prehistoric monuments by reporting on a similar piece investigating the systematic and mathematically complex distribution of Woolworths stores (Woolworths is a now defunct UK chain store). His point was that with 800 stores to choose from, it is easy to identify geometrically interesting patterns, but this occurs mainly through neglecting the majority of the data, whether intentionally or otherwise. The reporting of both difference and similarity therefore could offer a check on the unintentional bias and provides some evidence to counter any suspicions of intentional bias. Furthermore, with reference to the second factor of cognitive bias, as noted in Marchi and Taylor (2009b), there is the difficulty of what we termed the "corroboration drive", that is to say, the systematic search for elements that validate previous findings, which is a variant of the more general confirmation bias. As researchers, we naturally tend towards building on our work, we look for corroboration that what we have found is valid and less frequently do we think to look for falsification or contrasting findings. So, once again, we can argue that a "push" towards looking for what we are not expecting, that is, similarity in this case, may serve as a valuable check on that (natural) researcher instinct to focus on change and corroboration.

In summary, first, the search for similarity may help achieve a more complete picture of our data and cumulatively, our field of study. Second, it helps counterbalance the issues of cognitive bias. Third, the reporting of similarity data provides robustness to the analysis. This search for similarity cannot remove the researcher from the research process of course, or guarantee objectivity any more than any other form of triangulation, therefore our research will naturally continue to be "researcher-driven" (Taylor 2010), but, along with the key components of transparency and replicability, the search for similarity can help us achieve a more methodologically-sound analysis.

### 11.2.2 Classic ways of searching for difference in corpus linguistics

The classic corpus linguistic entry points to our data would include the analysis of concordances, collocates and keywords/key clusters and, more recently, key semantic domains. In particular, it is the popularity of the concept of keyness, and the provision of user-friendly software that can calculate keyness (e.g. *Wordsmith Tools*, *AntConc*), which has facilitated the analysis of difference. In addition, there are also tools which facilitate the comparison of collocates, such as *SketchEngines*'s *Sketch Difference* (discussed below) and the "compare" function in the BYU interface to the British National Corpus (Davies 2004) and other corpora. Both of these also allow for comparison across different corpora, for instance on the BYU BNC page it notes that "In addition, you can compare between registers – for example, verbs that are more common in legal or medical texts, or nouns near *break* that are more common in fiction than in academic writing" (Davies 2004), illustrating the (natural) emphasis on using the tools to search for difference. Because these tools are accessible and very user-friendly, they constitute a prime example of how the tools which are available shape and form the type of research which may be carried out, as argued by Partington:

> [...] in most modern physical science, the object of observation is only tangible, in a sense only exists for an observer (outside of a mathematical formula), through the instruments of study, which thus constrain not only what can be perceived but even the very questions that can usefully be put of the physical world. [...] There is a sort of indivisible hermeneutic package – the observer (including mind), the observational instruments, observations, object of observation. Alterations in any of the parts will affect the entire system, a process usually known as scientific advance. [...] Thus it is with corpus linguistics, just as it is for astrophysics or particle science. (2009a: 296)

Scott (1997: 235) puts forward a similar point in his discussion of how the category (word, sentence, text etc) which is chosen as a starting point will affect the research process. He writes that "The claim being made here is that the starting-point to a considerable degree determines the Corpus Linguistics tools; these determine the kinds of patterns which can be found" (1997: 235). For this reason, in the following section we discuss some of the ways in which we may start to systematically address similarity.

### 11.2.3 Ways of searching for similarity

In this section, we briefly survey some of the ways that we may search for similarity in the data. We start by considering what analytical tools are embedded within existing software and then focus mainly on notions or procedures that have been developed within corpus linguistics for this purpose. However, it should be added that a fundamental means of looking for similarity is by implementing the procedure of "looking both ways" as a standard practice and methodological principle. For instance Seale et al. (2007) carry out a keyword comparison of broadsheet and tabloid corpora containing articles referring to *sleep*, and note that:

> A disadvantage lies in the fact that the method identifies differences between texts rather than similarities or overlaps which could be relevant. It was therefore important also to read and become familiar with the content of the articles and to use this knowledge to influence our interpretations. Seale et al. (2007: 422)

In addition, although it is not explored here because the software was too expensive, there is potentially a very rich source of software packages and techniques within the neighbouring discipline of forensic linguistics, for example, *Copycatch*, CFL Software Ltd which permits the analyst to look for similarities in cases, for instance, of authorship identification.

#### 11.2.3.1 *Word comparison*

One of the tools which was mentioned earlier, *Sketch Difference*, allows us to analyse similarity as well as difference because it includes shared collocates, as illustrated in Figure 11.1, which displays the first part of the output for a comparison of GIRL and BOY in the BNC. The first two sets of figures indicate the frequency of co-occurrence with the first and second lemma, the second set show the salience. *Sketch Difference* first shows the shared collocates and then the unshared collocates which differentiate the items. Figure 11.1 shows the shared collocates, those shaded in grey in the image below, but in colour on screen, show those which collocate more strongly with one item than another.

**girl/boy** British National Corpus freqs = 23657/20493

girl 6.0 | 4.0 | 2.0 | 0 | -2.0 | -4.0 | -6.0 boy

| and/or | 3198 | 3035 | 1.1 | 1.2 |
|---|---|---|---|---|
| Pip | 0 | 7 | 0.0 | 6.1 |
| master | 0 | 11 | 0.0 | 4.6 |
| Chris | 0 | 6 | 0.0 | 4.5 |
| dog | 0 | 9 | 0.0 | 3.8 |
| girl | 81 | 737 | 6.1 | 9.3 |
| son | 6 | 18 | 2.7 | 4.2 |
| man | 56 | 118 | 3.5 | 4.6 |
| youth | 6 | 9 | 3.9 | 4.5 |
| child | 45 | 52 | 3.9 | 4.1 |
| husband | 8 | 9 | 3.4 | 3.6 |
| lad | 8 | 8 | 5.1 | 5.1 |
| brother | 8 | 7 | 3.4 | 3.3 |
| father | 14 | 12 | 3.4 | 3.2 |
| mother | 23 | 15 | 3.9 | 3.3 |
| baby | 19 | 7 | 5.2 | 3.7 |
| woman | 172 | 33 | 6.0 | 3.6 |
| boy | 738 | 84 | 9.5 | 6.4 |
| wife | 12 | 0 | 3.4 | 0.0 |
| pupil | 8 | 0 | 3.8 | 0.0 |
| daughter | 10 | 0 | 3.8 | 0.0 |
| Mary | 6 | 0 | 3.9 | 0.0 |
| sister | 12 | 0 | 4.5 | 0.0 |
| Anne | 6 | 0 | 4.5 | 0.0 |

| subject_of | 4323 | 3586 | 3.5 | 3.5 |
|---|---|---|---|---|
| climb | 0 | 20 | 0.0 | 6.1 |
| race | 0 | 14 | 0.0 | 5.9 |
| grin | 0 | 8 | 0.0 | 5.6 |
| kick | 0 | 10 | 0.0 | 5.3 |
| shout | 0 | 11 | 0.0 | 5.3 |
| sleep | 8 | 11 | 5.0 | 5.6 |
| grow | 28 | 34 | 5.2 | 5.5 |
| nod | 12 | 13 | 5.5 | 5.7 |
| stare | 19 | 18 | 5.8 | 5.8 |
| stand | 50 | 49 | 5.5 | 5.5 |
| walk | 42 | 34 | 6.0 | 5.8 |
| die | 60 | 45 | 6.4 | 6.1 |
| live | 45 | 34 | 5.5 | 5.1 |
| come | 167 | 112 | 5.3 | 4.7 |
| sit | 92 | 55 | 6.7 | 6.0 |
| stay | 25 | 13 | 5.5 | 4.6 |
| laugh | 28 | 14 | 6.6 | 5.7 |
| smile | 23 | 11 | 6.1 | 5.1 |
| cry | 18 | 8 | 6.0 | 5.0 |
| wear | 55 | 25 | 6.4 | 5.3 |
| squeal | 6 | 0 | 5.4 | 0.0 |
| scream | 11 | 0 | 5.7 | 0.0 |
| marry | 23 | 0 | 6.1 | 0.0 |

| adj_subject_of | 654 | 465 | 2.5 | 2.1 |
|---|---|---|---|---|
| pleased | 0 | 7 | 0.0 | 5.6 |
| happy | 0 | 7 | 0.0 | 4.4 |
| concerned | 0 | 10 | 0.0 | 4.2 |
| good | 8 | 12 | 1.9 | 2.5 |
| alone | 8 | 10 | 5.6 | 6.0 |
| able | 10 | 12 | 3.0 | 3.3 |
| likely | 18 | 19 | 4.1 | 4.2 |
| ill | 6 | 6 | 5.5 | 5.6 |
| dead | 11 | 9 | 5.3 | 5.0 |
| young | 18 | 14 | 4.2 | 3.8 |
| different | 8 | 0 | 2.4 | 0.0 |
| easy | 6 | 0 | 3.5 | 0.0 |
| older | 6 | 0 | 4.5 | 0.0 |
| aware | 9 | 0 | 4.5 | 0.0 |
| beautiful | 8 | 0 | 4.9 | 0.0 |
| willing | 6 | 0 | 5.0 | 0.0 |
| capable | 6 | 0 | 5.5 | 0.0 |
| interested | 12 | 0 | 5.6 | 0.0 |
| married | 7 | 0 | 5.6 | 0.0 |
| afraid | 11 | 0 | 6.3 | 0.0 |
| frightened | 6 | 0 | 6.6 | 0.0 |
| pretty | 10 | 0 | 6.7 | 0.0 |
| asleep | 9 | 0 | 6.9 | 0.0 |

**Figure 11.1.** Screenshot of the Sketch Difference output for the lemmas GIRL and BOY in *BNC*

However, most research using *Sketch Difference* has so far concentrated on the differences between items and as Pearce notes in his study of the collocational behaviour of MAN and WOMAN there is a risk of "the privileging of difference over similarity. Inevitably, with a tool (*Sketch Difference*) that is designed, as its name suggests, to reveal contrasts, the analyst is in danger of exaggerating the differences and overlooking similarities" (2008: 21).

The interface to the BYU corpora developed by Mark Davies also facilitates the comparison of collocates for different words by listing their collocates side by side, as shown in Figure 11.2, which is more likely to lead the researcher towards difference.

SEE CONTEXT: CLICK ON NUMBERS (WORD 1 OR 2) [HELP..

WORD 1 (W1): **GIRL** (1.02) | WORD 2 (W2): **BOY** (0.98)

| | WORD | W1 | W2 | W1/W2 | SCORE | | WORD | W2 | W1 | W2/W1 | SCORE |
|---|---|---|---|---|---|---|---|---|---|---|---|
| 1 | COOKIES | 85 | 0 | 170.0 | 166.4 | 1 | SONNY | 103 | 0 | 206.0 | 210.5 |
| 2 | GOSSIP | 78 | 0 | 156.0 | 152.7 | 2 | WHIPPING | 91 | 0 | 182.0 | 186.0 |
| 3 | TATTOO | 73 | 0 | 146.0 | 142.9 | 3 | BALLOON | 53 | 0 | 106.0 | 108.3 |
| 4 | COSMO | 39 | 0 | 78.0 | 76.3 | 4 | STABLE | 50 | 0 | 100.0 | 102.2 |
| 5 | GOSSIP | 30 | 0 | 60.0 | 58.7 | 5 | TH | 46 | 0 | 92.0 | 94.0 |
| 6 | PETITE | 30 | 0 | 60.0 | 58.7 | 6 | HUBBA | 44 | 0 | 88.0 | 89.9 |
| 7 | GUERRILLA | 29 | 0 | 58.0 | 56.8 | 7 | TEFLON | 34 | 0 | 68.0 | 69.5 |
| 8 | SERVING | 29 | 0 | 58.0 | 56.8 | 8 | OLE | 31 | 0 | 62.0 | 63.4 |

**Figure 11.2.** Screenshot of the Compare output for the words *boy* and *girl* in CoCA

### 11.3.2.2 *Consistency analysis*

*WordSmith Tools* allows for the creation of consistency lists when producing word lists, which will identify words which are shared across a number of texts, as illustrated in Figure 11.3.

WordList

File Edit View Compute Settings Windows Help

| N | Word | Total | Texts | que | mic | ition | ying | iatic | veen | aring | ting | stive | rpus | rpus | nent | main | ering | dent | i |
|---|---|---|---|---|---|---|---|---|---|---|---|---|---|---|---|---|---|---|---|
| 1 | IS | 5,657 | 47 | 312 | 74 | 51 | 108 | 144 | 104 | 70 | 77 | 44 | 144 | 64 | 87 | 96 | 45 | 111 | |
| 2 | THAT | 4,515 | 47 | 228 | 89 | 52 | 50 | 58 | 102 | 59 | 91 | 32 | 57 | 72 | 73 | 57 | 56 | 151 | |
| 3 | AS | 4,114 | 47 | 120 | 70 | 50 | 86 | 77 | 77 | 93 | 73 | 30 | 73 | 72 | 111 | 59 | 46 | 154 | |
| 4 | ARE | 3,066 | 47 | 57 | 77 | 21 | 49 | 71 | 66 | 33 | 62 | 22 | 83 | 30 | 58 | 45 | 61 | 36 | |
| 5 | BE | 2,734 | 47 | 117 | 36 | 36 | 46 | 56 | 41 | 42 | 69 | 15 | 58 | 47 | 61 | 22 | 53 | 51 | |
| 6 | THIS | 2,704 | 47 | 71 | 50 | 27 | 62 | 77 | 77 | 55 | 68 | 21 | 38 | 73 | 44 | 19 | 23 | 64 | |
| 7 | CORPUS | 2,701 | 47 | 35 | 34 | 105 | 50 | 52 | 8 | 50 | 37 | 26 | 55 | 128 | 41 | 132 | 68 | 328 | |
| 8 | IT | 2,593 | 47 | 138 | 37 | 25 | 77 | 22 | 36 | 34 | 49 | 15 | 47 | 29 | 47 | 29 | 26 | 54 | |
| 9 | LANGUAGE | 1,872 | 47 | 28 | 32 | 25 | 49 | 39 | 23 | 21 | 64 | 24 | 75 | 58 | 23 | 15 | 73 | 93 | |
| 10 | WE | 1,821 | 47 | 58 | 23 | 1 | 29 | 114 | 61 | 83 | 40 | 9 | 10 | 54 | 24 | 45 | 11 | 35 | |
| 11 | NOT | 1,805 | 47 | 86 | 15 | 14 | 16 | 38 | 37 | 29 | 39 | 15 | 24 | 28 | 42 | 25 | 12 | 54 | |
| 12 | WHICH | 1,742 | 47 | 126 | 19 | 38 | 47 | 50 | 36 | 31 | 18 | 13 | 21 | 25 | 30 | 14 | 32 | 26 | |
| 13 | ENGLISH | 1,487 | 47 | 7 | 22 | 22 | 11 | 41 | 35 | 6 | 85 | 17 | 42 | 52 | 128 | 23 | 67 | 48 | |
| 14 | I | 1,482 | 47 | 6 | 39 | 10 | 18 | 23 | 28 | 16 | 5 | 136 | 30 | 8 | 49 | 3 | 23 | 63 | |
| 15 | HAVE | 1,401 | 47 | 39 | 19 | 21 | 39 | 15 | 43 | 18 | 34 | 22 | 14 | 17 | 25 | 8 | 18 | 50 | |
| 16 | MORE | 1,319 | 47 | 22 | 33 | 16 | 20 | 20 | 45 | 22 | 26 | 7 | 27 | 32 | 36 | 7 | 16 | 54 | |

**Figure 11.3.** Partial screenshot showing consistency analysis of a corpus containing 47 corpus linguistics articles (prepositions and articles removed)

These consistency lists are useful when working with several corpora or corpora containing multiple files and, according to Scott and Tribble, the main uses are:

> First, in a general corpus like the BNC, to distinguish between word-types in terms of how consistently they get used in a mass of texts in the language. Second, if the scope of the research is the genre, to be able to locate lexical items which characterise certain genres or sub-genres. Third, to be able to study text variants (e.g. alternative translations or editions). (2006: 39)

Scott (2001) employs the function in illustrating how a teacher of ESP (English for Specific Purposes) might identify core lexis by looking for items which occur across a number of relevant subcorpora. Other examples come from research carried out by Cambridge ESOL (a major assessment organisation), for instance, Chambers (2008) uses consistency analysis to compare candidate output under computer-based and paper-based writing assessment procedures and Barker (2008) uses the program to study similarities in the lexical content of reading tasks from the various levels of the general suite of Cambridge English language exams (KET, PET, FCE, CAE, CPE). Overall, the review of the literature showed that this function has been used relatively infrequently to date. In this context, it is interesting to note that in the last two works cited there is likely to be a preference for finding similarity, whether demonstrating that the two modes of assessment delivery are equal or that the reading tasks effectively recycle lexis.

In addition to the tools mentioned above, which are integrated in software packages, researchers have developed a range of additional concepts and methodologies for searching for similarity, which have not (as yet) been formalised and integrated into corpus software.

#### 11.3.2.3 *Key keywords*

One concept which is useful for examining stasis is key keywords, introduced in Scott (1997), and defined in the *WordSmith Tools* guide as follows: "A 'key keyword' is one which is 'key' in more than one of a number of related texts. The more texts it is 'key' in, the more 'key key' it is" (Scott 2008). Rather like the procedure for consistency analysis, this is particularly useful when looking for repeated patterns across large numbers of sub-corpora.[3] In Scott's 1997 model, the calculation of key keywords subsequently allows for the identification of *associates*, that is "words found to be key in the same texts as a given key key word" (1997: 238), which form an alternative means of calculating collocation in the wider sense.

Key keywords have been recently employed in Bachman (2011), who also draws attention to the scarcity of studies employing this procedure (2011: 83). Bachman draws on McEnery's (2009) use of keywords to distinguish between transient and permanent key-keywords in moral panic discourse (McEnery 2009: 169) and applies them to his analysis of parliamentary debates in order to identify "a list of concepts that are representative of the debates as a whole" (2011: 87). In

3. The concept is modified somewhat in Scott & Tribble (2006), where it is claimed that key keywords are only more "key" than keywords when the corpora consist of a quite specific genre. However, this would depend on the kind of key keyness one was interested in analysing, and also on the definition of "same" genre? For instance, one might be interested in the key keyness of evaluative lexis in (a) book reviews (b) all reviews (c) all the magazine sections of a newspaper (d) the entire newspaper, as compared to others. Which is the "quite specific genre"?

other words, it becomes a method for avoiding spikes of data which do not give us information about constant features in the discourse.

A similar notion is used in Fitzsimmons-Doolan (2009) in a study which, remarkably, both sets out to look for similarity and falsifies its own hypothesis – the hypothesis being that there would be similarities in the lexical patterns of newspaper discourse about language policies, and newspaper discourse about immigration. Fitzsimmons-Doolan uses *Wordsmith Tools* for the calculation of keywords but adopts a manual analysis of what she terms the *keyest-keywords* by counting:

> how many of the top 10 keywords from each corpus were (a) in the top 20 and (b) in the top 500 keywords lists for each of the other corpora. These measures show the distribution of the "keyset" keywords from one corpus within each of the other corpora. (2009: 392)

After the analysis, she found little lexical overlap between the articles on language policies and those on immigration.

#### 11.2.3.4 *Consistent (or wide-distribution) collocates*

The identification of *consistent collocates* draws on Scott's notion of consistency (e.g. 1997) and the use of key-keywords to identify transient keywords discussed above, and was developed during work on the ESRC funded project "Discourses of refugees and asylum seekers in the UK press, 1996–2006" at Lancaster University. The concept of consistent collocates (c-collocates) was devised to describe the lexical items which collocated with *refugees/asylum seekers/immigrants/migrants* (RASIM) in at least seven out of the ten annual subcorpora which they had collected (described in Gabrielatos & Baker 2008). The consistent collocates were calculated in order to exclude *seasonal collocates*, that is, words which may have been triggered by particular events rather than being representative of newspaper discourse across the extended time period. To date, there seems to have been relatively little uptake of this notion although it is partially employed in Al-Hejin (2009).

The term *seasonal* is rather misleading, since seasons are events which return with regularity, something not intended by the term used in this way. Nor would "topic-related collocates" be appropriate, since very many c-collocates are also topic-related. The distinction lies not in a difference in what they express but in differences in location and distribution in linguistic space and time; c-collocates are widely distributed, another kind are more narrowly distributed. A better name for seasonal collocates might be "localised" collocates. In some circumstances one might adopt the terminology "wide-distribution" and "narrow-distribution" collocates (*w-collocates* and *n-collocates*). This would have the advantage of also underlining that the relation between the two is often more a cline rather than a binary distinction.

#### 11.2.3.5 *Lockwords*

As mentioned in the first case study, Baker (2011) further addresses the issue of search for similarity by introducing the concept of *lockwords*. This notion, and the procedure used for determining them, were conceived as a result of his observations of consistency of frequency in the BLOB, LOB FLOB and BE06 corpora. He notes that certain words "were so consistent in their frequencies that they appeared to be the opposite of Scott's (2000) concept of *keywords* – words which are highly frequent in one corpus when compared against another" (Baker 2011:73). Secondly, the notion of lockwords was conceived as a means of taking a more corpus-driven approach to diachronic language study, so that instead of starting with a specific item or set of items to investigate, the researcher may start with lists of items that have or have not changed over the time period under study. In coining the term lockword, Baker adds that:

> The term *lock* was chosen because it is related to *key* (*key* is the highest collocate of *lock* in the British National Corpus (using log likelihood)), and furthermore, *lock* is a good description of these words: they appear to be "locked" in place. (2011:73, emphasis in original)

In order to identify change in the corpora, Baker (2011) first used the *WordSmith Tools* detailed consistency list (11.3.2.2) to create lists of items for analysis, and then calculated the standard deviations with the expectation that "words with a high standard deviation would have changed in frequency over time a great deal, whereas those with low standard deviations would be more stable" (2011:72). However, this measure was not sufficiently satisfactory as standard deviation appeared to correlate with overall frequency and therefore the measure was changed to the coefficient of variance, which is the ratio of the sample standard deviation to the sample mean, and Baker notes that it is "easily calculated by dividing the standard deviation by the mean and then multiplying by 100" (2011:72). This measure does not specify whether the change is an increase or decline, so in the final stage, the results need to be manually sorted. We may summarise the lockword procedure as: (1) creation of detailed constancy lists, (2) calculation of coefficient of variance, (3) manual sorting. Although Baker used SPSS software, this procedure could also be replicated in *Microsoft Excel* which is more widely accessible to many researchers.

#### 11.2.3.6 *Alternative keyword calculations*

Another very fruitful method of calculating similarity/stability of ranking derives from work by Gabrielatos and Marchi (2011) into alternative calculations of keyness (also employed in Gabrielatos 2007; Gabrielatos & McEnery 2005). More specifically, they explore measuring keyness in terms of the size of difference between normalised frequencies of items in different corpora and provide an accessible, step-by-step guide to carrying out this procedure using *Wordsmith Tools* and basic *Microsoft Excel* functions. This measurement of difference may then be very easily employed in the search for similarity by identifying those items which had a very low percentage frequency difference because this would effectively be flagging up items which had very similar patterns of occurrence.

### 11.2.4 Previous research into the use of gender terms

Previous corpus linguistic research into the use of gender terms has tended to compare female terms to male terms synchronically (e.g. Pearce 2008) or compares the same gender terms over different time periods, with some combining the two. For instance, Macalister (2011) found that in writing for children *girl** was consistently more frequently pre-modified than *boy**, but he found no evidence that there was an evaluative difference in these adjectives. In contrast, Gesuato (2003) found that attributes for describing both WOMAN and GIRL were more likely to be negative or to focus on beauty (although it is not clear which dates were covered in the corpus). Baker (2010b) also found evidence from his analysis of BOY and GIRL that there were differences in representation which were indicative of gender stereotypes.

Holmes and Sigley (2001), Sigley and Holmes (2002) in particular, Gesuato (2003) and Baker (2010b) all discuss the use of GIRL to refer to adults and Baker (2010b) notes that this is an increasing trend for BOY too based on data in the 2006 BE06 Corpus of British English (Baker 2009).

In this case study, the focus is on the elements of stasis in the use of boy and girl, but there is also an element of difference as the findings for BOY and GIRL are presented side by side.

### 11.2.5 Data analysis

As would be the case with a difference-driven analysis, the first phase includes some basic analysis of the SiBol/Port corpora, starting with frequency counts, shown in Figure 11.4.

Figure 11.4 shows the relative frequency of the singular and plural forms of boy and girl (including occurrences of possessive forms) and some of their alternatives. The data is presented separately because Pearce (2008) notes a difference in the way that the singular and plural forms are used for MAN and WOMAN. The tendency for *women* to occur more frequently than *woman* in contrast with *man/ men* is also visible in Figure 11.4, but there does not seem to be a similar pattern for GIRL and BOY. The frequency of BOY and GIRL seems to be relatively stable over

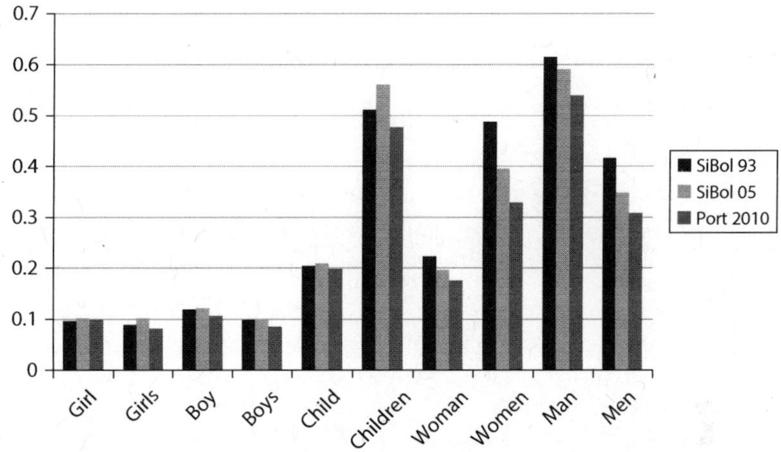


Figure 11.4. Relative frequency (per thousand words) of the search terms

the three time periods, although there is a pattern of decreasing mentions for BOY. There is no evidence in Figure 11.4 that the decreasing mentions of WOMAN are accounted for by an increasing use of GIRL. The investigation of the decrease of WOMAN and an analysis of which (if any) other terms are being employed would be an interesting area for future analysis.

The second basic analysis involved small-scale sampling to determine which age groups the search terms BOY and GIRL referred to. One hundred concordance lines for boy/s and girl/s in each corpus were read in context to determine whether they referred to children (under 11), adolescents (up to 17) or adults (18 and above) and the results are reported in Figure 11.5.

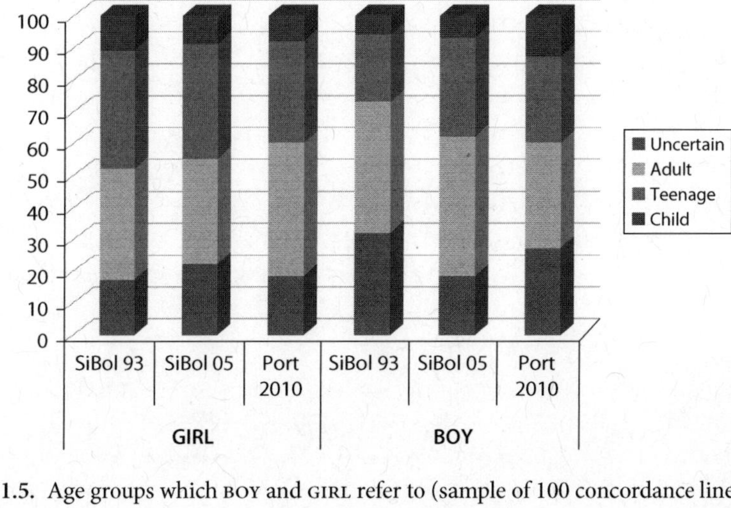


Figure 11.5. Age groups which BOY and GIRL refer to (sample of 100 concordance lines per bar)

This process showed that, in the sampled concordances, GIRL is more likely to refer to adults than BOY and this pattern is consistent over the time period. It also appears that GIRL is less frequently used to refer to adult women, while the reverse trend is seen for BOY but the sample is currently too limited to draw any firm conclusions. Although this was a small sample it was useful as a means of familiarisation with the data and revealed some differences, such as the tendency for BOY, when used to refer to adult males, to occur within sport contexts.

#### 11.2.5.1 *C-collocates*

The first starting point was the calculation and analysis of consistent collocates in order to identify which items have a relatively stable relationship with the search terms. In this paper, c-collocates are operationalised as items which co-occurred with the node lemma (either BOY or GIRL) more than ten times and with a z-score of more than fifteen. These cut-off points are arbitrary and could easily have been set at 20 and 20. However, this combination resulted in a manageable quantity of data. In order to calculate the c-collocates, *Wordsmith Tools* was used to identify the collocates, and then the three lists, one for each year, were manually compared in *Excel* and items which did not occur in all three lists were discarded (in future research, this stage could be made faster by using pivot tables).[4] In the next stage, the shared collocates were grouped into thematic sets. This final stage is therefore researcher-driven and subjective, but the data is presented transparently in Table 11.1, so that other patterns may, potentially, be identified.

From Table 11.1, we can see that c-collocates refer to people and relationships and the largest set consists of descriptions, referring to age, physical appearance, character and so on. There is also a set of items referring to violence, which is to be expected in newspaper discourse, given that negativity is a key news value (Galtung & Ruge 1965, Harcup & O'Neill 2001). A total of 119 of the collocates displayed in the table are shared by BOY and GIRL.

The items in the table that are marked in bold indicate those collocates which refer to sexual relations in some sense. For BOY, these items were: PUBESCENT, RENT, MOLEST, RAPE, SEXUAL, LOVE, MARRY. While for GIRL, the consistent collocates associated with sex were: BOYFRIEND, PUBESCENT, NAKED, SINGLE, PREGNANT, PROSTITUTE, GLAMOUR, RAPE, MOLEST, PROSTITUTION, SEX, SEXUAL, SEXUALLY, FANCY, KISS, LOVE, MARRY and, to some extent, the item *call* (formed *call girl* in 30% of occurrences). From this it is clear that over the

4. Gabrielatos, C. Personal communication made at ***Corpus Linguistics in the South:*** *Theoretical-methodological challenges in corpus approaches to discourse studies – and some ways of addressing them*, 5 November 2011, University of Portsmouth

**Table 11.1.** List of consistent collocates of BOY and GIRL for 1993, 2005, 2010 (numbers excluded). The items which have been grouped as processes may also be, in some cases, nouns. The collocates were not sorted for part of speech

| Category | GIRL | BOY |
|---|---|---|
| People | *BOY* ***BOYFRIEND*** father man mother *PARENT* WOMAN<br>FRIEND GANG | *BROTHER* FATHER *GIRL* MAN WOMAN MOTHER<br>FRIEND GANG |
| Age | ADOLESCENT AGE BABY CHILD *OLD* **PUBESCENT** TEENAGE *TEENAGER* YOUNG | ADOLESCENT AGE BABY CHILD **PUBESCENT** TEENAGE YOUNG |
| Description: | | |
| – physical | *BEAUTIFUL* BLONDE EYED GOLDEN HAIRED LITTLE ***NAKED*** | *BIG* BLONDE EYED *FAT* HAIRED LITTLE *SMALL* |
| – body parts | *EYE HAIR* HEAD | *FACE* HEAD |
| – character | BAD BRIGHT *LOVELY* NICE *SHY* | BAD BRIGHT *GOOD NAUGHTY* NICE |
| – epithet | ***SINGLE*** POOR *POSH* ***PREGNANT*** | *BLIND* |
| – classifier | *DADDY'S ENGLISH* JEWISH *ESSEX CONVENT* | *MUMMY'S* JEWISH |
| – functions / 'occupations' | ***PROSTITUTE*** *CHORUS* ***GLAMOUR*** *MODEL* | *ALTAR* CHOIR *SOLDIER BACKROOM BARROW MESSENGER* ***RENT*** |
| Violence | *ABDUCT* ABUSE ASSAULT *BURN* DEAD *DEATH* DIE DROWN INJURE *LURE* KIDNAP KILL **MOLEST** MURDER **RAPE** STAB SUFFER | ABUSE ASSAULT DEAD DIE DROWN INJURE KIDNAP KILL **MOLEST** MURDER **RAPE** STAB SUFFER *wound* |
| Clothing | *BLOUSE* CLOTHE *COSTUME* DRESS *SKIRT* TROUSER WEAR | CLOTHE DRESS *SHOE* TROUSER |
| Sex: Other | ***PROSTITUTION SEX SEXUAL*** **SEXUALLY** | **SEXUALLY** |
| Processes: sexual | ***KISS*** **LOVE MARRY** | **LOVE MARRY** |
| Police activity | ARREST | ARREST *CONVICT DETAIN* |
| Other childhood related | *SONG DOLL* STORY CONJURER SCOUT GUIDE | *TOY TRAIN BOOK* CONJURER *SCOUT* STORY *BIRTHDAY* |
| School | *CAMDEN COLLEGE COMPREHENSIVE* EDUCATE *EDUCATION* GRAMMAR *HEADMISTRESS PAUL'S SECONDARY* PUPIL SHERBORNE SCHOOL TEACH TEACHER CLASS *HIGH ST VI* | EDUCATE *ETON* GRAMMAR PUPIL *PLAYGROUND SCHOLARSHIP* SCHOOL *PAUL* TEACH TEACHER CLASS *JUNIOR* |
| Other material processes* | *DANCE* PLAY<br>ARRIVE ATTEND BEGIN BITE BRING BULLY COME DRINK FALL FIND *FOLLOW* GET GIVE GO GROW INCLUDE INVOLVE LEAVE *LIVE* LOSE SHOW *SLEEP* TAKE *TEAR* SIT TRY TURN *WORK* | PLAY *RUN SWIM THROW*<br>ARRIVE ATTEND *BEAT BEFRIEND* BEGIN BITE BRING BULLY COME *CRY EXCITE* FALL FIND GET GIVE GO GROW *HANG HOLD* INCLUDE INVOLVE *JOIN LEAD* LEAVE LOSE SEND SHOOT SHOW SIT TAKE TRY TURN *USE WALK WIN* |

(*Continued*)

**Table 11.1.** (Continued)

| Category | GIRL | BOY |
|---|---|---|
| Other mental processes* | DISCOVER DREAM *ENCOURAGE FRIGHTEN* HEAR KNOW LIKE OBSESS LOOK SEE *TERRIFY* THINK WANT WATCH | DISCOVER DREAM HEAR KNOW *LEARN* LIKE LOOK *READ* SEE THINK WANT WATCH |
| Verbal processes | ACCUSE ADMIT ALLEGE ASK CALL DESCRIBE SAY *SCREAM* TALK TELL SING WRITE | ACCUSE ADMIT ALLEGE ASK CALL *CLAIM* DESCRIBE *DENY PLEAD* SAY *SHOUT* SING TALK TELL *THREATEN WARN REFUSE* WRITE |
| Other relational processes* | BECOME SEEM | BECOME SEEM |
| Function words | A *ABOUT* AS AT DO *FOR* FROM *HER HERSELF I* IN *ME MY OF OUT SHE SHE'S* THAT THE *THEIR* TO UP WHO *WHOM* WHOSE WITH | A AND AS AT *BOTH BY* DO FROM *HE* MY IN OF *HE'S HIM HIS OTHER* THAT THE TO UP *WHEN* WHO WHOSE WITH |
| Misc. | *MISS* NAME *PHOTOGRAPH* ORPHAN *TIFFIN* YEAR | *LATE* NAME *NICKNAME* ORPHAN *SHOP* YEAR |
| Part of name / fixed phrase | – | *GOLDEN RACER WONDER DEL DEAR GEORGE PET OH OL OLD WHIP TEDDY BEACH* |

seventeen year period, there is a consistent association for both gender terms with some aspects of sexual relationships, with reference to both positive and negative contexts.

The items which are in italics are those which were not shared consistent collocates between BOY and GIRL and an examination of these items also reveals that items referring to sexual activity are more frequent in the GIRL collocates. Furthermore, the presence of items such as SINGLE, MARRY or GLAMOUR make it evident that GIRL is being used to refer to adult women throughout this period. This focus on stasis in the analysis of c-collocates shows that to talk of the increasing sexualisation of female children is somewhat problematic, given that the key term for referring to these individuals, GIRL, displays a stable history of association with sex in the broadsheet newspapers from 1993 to 2010. The somewhat higher presence of childhood-related collocates, such as SMALL, CHOIR, TRAIN (as in toys), and so on, in the BOY column also indicates that the age-coverage of the two gender terms is not equal. Other interesting items on the same topic include *whom* in the GIRL column, suggesting that GIRL is more frequently the object of some action (the most frequent pronoun collocating with GIRL + *whom*, occurring in a quarter of all instances, was *he*).

#### 11.2.5.2 *Word Sketches*

Another means of measuring collocation is through the *Word Sketches* available in *Sketch Engine* (see Kilgarriff & Tugwell 2001). For this stage, separate *Word Sketches* were created for GIRL and BOY over the three years. Then, the contents of the *Word Sketches* from the different years were manually compared in order to identify the items which appeared in the *Word Sketches* for all three years. The results are reported in Table 11.2 (GIRL) and Table 11.3 (BOY).

As can be seen from Tables 11.2 and 11.3, this process reveals similar patterns to the more labour intensive calculation of c-collocates in Section 3.3.1, for instance, Table 11.2 shows that the collocates relating to sex (marked in bold) are more frequent in the GIRL collocates, as are modifiers relating to physical appearance e.g. *beautiful, lovely, pretty*. In addition this stage highlights some of the BOY collocates which seem more closely associated with children, those which are not shared include: PLAY, *pupil, school, staff, small* and *care*. *Care* also fits with the negative contexts seen in the "object of" column.

**Table 11.2.** Items shared in the Word Sketches for GIRL in Sibol 93, Sibol 05 and Port 2010

| object of | subject of | and/or | adj subject of | a modifier | n modifier | modifies | possessed |
|---|---|---|---|---|---|---|---|
| ABUSE | DIE GROW | BOY | LIKELY | TEENAGE | BABY ***CALL*** | *FRIEND* | *BLOUSE* |
| AGE | *LIKE LIVE* | CHILD | *YOUNG* | *BEAUTIFUL* | *CHECKOUT* | *GROUP* | FATHER |
| ASSAULT | ***LOVE*** | *FRIEND* | | EIGHT-YEAR | *CHORUS* | *PUPIL* | *FRIEND* |
| BEAR | *SCREAM* | GIRL *GUY* | | OLD | *COVER* | *SCHOOL* | MOTHER |
| KIDNAP | TEND | MAN | | FIVE-YEAR | *DANCING* | | NAME |
| KILL | WANT | MOTHER | | OLD FOUR- | ***ESCORT*** | | PARENT |
| ***KISS*** | WEAR | PARENT | | YEAR OLD | ***GLAMOUR*** | | SCHOOL |
| ***MARRY*** | | WOMAN | | *JEWISH* | *MAKE-UP* | | |
| *MEET* | | | | LITTLE | *ORPHAN* | | |
| MURDER | | | | *LOVELY* | *PEASANT* | | |
| NAME | | | | *NICE* NINE- | ***PIN-UP*** | | |
| ***RAPE*** | | | | YEAR OLD | ***UNDER-AGE*** | | |
| *RESCUE* | | | | *PRETTY* | | | |
| | | | | SEVEN- | | | |
| | | | | YEAR OLD | | | |
| | | | | *SIX-YEAR* | | | |
| | | | | *OLD* | | | |
| | | | | TWO-YEAR | | | |
| | | | | OLD YEAR | | | |
| | | | | OLD YOUNG | | | |
| **pp in i** | **pp with i** | **pp at i** | **pp under i** | **pp from i** | **pp of i** | **pp than i** | **possessor** |
| CLASS | *HAIR* | SCHOOL | *AGE* | SCHOOL | AGE *DREAM* | *BOY* | *DADDY* |
| *DRESS* | | | | | | | |
| SCHOOL | | | | | | | |
| *WORLD* | | | | | | | |

**Table 11.3.** Items shared in the Word Sketches for BOY in Sibol 93, Sibol 05 and Port 2010

| object of | subject of | and/or | adj subject of | a modifier | n modifier | modifies | possessed |
|---|---|---|---|---|---|---|---|
| ABUSE | DIE *DO* | BOY | LIKELY | *BIG* | *ALTAR* | *GENIUS* | *CHAMPION* |
| AGE | GROW | CHILD | | EIGHT- | BABY | *KING* | *CLUB* |
| ASSAULT | *PLAY SIT* | *FAMILY* | | YEAR | *BACKROOM* | *NETWORK* | *DEATH* |
| BEAR | TEND | *FATHER* | | OLD | *BARROW* | *RACER* | *DREAM* |
| *BEAT* | *TRY* | GIRL | | FIVE-YEAR | *BOVVER* | *SCOUT* | FATHER |
| KIDNAP | *WALK* | MAN | | OLD | *BULLY* | *WONDER* | MOTHER |
| KILL | WANT | MOTHER | | FOUR- | *DELIVERY* | | NAME |
| *MOLEST* | WEAR | parent | | YEAR-OLD | *GRAMMAR* | | PARENT |
| MURDER | | *PUPIL* | | *GOLDEN* | *GRAMMAR-* | | SCHOOL |
| NAME | | *SCHOOL* | | LITTLE | *SCHOOL* | | *SINGLE* |
| | | *SON* | | *NAUGHTY* | *MESSENGER* | | *TITLE* |
| | | *STAFF* | | NINE-YEAR | ***RENT*** | | *TOY* |
| | | WOMAN | | OLD OLD | *SCHOLARSHIP* | | |
| | | | | SEVEN- | *SHEPHERD* | | |
| | | | | YEAR OLD | *TEDDY* | | |
| | | | | *SMALL* | | | |
| | | | | TEENAGE | | | |
| | | | | TWO-YEAR | | | |
| | | | | OLD | | | |
| | | | | *WHIPPING* | | | |
| | | | | YEAR-OLD | | | |
| | | | | YOUNG | | | |
| **pp in i** | **pp with i** | **pp at i** | **pp under i** | **pp from i** | **pp of i** | **pp than i** | **possessor** |
| *CARE* | | SCHOOL | | SCHOOL | AGE | *GIRL* | *MUMMY* |
| CLASS | | | | | | | *OL* |
| SCHOOL | | | | | | | |

Using these two different measures of analysing c-collocates may function as a form of methodological triangulation. Furthermore, given that the collocates here are grouped not by theme but by grammatical relationship there is the opportunity for the researcher to identify different sets of patterns in the data. To summarise, this second method is much quicker but the researcher has less control over the process.

#### 11.2.5.3 *Thesaurus*

Another starting point for this analysis could be through the use of the *Sketch Engine* distributional thesaurus, which identifies words which behave in similar ways to the search term (see Rychly & Kilgarriff 2007 for more detail on the algorithm used). In a similar way to that above, the thesaurus entries were calculated separately for BOY and GIRL for each of the three years and then manually compared. This time, the table shows the rankings for the three years side by side so that stability of ranking may be tracked.

From Tables 11.4 and 11.5 we can see that the lemma which behaves most like the search term is its gender equivalent, that is BOY for GIRL and vice versa, and the thesaurus candidates are similar over the three years and for the two items. Looking at the items below BOY/GIRL, we can see that WOMAN is near the top in each case. However, at this stage, a possible difference over time becomes evident as the position of WOMAN and CHILD inverts. In contrast, MAN is not seen to behave in

**Table 11.4.** Sketch thesaurus results for GIRL

| SiBol93 | | SiBol05 | | Port2010 | |
|---|---|---|---|---|---|
| BOY | 0.519 | BOY | 0.519 | BOY | 0.452 |
| CHILD | 0.385 | WOMAN | 0.413 | WOMAN | 0.370 |
| WOMAN | 0.383 | CHILD | 0.384 | CHILD | 0.345 |
| MOTHER | 0.364 | PERSON | 0.368 | MOTHER | 0.334 |
| WIFE | 0.353 | MOTHER | 0.368 | TEENAGER | 0.320 |
| PERSON | 0.346 | TEENAGER | 0.368 | PERSON | 0.320 |
| PARENT | 0.337 | KID | 0.360 | DAUGHTER | 0.315 |
| FRIEND | 0.336 | FRIEND | 0.358 | MAN | 0.311 |
| SOMEONE | 0.333 | MAN | 0.347 | PEOPLE | 0.306 |
| COUPLE | 0.332 | SOMEONE | 0.343 | WIFE | 0.306 |

**Table 11.5.** Sketch thesaurus results for BOY

| SiBol93 | | SiBol05 | | Port2010 | |
|---|---|---|---|---|---|
| GIRL | 0.519 | GIRL | 0.519 | GIRL | 0.452 |
| CHILD | 0.400 | CHILD | 0.385 | CHILD | 0.350 |
| PERSON | 0.358 | WOMAN | 0.380 | WOMAN | 0.337 |
| MOTHER | 0.354 | TEENAGER | 0.363 | MOTHER | 0.324 |
| WOMAN | 0.350 | KID | 0.360 | KID | 0.318 |
| SON | 0.348 | PERSON | 0.358 | TEENAGER | 0.318 |
| WIFE | 0.343 | MAN | 0.355 | SON | 0.317 |
| FRIEND | 0.340 | SON | 0.354 | PERSON | 0.317 |
| PARENT | 0.336 | FRIEND | 0.354 | MAN | 0.314 |
| SOMEONE | 0.336 | MOTHER | 0.348 | SOMEONE | 0.314 |

an analogous way in regard to BOY (it was in 14th position in the 1993 list). In fact, WOMAN is higher up the list of BOY entries for all three years.

#### 11.2.5.4 *C-clusters/c-ngrams*

In a similar way to the calculation of c-collocates in Section 3.4.2, another starting point would be the calculation of ngrams or clusters which remain stable over time. These are not fully reported here because the analysis of ngrams requires greater space as they cannot be grouped thematically. The 100 most frequent 3-grams for GIRL and BOY were calculated for each year and then compared. Out of these 100, it was found that there were 65 shared 3-grams for all three years for GIRL and 76 for BOY. In order to down-sample the total set of 3-grams available for analysis, we focus on those which appear to have the function of "grouping" e.g. *a group of girls, a quarter of boys*, because they were striking in the categorisation stage.

All occurrences of "noun + *of girls/boys*" were concordanced using *Wordsmith Tools* and manually sorted so that those which referred to *girls and boys/boys and girls* were deleted as were those in which *boys* or *girls* was functioning as a pre-modifier in a noun phrase. In the next stage, any instances in which the noun was not functioning to "group" were also deleted. So the remainder were made up of examples like "x per *cent of girls, a clutch of girls*". Figure 11.6 shows the number of patterns which were found for each year.

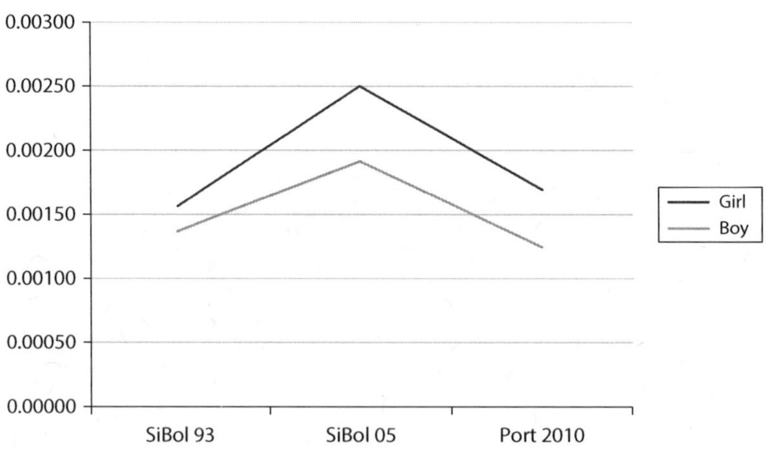


**Figure 11.6.** Number of occurrences (per thousand words) of 'grouping' phrases in each corpus

As can be seen, there was an increase for both *boys* and *girls* in 2005 followed by a decrease in 2010, and more corpora will be needed to test whether this is represents the peak in a trend or not. In all three years, *girls* appeared to be counted more frequently than *boys* and there was greater productivity/creativity in the grouping phrases for *girls* too; in total there were 84 different phraseologies for *girls* compared to 69 for *boys* (this pattern was stable for each of the three years). In all three years, for both *boys* and *girls*, phrases included: *per cent of, a group of, a quarter of* and expressions of proportion were the most common overall.

However, there were also qualitative differences in the type of "grouping" noun chosen for *boys* and *girls*. Phraseologies referring to groups which are described as "lines" included: *a succession of girls, a stream of girls, a rota of girls, a column of girls, a string of girls, a line of girls, rows of girls, a *run of girls,* and *a *stream of boys, a rota of boys, a queue of boys*. Groupings with a possible animal metaphor included: *a/her stable of girls, flock of girls, a breed of girls, a brace of girls, a gaggle of girls* and *a pack of boys, the pack of boys*. Metaphors with a "product" metaphor included: *supply of girls, a selection of girls, a *assortment of girls, a shortage of girls, a dearth of girls,* and *an excess of boys*. Taken individually, these were all low frequency items, but regarded as a set they are important in the representation of BOY and GIRL and help to emphasise the need to look for patterns beyond word repetition. Furthermore, one of the factors which made this section particularly interesting was the tendency for *boys* who were described with more typically *girl* counting nouns to refer to *boys* who were seen as sharing "feminine" characteristics in some way, for instance:

(35) Suddenly, *a gaggle of prancing boys* skips into the fray. (*Guardian* 2005)

(36) His early oils feature *a succession of* handsome, and *androgynous boys*. (*Guardian* 2005)

(37) Westlife and *a host of* other *wispy boys* who never looked like they'd want to do any of those things that a bad boy would want to do. (*Times* 2010)

This type of similarity would be another interesting area for future analysis.

### 11.2.6 Discussion and conclusions on *girl/s* and *boy/s*

In this section, we have presented several "starting points" for a CADS style analysis of the corpora, each of which focus on similarity. In a full analysis, each of these starting points would have been expanded and then explored through shunting between collocates, concordance and text. For instance, through concentrating initially on similarity, it has been possible to highlight the ways in which the lemma GIRL, over a very recent seventeen year period, is consistently associated with sexual contexts. However, only more detailed analysis can describe the ways in which this is both the result of female children being described in adult terms and also the result of adult females being infantilised. Having mapped some of the constants for the representation of BOY and GIRL, subsequent research would then go on to track the changes against this background of similarity. For instance, in this research there was strong evidence that GIRL is moving closer to WOMAN and BOY was starting to reflect the linguistic behaviour of GIRL. This short case study has also illustrated that in practice it is almost impossible to focus entirely on similarity in isolation, for instance here, while concentrating on the relationship of diachronic stability of frequency and ranking there has still been reference to difference in terms of how BOY and GIRL are constructed in the UK press.

## 11.3 Conclusion

Most comparative/contrastive studies of language, whether corpus-assisted or not, generally aim to highlight differences among the particular language varieties being studied. Cross-cultural studies usually seek to examine and explain divergence or variation among cultural practices. Diachronic linguistics often explicitly regards its scope as "[p]ertaining to linguistic *change* across time" (our emphasis, Trask 1993: 81). As regards CADS, the keywords comparison, so frequently the starting point of analyses, is specifically intended and designed to highlight difference and change.

In this chapter we have tried to show how it is possible to study both "change" and "sameness" and, especially, the relationship between the two, which can be complex. There are of course, a myriad of ways in which change can occur, semantic drift, changes in syntactic usage, changes in the real world of the referents of items (for example, in the precise nature of *university fees, ethical issue/s* or *US President/s*) or developments over time in discourses practices in particular contexts, as we saw in the previous chapter regarding UK newspaper discourse practices. But "sameness" too can occur in different ways. Indeed, when talking about sameness, or apparent absence of change, it is necessary to specify which particular variety is intended, of which there are at least three:

- Stasis, or immobility,
- Change but at a steady consistent rate (known technically as "inertia") for example, a word, expression or a discourse practice whose use increases or decreases at a regular rate,
- An overall statistical consistency (of, say, relative frequency of co-occurrence in two or more datasets), but where there are changes in meanings or context of use of an item.

Absolute stasis is rare since all parts of a language system are in constant flux. It is also, from a theoretical point of view, impossible to prove that no change at all has occurred in a particular part of the system; an infinity of tests would be needed. However, in more practical terms, we can speak of a system remaining in a similar state, as when we observed above that GIRL retains consistent collocates over time relating to sex and sexual attraction. We also saw how, in practice, in studying stasis we found it impossible not to notice change as well. The two are indivisibly linked, in fact neither has meaning without the other (which is Heraclitus's whole argument).

The second and third forms of "sameness" might well be described as "dynamic stasis". Steady, consistent evolution, especially if slow, can be very difficult for an observer to detect. However it can be revealed by the kind of MD-CADS methodology we have attempted to outline. The sister corpora can be envisaged as snapshots of a particular language system taken in different periods of time and the comparison of the snapshots can reveal even small changes. But to infer with any certainty whether the change was gradual or sudden, the observer needs more than two data points. For instance, to decide whether UK newspapers adopted verb contractions and reduced their use of honorifics gradually or suddenly, perhaps as an executive style decision, one would need to refer to data from at least three corpora. In the second case study in this chapter, a third dataset, a third parallel corpus, was required to lend confidence to the observation that BOY was starting, in recent newspapers, to reflect the linguistic behaviour of GIRL and to replicate the finding that *parent* had slipped out of the top thesaurus results for both GIRL and BOY in the recent newspaper data (see Tables 11.4 and 11.5).

Regarding the second type of dynamic stasis, apparent sameness masking covert change, as related in 11.1.1 one of the triggers of the research into antisemitism was Duguid's finding that *anti-semit** words had kept their exact places in the keyword lists she analysed. The present study has corroborated her hypothesis that items can retain their relative rankings in word frequency lists and thus their rate of occurrence as topic of discourse, but that the nature of those discourses can alter dramatically. Indeed the "sameness" in ranking concealed very considerable changes in the contexts in which anti-Jewish prejudices were being reported and discussed. As mentioned earlier, Baker (2011) has coined the term "lockword" to indicate items which retain their permanence (in frequency lists) over time but, by the principle of dynamic stasis, *lockwords* do not necessarily entail *lock-discourses*.

## Suggestions for further research

1. The SiBol/Port corpora are available via *Sketch Engine* and can be used as the source material for diachronic studies of social, political or cultural phenomenon as described here. Alternatively it is possible to download newspaper articles relating to your chosen topic via *Lexis Nexis*. The raw articles you collect can function as your corpora or you might well find it more appropriate to use the concordance-corpora technique described in this chapter. If you

are interested in discourses around prejudice, you might like to compare the findings here with those of a diachronic study of the discourse around *anti-Muslim** or *anti-Catholic**.

2. If you have previously worked on differences between corpora, for instance, using a keyword comparison, you may find it interesting to compare the same corpora but focussing on similarity this time.

3. In the same way, you may find it interesting to take a topic that is often discussed in terms of difference and then use some of the techniques discussed above to focus on similarities.

CHAPTER 12

# Conclusion

In this work we have tried to make connections of relevance between theory and practice, specifically between the advances in lexical-grammar theories to which corpus linguistics has contributed greatly and the kinds of language topics to which the techniques of CADS can usefully be applied. The first of these, the theories, include Sinclair's idiom versus open choice theory of discourse organisation and Hoey's theory of lexical priming, as well as the corpus-assisted work performed on the systems of evaluation in language (including evaluative prosody). As regards the second of these, the practice, we have tried to concentrate on themes often thought of as thorny issues for (semi-)automated or machine-mediated language analyses, for example, metaphor, irony and wordplay, or on enterprises which have been relatively neglected, such as the search for similarities rather than differences across language varieties. We have tried to include a range of different categories of themes and we have illustrated at some length a novel variety of CADS, namely modern-diachronic corpus-assisted discourse studies. We have also tried to be candid about the limitations of machine-assisted investigations into language, for example, as regards how much they can contribute to literary stylistics.

## 12.1 CADS and discourse theories

### 12.1.1 Discourse organisation and the idiom/open choice principles

We have seen evidence of how discourse is organised according to the two principles of idiom (phraseology) and open-choice (Chapter 1) and how these two organisational principles interact to produce discourses and how speakers and writers exploit this interplay for creative effect. We saw how there are different sorts of preconstructed phrases from fully fixed – *in other words, as a matter of fact*, and so on – to templates with a combination of fixed and variable elements. Sometimes the variable element allows a very limited choice, for example, *of some stature/standing*, sometimes a much wider set is possible, as in *the *est* [noun] *yet* and *efforts to* + [verb]. Sometimes the variable element is generally a member of one or more semantic sets as in *fraught with* + items indicating DANGER (dangers, peril, risks etc.), DIFFICULTY (problems, pitfalls, etc.), ANXIETY (anxiety, tension, etc.), COMPLICATION (contradictions, complexities, paradoxes, etc.).

In Chapter 2 we also saw how lexical elements both nested and embedded within other (semi-)preconstructed phrases and how (semi-)preconstructed phrases, just like single lexical items, very often expressed a particular evaluative polarity: *of some stature/standing* is patently positive, but sometimes the evaluation is less apparent and corpus evidence was required to show how the expression *end up* + [preposition] + place was very generally used to express negative evaluation.

In the final case study in Chapter 4 on phrasal irony and in the second case study in Chapter 5 on wordplay including metaphor, we examined how writers exploit the interaction of the two discourse organisational principles. Hearers/readers have certain predictions or expectations about how speakers/writers employ these principles, in particular our knowledge of the discourse type, our communicative competence, means we are primed to anticipate that (semi-)fixed phrases will be just that, fixed in certain specific and expected ways. It is these organisational expectations which wordplay upsets and exploits. As Hoey argues in discussing lexical priming, creativity with language is largely achieved by the deliberate overriding or exploiting of normal primings, to generate what elsewhere has been termed *unusuality* (Partington 1998: 121–143). As Hoey puts it "when a choice of one priming is overwhelmed by another, more dominant priming [the result] is either ambiguity or humour" (2005: 170), both of which are strongly associated, of course, with wordplay.

Sinclair argues that the idiom or phraseological principle of language is the dominant, default mode of both producing and interpreting discourse because it requires less time and effort on the part of both speakers and hearers. Giora shows, with examples from psycholinguistic studies, that listeners normally access idiomatic interpretations of phrases in preference to literal ones; as Sinclair, she argues that idiomaticity is more *salient* than literalness (Giora 2003: 18–21). However, should this process fail (in the sense of failing to explain the text), hearers retain the option of applying the open-choice principle. It is always possible to treat even tightly idiomatic phrases as if they were capable of analysis into smaller units, and it is this potential which playing on words exploits. Thus it is the interplay, the enforced switching from one mode of interpretation to another, from the idiom to the open-choice, which is at the heart of a great part of wordplay.

The clearest examples are perhaps the substitution by the evaluative opposite in well-known phrases (Chapter 4.9), such as *all-American villain*, *Christmas and new year tribulations* and [*snatch*] *defeat from the jaws of victory*; their effect clearly depends on upsetting strongly primed phrasal expectations; a fixed phrase has been broken up – or freed up – to produce an unusual even opposite sense, a process known as *relexicalisation* (Partington 1998: 133–135; 2009a). The other examples of phrasal irony we analysed function in a similar manner. The semi-fixed phrases *an outbreak of, in a fit of, the/an onslaught of* all set up strong primed expectations of something negative but these expectations can be exploited by writers to produce such versions as *an outbreak of honesty, in a fit of democracy, onslaught of hospitality*, and such like. Conversely, phrase templates like *do a good job of* and *a lot/much to be said for* which set up expectations of something positive were also relexicalised subversively to produce utterances such as *doing a good job of losing the war* and *much to be said for failure/acrimony/death.*

In Chapter 8, we first of all considered evidence that conversation very probably relies on fixed phrases even more than most types of writing and may well make use of many types of fixed phrases more or less particular to speech. We then examined a discourse type, press briefings, which relied very heavily on the employment, indeed at times deliberate *deployment* of fixed and semi-fixed phrases, to flood the discourse with particular suasive messages. In Chapter 9 we looked at the use of a number of set phrases generally associated with im/politeness, including *with due/great/the greatest (possible) respect, I* [not] *mean to be rude, if I may say so/put it like this*. Rather similar to the way the primed meaning of certain fixed phrases can be subverted or even reversed for rhetorical effect, we witnessed how several of the politeness markers were used in multiple fashions, often to express mock politeness, or even to be rude whilst remaining within the rules of the institutional setting.

### 12.1.2 Lexical priming

Just as we have tried to show the utility of Sinclair's idiom-open choice theory in describing overall discourse structure, we have attempted to demonstrate the power of Hoey's theory of lexical priming in describing in more detail how speakers and writers organise utterances. The theory is primarily psychological in that it outlines how speakers acquire, by regular exposure to and steady acquaintance with a particular discourse type, the communicative competence of knowing how to use items, that is, their usual positioning in the phrase, what other items they normally interact – or avoid interacting – with, and their functions and meanings, including evaluative meaning, in that discourse type. By metaphorical extension it also becomes a theory of discourse organisation in that we can, in addition, say that items themselves are primed for those uses in that discourse type. We saw then in Chapter 1 how priming theory explains speakers' knowledge of collocations, semantic preferences, prosodies, and so on.

In Chapter 2 we concentrated in particular on the evaluative primings of items, on how they are affected by point of view (adopted perspective) and also on how they interact with each other in texts to contribute very markedly to creating textual cohesion. In Chapters 2 and 3 we also speculated on the possible existence of what we might call "deep" or "existential" or even "phylogenetic" psychological primings common to all human beings and therefore all language. We found much evidence to suggest that uses of items which suggested that the party whose perspective is adopted was in control of events and their environment were very generally primed for positive evaluation, whilst lack of such control was very generally seen as negative. Other such existential phenomena which may affect language primings include *having/presence* is often better than *not having/absence*, and that *change* generally sets in gear a process of evaluation more frequently than *non-change*. The very drive and capacity to evaluate is itself the deepest phylogenetic priming ability of all.

In the three subsequent Chapters 4, 5 and 6, we also witnessed how writers and speakers upset and subvert the priming regularities and thus the expectations of their audience for rhetorical effect. The subversive relexicalisation of phrasal irony discussed in Chapter 4 and mentioned above – *onslaught of hospitality, much to be said for death*, and so on – are clear instances. Very similar are the surprise-effect figurative expressions employed by the humorous columnists we examined in Chapter 5, such as *rabble-soothing speech*, and so on, including and especially the subversion of templates generally employed for creating metaphor and similes, for example, *about as Swedish as a limerick* or *with the elegant body language of a beanbag* where, once again, evaluative expectations are upset for rhetorical effect. We might add that readers who are used to this discourse type are also "primed" in the more general psychological sense of the word to expect such effects and might be disappointed not to encounter them, whereas readers unused to it and without such expectations might well miss the point, that is, the humorous intent. In Chapter 6, in a corpus-assisted study of the humorous writings of Wodehouse, we introduced the term "creative collocational inappropriateness" or "clash" to describe the process in which primed collocational expectations are upset, where the clash in question is between positive and negative evaluation, as in "… deliberately love this girl" (*deliberately* very generally collocating with highly negative entities) and "upsetting [the table] with all the old thoroughness" (upsetting tables is usual negative but thoroughness is usually positive and *all the old* is marked, according to corpus evidence for [good: endearing]).

### 12.1.3 Evaluation

If Sinclair's idiom and open-choice theory and Hoey's theory of lexical priming *describe* the way language users organise discourse, evaluation has enormous potential in helping *explain* their motives for communicating in the first place and we have seen the expression of evaluations in discourse at every turn throughout this work. We discussed the role of evaluation in describing discourse organisation in Chapter 2, in showing how textual cohesion is largely created by connected strings of evaluative items. Texts have to make sense not just ideationally or conceptually, but also evaluatively. In other words speakers and writers must attempt to express not only the topic but their evaluation of the topic in a coherent interconnected fashion. In Chapter 2 we also attempted a rudimentary categorisation of types of evaluative realisation, from items whose evaluative force was inherent to those whose evaluation was realised through co-occurrence arrays with other items (evaluative prosody) to "neutral" items which took on an evaluative force according to the context they were used in and, of course, the intention of the speaker. In Chapter 3 we examined a good number of items whose evaluative function had been much discussed in the literature on prosody and showed how the contextual feature of the adopted perspective's being or not being in control of the event was crucial to the realisation or suppression or even reversal of the primed evaluation.

In Chapter 4 we saw how evaluation elucidates both the mechanism and the purpose of ironic utterances. If irony is defined merely as saying the opposite of what one means, then it would be simply perverse, barely distinguishable from lying or insanity. If however it is defined as expressing an evaluation and implying the opposite evaluation (very generally negative) for the precise communicative purpose of criticism – whether mild and jocular or severe and harsh – then we begin to appreciate both its role and its popularity. We also noted a specific subform of irony which depended on the reversal of exaggeration into understatement (or "litotes"), which is evidence of how closely hyperbole is associated with evaluation.

In Chapter 5 we emphasised how metaphors, whether in the form of conventional sets of metaphors such as ANTI-AMERICANISM IS A DISEASE or as novel and creative such as "Goldilocks on crack" or "a programme that oozes despair like a badly applied tourniquet" are chosen or invented to express evaluations. Indeed, we saw how, very often, metaphors are selected or forged to do little else but evaluate. In addition we considered how the presumption of shared evaluations of people, products, events and so on, can be used to create affiliation between columnist and readers to help sell newspapers.

Chapter 7 examined and compared the representations of racism and xenophobia as concepts in British and Italian newspapers, including how the newspapers orientated towards, or evaluated, these concepts.

Chapters 8 and 9 dealt mainly with evaluations in competition, in conflict even in certain forms of spoken discourse. We looked at how the evaluations of events and people's behaviours presented by different parties in discourse events such as press briefings and judicial inquiries were frequently (and frequently of necessity) very different, and at how speakers strived to have their evaluative version of events become the generally accepted one.

In Chapter 10 we noted how particular sets of overtly evaluative lexis had entered into the usage of the UK so-called quality press, lexis which twenty years ago was absent. We reflected that this change in prose style may well reflect both a general tendency to adopt familiar, colloquialised language in more and more social contexts in the UK and also an increasing trend for English "quality" newspapers to copy the discourse practices of their supposedly downmarket rivals, the tabloids. Finally, in Chapter 11 evaluations played a role in two other modern diachronic case studies. In the first, into discussions of antisemitism, anti-Jewish prejudice was understandably evaluated by all newspapers as negative, but the foci and loci of the evaluation was found to have altered dramatically over recent time. In the second we focussed on the consistency of evaluations over time of *boy/s* and *girl/s* in UK newspapers.

What these studies, as a set, have shown is how the Sinclairian discourse organisational principles, lexical priming and evaluation are not separate systems but are synergetic. The idiom principle predicts that we are primed with expectations about which items normally occur together in (semi) preconstructed lexical units or which items are normally permissible within a lexical template, whilst the principle of evaluative cohesion or harmony as described in Chapter 2 is one of the principle psycho-pragmatic forces influencing which items tend to – and we expect to – co-occur in texts.

## 12.2 The eclecticism of CADS research

One of the principal lessons we learned in writing this book was the necessity of tailoring the research procedures to the particular research questions and aims. CADS research is extraordinarily eclectic in its methodologies, a fact which is reflected in the number of different types of comparisons which can be carried out (and we have tried to stress throughout this work how important comparison is to discourse analysis).

One of the more standard sets of procedures is that followed in Chapter 6 on corpus-assisted stylistics. A corpus of relevant texts is compiled, one or more comparison corpora are compiled to which the target corpus is contrasted by means of keyword and key-cluster listing. These lists are then examined by the analyst and interesting items, particularly sets of similar items are then concordanced to examine more closely the contexts in which they are used. A somewhat similar methodology was described in Chapter 10, where three sister corpora containing texts of the same discourse types – UK newspaper prose – but from different periods of time were contrasted and the keyword lists were analysed under the hypothesis that changes in key lexis might reveal changes over time in discourse practices. In the case study on discussions of antisemitism in Chapter 11, instead, it was necessary to construct sub-corpora of the three sister corpora, that is concordance-corpora of text fragments containing mentions of *antisemit**, which were then contrasted for key lexis which might reveal differences over time. However, they were also each in turn contrasted with an external comparison corpus, the BNC, which served to reveal *similarities* among the three concordance-corpora and thus among the ways antisemitism has been discussed over time (what we have called "lock discourses"). In the second case study we presented a variety of procedures which can be used in the search for similarities between texts and collections of text, including a program which lists the shared as well as the unshared collocates of two lexical items, consistency listing, which will identify words which are shared across a number of texts and key keywords, which is of use in looking for repeated patterns across large numbers of sub-corpora.

In Chapter 11 we also discussed the important relationship between searching for differences and for similarities, which goes to the heart of linguistic practice. Linguistics in general is first and foremost a descriptivist endeavour, its aims being to describe the structure of language systems and the behaviour of language users (some forms of linguistics also attempt explanations, but unless these are based on sound initial description they will be at best speculative and at worst dishonest). Forms of text linguistics, of course, including corpus linguistics and CADS, describe the behaviour of users in attested, recorded circumstances.

All descriptivist science is in constant tension between searching for *differences* between phenomena and significant generalisations or *similarities* among phenomena, which allow the analyst to posit categories of items or events which enable us to make sense of the apparent chaos of the real world. As regards linguistic science, for instance, linguists must try to describe both what it is that makes adjectives different from adverbs, or amplifiers from emphasisers, or endearment terms from familiarisers, but also what it is that items which get included in any category have in common to justify the constitution of that category.

In Chapter 8 still other types of comparison were performed. In the first study, the frequency counts of lexical items from White House briefings relating to events in Libya, Syria and Egypt in 2011 could be tracked month by month which highlighted changes in the way governments or leaders were being represented.

In the second study, comparisons were made between the linguistic production of certain types of speakers.

Not all case studies involved comparisons quite so explicitly. Chapters 2 and 3 rely heavily on the concordancing of items to shed light on their evaluative behaviour. In Chapter 5 the concordances of the term *anti-American** from various corpora were analysed in order to categorise types of metaphor around the concept that writers employ and the comparison was made post-analysis to see whether variation seemed dependent on language or political orientation. Whilst in Chapter 9 a number of im/politeness markers are concordanced to shed light on the contexts in which forms of im/politeness are utilised and exploited by speakers.

Finally, the case study on irony in Chapter 4 employed a particular set of procedures. It was decided, first of all, that a reliable description was needed of what language users actually intend when they overtly signal a certain statement, situation or state-of-affairs as *ironic*, of what people actually consider irony to be. To this end, first of all, we examined the frequent collocates of *irony* and *ironic** in the SiBol corpora, as well as the use of explicit indicators of irony such as *the irony is* or *isn't it ironic that* in a spoken corpus of press briefings. It became clear that irony was felt to consist of a situation in which two narratives were being contrasted and where the apparent evaluation of the first was reversed in the second. In the next phase of research, episodes of implicit irony (that is, where there is no lexical marker such as *the irony is*) were collected by compiling a concordance corpus of episodes where laughter was signalled in the briefings transcription, given the well-documented observation that implicit irony is often seen as humorous, and examining this for episodes where some form of evaluation-reversal was being performed. These could then be analysed to discover what functions speakers used irony to perform. In each phase there was a productive interplay between the objective data produced by the software analysis and human interpretation of this data, which would then become the basis for further computer analysis in a recursive process.

On the subject of CADS eclecticism, we might also consider the variety of lexical elements used in analyses. In several of our case studies we have stressed how CADS research often utilises as data lengthier text fragments than is traditional in other forms of corpus linguistics. Or rather, depending on the aim of the research it utilises strings of all lengths from single words (frequency wordlists, keywords, collocates) to clusters, to KWIC concordances (occasionally) to sentence concordances (more frequently) to concordance-corpora in which the character span is generally at least 300 characters to entire text extracts, as in Chapter 2's study of the way textual cohesion is largely created by connected strings of evaluative items.

Lastly, we might also recall the wide variety of discourse types we have considered in this volume. There is, in theory, no limit to the sorts of discourse types CADS can take an interest in.

## 12.3 Corpus-assisted discourse studies: More than the sum of discourse analysis + computing

### 12.3.1 Adding value to discourse analysis: Keeping us honest and the "culture of the counterexample"

As in all research, there is a good deal which is subjective in CADS. We choose our research question, we decide what analyses to run and we interpret the eventual data output, and the sorts of comparisons we choose to perform will influence what we can see, as will our own personalities, beliefs and prejudices. However, one key criteria which CADS can endeavour to fulfil, to offset against this inbuilt subjectivity, is that of replicability. This may be attained both by making the procedures as transparent as possible, including descriptions of the statistical settings used for calculating collocation, key words and so on, and, where possible, by making the corpora available – as we have done with the SiBol/Port corpora which were employed several times in this work. Furthermore once the software is set in motion the researcher cannot interfere. There is therefore at least one phase of corpus-assisted research, the software analyses, whether they be keywording or concordancing or collocate collection or combinations of these, which the researcher cannot either consciously or unconsciously manipulate.

As a consequence, in common with other branches of corpus linguistics, we very often find ourselves with information which was not anticipated in our original hypothesis. One light-hearted example: in a corpus-assisted study of the language used by US Representatives about the conflict in Iraq, a concordance of the item *Hollywood* (which itself had been noted due to its appearance in a previous concordance) revealed that it was mentioned 28 times by Republicans but not once by a Democrat. The co-text showed that, in contrast to the relative mildness of their objections to negative press coverage of US intervention, what truly enraged a number of Republican speakers was the political meddling of cinema actors in current affairs. A more serious example is how the case study into the changing discussions of antisemitism reported in Chapter 11 was sparked by an earlier MD-CADS work into *anti-* prefixed words (Duguid 2010), where it was observed that *anti-semit** items had retained their ranking in frequency lists of these items between 1993 and 2005, but that a closer inspection of the concordance co-texts seemed to show distinct changes in the nature of these discussions. All corpus linguists have experience of these serendipitous discoveries, and although serendipity is not limited to inductive, data-gathering enterprises such as corpus linguistics, induction certainly creates a more fertile environment for it than unassisted introspection (Partington 2006a 12–13; 2009a:292). And yet even serendipity is not divorced from subjectivity. On the one hand:

> It provides a further stage of analyst abstraction from the data in that hypotheses can be *suggested by* the data rather than being *imposed on* the data.

but on the other, although it "casts the researcher in a new role" of reacting to novel and unexpected data, this role still has its subjective element:

> often the sheer variety of possible avenues which constantly open up means the researcher has to learn the skill of selecting and of predicting which they feel are likely to prove the most rewarding. (Partington 2006a: 12)

Further still, we often find ourselves, not simply with unanticipated, fresh information, but with actual *counterexamples* to our original hypotheses. We might say that, as a result of the objectivity of the software analysis phase, corpus linguistics thrives within a "culture of the counterexample". We say "thrives" because counterexamples, though sometimes vexing for the researcher, are an excellent thing for the research. Evaluative prosody is a particularly fruitful area to find examples to illustrate this, probably because our conscious introspections on prosody are very often incomplete.

In Chapter 2.7 we saw how, if a speaker wished to express the notion of "full of" something negative, s/he might well use *fraught with* and we mentioned in passing how, if a speaker wished instead to express the idea of "full of" something positive they might well, instead, choose to employ *brimming with*. The following concordance of the first twenty occurrences extracted by the program from the *Telegraph* section of SiBol 05 certainly bears witness to the item's positive prosody:

| | | |
|---|---|---|
| 1 | t they will be up against a side | **brimming with** all the good things in football. |
| 2 | generally cheap and periodically | **brimming with** bargains, drawing in low-to-middl |
| 3 | ited's manager, once left Monaco | **brimming with** bonhomie after a 0–0 only for Dav |
| 4 | c and metal waste packaging, and | **brimming with** bright colours and high spirits, |
| 5 | ssume that the BBC's coffers are | **brimming with** cash, and that therefore I need n |
| 6 | m feeling apologetic, Mr Bush is | **brimming with** confidence. He was flanked by his |
| 7 | s capable of fitting into a team | **brimming with** confidence. With Chelsea having l |
| 8 | Elsewhere, the music-making was | **brimming with** energy and passion. The first mov |
| 9 | land on the Windrush in 1948, is | **brimming with** excitement. Her agent, David Gros |
| 10 | "Autumn/winter collections are | **brimming with** heritage fabrics and country-hous |
| 11 | r possibly. Certainly hostelries | **brimming with** home-brewed beer and Cornish past |
| 12 | ughout recorded history, are now | **brimming with** hope. The world's two most populo |
| 13 | or every athlete. I'm absolutely | **brimming with** it, which is why I've worked so h |
| 14 | kling Thames. Craven Cottage was | **brimming with** its traditional goodwill, noisy, |
| 15 | us just how great and modern and | **brimming with** life-force as a screen actor Cagn |
| 16 | he season, which climaxed a move | **brimming with** refined thought, touch and moveme |
| 17 | tion proves, the British public, | **brimming with** seasonal bonhomie, do not seem to |
| 18 | f-mocking and original, her eyes | **brimming with** tears as she describes the dreadf |
| 19 | s is a genuinely brilliant work, | **brimming with** wit and wisdom, and I can hardly |
| 20 | er 30, Ponting's side are hardly | **brimming with** youth, once the trademark for Aus |

A concordance of the first 20 occurrence of *brimming with* from the *Telegraph* section of SiBol 05.

We can compare this with the concordance of *fraught with* in the Introduction, 0.4.3.

However, what should we make of line 18, "brimming with tears"? If we expand the co-text beyond 80 characters it becomes clear that these are not tears of joy: "her eyes brimming with tears as she describes the dreadful things she has witnessed". We are clearly faced with a counterexample to our introspective hypothesis of the positive prosody of this item. Do we therefore abandon the hypothesis? Probably not, but the occurrence requires an explanation. We note first of all that it is the least metaphorical of all the uses, the OED defines *brimming* as "being full to the brim, overflowing", with clear reference to liquids, and in the case in question, we have *tears*. The only other such reference to liquids is in line 11, but one doubts whether it is the hostelries themselves which are brimming with beer; it is a metonymic reference to the amounts they serve. We might begin to refine our original hypothesis and conclude that the positive prosody of *brimming with* may only apply to its figurative use (which is by far the most common use in newspaper material). Secondly, line 18 raises also the possibility that particular set phrases may have a different evaluation from the general use, either the opposite evaluation or a neutral one. The expression *brimming with tears* occurs five times in SiBol 05, three instances expressing sorrow, two happiness.

We then proceeded to make a similar concordance from the *Guardian* section of SiBol 05:

| | | | |
|---|---|---|---|
| 1 | ay be failing in class, but he's | **brimming with** | big ideas. But he also has romant |
| 2 | ches in Normandy. One young man, | **brimming with** | cheeky confidence, proudly told u |
| 3 | ust a pipedream. And Huckerby is | **brimming with** | confidence. "The United game was |
| 4 | omania's Andrei Pavel in a match | **brimming with** | drama and controversy. It seems t |
| 5 | achievable. A packed Edgbaston, | **brimming with** | excitement and confidence at the |
| 6 | ins a couple of copper cauldrons | **brimming with** | Gluhwein. Standing in a circle, w |
| 7 | ritish portraits – a masterpiece | **brimming with** | ideas in which death and life con |
| 8 | ply written, intelligently told, | **brimming with** | ideas and threaded with a sense o |
| 9 | ated. "Mark's a younger manager, | **brimming with** | ideas. He's brought in a lot of m |
| 10 | le from scratch n was absolutely | **brimming with** | jeopardy. It was a Matterhorn of |
| 11 | as "full of patriotic verve and | **brimming with** | juche". 11.30pm: Have I Got Good |
| 12 | that those who had just met were | **brimming with** | NGF, whereas people who had been |
| 13 | Are Forever – McAlmont's voice, | **brimming with** | pain and aching with desperate pe |
| 14 | n the cities, pavement cafes are | **brimming with** | pretty people, idling away the ho |
| 15 | n of the Pope's visit. Cafes are | **brimming with** | priests, nuns and monks, while yo |
| 16 | y, a 39-year-old mother of three | **brimming with** | self-assurance, is an altogether |
| 17 | streets and tube stations may be | **brimming with** | suspicion, fear and armed police, |
| 18 | hair at Brown university. "It is | **brimming with** | the same indifference to historic |
| 19 | topped a yacht in broad daylight | **brimming with** | valuable amphorae, or jars, as it |
| 20 | impact of those last four words | **brimming with** | violent possibilities. This idea |

A concordance of the first 20 occurrence of *brimming with* from the *Guardian* section of SiBol 05.

On this set of evidence alone the evaluative polarity would by no means be clear; *big ideas* and sports matches which have *excitement* and *drama* may be good, but *pain, fear* and *violent possibilities* certainly are not. A wider context is needed to interpret the evaluation of other cases, such as *self-assurance* and *cheeky confidence,* not to mention *pretty people* and *priests, nuns and monks.* Do we now have to abandon our initial introspective hypothesis of positive prosody?

The same type of 20-line concordance from *The Times*, however, corroborated the *Telegraph* data. Cities were brimming with *beautiful buildings* or *culture* or *culinary possibilities.* People are brimming with *optimism, energy, enthusiasm* and brilliant *ideas* (including on how to improve one's sex life), whilst herbs are said to be "brimming with a wide variety of cancer-fighting nutrients". There is yet again, however, a counter-instance: "people are sick of paying for albums brimming with fillers" (re-issued songs). Another possible counterexample might seem to be "brimming with used-car-dealer-nous and Estuary English", but the description is of the highly talented actor Bob Hoskins and the context is generally complimentary (yet more evidence of the need to look beyond the narrow KWIC concordance window).

How then do we interpret these counterexamples, especially the considerable number in the *Guardian* concordance? They appear to have much in common with the expressions examined in Chapter 4's final case study. In other words they are instances of phrasal irony, specifically of the type where the primed expectation that *brimming with* be followed by something positive is overturned and exploited for rhetorical effect, as was seen with *doing a good job of* <u>*losing*</u>, *much to be said for* <u>*failure*</u> and *gives* <u>*stupidity*</u> *a bad name*. It should be noted that *brimming with* displays two of the properties which we surmised might be used to predict an item's potential use for phrasal irony, an evaluative polarity marked enough to set up expectations and an inherent hyperbolic meaning ("full to overflowing"). A look at the wider context of some of the counterexamples shows how they often appear in texts, generally comment pieces where writers are striving to produce interesting effects, including humorous exaggeration (to which, as we said, irony is often connected), for instance:

(1) In truth, the project itself to build a restaurant [...] from scratch was absolutely **brimming with** jeopardy. It was a Matterhorn of jeopardy. (SiBol 05 *Guardian*)

not to mention a touch of the Guardian's colourful sarcasm about Catholicism (note the hyperbolic terms *gripped*, *fervour* and *roam the streets* along with *brimming with*; irony is often marked by hyperbole):

(2) Cologne has been gripped with religious fervour in anticipation of the Pope's visit. Cafes are **brimming with** priests, nuns and monks, while youths roam the streets wearing T-shirts bearing the slogan "I love Jesus". (SiBol 05 *Guardian*)

Thanks to the counterexamples provided by our analysis of data, then, our initial simple hypothesis has become considerable more detailed and nuanced. In general, *brimming with* is indeed used in combination with positive items to create a positive prosodic array. However, we have added to this that such evaluative behaviour may apply only to its figurative uses, that items used in set phrases may have different prosodic behaviour from that when used in more open-choice situations (as predicted by lexical priming theory) and that it is not unusual to find it employed in phrasal ironies for rhetorical effect, including for humour. Finally there is some indication that one of our newspapers, the *Guardian*, employs phrasal irony more often than its rivals, a conjecture worth further investigation.

### 12.3.2 Actively looking for counterexamples

Indeed we might go further still and advocate the active seeking out of counterexamples to test our hypotheses, in true Popperian fashion. The year 2005 was an election year in the United Kingdom and the Conservative party made immigration control one of its main campaign issues (see Example 4).

We might then test the hypothesis that the right-leaning *Daily* and *Sunday Telegraph* newspapers focussed on the issue of immigration and in a negative way. We could, of course, choose to look for articles where immigrants and immigration are criticised using searchwords such as *immigra** in association with, say, *negative* and *bad*. This, as it turned out, returned seven results, only one of which actually carried criticism of immigration, but even this is not averred by the newspaper itself, it is attributed to a *vox populi*:

(3) Her big voting issue is immigration, "I want to decrease the numbers coming in" said Miss Cosgrove. "It's not that immigrants in Poplar are bad, but housing is a big problem around here. It's more or less impossible to get a council flat now." (SiBol 05, *Telegraph*)

whilst four were critical of the Conservative's "negative campaign on immigration" (SiBol 05, *Telegraph* and see Example 6).

However, we would do well to test the hypothesis more thoroughly by searching for counterexamples, in other words, by looking for occasions on which the newspaper reported immigration in a positive light, perhaps using *immigra** in association with *positive* and *benefi** (*benefits/beneficial*). After winnowing out instances where *benefits* referred to social security payments, there were 18 occurrences. Four of these were references to a report by the anti-immigration thinktank *Migrationwatch* questioning the benefits of immigration whilst five others came in a letter, and discussions of it, from the Conservative leader, Michael Howard, himself the son of an immigrant, to the *Daily Telegraph*, in which he writes:

(4) Modern Britain is immeasurably better off as a result of the new Britons who have made their homes here over the last century. We all benefit from the social diversity, economic vibrancy and cultural richness which **immigration** has brought. But, if those benefits are to continue to flow, we need to ensure that immigration is effectively managed, in the interests of all Britons, old and new. (SiBol 05, *Telegraph*)

Our evaluation of this will depend on our judgment of Mr Howard's sincerity. But our hypothesis that the *Telegraph* was anti-immigration in 2005 has somehow to survive some very positive evaluations of immigration averred by the newspaper, for example:

(5) [...] it's hard to argue with Mr King's (elegantly disguised) conclusion: that orderly **immigration** by hard working people is a big net benefit to the economy. (SiBol 05, *Telegraph*)

(6) I doubt Mr Howard's new emphasis on immigration and asylum will do his party much good. There is always a danger, for a start, in lumping together the flaws in the asylum system with **immigration** – the economic benefits of which are richly appreciated by many businesses. (SiBol 05, *Telegraph*)

as well as its decision to publish letters from readers in praise of immigrants, both for their contribution to the UK economy:

(7) **Immigration** benefits

SIR – Given the febrile air surrounding immigration issues during the election campaign, it is important to recognise, a year on from the expansion of the European Union, the substantial contribution that migrant workers from the new member states have already made to Britain's economy. With seven per cent of British businesses taking advantage of the pool of eastern European labour, the contribution was recently lauded by, among others, the Royal Institute of Chartered Surveyers. (SiBol 05, *Telegraph*)

and for their contribution to someone's kitchen:

(8) **Immigration** benefits

SIR – Like Becky Barrow (report, Apr 30), I live in a part of west London that has long-standing links with the Polish community. I benefit hugely from their presence. While my friends in the Home Counties complain that it is impossible to find a builder, I have a pool of hard-working, highly skilled workers on my doorstep. The cupboards made by my Polish joiner are a work of art, over which I gloat daily. (SiBol 05, *Telegraph*)

This was also the year of the "Polish plumber", the metonymical east-European worker-migrant who, according the UK press, was causing anxieties among native French workers and trade unions. As serendipity would have it, the article from which Example (5) derives had the following headline ("King" is Sir Mervyn King, then Governor of the Bank of England):

(9) Governor: immigrants keep down inflation; 'Polish plumber' effect reduces pressure on wages, says King. (SiBol 05, *Telegraph*)

We decided to concordance *Polish plumber* in the 2005 *Telegraph*. There were eleven occurrences in none of which was the "plumber" depicted negatively. In five he was a positive figure, whilst any criticism is reserved for "French workers":

(10) Faced with the bogeyman of the cheap "Polish plumber'", French workers could only suggest laws and rules to keep that plumber out, or make him more expensive by harmonising taxes and working rules across the EU. (SiBol 05, *Telegraph*)

including the following dose of sarcasm at the expense of both French and British attitudes:

(11) If soundings of French public opinion are to be trusted, it is this innocuous, hardworking figure who is to be blamed for that country's great cry of "Non!'". The drains of la Patrie, they declared, are not to be trusted to the wrenches and sink-plungers of des cohortes trangres. In the UK, we take a different view. Without the Polish Plumber, and his apple-cheeked cousin, the Polish Cleaning Lady, our radiators would harbour dust-bunnies, and skeins of Andrex would float like seaweed through our drawing rooms each Bank Holiday weekend. (SiBol 05, *Telegraph*)

Finally, can it at least be argued that the *Telegraph* is more obsessed with immigration than other quality papers? In 2005, the phrase *illegal immigrants* appears 165 times in the *Daily and Sunday Telegraph*, 4.6 occurrences per million words and 218 times in the *Guardian* and *Observer*, or 4.0 p.m.w. However, the phrase *asylum seeker** appears just 339 times in the *Telegraph* papers (9.4 p.m.w) compared to 1,080 times in the *Guardian/Observer* (20.5 p.m.w). There is little evidence, then, of the formers' preoccupation with the topic.

These counter-instances to our hypothesis seem to show that the newspaper is not viscerally anti-immigration but allows pro-immigration voices too, even if they tend to be hard-nosed and practical in nature rather than socio-cultural ones emphasising the culturally enriching aspects of immigration. Moreover, we have also discovered that the paper does not, at least in this case, preach slavishly the policies of the Conservative party, with which it is often considered to align. Perhaps these observations should not surprise us overmuch. The *Telegraph* is a middle-class newspaper aimed especially at business people. Immigration is depicted, as we have seen, by the newspaper as providing inexpensive domestic labour, of filling skills gaps in the labour market and also of depressing wages of the work-force, all viewed as good things for the paper's target audience. It is by no means coy about reporting voices expressing the latter, as in Example (9) and the following:

(12) [...] there is always the hope that the Polish plumber's low-cost flexible model will frighten European workers into change. Competition from new Europe "may be causing distress to voters now, but in the end it will create dynamism," said Mr Murray.

Be all this as it may, the point to be underlined is that the active search for counter-data to an initial hypothesis has allowed us to refine it quite considerably.[1]

Finally, an obligatory word of caution. It must never be forgotten when studying socio-political issues, including representations of groups and potential prejudice towards them in newspaper texts, that negativity is one of the chief news values (Galtung & Ruge 1981). Wrongdoing makes the papers, normal good service rarely so. The corollary of this is that most social groups will, on a statistical level, be spoken about more often in negative contexts than in positive ones. A *reductio ad absurdum* is the "football supporters syndrome". On a simple statistical analysis, one would surmise that all newspapers were extremely prejudiced against football supporters since they only get mentioned when causing trouble. In making a case of media bias then it is necessary to meet a number of criteria. Firstly, to give strong evidence that the negativity is more frequent and more drastic than might normally be expected, perhaps by comparing the representation of one group with others, or the representation of the same group across different newspapers. Secondly, to not ignore out of hand counter-instances of positive evaluation; since these are relatively rare in newspapers they count for a good deal. Finally, to maintain a solid distinction between *negative representation* meaning "prejudiced representation" and *negative representation* meaning "reporting of negative events". The latter is what newspapers do for a living and rarely implies the former. For instance, in Port 2010 the term *Catholic priest** cooccurs 32 times with *abus** (whereas only once is mention made of care for the sick and dying), but even if only a tiny proportion of priests have ever

1. Morley and Taylor (2012) also find very little evidence of consistent anti-immigration prejudice on the UK broadsheet press. Baker et al. produce some evidence of a negative stance amongst UK popular newspapers "whereas broadsheets demonstrate a more balanced stance" (2008: 290).

come under suspicion of child abuse this does not necessarily imply prejudice against the Catholic Church. Nor do reports of homophobic or antisemitic statements by some Islamic cleric necessarily connote bigotry towards all Muslims, nor do reports about the rising costs to taxpayers of benefits payments necessarily mean prejudice against the unemployed. Yet far too often politicised discourse analysts have been happy to concoct dark agendas and media conspiracies simply on the basis of the press's meat-and-drink news value of negative reporting.

## 12.4 CADS: From research to the teaching of discourse analysis

All this has significant implications for teaching using corpus materials. It is insufficient, disingenuous and sometimes downright deceitful to pick texts and procedures to make a case, for example, trawling through the *Telegraph* subcorpus looking for anti-immigration articles to "prove" one's initial hypothesis. This must at least be balanced by looking for texts and procedures which might support a counter-case. As the physicist, Richard Feynman puts it in outlining the difference between science and "cargo cult science" (that is, going through the motions thinking you are doing science):

> The first principle is that you must not fool yourself–and you are the easiest person to fool [...] After you've not fooled yourself, it's easy not to fool other scientists. You just have to be honest in a conventional way after that [...] I'm talking about a specific, extra type of integrity that is not lying, but bending over backwards to show how you are maybe wrong.
> (Richard Feynman, Speech at Caltech, 1974 also known as "Cargo Cult Science")[2]

This of course is not to say that researchers must not steadily accumulate evidence in favour of an argument. This process of inductive research is the most usual one in observational sciences such as corpus linguists and indeed this book would be very slim without it. What Feynman is saying is that where the possibility of challenging a hypothesis is feasible it should be done, and that researchers should always be on the lookout for ways of doing so, not just because looking for counterexamples keeps us honest but also because, as we saw in the previous section, they are extremely valuable in refining our model of the object of research.

2. The whole speech can be read at ⟨http://www.lhup.edu/~DSIMANEK/cargocul.htm⟩

Finally, encouraging students to interrogate appropriate corpora (for example, containing a variety of newspaper texts from varying political standpoints) can expose them to a much wider range of diverse perspectives on any particular social issue, including ones which had not occurred to the teacher. Moreover, it allows students to collect evidence in support of their own case, should this differ from the preferred perspective of the teacher. This can even lead the teacher him/herself to a more sophisticated understanding. Moreover, it is, of course, entirely possible for different people to view the same data and reach very diverse conclusions. We ourselves are aware that another group might view the 2005 *Telegraph* data on immigration in a more negative way; why, for instance, was it necessary to mention at all the *Migrationwatch* report questioning the benefits of immigration?

Research schools which perform discourse analysis with socio-political aims, critical discourse analysis being the foremost example, run a considerable risk of failing to meet Feynman's criterion of integrity. If researchers and teachers impose a priori a particular ideological perspective and then perhaps use the corpus simply as a source of material to support that perspective, never looking for counter-data to that ideological perspective – even ignoring them if stumbled upon by accident – and, finally, if they constrain students to interpret the data within that perspective, then the chances are that very little that is new will be learned along the way. Researchers who work within the framework of CDA have stated that their form of research is more honest than others because they openly declare their political position. But such open declarations of stance are no more a guarantee of Popper-Feynman intellectual rigour and honesty than those of a politician or lawyer when they openly advocate their case, in fact, knowing that an interpretation is being argued from a particular political standpoint with no effort made to look for "inconvenient" data should make us more sceptical of it, not less. This is why we argue that replicability (and para-repicability, that is, following the same research procedures on a different data-set), where possible, is a key characteristic of CADS research – if the processes of data collection and data analysis are sufficiently transparent to be repeated, then claims can be tested and even perhaps analysed from a series of different ideological viewpoints.

As regards sociopolitical topics, then, the CADS that we envisage recalls an older tradition of liberal education, in which great value is attached to presenting students with differing points of view on social issues, allowing them to discover new ones by themselves, and teaching the techniques of evaluating them. The students' own work is then – ideally – assessed in terms of the quality of their evaluative capacities independently of whether their evaluations concur politically with those of the teacher. Dissenting ideas are welcome if they are rationally argued and supported. It is felt that this encourages students to have an open mind, to be tolerant of others' opinions and teaches them how to argue a case. It is also felt that competition among ideas is the best way to test their validity. Whilst recognising that researcher bias can never be eliminated, using the corpora honestly, making the analytic processes transparent, and carrying out the analysis in a variety of ways to let the data speak as far as possible for itself can help minimise, control and refine it.

# Appendix

## Resources

This Appendix is not intended to be a comprehensive list of all corpus linguistic resources available but as a guide to some of the software or corpora employed in this volume.

### 1. Corpus compilation

#### 1.1 BootCaT (Chapter 9)

*BootCaT* (Baroni & Bernardini 2004) is a tool which helps you to download corpora from the internet. The user specifies the searchwords to be used to build the corpus and it is possible to limit the search to certain websites or internet domains. It is free to use and can be downloaded from http://bootcat.sslmit.unibo.it/

### 2. Annotation and interrogation

#### 2.1 UAM Corpus Tool (Chapter 7)

*UAM Corpus Tool* (O'Donnell 2008) is a tool which helps you to annotate your corpus and also interrogate your corpus in the same interface. It is free to use and can be downloaded from http://www.wagsoft.com/CorpusTool

### 3. Mark up

If you are creating your own corpus and would like to share it with other users at some stage it is advisable to follow the TEI guidelines for mark up. For more information, see http://www.tei-c.org/Guidelines/

## 4. Corpus interrogation

There are a range of resources available and in this book we have used different software packages for different purposes. Here we simply supply some hints to help you choose the best tool for each specific job. The tools that we used in this book are:

### 4.1 AntConc (Chapter 9)

*AntConc* (Anthony 2011) is a freeware concordance programme which allows the user to perform the most common types of corpus analysis (wordlists, keywords, concordances, collocates). It can be downloaded from http://www.antlab.sci.waseda.ac.jp/software.html. There are versions for Windows, Mac and Linux.

### 4.2 Concgram (Chapter 5)

*Concgram* (Greaves 2009) is a software package that is designed to aid the identification of phraseologies. It is not freeware and can be purchased from John Benjamins.

### 4.3 Sketch Engine (Chapters 7)

*Sketch Engine* (Kilgarriff et al. 2004) is another set of software. The most distinctive features are the *Word Sketch*, which groups collocates by grammatical relation to the node, the *Sketch Difference*, which compares Word Sketches for 2 items and the *Distributional Thesaurus*. Unlike the other software packages described here, the user does not download the software but is given access to the interface online. This means that it is less flexible in terms of uploading your own corpora but it does include access to a wide range of part-of-speech (POS) tagged corpora in many languages. It is not freeware and can be purchased from http://www.sketchengine.co.uk. A one-month trial is available.

### 4.4 Wordsmith Tools (Chapters 4, 5, 6, 7, 9)

*WordSmith Tools* (Scott 2008) is one of the best-known software packages. It contains all the most frequently used corpus analytical tools and the latest version also allows for concgram searches. It is not freeware and can be purchased from http://www.lexically.net/wordsmith/

### 4.5 Wmatrix facilities (Chapter 5)

*Wmatrix* (Rayson 2009) is a software package which, like *Sketch Engine*, is accessed through a web interface. In addition to the usual tools, the most innovative feature of *Wmatrix* is the option of searching for, and comparing, semantic domains. When corpora are uploaded they are POS-tagged and, in addition, they are semantically tagged. It is not freeware and can be purchased from http://ucrel.lancs.ac.uk/wmatrix/ A one-month trial is available.

## 5. Publicly available corpora which are referred to in the book (alphabetical order)

In this section we have only listed corpora which can be accessed by researchers at any institution. Some of them require payment, but none are restricted access.

### 5.1 BASE (mentioned in Chapter 8)

The British Academic Spoken English (BASE) corpus and its counterpart, the British Academic Written English Corpus (BAWE) are both available through the Oxford Text Archive at http://ota.ahds.ac.uk and can also be accessed through the Sketch Engine interface.

### 5.2 BNC (mentioned in Chapter 8 and Chapter 11)

This is one of the best known English corpora and contains British English texts (spoken and written) from the 1960s–1990s. It can be searched at no cost from http://www.natcorp.ox.ac.uk/ and also available through the Brigham Young interface (see http://corpus.byu.edu/) and on Sketch Engine.

### 5.3 Brown Family of Corpora (mentioned in the Introduction and Chapter 6)

The Brown Family (which includes the Brown corpus, Frown, LOB and FLOB and BE06) are a set of corpora which contain British and American varieties of English and may be analysed diachronically. More information on each corpus may be found at http://www.helsinki.fi/varieng/CoRD/corpora/index.html

The Brown family has also inspired The International Corpus of English (ICE) which began work in 1990 with the primary aim of collecting material for comparative studies of English worldwide. Twenty-four research teams around the world are preparing electronic corpora of their own national or regional variety of English. See http://ice-corpora.net/ice/index.htm

### 5.4 Corpus of Contemporary American English (CoCA) (mentioned in a task for Chapter 5 and Chapter 9)

This is one of a family of large corpora which have been made freely available by Davies at Brigham Young University, see http://corpus.byu.edu/

### 5.5 CORD historical Corpus of English Dialogues (mentioned in Chapter 8)

The CORD Corpus contains historical data from 1560–1760. The texts it contains are written records of real speech events (for example, trial proceedings) and "constructed dialogue" (for example, plays). It can be accessed through the Oxford Text Archive.

### 5.6 Hong Kong Corpus of Conversational English (HKCCE) (mentioned in Chapter 8)

The HKCCE contains spoken English recorded in Hong Kong, it can be searched at no cost at http://rcpce.engl.polyu.edu.hk/HKCSE/

### 5.7 London-Lund (mentioned in Chapter 8)

The London-Lund corpus contains Spoken British English data from 1950s to 1970s and can be accessed through the Oxford Text Archive.

### 5.8 MICASE (mentioned in Chapter 8)

The Michigan Corpus of Academic Spoken English (MICASE) can be accessed online, at no cost, from www.hti.umich.edu/m/micase/

### 5.9 SiBol/Port (used throughout the book)

The SiBol/Port corpora are available through the Sketch Engine interface and more information is available from http://www3.lingue.unibo.it/blog/clb/?page_id=8

## 6. Selected resources for downloading data used in corpora employed in this book

In this section we only list recourses used for the corpora we created, the aim being to provide a starting point and to give newer researchers an idea of the wealth of material that is available through the internet.

6.1 Project Gutenburg was used to create the corpora containing data for the Jane Austen and contemporaries corpora mentioned in Chapter 3, the Wordsworth and contemporaries corpora mentioned in Chapter 6 and Wodehouse and contemporaries corpora used in Chapter 6. Access is free from http://www.gutenberg.org/

6.2 White House press briefings (discussed in Chapters 4 and 8, also in the construction of the CorDis corpus mentioned in those chapters) can be found at http://www.whitehouse.gov/briefing-room/press-briefings

## 6.3 UK parliamentary discourse (Chapter 9, also used in the CorDis corpus mentioned in Chapters 4 and 8) can be found at http://www.publications.parliament.uk/pa/cm/cmhansrd.htm

## 6.4 UK political interviews (used in Chapter 9)

The *Breakfast with Frost* transcripts were downloaded from the BBC website http://news.bbc.co.uk/1/hi/programmes/breakfast_with_frost/default.stm

## 6.5 Judicial inquiries

The Hutton Inquiry (used in Chapter 8) was downloaded from the official website www.the-hutton-inquiry.org.uk and the Saville Inquiry/Bloody Sunday Inquiry (Chapter 8) was downloaded from the official website www.bloody-sunday-inquiry.org.uk/

## 7. **Other resources**

Two very useful sources for finding existing corpora are:

The Corpus Resource Database (CoRD) compiled at the University of Helsinki which is a searchable database of information about major corpora http://www.helsinki.fi/varieng/CoRD/index.html

Xiao's survey of corpora, one version is available on the Lancaster University website http://www.lancs.ac.uk/fass/projects/corpus/cbls/corpora.asp

## **Appendix references**

Anthony, L. 2011. *AntConc (Version 3.2.2)* [Computer Software]. Tokyo: Waseda University. Available from http://www.antlab.sci.waseda.ac.jp/

Greaves, C. 2009. *ConcGram 1.0: A phraseological Search Engine*. Amsterdam: John Benjamins.

Kilgarriff, A., P. Rychly, P. Smrz & D. Tugwell. 2004. The Sketch Engine [Computer Software]. *Proc EURALEX 2004*, Lorient, France, 105–116.

Baroni, M. & S. Bernardini. 2004. BootCaT: Bootstrapping corpora and terms from the web. [Computer Software]. *Proceedings of LREC 2004*.

O'Donnell M. 2008. *UAM Corpus Tool 2.0*. [Computer Software]. *Madrid*.

Rayson, P. 2009. *Wmatrix: a web-based corpus processing environment*. Computing Department, Lancaster University. Available from http://ucrel.lancs.ac.uk/wmatrix/

Scott, M. 2008. *WordSmith Tools version 6*, Liverpool: Lexical Analysis Software. Available from: http://www.lexically.net/wordsmith/version6/index.html

# References


Adams, M. 2009. *Slang: The People's Poetry*. Oxford: OUP.

Ädel, A. 2010. How to use corpus linguistics in the study of political discourse. In *The Routledge Handbook of Corpus Linguistics*, M. McCarthy & A. O'Keeffe (eds), 591–604. London: Routledge.

Adolphs, S. 2008. *Corpus and Context: Investigating Pragmatic Functions in Spoken Discourse* [Studies in Corpus Linguistics 30]. Amsterdam: John Benjamins.

Adolphs, S. & Knight, D. 2010. Building a spoken corpus: What are the basics? In *The Routledge Handbook of Corpus Linguistics*, M. McCarthy & A. O'Keeffe (eds), 591–604. London: Routledge.

Ahl, F. 1988. Ars est caelare artem (Art in puns and anagrams engraved). In *On Puns: The Foundation of Letters*, J. Culler (ed.), 17–43. Oxford: Blackwell.

Aijmer, K. 1996. *Conversational Routines in English: Convention and Creativity.* Harlow: Longman.

Al-Hejin, B. 2009. What matters about Muslim women? A comparison of BBC news and Arab news. Paper delivered at *ICAME* 29 May 2009.

Allen, W. 1997. *Complete Prose*. London: Picador.

Alvarez-Cáccamo, C. & Prego-Vásquez, G. 2003. Political cross-discourse: Conversationalization, imaginary networks, and social fields in Galiza. *Pragmatics* 13(1): 145–162.

Anthony, L. 2011. AntConc (Version 3.2.2) [Computer Software]. Tokyo, Japan: Waseda University. Available from http://www.antlab.sci.waseda.ac.jp/

Archer, D. & Culpeper, J. 2009. Identifying key socio-pragmatic usage in plays and trial proceedings (1640–1760): An empirical approach via corpus annotation. *Journal of Historical Pragmatics* 10(2): 286–309.

Attardo, S. 1994. *Linguistic Theories of Humor*. Berlin: Mouton de Gruyter.

Attardo, S. 2000. Irony as relevant inappropriateness. *Journal of Pragmatics* 32: 793–826.

Bachman, I. 2011. Civil partnership – "Gay marriage in all but name": A corpus-driven analysis of discourses of same-sex relationships in the UK Parliament. *Corpora* 6(1): 77–105.

Backhouse, A. 1992. Connotation. In W. Bright (ed.), *The International Encyclopedia of Linguistics*. New York: Oxford University Press, 297–298.

Baker, M. & McCarthy, M. 1990. Multi-word units and things like that. Ms, University of Birmingham.

Baker, M., Francis, G. & Tognini-Bonelli, E. (eds). 1993. *Text and Technology: In Honour of John Sinclair*. Amsterdam: John Benjamins.

Baker, P. & McEnery, A. 2005. A corpus-based approach to discourses of refugees and asylum seekers in UN and newspaper texts. *Language and Politics* 4(2): 197–226.

Baker, P. 2005. *Public Discourses of Gay Men.* London: Routledge.

Baker, P. 2006. *Using Corpora in Discourse Analysis*. London: Continuum.

Baker, P. 2007. Discourses of refugees and asylum seekers in the UK press, 1996–2006: Full Research Report. ESRC End of Award Report, RES-000-22-1381. Swindon: ESRC.

Baker, P. 2009. The BE06 Corpus of British English and recent language change. *International Journal of Corpus Linguistics* 14(3): 312–337.

Baker, P. 2010a. *Sociolinguistics and Corpus Linguistics*. Edinburgh: EUP.

Baker, P. 2010b. Will Ms ever be as frequent as *Mr*? A corpus-based comparison of gendered terms across four diachronic corpora of British English. *Gender and Language* 4(1): 125–129.

Baker, P. 2011. Times may change but we'll always have money: A corpus driven examination of vocabulary change in four diachronic corpora. *Journal of English Linguistics* 39: 65–88.

Baker, P., Gabrielatos, C., Khosravinik, M., Krzyzanowski, M., McEnery, T. & Wodak, R. 2008. A useful methodological synergy? Combining critical discourse analysis and corpus linguistics to examine discourses of refugees and asylum seekers in the UK press. *Discourse and Society* 19(3): 273–306.

Barbe, K. 1993. "Isn't it ironic that...?": Explicit irony markers. *Journal of Pragmatics* 20: 578–590.

Barker, F. 2008. Exploring lexical differences in General English Reading papers. *Research Notes* 31: 22–25. University of Cambridge ESOL examinations. ⟨http://www.cambridgeesol.org/rs_notes/rs_nts31.pdf⟩

Barlow, M. 1996. Corpora for theory and practice. *International Journal of Corpus Linguistics* 1(1): 1–37.

Barlow, M. & Kemmer, S. 1994. A schema-based approach to grammatical description. In *The Reality of Linguistic Rules* [Studies in Language Companion Series 26], S. Lima, R. Corrigan & G. Iverson (eds), 19–42. Amsterdam: John Benjamins.

Baroni, M. & Bernardini, S. 2004. BootCaT: Bootstrapping corpora and terms from the web. Proceedings of LREC 2004.

Bartlett, F. 1932. *Remembering*. Cambridge: CUP.

Bayley, P. (ed.). 2004. *Cross-Cultural Perspectives on Parliamentary Discourse* [Discourse Approaches to Politics, Society and Culture 10]. Amsterdam: John Benjamins.

Bayley, P. 2006. 'Accountable' and 'accountability'. Talk given at the *Intune* Mid-term Meeting, 2–5 March, 2006. University of Bologna at Forlì.

Bayley, P. & Bevitori, C. 2009. 'Just war' or just war: arguments for doing the 'right thing'. In *Corpus-Assisted Discourse Studies on the Iraq Conflict: Wording the War*, J. Morley & P. Bayley (eds), 74–107. London: Routledge.

Bayley, P. & Williams, G. (eds). 2012. *European Identity: What the Media Say*. Oxford: OUP.

Bednarek, M. 2006. *Evaluation in Media Discourse: Analysis of a Newspaper Corpus*. London: Continuum.

Bednarek, M. 2008. *Evaluation in Media Discourse*. London: Continuum.

Bednarek, M. 2010. *The Language of Fictional Television*. London: Continuum.

Beeching, K. 2006. Politeness markers in French: Post-posed *quoi* in the Tourist Office. *Journal of Politeness Research* 2(1): 143–167.

Bell, A. 1991. *The Language of News Media*. Oxford: Blackwell.

Berber Sardinha, T. 2000. Semantic prosodies in English and Portuguese: A contrastive study. *Cuadernos de Filología Inglesa* 9(1): 93–110.

Bhatia, A. 2006. Critical discourse analysis of political press conferences. *Discourse & Society* 17(2): 173–203.

Bhatia, A. 2011. Finding faith and solidarity: Building community in political press conferences. *Iberica* 21: 117–139.

Biber, D. & Burges, J. 2001. Historical change in the language use of women and men: Gender differences in dramatic dialogue. *Journal of English Linguistics* 28: 21–37. Reprinted in Conrad, S. & Biber, D. (eds), 2001, 157–170.

Biber, D. & Conrad, S. 1999. Lexical bundles in conversation and academic prose. In *Out of Corpora*, H. Hasselgård & S. Oksefjell (eds), 181–190. Amsterdam: Rodopi.

Biber, D., Conrad, S. & Leech, G. 2002. *The Longman Student's Grammar of Spoken and Written English*. London: Longman.

Biber, D., Johansson, S., Leech, G., Conrad, S. & Finegan, E. 1999. *Longman Grammar of Spoken and Written English*. London: Longman.

Blas-Arroyo, J. 2003. "Perdóneme que se lo diga, pero vuelve usted a faltar a la verdad, señor González": Form and function of politic verbal behaviour in face-to-face Spanish political debates. *Discourse and Society* 14(4): 395–423.

Bolinger, D. 1976. Meaning and memory. *Forum Linguisticum* 1(1): 1–14.

Bondi, M. 2007. Key-words and emotions: A case study of the Bloody Sunday Inquiry. In *Discourse and Contemporary Social Change*, N. Fairclough, G. Cortese & P. Ardizzone (eds), 407–432. Bern: Peter Lang.

Brazil, D. 1995. *A Grammar of Speech*. Oxford: OUP.

Brazil, D. 1997. *The Communicative Role of Intonation in English*. Cambridge: CUP.

Brown, G. & Yule, G. 1983. *Discourse Analysis*. Cambridge: CUP.

Brown, P. & Levinson, S. 1987. *Politeness: Some Universal in Language Usage*. Cambridge: CUP.

Bublitz, W. 1996. Semantic prosody and cohesive company: "Somewhat predictable". *Leuvense Bijdragen* 85: 1–32.

Cameron, L. & Deignan, A. 2003. Combining large and small corpora to investigate tuning devices around metaphor in spoken discourse. *Metaphor and Symbol* 18(3): 149–160.

Cameron, L. & Deignan, A. 2006. The emergence of metaphor in discourse. *Applied Linguistics* 27(4): 671–690.

Carston, R. & Uchida, S. (eds). 1998. *Relevance Theory: Applications and Implications* [Pragmatics & Beyond New Series 37]. Amsterdam: John Benjamins.

Carter, R. 1995. *Keywords in Language and Literacy*. London: Routledge.

Carter, R. 2004. *Language and Creativity: The Art of Common Talk*. London: Routledge.

Carter, R., Goddard, A., Reah, D., Sanger, K. & Bowring, M. 1997. *Working with Texts: A Core Book for Language Analysis*, 1st edn. London: Routledge.

Carter, R. & McCarthy, M. 1997. *Exploring Spoken Discourse*. Cambridge: CUP.

Carter, R. & McCarthy, M. 2006. *The Cambridge Grammar of English: A Comprehensive Guide to Spoken and Written English. Grammar and Usage*. Cambridge: CUP.

Censis. 2010. *Dare casa alla sicurrezza: Rischi e prevenzione per i lavoratori domestici. Sintesi della ricerca*. Rome, 13 July 2010. ⟨www.censis.it⟩

Censis: Rapporto Sopemi Italia. 2010. *Immigrazione e Presenza Straniera in Italia, 2009–2010*, Rome, November 2010. ⟨www.censis.it⟩

Chambers, L. 2008. Computer-based and paper-based writing assessment: A comparative text analysis. *Research Notes* 34: 9–15. University of Cambridge ESOL examinations. ⟨http://www.cambridgeesol-winterthur.ch/pdf/Reseach_Notes/November08_CB_Testing.pdf⟩

Channell, J. 1994. *Vague Language*. Oxford: OUP.

Channell, J. 2000. Corpus analysis of evaluative lexis. In *Evaluation in Text*, S. Hunston & G. Thompson (eds), 38–55. Oxford: OUP.

Charteris-Black, J. 2004. *Corpus Approaches to Critical Metaphor Analysis.* Basingstoke: Palgrave Macmillan.

Charteris-Black, J. 2006. Britain as a container: Immigration metaphors in the 2005 election campaign. *Discourse & Society* 17: 563–581.

Cheng, W. & Warren, M. 1999. Inexplicitness: What is it and should we be teaching it? *Applied Linguistics* 20(3): 293–315.

Cheng, W., Greaves, C. & Warren, M. 2006. From n-gram to skipgram to concgram. *International Journal of Corpus Linguistics* 11(4): 411–433.

Cheng, W., Greaves, C. & Warren, M. 2008. *A Corpus-driven Study of Discourse Intonation* [Studies in Corpus Linguistics 32]. Amsterdam: John Benjamins.

Chomsky, N. 1957. *Syntactic Structures*. The Hague: Mouton.

Chomsky, N. 2000. *New Horizons on the Study of Mind.* Cambridge MA: The MIT Press.

Christie, C. 2002. Politeness and the linguistic construction of gender in parliament: An analysis of transgressions and apology behaviour. *Sheffield Hallam Working Papers on the Web: Linguistic Politeness and Context.* ⟨http://extra.shu.ac.uk/wpw/politeness/christie.htm⟩ (27 August 2010).

Cirillo, L., Marchi, A. & Venuti, M. 2009. The making of the *CorDis Corpus*: *Compilation and Markup*. In Morley & Bayley (eds), 13–33.

Clayman, S. 1993. Reformulating the question: A device for answering/not answering questions in news interviews and press conferences. *Text* 13(2): 159–188.

Clayman, S. & Heritage, J. 2002. *The News Interview: Journalists and Public Figures on the Air.* Cambridge: CUP.

Clift, R. 1999. Irony in conversation. *Language and Society* 28: 523–553.

Cohen, S. 1984. *That's Funny. You Don't Look Anti-Semitic*. Belfast: Beyond the Pale Publications.

Colston, H. & Keller, S. 1998. You'll never believe this: Irony and hyperbole in expressing surprise. *Journal of Psycholinguistic Research* 27: 499–513.

Colston, H. & O'Brien, J. 2000. Contrast and pragmatics in figurative language: Anything understatement can do, irony can do better. *Journal of Pragmatics* 32: 1557–1583.

Conrad, S. & Biber, D. 2000. Adverbial marking of stance in speech and writing. In *Evaluation in Text*, S. Hunston & G. Thompson (eds), 56–73. Oxford: OUP.

Cook, G. 1992. *The Discourse of Advertising*. London: Routledge.

Cotterill, J. 2003. *Language and Power in Court: A Linguistic Analysis of the O.J. Simpson Trial.* Basingstoke: Palgrave Macmillan.

Cotterill, J. 2004. Collocation, connotation, and courtroom semantics: Lawyers' control of witness testimony through lexical negation. *Applied Linguistics* 25(4): 513–537.

Coulthard, M. 1993. Beginning the study of forensic texts: Corpus, concordance, collocation. In *Data Description Discourse*, M. Hoey (ed.), 86–97. London: HarperCollins.

Coulthard, M. 2007. *An Introduction to Forensic Linguistics: Language in Evidence*. London: Routledge.

Crick, F. 1979. Thinking about the brain. *Scientific American* 9: 218–232.

Culpeper, J. 1996. Towards an anatomy of impoliteness. *Journal of Pragmatics* 25: 349–367.

Culpeper, J. 2002. Computers, language and characterisation: An analysis of six characters in Romeo and Juliet. In *Conversations in Life and in Literature*, C. Östman & M. Kytö (eds), 11–30. Uppsala: Universitetstryckeriet.

Culpeper, J. 2008. Reflections on impoliteness, relational work and power. In *Impoliteness in Language*, D. Bousfield & M. Locher (eds), 17–44. Berlin: Mouton de Gruyter.

Culpeper, J. 2009. Keyness: Words, parts-of-speech and semantic categories in the character-talk of Shakespeare's *Romeo and Juliet*. *International Journal of Corpus Linguistics* 14(1): 29–59.
Culpeper, J. 2010. Conventionalised impoliteness formulae. *Journal of Pragmatics* 42(12): 3232–3245.
Culpeper, J., Bousfield, D. & Wichman, A. 2003. Impoliteness revisited: With special reference to dynamic and prosodic aspects. *Journal of Pragmatics* 35: 1545–1579.
Culpepper, J. & Kytö, M. 2010. *Speech in Writing: Explorations in Early Modern English Dialogues*. Cambridge: CUP.
Darwin, C. 1901[1874]. *The Descent of Man*. London: Murray.
Davies, M. 2004. *BYU-BNC: The British National Corpus*. ⟨http://corpus.byu.edu/bnc/⟩
Deignan, A.H. 2005. *Metaphor and Corpus Linguistics*. John Benjamins.
Dent, S. 2005. *Fanboys and Overdogs: The Language Report*. Oxford: OUP.
Dews, S., Kaplan, J. & Winner, E. 1995. Why not say it directly? The social functions of irony. *Discourse Processes* 19: 347–367.
Dews, S. & Winner, E. 1995. Muting the meaning: A social function of irony. *Metaphor and Symbolic Activity* 10: 3–19.
Drew, P. & Heritage, J. (eds). 1992. *Talk at Work: Interaction in Institutional Settings*. Cambridge: CUP.
Dugalès, N. & Tucker, G. 2012. Representations of representation: European institutions in the French and British Press. In Bayley & Williams (eds), 21–54.
Duguid, A. 2007. Men at work: How those at Number 10 construct their working identity. In *Discourse, Ideology and Specialized Communication*, G. Garzone & S. Sarangi (eds), 453–484. Bern: Peter Lang.
Duguid, A. 2010a. Newspaper discourse informalisation: A diachronic comparison from keywords. *Corpora* 5(2): 109–138.
Duguid, A. 2010b. Investigating anti and some reflections on Modern Diachronic Corpus-Assisted Discourse Studies (MD-CADS). *Corpora* 5(2): 191–220.
Edwards, J. 1992: Principles and contrasting systems of discourse transcription. In *Talking Data – Transcription and Coding in Discourse Research*, J. Edwards & M. Lampert (eds), 3–32. Hillsdale NJ: Lawrence Erlbaum Associates.
Fairclough, N. 1995. *Media Discourse*. London: Edward Arnold.
Fairclough, N. 1996. Technologisation of discourse. In *Texts and Practices: Readings in Critical Discourse Analysis*, C. Caldas-Coulthard & M. Coulthard (eds), 71–83. London: Routledge.
Fairclough, N. 2000. *New Labour, New Language?* London: Routledge.
Farr, F. 2010. *The Discourse of Teaching Practice Feedback. An Investigation of Spoken and Written Modes*. New York NY: Routledge.
Fillmore, C. 1992. Corpus linguistics or computer-aided armchair linguistics. In *Directions in Corpus Linguistics. Proceedings of Nobel Symposium 82*, Stockholm, 4–8 August 1991, J. Svartvik (ed.), 13–38. Berlin: Mouton de Gruyter.
Fischer-Starcke, B. 2010. *Corpus Linguistics in Literary Analysis: Jane Austen and Her Contemporaries*. London: Continuum.
Fishman, J. 1980. Minority language maintenance and the ethnic mother tongue school. *Modern Language Journal* 64(2): 167–172.
Fitzsimmonds-Doolan, S. 2009. Is public discourse about language policy really public discourse about immigration? A corpus-based study. *Language Policy* 8: 377–402.

Foxman, A. 2003. *Never Again? The Threat of the New Anti-Semitism*. San Francisco CA: Harper.

Francis, G. 1994. Labelling discourse: An aspect of nominal group lexical cohesion. In *Advances in Written Text Analysis*, M. Coulthard (ed.), 83–10. London: Routledge.

Franconi, M. 2011. L'ingegneria linguistica dei briefings: Come viene gestito il dibattito tra la casa bianca e la stampa sulle sommosse arabe. Ph.D. dissertation, Bologna University.

Freake, R. 2011. Methodological challenges in bilingual corpus-assisted discourse analysis. Presentation at *Corpus Linguistics 2011*, Birmingham, UK, 20–22 July.

Freake, R., Gentil, G. & Sheyholislami, J. 2011. A bilingual corpus-assisted discourse study of the construction of nationhood and belonging in Quebec. *Discourse & Society* 22(11): 1–27.

Friginal, E. 2009. *The Language of Outsourced Call Centers: A Corpus-based. Study of Cross-Cultural Interaction* [Studies in Corpus Linguistics 34]. Amsterdam: John Benjamins.

Fung, L. & Carter, R. 2007. Discourse markers and spoken English: Native and learner use in pedagogic settings. *Applied Linguistics* 28(3): 410–439.

Gabrielatos, C. 2007. *If*-conditionals as modal colligations: A corpus-based investigation. Paper presented at *Corpus Linguistics 2007*, University of Birmingham, UK, 28–30 July. ⟨http://eprints.lancs.ac.uk/965/⟩

Gabrielatos, C. & Baker, P. 2008. Fleeing, sneaking, flooding: A corpus analysis of discursive constructions of refugees and asylum seekers in the UK Press (1996–2005). *Journal of English Linguistics* 36(1): 5–38.

Gabrielatos, C. & Marchi, A. 2011. Keyness: Matching metrics to definitions. Paper presented at Corpus Linguistics in the South: Theoretical-methodological challenges in corpus approaches to discourse studies – and some ways of addressing them, University of Portsmouth, 5 November 2011. ⟨http://eprints.lancs.ac.uk/51449/⟩

Gabrielatos, C. & McEnery, T. 2005. Epistemic modality in MA dissertations. In *Lengua y Sociedad: Investigaciones recientes en lingüística aplicada* [Lingüística y Filología 61], P. Fuertes Olivera (ed.), 311–331. Valladolid: Universidad de Valladolid.

Galtung, J. & Ruge, M. 1965. The structure of foreign news: the presentation of the Congo, Cuba and Cyprus crises in four Norwegian newspapers. *Journal of International Peace Research* 1: 64–91.

Galtung, J. & Ruge, M. 1973. Structuring and selecting news. In *The Manufacture of News: Social Problems, Deviance and the Mass Media*, S. Cohen & J. Young (eds), 62–72. London: Constable.

Galtung, J. & Ruge M. 1981. Structuring and selecting news. In *The Manufacture of News: Social Problems, Deviance and the Mass Media*, 2nd edn, S. Cohen & J. Young (ed.), 52–63. London: Constable.

Gavioli, L. 2005. *Exploring Corpora for ESP Learning*. Amsterdam: John Benjamins.

Gee, J. 1999. An introduction to discourse analysis: Theory and method. London: Routledge.

Gellner, E. 1959. *Words and Things*. London: Gollancz.

Gesuato, S. 2003. The company women and men keep: What collocations can reveal about culture. In *Proceedings of the Corpus Linguistics 2003 Conference*, D. Archer, P. Rayson, A. Wilson & T. McEnery (eds), 253–262. Lancaster: Lancaster University.

Gibbs, R. 1993. Process and products in making sense of tropes. In *Metaphor and Thought*, A. Ortony (ed.), 252–276. Cambridge: CUP.

Gibbs, R. 2000. Irony in talk among friends. *Metaphor and Symbol* 15: 5–27.

Gibbs, R. & O'Brien, J. 1991. Psychological aspects of irony understanding. *Journal of Pragmatics* 16: 523–530.

Giora, R. 2003. *On Our Mind: Salience, Context and Figurative Language*. Oxford: OUP.

Goatly, A. 1997. *The Language of Metaphors*. London: Routledge.

Goffman, E. 1955. On face-work: An analysis of ritual elements of social interaction. *Psychiatry: Journal for the Study of Interpersonal Processes* 18(3): 213–231.

Goffman, E. 1967. *Interaction Ritual: Essays on Face-to-Face Behaviour.* New York NY: Pantheon Books.

Goffman, E. 1981. *Forms of Talk*. Oxford: Blackwell.

Golab, J. 2004. Frame-based Analysis of Humorous Dialogues from the Novel *Much Obliged Jeeves*, and its Polish Translation. Ph.D. dissertation, Jagiellonian University, Krakow.

Goldacre, B. 2010. Did aliens help to line up Woolworths stores? *The Guardian*, Saturday 16 January. ⟨http://www.guardian.co.uk/science/2010/jan/16/ben-goldacre-bad-science-aliens-woolworths⟩

Greaves, C. 2009. *Concgram 1.0: A Phraseological Search Engine*. Amsterdam: John Benjamins.

Grice, H. 1975. Logic and conversation. In *Syntax and Semantics: Speech Acts*, Vol. 3, P. Cole & J. Morgan (eds), 41–58. New York NY: Academic Press.

Grundmann, R. & Krishnamurthy, R. 2010. The discourse of climate change: A corpus-based approach. *Critical Approaches to Discourse Analysis Across Disciplines* 4(2): 125–146.

Hall, R. 1974. *The Comic Style of P.G. Wodehouse*. Hamden CT: Archon Books.

Halliday, M. 1985. *An Introduction to Functional Grammar*, 1st edn. London: Arnold.

Halliday, M. 1994. *An Introduction to Functional Grammar*, 2nd edn. London: Arnold.

Halliday, M. & Hasan, R. 1976. *Cohesion in English*. Harlow: Longman.

Halliday, M. & Matthiessen, C. 2004. *An Introduction to Functional Grammar*. London: Arnold.

Hamamoto, H. 1998. Irony from a cognitive perspective. In R. Carston & S. Uchida (eds), 257–270.

Hanks, P. 2000. Do word meanings exist? *Computers and the Humanities* 34: 205–215.

Hanks, P. 2004. The syntagmatics of metaphor and idiom. *International Journal of Lexicography* 7(3): 245–274.

Hanks, P. 2010. How people use words to make meanings. In *NLPCS 2010 Proceedings*, B. Sharp & M. Zock (eds), 3–13. Funchal: SciTePress.

Harcup, T. & O'Neill, D. 2001. What is news? Galtung and Ruge revisited. *Journalism Studies* 2(2): 261–280.

Hardaker, C. 2010. Trolling in asynchronous computer-mediated communication: From user discussions to academic definitions. *Journal of Politeness Research* 6(2): 215–242.

Harris, S. 1991. Evasive action: How politicians respond to questions in political interviews. In *Broadcast Talk*, P. Scannell (ed.), 76–99. London: Sage.

Harris, S. 1995. Pragmatics and power. *Journal of Pragmatics* 23(2): 117–135.

Harris, S. 2001. Being politically impolite: Extending politeness theory to adversarial political discourse. *Discourse and Society* 12: 451–472.

Hasan, R. & Halliday, M. 1989. *Language, Context, and Text: Aspects of Language in a Social-semiotic Perspective,* 2nd edn. Oxford: OUP.

Haverkate, H. 1990. A speech act analysis of irony. *Journal of Pragmatics* 14: 77–109.

Herbart, J. 1898. *Letters and Lectures on Education*. London: Sonneschein.

Hockey, Susan. 1980. *A Guide to Computer Applications in the Humanities*. London: Duckworth.

Hoey, M. 2005. *Lexical Priming: A New Theory of Words and Language*. London: Routledge.

Hoey, M. 2007. Lexical priming and literary creativity. In *Text, Discourse and Corpora*, M. Hoey, M. Mahlberg, M. Stubbs & W. Teubert (eds), 7–30. London: Continuum.

Hoey, M. 2009. Corpus-driven approaches to grammar: The search for common ground. In *Exploring the Lexis-Grammar Interface* [Studies in Corpus Linguistics 35], U. Römer & R. Schulze (eds), 33–47. Amsterdam: John Benjamins.

Holmes, J. & Sigley, R. 2001. What's a word like *girl* doing in a place like this? In *New Frontiers of Corpus Linguistics*, A. Smith & P. Peters (eds), 247–263. Amsterdam: Rodopi.
Hori, M. 2004. *Investigating Dickens' Style. A Collocational Analysis*. Basingstoke: Palgrave.
Hundt, M. & Mair, C. 1999. "Agile" and "upright" genres: The corpus based approach to language change in progress. *International Journal of Corpus Linguistics* 4(2): 221–242.
Hunston, S. & Thompson, G. (eds). 1999. *Evaluation in Text*. Oxford: OUP.
Hunston, S. & Francis, G. 2000. *Pattern Grammar: A Corpus-driven Approach to the Lexical Grammar of English* [Studies in Corpus Linguistics 4]. Amsterdam: John Benjamins.
Hunston, S. & Sinclair, J. 2000. A local grammar of evaluation. In *Evaluation in Text*, S. Hunston & G. Thompson (eds), 75–101. Oxford: OUP.
Hunston, S. & Thompson, G. (eds). 2000. *Evaluation in Text*. Oxford: OUP.
Hunston, S. 2000. Phraseology and the modal verb: A study of pattern and meaning. In *Words in Context* [English Language Research Discourse Analysis Monograph 18], C. Heffer & H. Staunton (eds), 234–248. Birmingham: University of Birmingham.
Hunston, S. 2002. *Corpora in Applied Linguistics*. Cambridge: CUP.
Hunston, S. 2004. Counting the uncountable: Problems of identifying evaluation in a text and in a corpus. In *Corpora and Discourse*, A. Partington, J. Morley & L. Haarman (eds), 157–188. Bern: Peter Lang.
Hunston, S. 2007. Semantic prosody revisited. *International Journal of Corpus Linguistics* 12(2): 249–268.
Hunston, S. 2010. *Corpus Approaches to Evaluation: Phraseology and Evaluative Language*. London: Routledge.
Hutchby, I. 2005. *Media Talk: Conversation Analysis and the Study of Broadcasting*. London: McGraw-Hill International.
Hymes, D. 1971. *On Communicative Competence*. Philadelphia PA: University of Pennsylvania Press. Reprinted in Pride J. & Holmes, J. 1972. *Sociolinguistics*, 269–293. Harmondsworth: Penguin.
Ilie, C. 2004. Insulting as (un)parliamentary practice in the British and Swedish parliaments. A rhetorical approach. In *Cross-Cultural Perspectives on Parliamentary Discourse* [Discourse Approaches to Politics, Society and Culture 10], P. Bayley (ed.), 45–86. Amsterdam: John Benjamins.
Isernia, P. 2005. Anti-Americanism and European public opinion. In *America Contested. American Unilateralism and European Discontent*, S. Fabbrini (ed.), 130–158. London: Routledge.
Iyeiri, Y., Yaguchi, M. & Okabe, H. 2005. Gender and style: The discourse particle *like* in the corpus of spoken professional American English. *English Corpus Studies* 12: 37–51.
Jaworski, A. & Coupland, N. 2006. *The Discourse Reader*, 2nd edn. London: Routledge.
Johnson, A. 2002. So…?: Pragmatic implications of *so*-prefaced questions in formal police interviews. In *Language in the Legal Process*, J. Cotterill (ed.), 91–110. Basingstoke: Palgrave Macmillan.
Johnson, J. 2010. A Corpus-assisted study of PARERE/SEMBRARE in Grazia Deledda's *Canne al Vento* and *La Madre*. Constructing point of view in the source texts and their English translations. *Textus* 23: 283–302.
Johnson-Laird, P. 1981a. Mental models of meaning. In *Elements of Discourse Understanding*, A. Joshi, I. Sag & B. Webber (eds), 106–126. Cambridge: CUP.
Johnson-Laird, P. 1981b. Comprehension as the construction of mental models. *Philosophical Transactions of the Royal Society, Series B* 295: 353–374.
Johnson-Laird, P. 1983. *Mental Models*. Cambridge: CUP.
Julius, A. 2010. *Trials of the Diaspora*. Oxford: OUP.

Kennedy, G. 1998. *An Introduction to Corpus Linguistics*. London: Longman.

Kilgarriff, A. & Tugwell, D. 2001. WORD SKETCH: Extraction and display of significant collocations for lexicography. In *Proc. ACL workshop on COLLOCATION: Computational Extraction, Analysis and Exploitation*, Toulouse, July, 32–38. ⟨http://www.kilgarriff.co.uk/Publications/2001-KilgTugwell-ACLcollos-Sketches.pdf⟩

Kilgarriff, A., Rychly, P. Smrz, P. & Tugwell, D. (2004). The Sketch Engine [Computer Software]. *Proc EURALEX 2004*, Lorient, France, 105–116.

Koestler, A. 1964. *The Act of Creation*. London: Hutchinson.

Kohnen, T. 2008. Linguistic politeness in Anglo-Saxon England? A study of Old English address terms. *Journal of Historical Pragmatics* 9(1): 140–158.

Kreuz, R. Long, D. & Church, M. 1991. On being ironic: Pragmatic and mnemonic implications. *Metaphor and Symbolic Activity* 6: 149–162.

Kreuz, R. & Roberts, R. 1995. Two cues for verbal irony: Hyperbole and the ironic tone of voice. *Metaphor and Symbol* 10: 21–31.

Krishnamurthy, R. 1996. Ethnic, racial and tribal: The language of racism? In *Texts and Practices: Readings in Critical Discourse Analysis*, C.R. Caldas-Coulthard & M. Coulthard (eds), 129–149. London: Routledge.

Kruez, R. & Glucksberg, S. 1989. How to be sarcastic: The echoic reminder theory of verbal irony. *Journal of Experimental Psychology: General* 118(4): 374–386.

Kuhn, T. 1970. *The Structure of Scientific Revolutions*, 2nd edn. Chicago IL: University of Chicago Press.

Haarman, L. & Lombardo, L. (eds). 2009. *Evaluation and Stance in War News: A Linguistic Analysis of American, British and Italian Television News Reporting of the 2003 Iraqi War*. London: Continuum.

Labov, W. 1972. *Language in the Inner City*. Philadelphia: University of Pennsylvania Press.

Lakoff, R. 1975. *Language and Woman's Place*. New York NY: Harper and Row.

Leech, G. 1992. Corpora and theories of linguistic performance. In *Directions in Corpus Linguistics. Proceedings of Nobel Symposium 82, Stockholm, 4–8 August 1991*, J. Svartvik (ed.), 105–122, Berlin: Mouton de Gruyter.

Leech G. & Short, M. 1981. *Style in Fiction. A Linguistic Introduction to English Fictional Prose*. Harlow: Pearson Education.

Leech, G. & Smith, N. 2006. Recent grammatical change in written English 1961–1992: Some preliminary findings of a comparison of American with British English. In *The Changing Face of Corpus Linguistics*, A. Renouf & A. Kehoe (eds), 186–204. Amsterdam: Rodopi.

Lerner, G.H. 2003. Selecting next speaker: The context-sensitive operation of a context-free organization. *Language in Society* 32(2): 177–201.

Levinson, S. 1988. Putting linguistics on a proper footing: Explorations in Goffman's concepts of participation. In *Erving Goffman: Exploring the Interaction Order*, P. Drew & A. Wootton (eds), 161–227. Cambridge: Polity Press.

Lewandowska-Tomaszczyk, B. 1996. Cross-linguistic and language-specific aspects of semantic prosody. *Language Sciences* 18(1–2): 153–178.

Lewis, J., Williams, A., Franklin, B., Thomas J. & Mosdell, N. 2008. *The Quality and Independence of British Journalism: Tracking the Changes over 20 years*. Cardiff: Cardiff University Press.

Liu, D. 2003. The most frequently used spoken American English idioms: A corpus analysis and its implications. *TESOL Quarterly* 37: 671–700.

Locher, M.A. 2004. *Power and Politeness in action. Disagreements in Oral Communication*. Berlin: Mouton de Gruyter.

Locher, M. & Watts, R. 2005. Politeness theory and relational work. *Journal of Politeness Research* 1(1): 9–33.

Locke, J. 1961 (1690). *Essay Concerning Human Understanding*, J.W. Holden (ed.). London: Dent.

Lodge, D. 2008. *Deaf Sentence*. London: Penguin.

Lombardo, L. 2001. *Selling It and Telling It: A Functional Approach to the Discourse of Print Ads and TV News*. Rome: Istituto di Lingue Moderne, Luiss.

Louw, W. 1993. Irony in the text or insincerity in the writer? - The diagnostic potential of semantic prosodies. In *Text and Technology. In honour of John Sinclair*, M. Baker, G. Francis & E. Tognini-Bonelli (eds), 157–176. Amsterdam: John Benjamins.

Louw, W. 2000. Contextual prosodic theory: Bringing semantic prosodies to life. In *Words in Context* [English Language Research Discourse Analysis Monograph 18], C. Heffer & H. Staunton (eds), 48–95. Birmingham: University of Birmingham.

Lyons, J. 1977. *Semantics*. Cambridge: Cambridge University Press.

MacAlister, J. 2011. Flower-girl and bugler-boy no more: Changing gender representation in writing for children. *Corpora* 6(1): 25–44.

*Macmillan Online Dictionary* ⟨http://www.macmillandictionary.com⟩

MacShane D. 2008. *Globalising Hatred: The New Anti-Semitism*. London: Weidenfeld & Nicolson.

Mahlberg, M. 2007. Corpus stylistics: Briging the gap between linguistic and literary studies. In *Text, Discourse and Corpora*, M. Hoey, M. Mahlberg, M. Stubbs & W. Teubert (eds), 219–246. London: Continuum.

Marchi, A. & Taylor, C. 2009a. If on a winter's night two researchers … A challenge to assumptions of soundness of interpretation. *CADAAD Journal* 3(1): 1–20.

Marchi, A. & Taylor, C. 2009b. Establishing the EU: The representation of Europe in the press in 1993 and 2005. In *Corpora: Pragmatics and Discourse. Papers from the 29th International Conference on English Language Research on Computerized Corpora* A. Jucker, M. Hundt & D. Schreier (eds), 201–224. Amsterdam: Rodopi.

Martin, J. & Rose, D. 2003. *Working with Discourse: Meaning Beyond the Clause*. London: Continuum.

Martin, J. & White, P. 2005. *Language of Evaluation: Appraisal in English*. Basingstoke: Palgrave.

Martin, R. 1992. Irony and universe of belief. *Lingua* 87: 77–90.

McCarthy, M. & Carter, R. 2004. "There's millions of them": Hyperbole in everyday conversation. *Journal of Pragmatics* 36(2): 149–184.

McDonald, S. 1999. Exploring the process of inference generation in sarcasm: A review of normal and clinical studies. *Brain and Language* 68: 486–506.

McEnery, T. 2006. *Swearing in English: Bad Language, Purity and Power from 1586 to the Present*. London: Routledge.

McEnery, T. 2009. Keywords and moral panics: Mary Whitehouse and media censorship. In *What's in a Word: Investigating Word Frequency and Keyword Extraction*, D. Archer (ed.), 93–124. Farnham: Ashgate.

McEnery, T., Baker, P. & Cheepen, C. 2002. Lexis, indirectness and politeness in operator calls. In *Language and Computers, New Frontiers of Corpus Research. Papers from the Twenty First International Conference on English Language Research on Computerized Corpora Sydney* 2000, P. Peters, P. Collins & A. Smith (eds), 53–69. Amsterdam: Rodopi.

McEnery, T. & Hardie, A. 2011. *Corpus Linguistics: Method, Theory and Practice*. Cambridge: CUP.

McEnery T. & Wilson, A. 1996. *Corpus Linguistics*. Edinburgh: EUP.

McIntyre, D. 2010. Dialogue and characterisation in Quentin Tarantino's Reservoir Dogs: A corpus stylistic analysis. In *Language and Style*, D. McIntyre & B. Busse (eds), 162–182. Basingstoke: Palgrave.

McIntyre, D. 2012. Prototypical characteristics of blockbuster movie dialogue: A corpus stylistic analysis. *Texas Studies in Literature and Language* 54(3): 402–425.

McNair, N. 1996. *News Journalism in the UK*. London: Routledge.

McNair, N. 2003. *News Journalism in the UK*. London: Routledge.

Miller, D. & Johnson, J. 2009. Strict vs. nurturant parents? A corpus-assisted study of congressional positioning on the war in Iraq. In *Corpus-Assisted Discourse Studies on the Iraq Conflict: Wording the War*, J. Morley & P. Bayley (eds), 34–73. London: Routledge.

Miller, G. 1993. Images and models, similes and metaphors. In *Metaphor and Thought*, A. Ortony (ed.), 357–400. Cambridge: CUP.

Mills, S. 2002. Rethinking politeness, impoliteness and gender identity. In *Gender Identity and Discourse* [Discourse Approaches to Politics, Society and Culture 2], L. Litosseliti & J. Sunderland (eds), 69–89. Amsterdam: John Benjamins.

Minsky M. 1975. A framework for representing knowledge. In *The Psychology of Computer Vision*, P.H. Winston (ed.), 211–277. New York NY: McGraw-Hill.

Montgomery, M. 2007. *The Discourse of Broadcast News: A Linguistic Approach*. London: Routledge.

Moon, R. 1998. *Fixed Expressions and Idioms in English: A Corpus-Based Approach*. Oxford: Clarendon.

Morley, J. 2004a. More than meets the naked eye: From semantic prosody to rhetorical prosody. Talk given at the 25th ICAME Conference, May 2004. University of Verona.

Morley, J. 2004b. The sting in the tail: Persuasion in English editorial discourse. In *Corpora and Discourse*, A. Partington, J. Morley & L. Haarman (eds), 239–255. Bern: Peter Lang.

Morley, J. 2007. Ask not for whom Big Ben bongs: It tolls for ITV. In *Cityscapes: Islands of the Self*, Vol. 2, L. Jottini, G. Del Lungo & J. Douthwaite (eds), 23–42. Cagliari: Cooperativa Universitaria Editrice Cagliaritana.

Morley, J. & Bayley, P. (eds). 2009. *Corpus-Assisted Discourse Studies on the Iraq Conflict: Wording the War*. London: Routledge.

Morley, J. & Partington, A. 2009. A few Frequently Asked Questions about semantic – or *evaluative* – prosody. *International Journal of Corpus Linguistics* 14(2): 139–158.

Morley, J. & Taylor, C. 2012. 'Us' and 'them'. How immigrants are constructed in the British and Italian press. In *European Identity: What the Media Say*, P. Bayley & G. Williams (eds), 190–223. Oxford: OUP.

Moschonas, S. & Spitzmuller, J. 2010. Prescriptivism in and about the media: A comparative analysis of corrective practices in Greece and Germany. In *Language Ideologies and Media Discourse: Texts, Practices, Politics*, S. Johnson & T.M. Milani (eds), 17–40. London: Continuum.

Mullany, L. 2002. "I don't think you want me to get a word in edgeways do you John?" Re-assessing (im)politeness, language and gender in political broadcast interviews. *Sheffield Hallam Working Papers on the Web: Linguistic Politeness and Context*. ⟨http://extra.shu.ac.uk/wpw/politeness/mullany.htm⟩ (1 September 2008).

Munday, J. 2011. Looming large: A cross-linguistic analysis of semantic prosodies in comparable reference corpora. In *Corpus-Based Translation Studies*, A. Kruger, K. Wallmach & J. Munday (eds), 169–86. London: Continuum.

Murphy, A. 2005. Markers of attribution in English and Italian opinion articles: A comparative corpus-based study. *ICAME* 29: 131–150.

Nattinger, J. & DeCarrico, J. 1992. *Lexical Phrases and Language Teaching*. Oxford: OUP.

Nelson Francis, W. 1982. Problems of assembling and computerizing large corpora. In *Computer Corpora in English Language Research*. S. Johannson, 7–24. Bergen: Norwegian Computing Centre for the Humanities.

Nelson, M. 2006. Semantic associations in business English: A corpus-based analysis. *English for Specific Purposes* 25: 217–234.

Norrick, N. 2003. Issues in conversational joking. *Journal of Pragmatics* 35: 1333–1359.

O'Barr, W.M. & Atkins, B.K. 1980. Women's language or powerless language? In *Women in Language and Society*, S. McConnell-Ginet, B. Borker & N. Furman (eds), 193–110. New York NY: Praeger.

O'Donnell, M. *UAM CorpusTool* ⟨http://www.wagsoft.com/CorpusTool/⟩

O'Keeffe, A. 2006. *Investigating Media Discourse*. London: Routledge.

Partington, A. 1995. 'Kicking the habit': The exploitation of collocation in literature and humour. In *Linguistic Approaches to Literature* [English Language Research Journal 17], J. Payne (ed), 25–44. Birmingham: University of Birmingham.

Partington, A. 1998. *Patterns and Meanings: Using Corpora for English Language Research and Teaching* [Studies in Corpus Linguistics 2]. Amsterdam: John Benjamins.

Partington, A. 2003. *The Linguistics of Political Argument*. London: Routledge.

Partington, A. 2004a. Corpora and discourse: A most congruous beast. In *Corpora and Discourse,* A. Partington, J. Morley & L. Haarman (eds), 11–20. Bern: Peter Lang.

Partington, A. 2004b. "Utterly content in each other's company": Semantic prosody and semantic preference. *International Journal of Corpus Linguistics* 9(1): 131–156.

Partington, A. 2006a. *The Linguistics of Laughter: A Corpus-assisted Study of Laughter-talk*. London: Routledge.

Partington, A. 2006b. Metaphors, motifs and similes across discourse types: Corpus-Assisted Discourse Studies (CADS) at work. In Stefanowitsch & Gries (eds), 267–304.

Partington, A. 2009a. Evaluating evaluation and some concluding reflections on CADS. In *Corpus Assisted Discourse Studies on the Iraq Conflict: Wording the War*, J. Morley & P. Bayley (eds), 261–303. London: Routledge.

Partington, A. 2009b. A linguistic account of wordplay: The lexical grammar of punning. *Journal of Pragmatics* 41: 1794–1809.

Partington, A. 2010. Modern Diachronic Corpus-Assisted Discourse Studies (MD-CADS) on UK newspapers: An overview of the project. *Corpora* 5(2): 83–108.

Partington, A. (ed.). 2010. *Modern Diachronic Corpus-assisted Studies (MD-CADS). Corpora* 5(2), special issue.

Partington, A. 2012. Corpus analysis of political language. In *The Encyclopedia of Applied Linguistics*, C. Chapelle (ed.). Wiley Online ⟨http://onlinelibrary.wiley.com/book/10.1002/9781405198431⟩

Partington, A. & Morley, J. 2004. At the heart of ideology: Word and cluster/bundle frequency in political debate. In *PALC 2003: Practical Applications in Language Corpora*, B. Lewandowska-Tomaszczyk (ed.), 179–192. Frankfurt: Peter Lang.

Partington, A., Morley, J. & Haarman, L. (eds). 2004 *Corpora and Discourse*. Bern: Peter Lang.

Partington, A. & Taylor, C. 2010. *Persuasion in Politics,* 2nd edn. Milano: LED edizioni.

Partridge, C. & Geaves, R. 2008. Antisemitism, conspiracy culture, Christianity, Islam. In *The Invention of Sacred Tradition*, J. Lewis & O. Hammer (eds), 75–95. Cambridge: CUP.

Pawley, A. & Syder, H. 1983. Two puzzles for linguistic theory: Nativelike selection and nativelike fluency. In *Language and Communication*, J. Richards & R. Schmidt (eds), 191–226. London: Longman.

Pearce, M. 2008. Investigating the Collocational Behaviour of MAN and WOMAN in the BNC using Sketch Engine. *Corpora* 3(1): 1–29.

Perez de Ayala, S. 2001. FTAs and Erskine May: Conflicting needs? Politeness in Question Time. *Journal of Pragmatics* 33: 143–169.

Piirainen-Marsh, A. 2005. Managing adversarial questioning in broadcast interviews. *Journal of Politeness Research* 1(2): 193–217.

Quine, W. 1940. *Mathematical Logic*. Boston MA: Harvard University Press.

Quirk, R. Greenbaum, S., Leech, G. & J. Svartvik. 1985. *A Comprehensive Grammar of the English Language*. Harlow: Longman.

Rayson, P. 2009. *Wmatrix: A web-based corpus processing environment.* ⟨http://ucrel.lancs.ac.uk/wmatrix⟩

Reershemius, G. 2012. Research cultures and pragmatic functions of humor in academic research presentations: A corpus-assisted analysis. *Journal of Pragmatics* 44(6–7): 863–875.

Riccio, G. 2009. White House press briefings as a message to the world. In *Corpus-Assisted Discourse Studies on the Iraq Conflict: Wording the War*, J. Morley & P. Bayley (eds), 108–140. London: Routledge.

Ritchie, G. 2004. *The Linguistic Analysis of Jokes*. London: Routledge.

Rogers, S. (ed.). 2004. *The Hutton Inquiry and its Impact.* London: Politico's.

Römer, U. 2006. Where the computer meets language, literature, and pedagogy: Corpus analysis in English Studies. In *How Globalization Affects the Teaching of English: Studying Culture Through Texts*, A. Gerbig & A. Müller-Wood (eds), 81–109. Lampeter: E. Mellen Press.

Rühlemann, C. 2010. What can a corpus tell us about pragmatics? In *The Routledge Handbook of Corpus Linguistics*, A. O'Keeffe & Michael McCarthy (eds), 288–301. London: Routledge.

Rychly, P. & Kilgarriff, A. 2007. An efficient algorithm for building a distributional thesaurus. *Proc ACL*. Prague, Czech Republic. ⟨http://www.kilgarriff.co.uk/Publications/2007-RychlyKilg-ACL-thesauruses.pdf⟩

Scannell, P. 1991. *Broadcast Talk*. London: Sage.

Schank, R. 1986. *Explanation Patterns: Understanding Mechanically and Creatively*. Hillsdale NJ: Lawrence Erlbaum Associates.

Schank, R. 1991. *Tell Me a Story: A New Look at Real and Artificial Intelligence*. New York NY: Simon & Schuster.

Schank, R. & Abelson, R. 1977. *Scripts, Plans, Goals and Understanding*. Hillsdale NJ: Lawrence Erlbaum Associates.

Schauer, G. & Adolphs, S. 2006. Expressions of gratitude in corpus and DCT data: Vocabulary, formulaic sequences, and pedagogy. *System* 34(1): 119–134.

Schmitt, N. & Carter, R. 2004. Formulaic sequences in action: an introduction. In *Formulaic Sequences* [Language Learning and Language Teaching 9], N. Schmitt (ed.), 1–22. Amsterdam: John Benjamins.

Scott, M. 1997. PC analysis of key words – And key key words. *System* 25(2): 233–245.

Scott, M. 1999. *WordSmith Tools*. Version 3. Oxford: OUP.

Scott, M. 2000. Focusing on the text and its key words. In *Rethinking language pedagogy from a corpus perspective vol. 2*, L. Burnard & T. McEnery (eds), 103–122. Frankfurt: Peter Lang.

Scott, M. 2001. Comparing corpora and identifying key words, collocations, frequency distributions through the WordSmith Tools suite of computer programmes. In *Small Corpus Studies and ELT: Theory and Practice*, M. Ghadessy, A. Henry & R. Roseberry, R. (eds.), 47–67. Amsterdam: John Benjamins.

Scott, M. 2008, *WordSmith Tools*. Version 5. Liverpool: Lexical Analysis Software.

Scott, M. 2010. *WordSmith Tools User Guide* (v.5). Liverpoll: Lexical Analysis Software.

Scott, M. & Tribble, C. 2006. *Textual Patterns: Key Words and Corpus Analysis in Language Education* [Studies in Corpus Linguistics 22]. Amsterdam: John Benjamins.

Seale, C., Boden, S., Williams, S., Lowe, P. & Steinberg, D. 2007. Media constructions of sleep and sleep disorders: A study of UK national newspapers. *Social Science & Medicine* 65: 418–430.

Semino, E., Heywood, J. & Short. M. 2004. Methodological problems in the analysis of metaphors in a corpus of conversations about cancer. *Journal of Pragmatics* 36: 1271–1294.

Semino, E. & Short, M. 2004. *Corpus Stylistics. Speech, Writing and Thought Presentation in a Corpus of English Writing*. London: Routledge.

Seto, K. 1998. On non-echoic irony. In Carston & Uchida (eds), 240–255.

Simpson, R., Briggs, S., Ovens, J. & Swales, J. 2002. *The Michigan Corpus of Academic Spoken English*. Ann Arbor MI: University of Michigan.

Sinclair, J. 1975. The linguistic basis of style. In H. Ringbom (ed.), *Style and Text*. Stockholm: Skriptor AB, 75–89.

Sinclair, J. 1987a. Collocation: a progress report. In *Language Topics: Essays in Honour of Michael Halliday*, R. Steele & T. Threadgold (eds), 319–331. Amsterdam: John Benjamins.

Sinclair, J. 1987b. The nature of the evidence. In Sinclair (ed.), *Looking Up* 150–159. London: Collins.

Sinclair, J. 1988. Mirror for a text. *Journal of English and Foreign Languages* 1: 15–44.

Sinclair, J. 1991. *Corpus, Concordance, Collocation*. Oxford: OUP.

Sinclair, J. 1994. Trust the text. In *Advances in Written Text Analysis*, M. Coulthard (ed.), 12–25. London: Routledge.

Sinclair, J. 1996. The search for units of meaning. *Textus* 9(1): 75–106.

Sinclair, J. 1998. The lexical item. In *Contrastive Lexical Semantics* [Current Issues in Linguistic Theory 171], E. Weigand (ed.), 1–24. Amsterdam: John Benjamins.

Sinclair, J. 2004. *Trust the Text: Language, Corpus and Discourse*. London: Routledge.

Sinclair, J. 2003. *Reading Concordances: An Introduction*. London: Longman.

Sinclair, J. & Hunston, S. 2000. A local grammar of evaluation. in *Evaluation in Text and the Construction of Discourse*, S. Hunston & G. Thompson (eds), 74–101. Oxford: OUP.

Sigley, R. & J. Holmes. 2002. Looking at girls in corpora of English. *Journal of English Linguistics* 30: 138–157.

Sperber, D. & Wilson, D. 1995. *Relevance*, 2nd edn. Oxford: Blackwell.

Sperber, D. & Wilson, D. 1998. Irony and relevance: A reply to Drs Seto, Hamamoto and Yamanashi. In Carston & Uchida (eds), 283–293.

Stefanowitsch, A. 2006. Corpus-based approaches to metaphor and metonymy. In Stefanowitsch & Gries (eds), 1–16.

Stefanowitsch, A. & Gries, S.T. (eds). 2006. *Corpus-Based Approaches to Metaphor and Metonymy*. Berlin: Mouton de Gruyter.

Stenstrom, A.-B. 1994. *An Introduction to Spoken Interaction*. Harlow: Longman.

Stewart, D. 2010. *Semantic Prosody: A Critical Evaluation*. London: Routledge.

Stubbs, M. 1983. *Discourse Analysis*. Oxford: Blackwell.

Stubbs, M. 1993. British traditions in text analysis: From Firth to Sinclair. In *Text and Technology: In Honour of John Sinclair*, M. Baker, F. Francis & E. Tognini-Bonelli (eds), 1–36. Amsterdam: John Benjamins.

Stubbs, M. 1995. Collocations and semantic profiles: On the cause of the trouble with quantitative studies. *Functions of language* 2(1): 23–55.

Stubbs, M. 1996. *Text and Corpus Analysis: Computer-assisted Studies of Language and Culture*. Oxford: Blackwell.

Stubbs, M. 2000. Using very large text collections to study semantic schemas: A research note. In *Words in Context* [ELR Monograph 18], C. Heffer & H. Sauntson (eds), 1–9. Birmingham: University of Birmingham.

Stubbs, M. 2001. *Words and Phrases: Corpus Studies of Lexical Semantics*. Oxford: Blackwell.

Stubbs, M. 2005. Conrad in the computer: Examples of quantitative stylistic methods. *Language and Literature* 14(1): 5–24.

Stubbs, M. 2006. Corpus analysis: The state of the art and three types of unanswered questions. In *System and Corpus*, G. Thompson & S. Hunston (eds), 15–36. London: Equinox.

Stubbs, M. 2007. On texts, corpora and models of language. In *Text, Discourse and Corpora*, M. Hoey, M. Mahlberg, M. Stubbs & W. Teubert, 127–162. London: Continuum.

Stubbs, M. 2009. Technology and phraseology: with notes on the history of corpus linguistics. In *Exploring the Lexis-Grammar Interface* [Studies in Corpus Linguistics 35], U. Römer & R. Schulze (eds), 33–47. Amsterdam: John Benjamins.

Stygall, G. 2001. A different class of witnesses: Experts in the courtroom. *Discourse Studies* 3(3): 327–349.

Tadros, A. 1993. The pragmatics of text averral and attribution in academic texts. In *Data, Description, Discourse,* M. Hoey (ed.), 98–114. London: HarperCollins.

Taylor, C. 2005. Electronic corpora in language study. *Daf-werkstatt* 6: 71–84.

Taylor, C. 2006. Powerless language? Witness strategies in the Hutton Inquiry. In *Studies in Specialized Discourse*, M. Gotti & J. Flowerdew (eds), 263–287. Bern: Peter Lang.

Taylor, C. 2008. What is corpus linguistics? What the data says. *ICAME Journal* 32: 179–200.

Taylor, C. 2009a. Interacting with conflicting goals: Facework and impoliteness in hostile cross-examination. In *Corpus Assisted Discourse Studies on the Iraq Conflict: Wording the War*, J. Morley & P. Bayley (eds), 208–233. London: Routledge.

Taylor, C. 2009b. The representation of immigrants in the Italian press. *CirCap Occasional Papers* 21. Siena: University of Siena.

Taylor, C. 2010. Science in the news. A diachronic perspective. *Corpora* 5(2): 221–250.

Taylor, C. 2011. Negative politeness features and impoliteness functions: A corpus-assisted approach. In *Situated Politeness,* B. Davies, A. Merrison & M. Haugh (eds), 209–231. London: Continuum.

Taylor, C. 2012. A corpus linguistic approach to analysing mock politeness in English and Italian. Paper presented at *IVACS Conference*. Leeds, June 21.

Teubert, W. 2005. My version of corpus linguistics. *International Journal of Corpus Linguistics* 10(1): 1–13.

Thompson, G. 1997. *Introducing Functional Grammar*. London: Arnold.

Thompson, G. & Hunston, S. 2000. Evaluation: An introduction. In *Evaluation in Text,* S. Hunston & G. Thompson (eds), 1–27. Oxford: OUP.

Thompson G. & Hunston S. 2006. System and corpus: Two traditions with a common ground. In *System and Corpus: Exploring Connections*, G. Thompson & S. Hunston (eds), 1–16. London: Equinox.

Thornborrow, J. & Wareing, S. 1998. *Patterns in Language: An Introduction to Language and Literary Style*. London: Routledge.

Thornborrow, J. 2002. *Power Talk: Language and Interaction in Institutional Discourse*. London: Longman.

Thornborrow, J., Haarman, L. & Duguid, A. 2012. Discourses of European Identity in British, Italian, and French TV News. In *European Identity: What the Media Say*, P. Bayley & G. Williams (eds), 84–117. Oxford: OUP.

Tognini-Bonelli, E. 2001. *Corpus Linguistics at Work* [Studies in Corpus Linguistics 6]. Amsterdam: John Benjamins.

Tognini Bonelli, E. & Manca, E. 2002. Welcoming children, pets and guests. A problem of non-equivalence in the languages of Agriturismo and Farmhouse Holidays. *Textus* 15(2): 317–334.

Trask, R. 1993. *A Dictionary of Grammatical terms in Linguistics*. London: Routledge.

Tucker, G. 2006. The lexicogrammar of 'representation'. Talk given at the *Intune* Mid-term Meeting, 2–5 March, 2006. University of Bologna at Forlì.

Ulrych, M. 1992. *Translating Texts: From Theory to Practice*. Rapallo: CIDEB.

Van Dijk, T. 1992. Discourse and the denial of racism. *Discourse and Society* 3(1): 87–118.

Watts, R. 2003. *Politeness*. Cambridge: CUP.

Watts, R., Ide, S. & Ehlich, K. 1992. Politeness in Language: *Studies in its History, Theory, and Practice*. Berlin: Mouton de Gruyter.

Whitsitt, S. 2005. A critique of semantic prosody. *International Journal of Corpus Linguistics* 10(3): 283–305.

Wimsatt, W. & Beardsley, M. 1946. The intentional fallacy. *Sewanee Review* 45(3): 469–470.

Wynne, M. 2006. Stylistics: Corpus approaches. In *Encyclopedia of Language and Linguistics*, 2nd edn., K. Brown (ed.), 223–226. Oxford: Elsevier.

Xiao, R. & McEnery, T. 2006. Collocation, semantic prosody, and near synonymy: A cross-linguistic perspective. *Applied Linguistics* 27(1): 103.

Zgusta, L. 1967. Multi-word lexical units. *Word* 23: 578–587.

# Author index

# Subject index